This is the book I've been waiting for. Building on the author's previous scholarship, this volume is an important contribution to the under-researched field of the history of language education in the UK. Much more than 'just' a history, this is a rich and insightful account of issues still very alive today, from assessment to arguments about effective pedagogy, and breaks new ground in its astute narrative of language advocacy. McLelland succeeds in being both erudite and highly enjoyable to read; the book is full of delightful gems as well as providing a valuable and comprehensive source of references to aid other researchers in the field.
–Simon Coffey, Senior Lecturer in Modern Languages Education, King's College London

Nicola McLelland's new book is an invaluable resource for anyone interested in reading about or studying the history of language learning and teaching in Britain. It is packed with concise information on a wide range of languages, periods, contexts, and topics, some of which have not received much attention so far. Thus it provides a fascinating comprehensive overview and will without doubt stimulate further historical research.
–Friederike Klippel, Chair of TEFL (until 2015), Ludwig-Maximilians-University Munich, Germany

Congratulations to Nicola McLelland on this important accomplishment! Her book will be of great interest to foreign language scholars and professionals in Britain. More important, perhaps, is that Professor McLelland has provided an excellent model for how to craft similar histories of foreign language education in other national contexts and indeed from transnational perspectives. Language specialists have written their own, more limited histories of the profession, typically focusing on how languages have been taught. Professor McLelland's book provides a much richer perspective by tracing which languages have been taught in Britain and why, the changing social contexts in which they have been taught, a nascent history of language assessment, and an engaging historical perspective on language education policy advocacy. In addition to its analytical breadth, the book expands its historical perspective beyond the nineteenth century. This allows Professor McLelland to draw more compelling conclusions about the nature of foreign language education and the challenges facing scholars, professionals, and students of it.

–Jeff Bale, Associate Professor of Language and Literacies Education, Ontario Institute for Studies in Education, University of Toronto

Teaching and Learning Foreign Languages

Teaching and Learning Foreign Languages provides a comprehensive history of language teaching and learning in the UK from its earliest beginnings to the present. McLelland offers the first history of the social context of foreign language education in Britain, as well as an overview of changing approaches, methods and techniques in language teaching and learning. The important impact of classroom-external factors on developments in language teaching and learning is also taken into account, particularly regarding the policies and public examination requirements of the twentieth century.

Beginning with a chronological overview of language teaching and learning in Britain, McLelland explores which languages were learned when, why and by whom, before examining the social history of language teaching and learning in greater detail, and addressing topics including the status that language learning and teaching have held in society. McLelland also provides a history of how languages have been taught, contrasting historical developments with current orthodoxies of language teaching. Experiences outside school are discussed with examples from adult education, teach-yourself courses and military language learning.

Providing an accessible, authoritative history of language education in Britain, *Teaching and Learning Foreign Languages* will appeal to academics and postgraduate students engaged in the history of education and language learning across the world. The book will also be of interest to teacher educators, trainees and practising teachers, policymakers and curriculum developers.

Nicola McLelland is a Professor in German and History of Linguistics at the University of Nottingham and Editor of the journal *Language & History*. Her interests span the history of linguistics and sociolinguistics (past and present), as well as the history of language learning and teaching.

Routledge Research in Language Education

For a full list of titles in this series, please visit www.routledge.com

The *Routledge Research in Language Education* series provides a platform for established and emerging scholars to present their latest research and discuss key issues in Language Education. This series welcomes books on all areas of language teaching and learning, including but not limited to language education policy and politics, multilingualism, literacy, L1, L2 or foreign language acquisition, curriculum, classroom practice, pedagogy, teaching materials, and language teacher education and development. Books in the series are *not* limited to the discussion of the teaching and learning of English only.

Books in the series include:

Teaching and Learning Foreign Languages
A History of Language Education, Assessment and Policy in Britain
Nicola McLelland

Teaching Chinese Literacy in the Early Years
Psychology, Pedagogy, and Practice
Hui Li

Pronunciation for English as an International Language
From Research to Practice
Ee-Ling Low

The Role of English Teaching in Modern Japan
Diversity and Multiculturalism through English Language Education in a Globalized Era
Mieko Yamada

Advances and Current Trends in Language Teacher Identity Research
Edited by Ying Ling Cheung, Selim Ben Said and Kwanghyun Park

Language, Ideology, Education
The Politics of Textbooks in Language Education
Edited by Xiao Lan Curdt-Christiansen and Csilla Weninger

Teaching and Learning Foreign Languages
A History of Language Education, Assessment and Policy in Britain

Nicola McLelland

Routledge
Taylor & Francis Group

LONDON AND NEW YORK

First published 2017 by Routledge

2 Park Square, Milton Park, Abingdon, Oxfordshire OX14 4RN

52 Vanderbilt Avenue, New York, NY 10017

Routledge is an imprint of the Taylor & Francis Group, an informa business

First issued in paperback 2018

Copyright © 2017 Nicola McLelland

The right of Nicola McLelland to be identified as author of this work has been asserted by her in accordance with sections 77 and 78 of the Copyright Designs and Patents Act 1988.

All rights reserved. No part of this book may be reprinted or reproduced or utilised in any form or by any electronic, mechanical, or other means, now known or hereafter invented, including photocopying and recording, or in any information storage or retrieval system, without permission in writing from the publishers.

Notice:
Product or corporate names may be trademarks or registered trademarks, and are used only for identification and explanation without intent to infringe.

British Library Cataloguing-in-Publication Data
A catalogue record for this book is available from the British Library

Library of Congress Cataloging-in-Publication Data
Names: McLelland, Nicola, 1970– author.
Title: Teaching and learning foreign languages : a history of language
 education, assessment and policy in Britain / Nicola McLelland.
Description: Milton Park, Abingdon, Oxon ; New York, NY :
 Routledge, [2017]
Identifiers: LCCN 2016055460 | ISBN 9781138651289 (hardback) |
 ISBN 9781315624853 (ebook)
Subjects: LCSH: Language and languages—Study and teaching—
 English speakers—Great Britian. | Language policy—Great
 Britian—History.
Classification: LCC PE1128.A2 M424 2017 | DDC 418.0071/041—dc23
LC record available at https://lccn.loc.gov/2016055460

ISBN: 978-1-138-65128-9 (hbk)
ISBN: 978-0-367-17791-1 (pbk)

Typeset in Galliard
by Apex CoVantage, LLC

Visit the eResources: www.routledge.com/9781138651289

For Tom, Patrick, and Mary

Why do we learn foreign languages? For two reasons, a lower and a higher – the lower simply utilitarian, the higher to acquire a new soul by penetrating into a new realm of thought.

(Widgery, *The Teaching of Languages in Schools*, 1888: 1)

Contents

List of tables and figures   x
Acknowledgements   xi

1 Introduction   1

2 Which languages do English speakers want to learn? Answers from history   5

3 A sociocultural history of language learning: Why, who, where?   39

4 How languages have been taught and learned   85

5 Assessment   127

6 Making the case for languages: A history of advocacy and policy   174

7 Conclusions – applying lessons from the past to the present and future   217

Bibliography   226
Index   253

Tables and Figures

Tables

2.1	Language candidates at the Cambridge Local Examinations, December 1888 (Juniors and Seniors)	8
2.2	GCSE Examination figures for so-called community languages in 2005	29
2.3	Most popular combinations of two or more modern foreign languages at GCSE in 2007	31
2.4	A-level entries for French, German and Spanish (1938–2010)	33
3.1	Uptake of combinations of modern foreign languages by school type (percentages of students)	54
3.2	Number of higher education institutions in the UK offering particular languages in 1963 and 1996	74
5.1	An overview of test requirements in some non-school and school examinations in 1970	134
5.2	Relative weightings of test components at O-level/GCSE 16	135
5.3	Opening sentences of the passage for translation into German in Senior/Higher/A-level examinations for selected years, 1858–1994, from UCLES/Cambridge Assessment	136
5.4	Grammatical structures required in the French GCSE	142
5.5	Writing assessment criteria in various schemes	158
5.6	Attainment targets for writing in the National Curriculum, 1992–present	161

Figures

2.1	Ludolf's *Grammatica russica* (1696: 54–55)	24
3.1	The Dutch Schoole-Master (*Le Mayre 1606*)	41
3.2	*Lamartine's* Pictorial French Course shows 'The family in the living-room' (14th ed. 1914: 1)	57
4.1	*Arte de la lengua chio chiu* (ca. 1620), f. 5r	91
4.2	The first exercise in Wanostrocht's *Practical Grammar of French* (London, 1780: 13)	98
4.3	A picture story from *En Avant* Nuffield Introductory French Course Stage 4b (Nuffield 1971: 17)	113

Acknowledgements

Thanks to the British Academy for a 12-month British Academy Mid-Career Fellowship in 2015, during which this book was written. I hope that it will add to the energetic efforts of the Academy to help to promote interest in learning and studying languages in the UK – and beyond.

Warm thanks to Lesley Hagger-Vaughan, Bernadette Holmes and Rosamond Mitchell, whose comments on earlier drafts of some of the chapters in this book were invaluable.

Finally, my heartfelt gratitude goes to my colleagues in German Studies at the University of Nottingham, who were unfailingly supportive and encouraging, and who carried on the daily business of the department while somehow forbearing from telling me any of the myriad administrative concerns and crises of the modern academic hurly-burly.

Thanks to the following for kind permission to reproduce textbook images and examination papers: AQA, Cambridge Assessment, Cambridge University Library, Trinity College Dublin, University of Barcelona Library, University of Birmingham Library.

1 Introduction

This history of language learning and teaching in Britain – the first such history for Britain and indeed for any English-speaking country[1] – brings together several threads that have previously been treated separately, by scholars from different disciplines: the place of language teaching and learning in society as considered by cultural historians (e.g. Cohen 1996, Gallagher 2014); the history of learning individual languages as researched by language specialists, whether for England in particular (e.g. Kibbee 1991 for French, Muckle 2008a for Russian, McLelland 2015a for German)[2] or taking a wider view (e.g. Glück 2002, 2013 on the history of German as a foreign language in Europe and beyond); and the history of language teaching methods written by language pedagogues (e.g. Titone 1968 and Kelly 1969, Wheeler 2013, as well as historical sections in Stern 1983 and Hawkins 1987, 1996). Drawing on these various threads, the five chapters that follow each tackle the history of language learning from a different perspective. Chapter 2 provides a chronological overview of Britain's language learning choices – which languages began to be learnt when, and why? Chapter 3 examines the social history of language teachers and learners and the social status of language learning. Chapter 4 is a history of *how* languages have been taught, how that has changed over time, and why. The final two chapters tackle areas whose histories have barely begun to be charted anywhere in the world: Chapter 5 deals with the history of assessment and Chapter 6 with the history of advocacy and policy.

My chronological reach is deliberately wide, including the pre-modern period is a corrective to some language teaching histories that tend to emphasize developments since the nineteenth century, or since the Reform Movement of the late nineteenth century only, thus making the twentieth century's gradual shift in favour of communicative skills appear an unprecedented improvement rather than a swing of the pendulum (though with important differences) back to pre-modern priorities. Equally, my emphasis in the later chapters on twentieth-century assessment, advocacy and policy addresses both a period and key themes that have thus far received little attention from language teaching historians.

A word on my methodology and sources: published prescriptions for teaching and learning may suggest revolutionary changes in practice, but may not match the everyday reality, where there may be greater continuity than precepts "from above" may suggest. To get at this history of language teaching "from below" (McLelland 2015a: 2), I have not only drawn on institutional materials (e.g. government reports, policy documents, syllabi, curricula), professional journal articles and other "expert" writings, but have tried (as already in McLelland 2015a) to strike a balance between the pronouncements of authorities on what should be done, and other sources that reflect practice, including textbooks (and their authors' prefaces), examiners' reports and, to a limited extent, memoirs, letters and press coverage. (On sources for historiographers of language learning and teaching, see Smith 2016).

My focus is on the history of language learning in Britain and, indeed, often largely only England. But Britain's language learning history is part of Europe's cultural and social history, whether in the much-shared and oft-recycled bilingual and polyglot manuals of the early modern period (Chapter 2, 4), in the social cachet of the multilingual Grand Tourist and the discovery of other nations' literary and intellectual cultures (Chapter 3), or in the more recent shared history of European Union and Council of Europe initiatives in language learning assessment and policy (Chapters 5 and 6). The development of teaching methodologies – whether in British schools or in other settings – is part of an international history too, one that at the very least encompasses Europe and the USA, but perhaps also former British colonies (though very little work has been done on their language learning histories to date). The teacher-led initiatives of the newly professionalizing language teachers in the late nineteenth century and beyond, discussed in Chapter 3, provide examples that arguably set the direction of developments in the twentieth century across Europe and North America: the Reform Movement's renewed focus on the spoken language (amongst other innovations), as well as student exchanges, assistantships and pen-friendships that developed around 1900. Likewise, twentieth-century experiments in language teaching in Britain were inspired in some cases by developments in the USA (Chapter 4). There are potential parallels in policy amongst English-speaking countries too, where the answers to the questions "why learn a language?" and "which language first?" have had to be answered differently compared to those countries where the status of English as first foreign language is obvious, in recent history, at least. Against this background, the history of advocacy for Spanish in the USA, discussed in Chapter 6, offers an illuminating parallel with advocacy for Spanish in the UK and its subsequent steep rise in popularity.

The history of language assessment is in its infancy, but Weir and O'Sullivan note significant differences in the history of *English* language testing between Europe and the USA (p.c; see now also O'Sullivan & Weir 2016). We simply know too little about the history of modern languages assessment anywhere to make a similar judgement for languages other than English yet, but I hope that the case study of Modern Languages assessment in England presented in Chapter 5 will alert readers to similarities and differences compared with their own contexts; I hope, too, and that it will inspire similar case studies that will, ultimately, allow us to chart an international comparative history of languages testing: of the changing assumptions made about its goals, about what can and should be tested, and about the methods for doing so.

A history of language learning and teaching in Britain is a valid undertaking for its own sake, and I hope that readers will appreciate discovering how language teaching and learning have both mirrored and shaped Britain's cultural and social development, as well as its relationships with Europe and the rest of the world through trade, colonization and cultural exchange (cf. Hüllen 2005: 7). However, I also hope to equip readers to analyse the present state of language teaching and learning, and to debate decisions for the future, since – whether we intend it or not – our beliefs about the past guide our views of the present and of what is possible in future. It is easy to assume that the way we teach languages now is, if not the only way, then probably the best way there is; or we may look back with affection on own experience as learners as an ideal learning experience. Neither of these attitudes is good for teachers, learners, testers, or decision makers of whatever kind. First, decisions may rest on false assumptions about what is possible, or about what actions are likely to have what kind of effect. Second, when things change – changes in policy, or changed views about effective methods of teaching or assessment – it is all too easy for teachers to feel disorientated and to lose confidence in their ability to teach under these new "rules". One aim of this history of foreign language learning and teaching, then, is to furnish readers from all these constituencies with a wider historical context in which to view today's orthodoxies and tomorrow's revolutions, to enable more informed decision making, and to ease anxieties when change comes.

The history of language teaching and learning reveals – with the benefit of critical distance – how the day-to-day work of language teaching, assessment and planning is determined by core beliefs and assumptions that are scarcely questioned and are often simply accepted as "facts". In reality, as this book will show, those beliefs have changed greatly over time; what seems inevitable and self-evident now, has not always been so, and will not always be so. I end this introduction, therefore, with six questions where knowledge of the past can inform decisions today, and which I encourage readers to bear in mind as they read the following chapters:

1   Why do we teach languages, and how and why have the answers to the question changed over time?
2   What determines choices about which languages to learn?
3   Are English speakers a special case when it comes to language learning?
4   What is the right kind of learner, the right kind of teacher?
5   What affects what goes on in the languages classroom?
6   How do we measure language learning success?

We shall then return to these questions – and the changing answers to them – in Chapter 7.

4 *Introduction*

Notes

1 While it is the first such history of Britain, there is important work on the history of language learning and teaching in other parts of Europe. For example, see Schröder's bio-bibliographical compendium of foreign language teachers in the German-speaking world (Schröder 1987–99); Puren (1988, 1994) on language learning in France; Maréchal (1972) for Belgium up to the early twentieth century; Hulshof, Kwakernaak and Wilhelm (2016) for the Low Countries as a whole. See also the overviews of the history of language teaching and learning in the Low Countries, Germany, France, Spain, Italy and Portugal in McLelland and Smith (2017b). Two recent overviews of the history of language learning in Europe as a whole are given by Hüllen (2005), in German; and in French, and only up to 1800, Caravolas (1994, 2000, particularly 1994: 100–117 and 2000: 3–40).
2 For similar language-specific histories for other parts of Europe, see Rjéoutski & Tchoudinov (2013) for the learning of French in Eastern Europe from the seventeenth to nineteenth century, Kuhfuß (2014) for French learning in early modern Germany, de Boer (2012) on Italian in the Low Countries, Kok Escalle and Strien-Chardonneau (2010) for the history of French in the Low Countries and Hammar (1991) for French in Sweden. For Germany, key studies include a three-volume history of the methods of teaching English in Germany from 1800–1960 (Macht 1986–1990), and Klippel's study of English learning in nineteenth-century Germany (Klippel 1994). Chapters 2 and 3 also include suggestions for further reading on the history of learning and teaching specific languages, and of the sociocultural history of language learning and teaching.

2 Which languages do English speakers want to learn?
Answers from history

2.1 Introduction

One of the first – and the most crucial – choices made by learners, schools and policy bodies is which language(s) to learn or teach. This chapter looks at the history of language learning choices made by English speakers that have led to today's *status quo*. That history is better researched for some languages than for others, and since it is not possible to deal with every language learned, it is a somewhat uneven and incomplete history (but see suggestions for further reading in 2.14). Still, as the first such overview of the history of language learning choices made by English-speaking learners from 1500 to the present, it can shed light on the historical background to our current patterns of choice.

In the 1630s, a learning manual that was very popular throughout Europe was printed in two editions in England (Berlaimont 1637, 1639). Such 'polyglot' manuals catered to a growing language learning market by presenting multiple languages alongside one another, thus claiming to help learners tackle any one of several languages in a single volume. This was a valuable promise at a time when the new availability of printed materials was revolutionizing language teaching, but when books were still very expensive and when it was still widely acknowledged that once across the Channel, English was "worth nothing", as John Florio (1578: 1) wrote, a situation which continued well into the eighteenth century (Sumillera 2014: 61).[1] So which languages did these polyglot manuals offer alongside English? Latin, French and Dutch in the first case; Latin, French, Dutch, German, Spanish, Italian and Portuguese in the second. Those two lists are unlikely to match the first three foreign languages, or the first seven, that we would think of today. The aim of this chapter is to examine, and help explain, such changes in priorities, and so to consider how they might change again in future.

The chapter is roughly chronological, treating languages in the approximate order that they gained a foothold as foreign languages in Britain. That places Latin first (2.2), followed by French (2.3), then Italian (2.4), Spanish (2.5), Dutch (2.6), Portuguese (2.7), English as a Foreign Language (2.8), German (2.9), Russian (2.10) and so-called community languages such as Urdu (2.11) and Chinese (2.12). As we shall see, one continuity over the whole period is that French was, and still is, the first foreign language. Another, perhaps more surprising continuity, is that Urdu's place remains almost as marginal in formal education as it was in the eighteenth century, despite the large community that speaks it. There has been change, too. For example, Dutch, once a prominent language choice, has virtually no profile as a foreign language today; Chinese, a latecomer only in the nineteenth century, is starting to challenge traditional assumptions that "Modern Languages" are European languages. Politics, commerce and war all inform choices about which languages are promoted, but the most enduring trends in language learning nevertheless seem determined by the strength of lasting cultural affinities.

2.2 The first language taught – Latin

Language learning has been going on for as long as we can trace our written history. Around 731 AD, the monk and historian Bede listed the five languages of Britain as English, British, Irish, Pictish and Latin (Bede's *History*, Book I, Chapter 1). While he said nothing about how these different language communities communicated with each other, he implied that they all used Latin. Viking England was arguably a bilingual Danish-English society; some contemporary writers distinguished these as different languages, but in practice there was little need for language learning because the languages were mutually intelligible – each would speak their own language (like Swedes and Danes today, for example) (Townend 2002: 185–186). Travel and mixed marriages (especially amongst the elite) would have meant that some language learning went on, but we have no evidence of language *teaching* during this early period for any language except Latin. So the oldest tradition of formal language learning for English-speaking learners concerned a language that is not one of today's modern languages at all. Still, in Antiquity, the experience of learning Latin in Europe was much more like that of learning an "ordinary" foreign language than it is today, when Latin is by definition a "dead" language. Under the Roman Empire, Latin as a foreign language had already been a major educational challenge: children in Greece and other parts of the empire were "sent to Roman schools so that they would learn Latin and pick up the trappings of civilisation, and more importantly, be assimilated into the dominant culture" (Law 2003: 83). When the Empire was Christianized, Latin became the language not only of civil administration but also of the church. Since imparting literacy was exclusively in the hands of the church, Latin also became the language of education and scholarship across Europe, including Britain. Throughout this period, for the small number of boys (hardly ever girls) who learned Latin, the environment might have been not unlike that of a child today whose family uses another language at home, encountering English as their school language. The experience was, probably, similarly immersive. There are differences, however. To judge from the surviving materials, most learners began with methods that had originated to teach Latin to native speakers, with few concessions made to the needs of foreign learners. The most widely used beginners' text in Latin was the *Ars minor* of Aelius Donatus, studied continuously throughout Europe from when it was written, ca. 350 AD, up until the sixteenth century, and its influence can still be felt in Kennedy's *Latin Primer* used well into the twentieth century in Britain (Law 2003: 65). The *Ars minor* is a grammar of about 11 pages, in a question-and-answer format. It uses the "target language" from the start. The beginning pupil would have been expected to learn the text off by heart, starting as follows, by asking how many parts of speech there are (eight) and then what they are:

partes orationis quot sunt? octo. quae? nomen pronomen verbum adverbium participium conjunctio praepositio interjectio.
"How many parts of speech are there? Eight. What are they? Noun pronoun verb adverb participle conjunction preposition interjection."[2]

The *Ars minor* then deals with each part of speech in turn, supplying answers to questions – for the noun, the questions and answers tackled the cases, genders, number, etc. The beginning learner of Latin, then, was expected to learn about Latin grammar *through* Latin, although tutors also used glossaries (word-lists). Some at least also used model conversations, like the tenth/eleventh-century bilingual Anglo-Saxon/Latin one whose beginning is given next.

We cildra biddaþ þe, eala lareow! Þæt þu tæce us sprecan, for þam ungelþrde we $_7$ syndon gewæmmodliche we sprecaþ.
Nos pueri rogamus te, magister, obnixe, ut doceas nos loqui Latialiter recte, quia idiote sumus et corrupte loquimur.
"Master, we young men would like you to teach us how to speak properly and with a wide vocabulary, for we are ignorant and badly spoken."
(Stevenson 1929: 75)

In modern English translation, the dialogue continues:

Teacher: How would you like to speak?
Pupils: We are concerned about the way we speak, as we want to speak correctly and with meaning, and not with meaningless base words. Would you beat us and make us learn? For it is better for us to be beaten to learn than to remain ignorant. However, we know that you are a kind-hearted man who would not wish to inflict blows on us unless we ask for them.
Teacher: I ask you to tell me what work you do. I am a monk by profession. I sing seven psalms during the day, and spend my time in reading and singing; but, however, I should like you, in the meanwhile, to learn to converse in the Latin language. What skills do your workmates possess?
Pupils: Some are ploughmen, some are shepherds, others are oxherds, hunters, fishermen, fowlers, merchants, leather workers, salters and bakers.
Teacher: Can you tell us, ploughman, how you do your work?
(translation by Ann. E. Watkins from www.kentarchaeology.ac)

Aside from a ready acceptance of corporal punishment as a teaching technique (!), the dialogue shows us that regular and repeated exposure to Latin through the daily liturgical rhythm (including singing seven psalms in Latin every day) was not necessarily enough to "learn to converse in the Latin language", at least not about everyday matters. For these, vocabulary and conversation practice must be provided separately, beginning here with a ploughman's description of his work routine. It is difficult to know how widely such conversations were used in the Middle Ages. Still, we can say that English speakers' first experiences of learning a language formally began with a grammar, supported by word-lists and, sometimes, model dialogues.

Latin continued to be the mainstay of boys' education until the twentieth century. It was so obviously central that King Henry VIII commissioned a committee to produce a suitable grammar for schools, *A Shorte Introduction of Grammar*, compiled in about 1540 – the fact that *Latin* grammar was its object was so self-evident that it did not need to be stated. This grammar dominated the teaching of Latin for more than three centuries as an obligatory textbook in English schools (Gwosdek 2013). When the first Public Schools were established in the first half of the nineteenth century in Britain, Latin was still unquestioned as the core of the curriculum. Pupils learnt grammar, rhetoric, style – all through Latin. By the later nineteenth century, however, Latin was losing its stranglehold, as we can see from the numbers of candidates for the Oxford and Cambridge "Local" Examinations, intended for pupils not progressing to university. In the Cambridge Senior School Certificate examinations of December 1888, for example, almost three times as many pupils took French (2014) as Latin (696), only slightly more candidates than German, with 625 (see Table 2.1).[3] Likewise, at the equivalent Oxford examinations in 1895, the figures stood at 1,244 for French, 397 for Latin and 348 for German (Ortmanns 1993: 34).

Yet Latin continued to be the gateway to university study. Cambridge University, for example, continued to require Latin for entry until 1960 (or Ancient

Table 2.1 Language candidates at the Cambridge Local Examinations, December 1888 (Juniors and Seniors) (Source: "Papers, class lists, reports", Cambridge Library cam.c.11.51). Percentage figures in brackets indicate the relative proportions of female and male candidates for each subject.

Junior	Total no. of candidates	Latin		Greek		French	German
		Virgil	Caesar	Xenophon	Euripides		
Total boys	5,224	1,268 (91.9%)	2,292 (91.9%)	261 (98.9%)	136 (100%)	4,458 (63.5%)	352 (35.7%)
Total girls	2,660	111 (8.1%)	203 (8.1%)	3 (1.1%)	0 (0%)	2,558 (36.5%)	633 (64.3%)
Total number of Junior candidates	7,884	1,379	2,495	264	136	7,016	985

Senior		Latin	Greek	French	German
Total boys	1,498	484 (69.5%)	170 (93.9%)	551 (27.4%)	59 (9.4%)
Total girls	645	212 (30.5%)	11 (6.1%)	1,463 (72.6%)	566 (90.6%)
Total number of Senior candidates	2,143	696	181	2,014	625

Greek, though far fewer pupils took it).[4] Even leading advocates of Modern Languages still fully accepted the importance of the classical languages at the dawn of the twentieth century. Otto Siepmann, who taught French and German at Clifton College and was a pioneer in the introduction of new approaches to language teaching around 1900 (Whitehead 2004), wrote in 1902 to his son – then preparing for the scholarship examination for Rugby School – that "your future rests on the classical languages. In Rugby you will be tested in German and French too, it's true, but Latin and Greek are the main thing".[5]

Today, by contrast, Latin is not offered at all in most primary or secondary schools outside the private sector. Still, lobbying ensured that with the requirement from 2014 that all pupils learn a language from the age of eight (at "Key Stage 2"), ancient languages (Latin or Greek) were deemed acceptable. However, at Key Stage 3 (i.e. age 11–14), the National Curriculum for England requires a *modern* foreign language; there, Latin does not "count"(on this policy see 6.3.3).

2.3 French – the first foreign language

After the Norman Conquest of Britain in 1066, French was the language of the aristocracy, but the evidence suggests that it played virtually no role in everyday life until at least the mid-twelfth century, and very few English people knew French. But in 1166, a new law allowed freemen the right to appeal to the highest court, which operated in French,[6] and so a "professional class of pleaders" emerged, who needed to be able to read and write French – the very earliest text for learning French is a twelfth-century English-French legal glossary (Kibbee 1991: 11–15, 30–31).[7] The following is an example of a thirteenth-century model of how to record an interrogation in French (from *Placita corone* ca. 1280, ed. by Kaye 1966, cited by Kibbee 1991: 33). Most witnesses in fact gave their evidence in English, but the model interrogation is given in French because that was the language of legal record. (One might compare the case to Chinese, where, until the twentieth century, conversational exchanges in Chinese would automatically be rendered into – rather different – classical Chinese if they were to be written down.)

Visconte, pur que est cet homme pris?	Vicount, for what has this man been seized?
Sire, pur suspecion de bestes prises et emblees et en le pays priveement recettes	Sire, on suspicion of beasts taken away and secretly received in the country.
Avez rin trove oveke ly dont vous eiez mauveise suspecion?	Have you found anything of which you have a bad suspicion?
Sire, oil: ii vaches ke ci sunt presentes	Sire, yes: two cows which here are present.
Coment avez non, beaus amys?	What is your name, fair friend?
Nichole de C., Sire, ay a non	Nichole de Ca. is my name, sire.
Ou naquiste vous?	Where were you born?
Sire, en le Conte de C.	Sire, in the County of C.

French was not just used in the legal domain in the later Middle Ages. It was a "second language of culture" used by the literate minority who kept administrative, commercial, diplomatic, ecclesiastical, and social records in French too (Rothwell 1992: 7). However, this French was becoming very different in its vocabulary and semantics from the French of France. By the mid-thirteenth century, therefore, the descendants of the Normans living in England fell victim to a "cultural cringe". They felt a need to learn "proper", continental French, rather than their own, lower prestige, Anglo-Norman French, and there is much evidence of concern over children's "bad" French. (One might compare the experiences of second and later generations of migrants today in Britain and elsewhere – how anxious are they, or their parents, about their mastery of, say, Gujarati, Urdu, or Polish?). For example, Kibbee (1991: 25) cites the thirteenth-century Anglo-French romance *Blonde d'Oxford*, where young Blonde's English origins are betrayed by her French, until a French page tutors her:

> *Un peu parroit a son langage*
> *Que ne fus pas née a Pontoise*

"Her language showed somewhat that she was not born at Pontoise" (i.e. in the heart of France; Pontoise is a town now in the suburbs of Paris).

> Le tienent d'aprendre françois
> Et en milleur françois le mist.

"He gave lessons to her in French, and put her French in better order".[8]

Speaking French "badly" – differently to the prestige Parisian variety – continued to be a source of amusement. In his *Canterbury Tales*, written in the late fourteenth century, Geoffrey Chaucer describes the Prioress's French with an implied smile (Kibbee 1991: 69):

> *And French she spak ful faire and fetisly*
> *After the scole of Stratford atte Bowe,*
> *For French of Paris was to her unknowe.*
>   (Prioress's Tale, 124–126)

An additional motivation to learn French during the Hundred Years' War (1337–1453) was in order to serve in what Kibbee (1991: 61) calls the colonial administration, particularly its military force" of the French territories held by England. The status of French began to decline, however, after the Hundred Years' War, as it became clear that England would not be able to maintain its "cross-channel empire (Kibbee 1991: 62). By the fifteenth century, French was a foreign language for all, but it was still used as the language of record in government, church, literature and correspondence, as well as law. The paradoxical status of French is summed up in the fact that in 1362, a statute was passed under which French was no longer to be the language of government because it was "too poorly understood", but the statute was itself recorded in French (Kibbee 1991: 58)!

Another group who needed French were merchants, especially in the cloth trade with Flanders. One of the earliest textbooks for English speakers to learn French was a translation, published by the pioneering printer William Caxton around 1483, of an originally French-Flemish manual, the *Livre des Mestiers*, with bilingual dialogues and vocabulary (Howatt 1984: 6–7). Its dialogues are rather minimal – some of them are really contextualized word-lists. For example, the following is a vignette of Martin the grocer taken from the second half of the book (cited by Howatt 1984: 7), which contains descriptions of tradespeople and so allows listings of their accoutrements.

Martin le especier	Martin the grocer
Vent pluiseurs especes	Selleth many spyces
De toutes manieres de pouldre	Of all manners of poudre
Pour faire les brouets,	For to make browettys (i.e. *broths*)
Et a moult de boistes pointes	And hath many boxes paynted
Plaines de confections,	Full of confections,
Et moult de cannes	And many pottes
Plaines de beuurages.	Full of drynkes.

There are also basic dialogues for greetings and farewells, and for asking the way; a more detailed dialogue for bargaining over the price of cloth reveals the manual's origins as a manual for Flemish cloth-merchants in Bruges. A few years later, Caxton's assistant Wynken de Worde published a similar *Lytell Treatise for to lerne Englisshe and Frensshe* (1498), laid out in alternating lines of French and English (rather than in adjacent columns, as mentioned above, which became the norm for bilingual dialogues across Europe). It begins,

Here is a good boke to lerne to speke Frenshe
Vecy ung bon livre apprendre parler françoys
[. . .]
Soo that I maye doo my merchandise
Affin que je puisse faire ma marchanchise
In Fraunce & ells whereh in other londes
En France et ailleurs en aultre pays
There as the folk speke Frensshe.
La ou les gens parlen françoys
                    (cited by Howatt 1984: 8)

Over the coming centuries, interest grew in other languages besides French, as we shall see below. However, French remained in first place. In every decade from 1480 to 1720, manuals for French outnumber those of any other single language (see Gallagher 2014: 33). French still remains the "first" foreign language in

Britain today. It is still most likely to be the first foreign language that a child encounters in school. For many people it is the only foreign language they ever learn, and it is the one taken by the largest number of pupils and students. In 2014–2015, the first year that primary schools were required to teach a foreign language, French was offered by 77% of primary schools, further consolidating its place as the "first" foreign language in Britain (Board & Tinsley 2015: 121).

2.4 Italian – a language of refinement?

Despite the primacy of French, by the sixteenth century, as more people began to travel and correspond more widely, French was not *always* the first modern language to be learnt (Kibbee 1991: 106). In the second half of the sixteenth century, both Italian and Spanish vied for attention, though for somewhat different reasons (on Spanish, see 2.5). The flowering of courtly culture in the High Middle Ages made French a prestige foreign language, as well as a useful one, in Britain as in other parts of Europe. The Renaissance, which gradually spread northwards from Italy through Europe, did the same for Italian. Italian became known as the language of Dante, Boccaccio and others. English speakers' interest in Italian was also, indirectly, helped on its way by their ties with French culture, because at the French court, Italian had become the prestige vernacular. After the Inquisition was established in Italy in 1542, Italian Protestant refugees provided a reservoir of potential teachers of Italian in England. Michael Angelo Florio, one such Protestant refugee, was the first to offer Italian lessons to the English public, and his well-connected son, John Florio, was, besides being tutor to Lady Jane Grey, the author of textbooks for learning Italian (*First Fruits, which yield Familiar Speech, Merry Proverbs, Witty Sentences, and Golden Sayings* 1578, a *Second Fruites* 1591 with about 6,000 proverbs, and the *World of Words* 1598). However, the first Italian textbooks published were written by Englishmen: Thomas's *Principal Rules of the Italian Grammer* [sic] 1550, followed by Granthan's *An Italian Grammar*, which was a translation of a grammar first written by Scipio Lentulo in Latin (Kibbee 1991: 107), and John Sanford's *Introduction to the Italian Tongue* (1605). The French Huguenot refugee Claudius Hollyband published *The Italian Schoolemaister* (1583) (see Caravolas 1994: 112–114 for these and numerous other examples; also Watson 1909: 444–467).

Florio's *First Fruits* was clearly directed at gentlemen – and women. In it, Italian is taught as a language of social aspiration, a language of courtly society and of fashionable literature. Topics of conversation in the early dialogues include attending court, listening to a concert of viols and lutes, choosing clothes (including white stockings, well-perfumed gloves and good garters) and leisured travel around France, Spain, Italy and Germany (the "Grand Tour"):

Io ho visto, toccata, sentito molte cose strane, e speso i miei danari	I have scene [sic], felt, heard many strange things, and spent my money

(Florio 1578: 8)

Much of the book consists of proverbs, which were a fascination of educated, Humanist Europe, as in these examples:

> Chi bien siede, mal pensa.   Who sitteth wel, thinketh yl.
> Chi lascia la via vechia,   Who leaueth an olde way
> per pa nuoua, spesse   for a new, oftentimes doth
> volte inganato si ritrova   finde hymselfe deccyued
>   [i.e. *deceived*]
>   (Florio 1578: 26)

Despite the prestige of Italian in the second half of the sixteenth century, it had mixed fortunes in the seventeenth century. Gallagher (2014: 36–37) finds only two English-Italian texts published between 1600 and 1619, and none at all for the next two decades. Italian re-emerged in 1640 with Giovanni Torriano's *Italian Tutor or a new and most compleat Italian grammer*. Its author appealed to "the good of all the English Nation", but, significantly, especially to "you who are in a continuall commerce with most parts of Italy, as well as Turkey, where the Italian Tongue is all in all" (Torriano 1640, dedication "To the right worshipfull and now most flourishing Company of Turkey Marchants"). The expansion of England's Mediterranean trade now briefly replaced cultural prestige as the main reason to learn Italian: it was a language which could serve as a lingua franca throughout the Mediterranean, from the Italian peninsula to the Barbary coast (i.e. North and North-Western Africa) and to Turkey, and beyond.

Yet Italian was also the foreign language most likely to be seen particularly as a ladies' accomplishment. Torriano wrote in his *Della Lingua Toscana-Romana* that after a decline in interest, the study of the language had been made popular again amongst women by 'several Ladies of qualitie' (1657: A2r, cited by Gallagher 2014: 38), and it enjoyed a further flowering when opera reached England. A few eighteenth-century titles were directed at female learners in particular, including Baretti's *Small talk for the use of young ladies that wish to learn the colloquial part of the Italian language* (1775) and *The Ladies' New Italian Grammar* (Grimani 1788), whose author also published French-Italian conversations. A century later, when Cambridge introduced its Examination for Women in 1869 (a higher qualification than the Junior and Senior school examinations, and envisaged as a qualification for intending governesses, for example), Italian was one of the languages offered alongside French and German, even though it was not yet available in the normal school examinations taken overwhelmingly by boys. However, when the Higher School Certificate was introduced in 1918, Italian was added, alongside Russian, as a new subsidiary subject.[9] Lepschy et al. (1974: 6) found Italian in "over 250" schools, and there were 37 departments of Italian at British universities in 1974, in addition to a presence in 18 polytechnics. Italian is still not very widely taught in schools, but remains well established in many universities today.

2.5 Spanish – from fourth to third to second

Spanish is now the second most popular foreign language in British schools, after French. It is also the most studied language in the USA, where the number of students taking Spanish language studies in higher education in autumn 2013 outnumbered the combined total taking all other languages (790,756 vs. 771,423 students; source Goldberg et al. 2015). In the USA, the reasons are obvious – Spanish is the most widely spoken language after English, and the USA has close links of all kinds, including strong family ties, with Central and South America.[10] In Britain, the reasons for the popularity of Spanish are less immediately obvious. This section reviews the growth in interest in Spanish, from its slow beginnings in the sixteenth century to its position as second foreign language today.

The first evidence of a market for Spanish learning materials comes from two Spanish-English conversation manuals that appeared in the 1550s, the decade during which Queen Mary Tudor (the daughter of the Spanish-born Catherine of Aragon and Henry VIII) married Phillip of Spain in 1554 (who became King of Spain in 1556). However, when Mary Tudor's death in 1558 brought the Protestant Queen Elizabeth I to the throne, it became riskier to show an interest in Catholic Spain; the Spanish Armada (1588) marked a low-point in Anglo-Spanish relations. But from 1614 to 1623, there were lengthy negotiations for a potential match between the son of King James I and the daughter of King Philip III of Spain, and there was another "flurry of texts" for learning Spanish (Gallagher 2014: 35). Two further texts appeared in the early eighteenth century when England was caught up in the War of the Spanish Succession: one by a Captain John Stevens, the other by a teacher of Spanish in London, writing, he said, "To the Service of the Nobility and Gentry of England, that upon the Occasion of the War go to Spain" (cited by Gallagher 2014: 36).

Spanish arts and literature were also enjoying their golden age in the sixteenth and seventeenth centuries and had some influence in Britain; Ben Johnson (1572–1637) made fun of the fashion for Spanish styles in one of his plays, for example (Spauling 1948: 174). John Minsheu, self-proclaimed "Professor of Languages in London", published aids to reading difficult classical or contemporary Spanish texts (Salmon 2003: 262), by providing passages

> expounded out of diuers [i.e. *diverse*] authors, setting downe the line and the leafe where in the same bookes they shall finde them, whereby they may not onely vnderstand them, but by them vnderstand others, and the rest as they shall meete with them.
> (Minsheu 1599: *A dictionarie in Spanish and English* [. . .]: taken from the full title of the work)

So some learners, at least, were reading Spanish literature. Whether, without the additional political and dynastic connections to Spain, its Golden Age would have been enough to spark an interest in the study of the language is unclear. As

Gallagher writes, "It seems Spanish language competence was mainly considered an acceptable accomplishment at times of Anglo-Spanish détente or heightened conflict" [. . .] "anxieties about Spanish power, English national security, and Catholicism [. . .] may account for the relative paucity of Spanish language-learning texts in English" in the early modern period" (Gallagher 2014: 36).

The Peninsular War against Napoleon in 1807–1814 (known in Spanish as the Spanish War of Independence) prompted renewed British interest in Spanish. This war of independence captured the imagination in the age of emerging nationalism in Europe, especially amongst British Romantics such as the poet Lord Byron (1788–1824) and Robert Southey (1774–1843), who published a history of the Spanish Peninsula war in 1823 (Martínez 2014: 144). The novelist Walter Scott read Spanish literature, and called for a new English translation of *Don Quixote*, a need supplied in 1822 by the Oxford don John Gibson Lockhart (1784–1854), making a significant contribution to popularization Spanish literature in Britain (Martínez 2014: 145); other translations followed. After the Spanish colonies of South America gained independence in the mid-nineteenth century (e.g. Mexico 1821, Argentina 1861), British business and industrialists recognized the potential of new markets in Latin America. So it is not surprising that Spanish could be taken, along with Italian, French and German, as a language in the Commercial Certificate language examinations briefly offered by Cambridge in the 1880s and early 1890s (see McLelland 2015a: 79–81). It was also the first additional foreign language to be offered alongside French and German in the main Junior and Senior school examinations set by the Oxford and Cambridge boards in 1894–1895 (Oxford) and 1895–1896 (Cambridge).

The first chairs of Spanish, established by University College London and King's College London in the 1830s, were held by Spanish ex-patriates, but British Hispanists soon found their own place. Captain George Gilmour, who had strong business links with Argentina, endowed a chair of Spanish at the newly independent University of Liverpool in 1908, with the specific requirement that the new professor should teach the variety of Spanish used in Argentina; Spanish had already been taught in the School of Commerce of the university's predecessor, the University College Liverpool (whose degrees were conferred by the University of London). Another industrialist, Weetman Pearson, who had made his money in Mexican railways, amongst other things, endowed a new Chair in Spanish Language and Literature at the University of Leeds in 1916. In the same year, an "Anglo-Spanish Society" was formed in Oxford, with branches soon following in other cities too; Cambridge University established a department of Spanish in 1919 (Martinez 2014: 157–159). A specialist journal, the *Bulletin of Spanish Studies*, was founded by Edgar Allison Peers in 1923. The timing of these key steps to establish not just Hispanophiles but qualified Hispanists around the turn of the twentieth century was crucial – they came just as the other modern languages were also only beginning to establish themselves in universities (for example, the Schröder chair of German at Cambridge was endowed by a merchant bank only in 1909). Henry Butler Clarke, appointed Teacher of Spanish at Oxford from 1890, lost no time in producing materials suitable for school pupils to learn Spanish, not just for students: a reader, a grammar and an 'elementary handbook' of literature (published 1891, 1892, 1893). All this groundwork at university level meant that Spanish was well-placed to respond to growing interest in learning Spanish in schools from the turn of the twentieth century onwards.

The endowment of Spanish chairs at Liverpool and Leeds by business interests already attests to the commercial importance of Spanish, and the commercial case was also made in public policy discussions in the Leathes Report on Modern Studies (1918 – see 6.3.4). However, Spanish at first grew only slowly in schools. In 1895, the first year it was available, there were four Junior and three Senior candidates in the Oxford board's examinations. In 1928, at the Secondary School Certificate examination, 719 candidates took Spanish, but this was still only about 1% of the number who took French, and a fifth of the number who sat German (Phillips & Filmer-Sankey 1993: 15–16). But in 1952–1953, when the Royal Society of Arts (RSA) set French, German and Spanish papers as part of its School Commercial Certificate, Spanish candidates (40) outnumbered those for French and German (19 and 0). Although 34 of the 40 failed, their existence is further evidence of the perception of Spanish as a subject with commercial relevance; even for Spanish as an "ordinary" subject in the RSA's examinations, the 528 candidates outnumbered the 445 for German in 1952 (RSA Programmes of Examinations, 1950–1953 PR.ED/100/17/30, p. 44).

Yet Spanish seems to have grown in popularity in schools only once Spain became culturally more familiar to a larger number of people, as from the 1960s Spain became an affordable and popular holiday destination (joined much more recently by growing interest in South America too), and a generation of parents had some affinity to the language. Once larger numbers started to learn it, Spanish seems often to have been perceived as an easier second language than German. Already in 1930, a Board of Education report noted that "Spanish is a language of unusual simplicity and facility", its syntax "clear and easy" (Board of Education 1930b: 33–34). This was perhaps especially a factor in its growth in popularity in the 1980s and 1990s, during which little formal English grammar was taught in British schools, so that pupils were arguably ill prepared for the more complex case system and word order rules of German. Still, even in the 1980s Spanish was taken by only about a quarter of the number of pupils who sat German in their General Certificate Examination (GCE); it overtook German only in 2001 (and Table 2.4 on p. 33 confirms the continuing trend). However, when primary languages provision became obligatory in primary classrooms from 2014, Spanish was offered in one in five primary schools, cementing its place as the new second foreign language, well ahead of German, which was offered in just 4% of primary schools sampled (Board & Tinsley 2015: 121).

2.6 Dutch – a surprising fourth

The British Library holds a 1783 pamphlet advertising a ladies' boarding school in Oxford where young boarders might learn, alongside the offerings of English, French and Italian, also Flemish:

At Mr. Christopher Towles, in High-Street, in Coventry, and at Miss Towles, in Penny-Farthing-Street, in Oxford. Young ladies are genteely boarded, and taught [. . .] Mr. Towle, teaches all sorts of English, French, Italion [sic], and Flemish, slow and quick dances.

The fact that languages are mentioned – in the same breath as dancing – as *ladies'* accomplishments may be less surprising to readers today than the mention of Flemish (i.e. the Dutch of Flanders, in today's Belgium) as one of the three modern languages on offer. In 2004, Salverda (2004) was able to quote a survey according to which 0.5% of the British population (i.e. some 300,000 people at the time) claimed to "know Dutch", but Dutch is nowadays virtually invisible in schools, and it is also rare to offer it to degree level in British universities (University College London, Sheffield and Nottingham are currently the three main centres – only the first has its own Dutch section).

Yet Dutch has a secret history of being more widely learnt in Britain. One reason for its past wider availability is that the Flemish and Dutch were themselves avid language learners. In the early fourteenth century, Flemish administrators were expected to be trilingual (in French, Latin and Flemish), and in addition, English was useful for trade. The many bilingual English-Dutch conversational manuals produced for this market on the continent could be adapted for use by English people wanting to learn Dutch, as could polyglot manuals. So when, as early as 1606, the *Dutch Schoolmaster* appeared (74 years before the first manual of German for English speakers!), its author Marten Le Mayre was able to draw on Dutch predecessors (Dibbets 1971–1972),[11] and his work was designed to be suitable for both Dutch and English learners. Typically for many of the Dutch-English materials of the seventeenth and eighteenth centuries, it includes a dialogue on buying and selling cloth, for the cloth trade between England and Flanders, a major weaving centre, was particularly important. (The opening pages of the dialogue are given in Figure 3.1 in the next chapter.) Four Dutch-English manuals or grammars were published in London between 1600 and 1800, in addition to one in New York; another, published in Amsterdam, was "very influential" amongst English learners (see Loonen 1991: 321–324, cited p. 324). Indeed, from 1630 onwards, at least one Dutch-English bilingual manual was published in every decade until the 1710s, although only three of 15 bilingual manuals between 1606 and 1807 were written by English, rather than Dutch, native speakers (Gallagher 2014: 34, 46–47). There were also strong family trade links between the Netherlands and the east coast of England. Colchester, for example, still has an area known as the "Dutch Quarter", a reminder of when about 15%–20% of the town's population were Flemish or Dutch; its Dutch church survived into the nineteenth century, even after the families had otherwise been assimilated into the native population. Several thousand English and Scots served in the Dutch Army throughout the seventeenth century. Religious ties were also important; for example, a huge volume of 1662 farewell sermons by Puritan ministers ejected from the Church of England was faithfully translated and published as *Versameling van Afscheytspredicatien, Gepredikt van Mr. Calamy*

[. . .] (Amsterdam 1662). Several of those ejected ministers immigrated to the Netherlands, to help run longstanding English churches there, serving both the military and the commercial communities in Leiden and elsewhere. Many gentlemen sent their sons to study at the universities of Utrecht and Leiden (particularly nonconformist gentry after 1662).[12] The importance of such religious ties would explain the relatively prominent religious content in Le Mayre's manual, which contains, following the usual dialogues, the Lord's Prayer, the twelve Articles of Faith, the Ten Commandments, two psalms, and prayers.

Some interest in Dutch continued through the eighteenth century (the advertisement cited on p. 17 dates from 1783), but Dutch seems to have declined as French and German became established as the two main foreign languages in young people's education toward the end of the eighteenth century and in the first half of the nineteenth century. I am not aware of any Dutch materials for learners in England published between 1788 and the 1880s. However, in the later nineteenth century, Dutch enjoyed renewed interest, and the dominant textbook appears to have been the *Elements of Dutch* of Jan Marius Hoogvliet (1860–1924), with at least four editions between 1887 and 1908.[13] Dutch was now of interest for two completely new reasons. First, Dutch could be useful to serious students of the history of English, as part of the nineteenth-century interest in historical-comparative philology. As Hoogvliet (1908: 2) explained, Dutch is very similar to English, especially if one looks at English in "its ancient and original form, in which it is generally called the Anglo-Saxon language" (p. 2). For example, in Anglo-Saxon *Where is my daughter?* is *Hwar is mín dohtor?*, which is similar to *Waar ist mijn dochter?* Hence "some knowledge of Dutch will prove very useful to any Englishman interested in the nature of his own language; to a scientific student of English and Anglo-Saxon [. . .] it is an indispensable support" (p. 3). Indeed, Hoogvliet cited praise of the grammar from Henry Sweet, the Anglo-Saxon specialist and language teaching reform advocate (Hoogvliet 1908 ed., front matter).

The second new spur to learn Dutch in the later nineteenth century was the uneasy co-existence of Dutch and British imperial interests, especially in southern Africa, resulting in the Boer Wars (1880–1881 and 1899–1902). At some point between the 1888 and 1908 editions of his *Elements of Dutch*, Hoogvliet added the tale of a Boer's encounter with a lion in the Transvaal (Hoogvliet 1908: 191–196) and included notes on peculiarities of Cape Dutch (i.e. what would become Afrikaans), such as the fact that Cape Dutch has just one gender, with one form of the article, *di* (Hoogvliet 1908: 22). Another text clearly aimed at those encountering Dutch in the colonies was Carroll's *The Dutch Language Simplified*, published in 1898 in Cape Town. This colonial interest meant that in 1911, Dutch was the fourth (of four) modern languages routinely available in the Cambridge Syndicate's Junior (under 16) School Certificate examinations. Spanish, with 62 candidates, was "only" three times more popular than Dutch (21), though both were overshadowed by German (588), which was in turn dwarfed by French (7332).[14] It is telling that 19 of the 21 candidates for Dutch in 1911 were "Colonial" – i.e. sitting the paper in one of Britain's overseas colonies, presumably those where Dutch or Cape Dutch might be encountered. When the new School Certificate and Higher School Certificate were introduced in 1918, Dutch was still one of only four modern languages that could be chosen (alongside French, German and Spanish). From that modest high point, however, the status of Dutch amongst school-age learners declined in the twentieth century. In 2004, with 380 entries at General School Certificate of Education (GCSE), Dutch had the fewest candidates out of the 16 "community languages" for which CILT (2005: 2) provides figures. Oxford, Cambridge and RSA Examinations (OCR), the one examination board that offered GCSE assessment in Dutch, has now announced that it will no longer offer Dutch after 2018.

2.7 Portuguese – England takes a lead in Europe

Portuguese is, surprisingly, one language for which the British can lay claim to have taken the lead in Europe, for Europe's first grammar of Portuguese as a foreign language was printed in London, *A Portuguez Grammar: or, Rules shewing the True and Perfect way to learn the said language*. It was published in 1662, on the occasion of the marriage of Catherine of Bragança to Charles II of England, and was intended to cater to "two sorts of Persons in England: to people of Traffique and Commerce (. . .) And to Persons of the Court" (De la Mollière 1662: A$_2$v; see Fonseca 2017). Early in the eighteenth century, a bilingual *Grammatica Anglo-Lusitanica: or a short and compendious system of an English and Portugueze grammar* was published by a certain A. J. in London, 1702 (2nd ed., Lisbon 1705; Gallagher 2014: 33, n. 30). This pocket-sized (octavo) manual contained information on grammar and syntax, together with a vocabulary and "[u]seful Dialogues and Colloquies, agreeable to common Conversation".[15] Its full title stated that it was "Designed for, and fitted to all Capacities, and more especially such whose Chance or Business may lead them into any part of the World, where that Language is used or esteemed" (Gallagher 2014: 55).

The production and circulation of such grammars of Portuguese as a foreign language, written in English and printed in London, increased during the eighteenth and nineteenth centuries (e.g. the grammars of Jacob Castro (1731) and António Vieira (1786)). However, in the nineteenth century, the works published were either multi-purpose (i.e. marketed at learners of Portuguese and at least one other language), or they were written according to a well-marketed language learning textbook formula or patented "method" such as that of Franz Ahn (on such methods see 4.5). This suggests that interest in Portuguese remained rather marginal. Examples of the first category are Richard Woodhouse's grammar of Spanish, Portuguese and Italian (Woodhouse 1815) and Luís Francisco Midosi's grammar in two parts: one for Portuguese and one for English (1832). Examples of the second category are Alfred Elwes's grammar of "the pleasant language of Portugal and Brazil" (Elwes 1876, preface, n.p.), building on the previous success of his grammars of Italian and Spanish and the *Practical Grammar on Dr. Otto's Conversational System* (1882) of Charles Henry Wall. Wall defended

Portuguese against the charge that it was a "mongrel" language, and drew attention to its "beauties and power" (Wall 1882: [vii]). "Knowing that many will study the language only in the interests of their business, I have endeavoured to make the exercises and conversations of as practical a character as possible", Wall wrote (p. ix). His success was mixed. Early conversational phrases include the practical *Ônde está a cervêja?* "Where is the beer?", but the work abounded in decontextualized sentences for translation, connected only by the grammatical point that they were all intended to practise, as in these sentences, for comparatives and superlatives: *The strength of the strongest man is far less than that of an elephant. It will cost you twenty dollars at most. The more frequently you practise what you read in your book, the better you will be* (p. 170). It thus typified an approach railed against by the Reform Movement in language teaching, launched in the same year that Wall's grammar appeared, by Wilhelm Viëtor's pamphlet (Viëtor 1882; see 4.6).

In the twentieth century, Portuguese remained a very low priority. Early issues of the Institute of Linguists' magazine in the 1920s contained "a serial course in Portuguese" by Cozens Elliott (cf. 3.1; see Smith et al. 2010: 15), but in the Cambridge Local Examinations, as late as 1930, when the range of languages offered had expanded to include Russian and "Oriental" languages (and even African languages by 1940), Portuguese was still not listed; no candidates took it at GCSE in 1960 at the Cambridge Board. However, the Portuguese-speaking population of Britain began to increase in the second half of the twentieth century, especially after Portugal joined the European Union in 1986 as one of its poorest countries. Portuguese-speaking migrants from Portugal's former colonies in Africa and the Indian subcontinent, as well as from Brazil, also began to arrive in Britain in significant numbers. When a guide to learning Portuguese was published in 1982, it listed half a dozen universities where it was possible to take Portuguese as a degree subject (CILT 1982: 35–37), but Portuguese was clearly not available in schools. In 2005, about a thousand pupils took a GCSE in Portuguese, but only 65 of these did so through a mainstream school (see Table 2.2 on p. 29); in 2007, the number was 973 (Rodeiro 2009: 5), and only around 10% of those candidates had English as their mother tongue (Rodeiro 2009: 5, 8). Its profile is still relatively low, and it narrowly avoided the fate of Dutch at GCSE – it was, like Dutch, dropped by the OCR board, but Pearson Education has agreed in principle to offer the qualification instead.[16] But Portuguese has at any rate improved in status since 1662, when James Howell described it as a "sub-dialect" of Spanish, and compared the relationship of Portuguese and Spanish to that of Scots and English (Sánchez Escribano 2006: 126).

2.8 English as a foreign or second language

This book is not about English language learning, but we should note that English, too, has been learnt as a foreign or second language in Britain. Howatt (1984: 53) dates the beginnings of teaching English as a foreign language in England to the late seventeenth century. After 1685, when Louis XIV revoked the 1598 Edict of Nantes that had protected Protestants in Catholic France, the number of French Protestant refugees (the so-called Huguenots) increased, and they needed to learn English. Howatt (1984: 54) singles out Guy Miège's *Nouvelle Méthode* (1685) as "a landmark in the development of English language teaching", taking advantage of insights from earlier works, including those of native speaker phoneticians and grammarians. Non-native speakers were sensitive to aspects of English which the natives tended to overlook, and Howatt cites Miège's handling of the present continuous tense in his 1688 *English Grammar* (his own translation of the *Nouvelle Méthode*):

> When we speak of a Thing that was a doing, but interrupted upon some Incident, then we properly use the Verb *I was* with a Participle of the Present Tense. As, *I was speaking of you when you came in; I was writing a Letter when you knock't at the Door.*
>
> (Howatt 1984: 57, 60)

Howatt (1984: 59) also observes that the dialogues, with their practical information on the culture of coffee-houses and their free newspapers, would have been useful to newly arrived refugees. In addition to the usual bilingual layout with columns in French and English, a third column provided an attempt to indicate English pronunciation to French speakers – e.g. "You shall mark that those letters must be pronounced long, which be noted with an accent grave [. . .] *you chàl mark, dat dòs letters must by prònònced long houitch by noted ours an accent gràf, è*" (Bellot 1580: 4).

Refugees came not only from France. In 1709, some 13,000 German refugees arrived in England from the German Palatinate, fleeing repeated invasions by the French. The rapid influx caused tensions, but at least one textbook sought to provide materials for them to learn English: *A Short and Easy Way for the Palatines to Learn English. Oder Eine kurze Anleitung zur Englischen Sprach, Zum Nutz der armen Pfältzer/nebst angehängten Englischen und Teutsche ABC* (Anon. 1710, noted by Gallagher 2014: 34). However, most English as a Foreign Language materials were published abroad over the following centuries, until a revival from the late nineteenth century onwards (Howatt 1984: 60). It is impossible to rehearse the history of this renewed English Language Teaching (ELT) in Britain, which has become today a vast enterprise. Still, we should note that a leading figure in its rebirth around 1900 was Walter Rippmann (anglicized to Ripman during World War I), born in England to German parents, who was the University of London's director of Holiday Courses for Foreigners.[17] When, in 1901, a special course for foreign students was established at Queen's College, London, Rippmann began it with a series of lectures on the pronunciation of English (Kaye 1972: 141–142), also teaching English phonetics and publishing phonetic teaching materials for English too: *The Sounds of Spoken English* (1906), *English Sounds: A Book For English Boys and Girls* (1911) and *A First English Book for Boys and Girls Whose Mother-Tongue Is Not English* (1920). Rippmann was later joined by key figures such as Harold E. Palmer, whom Howatt credits with making a British approach to ELT that "was no longer merely a junior branch of modern language teaching, but an independent profession which led the way in applied linguistic innovation" (Howatt 1994: 1915, cited by Smith 1999: 1; see Howatt 1984: 230–244 and Smith 1999).

2.9 German – a late start but a strong finish, until 2001

German was the "second" modern language in Britain since at least the 1850s, when French and German were the two modern languages offered in the first public examinations for school pupils.[18] Yet German comes relatively late in our chronological history of language learning in Britain. Trade between Germany and England in the late Middle Ages thrived under the control of the German Hanseatic League, but it depended on German merchants learning English, not the other way around (see Schröder 2000: 724). The first textbook of German for English speakers, *The High Dutch Minerva* by Martin Aedler, appeared only in 1680. It sold poorly and ultimately bankrupted its unfortunate author, who was forced to marry the widow to whom he was indebted. The marriage was not a happy one, and Aedler died alone and in poverty at the age of 81 (Van der Lubbe 2007: 72, 104). It was not a particularly auspicious start to the history of promoting German to English learners. A number of factors might explain the failure of Aedler's pioneering venture. First, his title, *High Dutch Minerva*, was rather obscure – when bookseller William Cooper bought up the unsold copies in 1685, he gave them a new title page, *High-Dutch Grammer* [sic], which suggests an attempt to reach a less learned audience (Van der Lubbe 2007: 73). Second, Aedler's textbook was unusual for a language manual at the time because he chose not to include any dialogues. He considered it more important to offer lists of idioms, whose meanings could be hard to guess. Finally, learners might also have been put off by Aedler's choice of spelling conventions which, though theoretically justifiable, were rather different to the spelling more commonly used for German at the time. In his account of German pronunciation, for example, Aedler gives the opening line of the Creed in his spelling, as shown below (note *ih* for *ich* "I", *shoepfer* for *Schöpfer* 'creator'). The second line is a notation intended to help an English speaker pronounce the unfamiliar German correctly – see, for example, *dare* for German *der* "the".

> *ih glaube an Gott den vater allmaehtigen shoepfer des himmels und der erden.*
> ig ghlòu-wey aun Gut dane vàuter, oll-maght-e-ghen, shoepf-er das him-mels und dare arden. (Aedler 1680: 43)
> "I believe in God the almighty father, creator of heaven and earth".

Despite Aedler's failure, interest in German gradually grew in the eighteenth century. The British monarchy passed to the German House of Hanover from 1714, beginning with George I, and this no doubt helped the cause of German amongst "families of distinction" such as those that William Render boasted of having taught German in London and Cambridge for several years (Render 1799: x). Germany's growing reputation in literature in the later eighteenth century helped too, for this was the age of writers like Lessing (1729–1781), Schiller (1759–1805) and Goethe (1749–1832). Nor was it just Germany's achievements in literature that were gaining notice – Render (1799: vi–viii) gave many examples of the international reputation of Germans in fields including philosophy, chemistry and medicine, law and divinity (McLelland 2015a: 66–67).

It is a historical accident that when school education became formalized in the nineteenth century, German happened to be in its ascendancy. German scientific achievements were very well-regarded – in the natural sciences, as well as in linguistics and in education – and much scientific publishing internationally was in German (see Reinbothe 2006, McLelland 2016). Thus it was that German, rather than Spanish, Italian or Dutch, became the second foreign language alongside French. As we have seen, German was always a very distant second to French, but it was soon rivalling Latin as the second language in schools. In Ireland, German benefited from the ideological function of modern languages. As one commentator remarked in 1908, "To free ourselves from the intellectual control of England is the main purpose with which the study of modern languages can be recommended" (cited by Fischer 2000: 467), and German especially seems to have been adopted by this Irish nationalist, de-Anglicizing current. In 1930, for example, 42.5% of candidates answered their German examinations through the medium of Irish, but only 5.5% of pupils taking French did so (Fischer 2000: 468–469). In other words, those in Irish-medium education disproportionately chose German.

The status of German suffered a considerable setback internationally as a result of its defeat in World War I. Many international scientific organizations in fields that had previously been trilingual (French, German, English) excluded German, more or less explicitly, as an official language (Reinbothe 2006). The contrast before and after World War I is at its most stark in the USA, where German had been particularly strong in schools because of the large numbers of pupils of German descent in certain states. At the 1910 census, over a third of Wisconsin and Ohio inhabitants were "of German stock" – i.e. with at least one parent born in Germany (Eichhoff 1971: 47) – and German was, until 1917, "the most widely studied language at universities and colleges" in the USA (Kloss 1971: 118). In 1915, more than a quarter of all high school students were studying German: 284,000 compared to 103,000 French and only 32,000 Spanish. "Up to 1917, German in the United States enjoyed unequalled prestige as *the* language of education and learning [. . .] the ability to read German was indispensable to many disciplines" (Kloss 1971: 119). After World War I, the number of USA high school pupils learning in German plummeted to a tiny 0.7% in 1922 (Thierfelder 1957 II: 369). In Britain, the decline was less dramatic, because German had never held such a strong position in schools, but it was still very noticeable. German recovered in the 1930s and, despite World War II, which again created negative attitudes to German and Germans, it maintained its place as second foreign language until Spanish overtook it in 2001. In the twenty-first century, a question mark seems again to hang over the viability of German in schools, much as it did in the early twentieth century (cf. O'Grady's tentatively titled article "German?" (1906), and Saunders' "Plea for the Study of German" (1919–1920); see McLelland 2014, 2015c).

2.10 Russian – mixed fortunes

The history of learning Russian in Britain begins relatively late, and yet the first grammar of Russian published in England is also the earliest surviving grammar of Russian anywhere in the world. It was published in 1696, not by a Briton, nor by a Russian, but by a German: Heinrich Ludolf's *Grammatica russica*. Only 300 copies were printed, but it seems likely that Ludolf used it in 1698 when he taught Russian in Germany to adherents of Pietism (a branch of Lutheranism), preparing them to work as teachers and missionaries in Russia (Koch 2002: 173, n.17). Ludolf's grammar is in Latin, but with additional German glosses of the Russian-Latin dialogues (see Figure 2.1). We have no evidence of how widely it was used by Britons, and not a single further grammar or dictionary of Russian appeared in England in the whole of the eighteenth century (Muckle 2008a: 13); the first English translation of a Russian work of literature appeared only in 1793. However, the British government did send a young man, John Maddison, to St Petersburg in 1762 in order to learn Russian so that he could be employed in

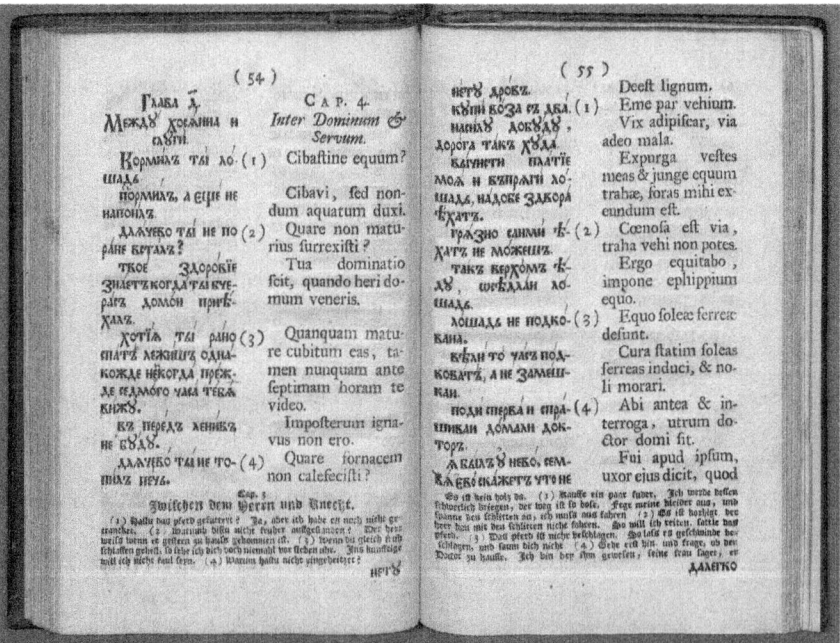

Figure 2.1 Ludolf's *Grammatica russica* (1696: 54–55). Reproduced by kind permission of the University of Birmingham

copying and translating Russian letters, sometimes also decoding letters in cipher (Muckle 2008a: 14–15). Still, Maddison's case was highly unusual. Even Britons travelling to or living in Russia seem to have felt no need to learn Russian, finding that French was widely used in polite society anyway. When, in 1800, a so-called *Commercial Dictionary* of Russian was published in London (Kroll 1800), it listed only about 650 words, all transliterated, and some words and phrases are garbled (e.g. *kneega* was translated as "books", although the transliteration is of the singular книга, 'book'). For Muckle, "it is hard to believe that this can have been much use to those seeking to sell their wares in Russia", but the book did contain much useful practical information about trading with Russia, including information on coins, weights and measures, lists of goods prohibited from import or export, translations of government edicts on trade, etc. (Muckle 2008a: 19–20).

The first two grammars of Russian intended specifically for English-speaking learners appeared in the 1820s, and both were clearly aimed at self-instructional learners, rather than learners who might be able to find a teacher. The first (by a certain W.H.M.D., not further identified, and published in 1822), was intended for English residents in Russia, but had many shortcomings. Its account of pronunciation was apparently "grossly inaccurate", and there was no treatment of the crucial matter of verbal aspect, whereas the pluperfect tenses that had not been used for centuries were explained, and there were very few examples of current usage. In sum, "it would be well-nigh impossible to learn much Russian from it" (Muckle 2008a: 22). The second work is a *Practical Grammar of the Russian Language* (Head 1827). Head had been enticed to set up a school on the estates of a certain Count Rumiantsev in Russia, and so was largely self-taught in Russian. His work was in the typical style of the "practical grammar" that became popular throughout Europe in the late eighteenth and early nineteenth century, with each point of grammar followed by practical exercises, an important innovation at the time (see 4.5). Others followed, including an English version of a work originally for German-speakers (Reiff 1853).

Russian increasingly became of interest for military and diplomatic purposes, as Britain fought Russia in the Crimean War (1853–1856), and then Russian and Britain wrangled for influence in Afgahnistan in the 1870s, leading to fears that Russia might threaten British India (Muckle 2008a: 32). The War Office and Admiralty began to encourage the learning of Russian by some of its officers, and in 1885, for the first time, a Russian examiner was listed in the annual report of the Civil Service Commission which had charge of examining officers. Russian began to find a modest place in the universities from 1848, when the first professor of Modern Languages at Oxford, Francis Trithen, gave his first course of lectures on "the language and literature of Russia", although the first student to graduate in Russian at Oxford did so only in 1903; at Cambridge, Russian was available within Modern and Medieval Languages from 1907 (Muckle 2008a: 40 [citation], 42–43).

As with German, attitudes towards learning Russian were greatly affected by geopolitical factors. With the outbreak of war in 1914, business interests had an eye to the markets previously dominated by the Germans. As the novelist H. G. Wells wrote to the *Times Education Supplement* in 1914, "I want my boys to learn Russian. [...] It is clear that this war will make Russia a land of unprecedented opportunity for enterprising young Englishmen in business [...]" (cited by Muckle 2008a: 52). Russian expanded in evening, commercial and technical colleges after 1914, especially in Scotland (Glasgow, Dundee and Aberdeen). Relatively large numbers in Bradford taking Russian reflected the desire of the textile industry there to improve relations with Russia (Muckle 2008a: 60). A dozen or so schools (mainly Public Schools or grammar schools) also introduced Russian (Muckle 2008a: 65), though Muckle suggests that efforts were hampered by the lack of suitable materials for children, as well as the difficulty of ensuring that teachers were adequately qualified. There was an anti-Semitic tint to suggestions that some Russian and Polish Jews who put themselves forward as teachers had only "imperfect knowledge" of the language; other teachers might be suspect as "revolutionary exiles and political adventurers" (*The Times*, 7.9.1915, p. 10, cited by Muckle 2008a: 69).

The Revolution of 1917 made the teaching of Russian all the more attractive to some, but decidedly suspect to others. The Leathes Report on Modern Studies in 1918 listed Russian as one of five languages, alongside French, German, Italian and Spanish, that "deserve a First-Class place in the Modern Studies of our Universities"; the same list should also be available in schools, as optional languages after French (Leathes 1918, para. 68, cited by Muckle 2008a: 90). At the same time, the report noted that Russian was "a difficult language"; its literature was "of little educational value", its history "obscure, unaccented and uninspiring" (para. 67, cited by Muckle 2008a: 89–90). Still, Russian was added to the list of possible subjects for examination in the Cambridge Local Examinations in 1918, when the new School Certificate was introduced (alongside French, German and Spanish; Italian was the other new addition).[19] Certainly, some adult learners of Russian were motivated by political sympathies. In an article in the first volume of a magazine called *The Adult Student* (1934), apparently aimed at the workers of Glasgow, Russian was ostentatiously listed first amongst the languages one might want to learn (Bischoff 1939: 188).

Interest in Russian declined in the inter-war years, but revived again in and after World War II with the teaching of Russian to national service conscripts in the 1950s, which equipped unprecedented numbers of people with good knowledge of Russian (see 3.1.3); the establishment of an Association of Teachers of Russian in 1959 (Muckle 2008a: 151); a government-commissioned report on the teaching of Russian (Annan 1962); and ambitious Russian language teaching and research projects in the 1960s and early 1970s (as part of the Nuffield Foreign Languages Teaching Materials Project, and the Contemporary Russian Language Analysis Project at the University of Essex: see Muckle 2008a: 154–156). The hopes of some, of expanding the teaching of Russian to rival that of German, were not fulfilled, however, although interest in the subject revived again after the collapse of the Soviet Union in 1991.

Overall, the history of Russian learning is characterized by a "high degree of instability" – 44% of schools listed in a 1992 survey of Russian teaching were not on an equivalent list in 1988. It seems probable that more pupils had the opportunity to experience at least a "taster" course in Russian from the 1980s onwards, which, however cursory, could often have a positive effect on the decision to study Russian at university later (Muckle 2008a: 196–197). In 2005, Russian had 1736 candidates at GCSE and 79 at A-level (CILT 2005: 2). Meanwhile, in the Republic of Ireland, Russian first became available for the Leaving Certificate (equivalent of A-level) in 2003; in 2005, 111 candidates sat for it, more than the number of A-level candidates in the whole of Britain (although the comparison is not an equal one: the Leaving Certificate requires pupils to take six subjects, most take seven); the excellent results suggest that most candidates in Ireland were children of Russian immigrants. In Britain, by contrast, nearly two-thirds of candidates for Russian at GCSE in 2007 had English as their first language (Rodeiro 2009: 8).

2.11 From languages of empire to "community languages"

We have so far considered the major European languages in the history of language learning in Britain. There is, however, a less visible history of language learning, the history of learning so-called community languages – i.e. "languages in use in the UK other than the official languages of the state (English and, in Wales, Welsh) and including British Sign Language" (CILT 2005: 4). Not all of the languages conventionally listed under this heading fit the definition neatly; the label can also reinforce the perception of these languages as having a place "out in the community" but not inside the walls of mainstream education. Some of the languages treated as "community languages", such as Russian and Dutch, have a hybrid history in the British Isles, taught both as foreign languages and as community languages – consider the status of Russian at the Irish Leaving Certificate, apparently taken mainly by heritage speakers, compared to its status as a somewhat elitist subject in the UK, where 71% of A-level entries came from the independent sector in 2014 (Board & Tinsley 2015: 32).[20] Others languages, such as languages of the Indian subcontinent, have very little established history within mainstream schools, but have a history of being learned by the British under the Empire. For example, the East India College (later renamed Haileybury College) was an elite training college established in Hertford Heath in 1806 to prepare young gentlemen, generally admitted at age 16–19, to become clerks for the East India Company in the colonies.[21] Alongside a wide curriculum of subjects intended to prepare candidates for their future service overseas, and a liberal education including classics, mathematics, law, political economy and history, students also took "Oriental Studies," which included Hindu literature, the history of Asia and languages. Sanskrit, Persian and Hindustani were compulsory, while other languages including Arabic, Bengali, Telugu, Hindi and Marathi were optional (Lowell 1900: 12). Sanskrit was deemed so challenging that although every student intended to serve in Madras was required to *begin* it, they were to be allowed to drop it after two months if the professor deemed it "expedient"

(1814 regulations, cited by Rocher 1968: 67). For the first few years, students were not examined in the Asian languages and therefore seem not to have taken their studies seriously, but from 1814 onwards, an external "Visitor" examined the students in writing, grammar, reading, translating and parsing an easy passage (Fisher 2001).[22]

Hindustani was considered essential for British officers destined to serve in the Indian Army, so was offered at the East India Company Military Seminary at Addiscombe House until 1861. The cadets were examined in Hindustani in the presence of a noble Indian civil servant or prince, who apparently confirmed that the accents of the cadets were very well affected.[23] After Sandhurst Military College took over the training of officers for the Infantry and Cavalry arms of the Indian Army, it continued to offer Hindustani, until officer training was cut to three months at the outbreak of World War I, leaving insufficient time to learn Hindustani; thereafter, cadets needing to learn Hindustani were sent to one of the Army Staff Colleges in India (Morton 2014: 28–29).

From the early twentieth century, Persian, Arabic, Sanskrit, Urdu and Chinese could all be taken by pupils at the School Certificate.[24] A planned Institute of Phonetics at University College London was partly justified in effusive media coverage in 1919 by the somewhat overblown claim that it would help those who needed to learn the languages of empire and so give Britain a commercial advantage. A headline in *The Daily Chronicle* called it an "Empire language 'factory'", and the director of the School of Oriental Studies was quoted in *The Observer* as saying,

> Many big banks and business houses are sending their representatives to evening classes here in order that before they go out to the East they may get an introduction to the vernacular. [. . .] It is of the utmost advantage to him [the Englishman], particularly where commerce is concerned, to know what the natives are saying with whom he is to do business. Talking amongst themselves to their own people in their own language they may be saying that the article he is showing them is worth £10, but they will offer him £5.
> (cited by Ashby & Przedlacka 2017: forthcoming)

In the later twentieth century, as the countries of Britain's empire gradually gained independence, many of the "colonial" languages began to be taught as heritage languages to the school-age children of the migrant communities who already spoke them (Urdu, Panjabi, Bengali, Gujarati). They were usually taught in supplementary schools (such as Saturday schools). In the late 1960s, the Committee on Research and Development in Modern Languages (CDRML) approved funds to develop teaching materials for Hindi/Urdu, Arabic and Turkish; the Arabic materials were intended to be suitable for home or language laboratory use and to provide a one-year intensive course for students from H.M. Forces and government departments (CRDML 1968: 12–13, 1971: 6, 25). Yet these languages are still rarely taught in mainstream schools, or even universities. Manchester Metropolitan University was the only university listed by the UCAS search tool for courses in Urdu in 2016.[25] For example, despite the fact that Urdu headed the list of community languages taken at GCSE in 2005 (see Table 2.2). Arabic, by contrast, is now offered by 16 universities.

Under England's National Curriculum introduced in 1988, community languages were placed under the heading of Modern Foreign Languages. In one way, this was problematic, because the goals and needs of more or less bilingual community language speakers are clearly very different to those beginning a foreign language from zero. Furthermore, initially, at least, community languages could only be offered by a school if it was also offering at least one European Union (EU) language (Geach 1996: 149). However, the move did make space for these languages *within* the curriculum. Accordingly, curriculum guides for 11 community languages were published by Centre for Information on Language Teaching (CILT) in the first decade of the twenty-first century: Gujarati, Tamil, Punjabi, Yoruba, Somali, Cantonese, Arabic and Urdu. The National Languages Strategy, published in 2002, deliberately encompassed all languages, not just those traditionally taught in mainstream schools,[26] and was "inclusive,

Table 2.2 GCSE Examination figures for so-called community languages in 2005 (from CILT 2005: 2)

Language	All GCSE entries 2005	% change in all entries from 2001 to 2005	% of all 2004 GCSE candidates from English mainstream schools**	% change in the number of English school entries from 2001 to 2004	All A-level entries 2005 (2001)
Urdu	6,334	−1	88	−12	739 (485)
Chinese	3,091	+40	59	−12	2,062 (1,375)
Irish	2,507	−5	0	0	306 (275)
Arabic	2,183	+63	69	−7	429 (275)*
Bengali	1,865	−17	93	−21	83 (58)
Russian	1,736	−1	79	−25	636 (469)
Panjabi	1,341	−15	89	−15	203 (226)
Turkish	1,337	+30	75	−1	362 (234)*
Japanese	1,120	+74	67	−3	251 (221)
Gujarati	1,080	−26	100	−10	46 (41)*
Portuguese	1,028	+57	65	−6	175 (111)
Greek	604	+17	90	+14	159 (125)
Hebrew	442	+9	100	+16	40 (16)
Persian	441	+37*	72	+32	170 (112)*
Polish	405	+35	76	+33	126 (97)
Dutch	380	+31*	66	+6	119 (37)
Total 25,894	+9	80***	−11	5,906	

* Comparison is with 2002, figures not available for previous years. ** This column shows entries from 15-year-olds in schools in England in 2004 as a proportion of total entries across all sectors of education in the UK 2004. Note that all entries include a relatively small number of candidates (under 2.5%) from Wales and Northern Ireland. The figures do not show whether candidates were external or internal, or whether they received tuition. *** % base excludes Irish, for which almost all candidates were in Northern Ireland.

not restrictive", in allowing the entitlement for language provision in primary schools to be fulfilled by offering a community language, as Lid King noted in his foreword to a curriculum guide for Punjabi (CILT 2007: 6). Yet when the requirement for primary languages provision came into effect in 2014–2105, Board & Tinsley (2015: 121) found that of the 648 primary schools in its sample, only one school taught Urdu within class time in the final two years of primary school, one Punjabi, and one Arabic. These numbers are tiny. Still, their formal presence at all may help build their status as subjects that can be taken in mainstream education.[27]

2.12 Chinese – changing status

The status of Chinese as a learned language in Britain has been changing rapidly. The histories of both Mandarin and Cantonese in Britain begin as languages of colonialism or of mission, learnt almost exclusively by adults preparing for a career in government, business or the church in China or Hong Kong (McLelland 2015b). The first grammar of Chinese for European learners, Martini's *Grammatica sinica* (in Latin) appeared in 1696, but it was not until the early decades of the nineteenth century that the first manuals of Chinese for English speakers appeared, beginning with Marshman's *Clavis Sinica* (1814) and Morrison's *A Grammar of the Chinese Language* (Morrison 1815, rpt. 2008). Britain's first Professor of the Chinese Language and Literature, Samuel Kidd, was appointed at University College, London in 1837. He had, like Marshman and Morrison, learnt his Chinese as a Protestant missionary (Douglas 2004). The potential importance of Chinese was recognized by the Committee on Research and Development in Modern Languages, which funded work on intensive methods of teaching Modern Chinese (CRDML 1971: 6, 7) and signalled the desirability of an "inter-universities Chinese language school" (CRDML 1971: 6–7), given the lack of qualified staff in individual universities, though this suggestion was not implemented. The Committee for Research and Development in Modern Languages (CRDML) considered that "in view of the lack of properly qualified teachers and of teaching material of all kinds, it would be unwise to encourage an expansion of the teaching of Chinese in schools at this time" (CRDML 1968: 23).

In recent decades both Mandarin and Cantonese have become community languages as a result of migration. At the same time, interest in Mandarin Chinese as a foreign language has grown considerably. Over 20 universities now offer degrees in Chinese as foreign language, usually from beginner level, and it has experienced rapid growth in secondary schools too, as a core subject within the curriculum. In 2014, only 5% of state schools offered it at GCSE and 5% at A-level, 20% of independent schools offered it at GCSE, and 22% at A-level (Board & Tinsley 2015: 127). (The big difference here between school types raises the question of social class and equality of opportunity in language learning – see 3.2.1). China's establishment of 29 Confucius Institutes in Britain over the past decade or so has also made Mandarin Chinese much more visible. Affiliated with universities, the Institutes offer Mandarin Chinese in evening classes

Table 2.3 Most popular combinations of two or more modern foreign languages at GCSE in 2007 (out of a total of 225 language combinations; from Rodeiro 2009: 6).

Combinations	Frequency	Percentage (of candidates who took at least one modern language)
French – Spanish	14,259	4.69
French – German	13,759	4.53
German – Spanish	1,762	0.58
French – Italian	1,169	0.38
French – German – Spanish	569	0.19
French – Chinese	505	0.17
French – Russian	456	0.15
French – Arabic	421	0.14
Arabic – Urdu	377	0.12
French – Gujarati	322	0.11
Total (of the top-ten combinations)	33,599	11.06

and have numerous outreach activities into nurseries, primary and secondary schools. Still, despite the growing visibility of Chinese in public discourse about languages needed in business, less than 1% of GCSE Modern Languages candidates took Chinese in 2011–2012 and, to judge by the very good results, many had some kind of native speaker background: 97% achieved a "good" grade (between A* and C), compared to 71% for any modern language, and 70% and 75% for French and German, respectively.[28] Just as German evolved from a marginal interest in the late seventeenth century to become *the* second modern language in the nineteenth and twentieth centuries, Chinese is arguably part way through a similar transformation in status. It is also raising questions of what is meant by "modern languages" – Mandarin is offered as a modern foreign language at school level, and, indeed, in 2007, French-Chinese was the sixth most popular language combination at GCSE (see Table 2.3). Yet at university level, Chinese is not always housed in modern language units, where the label "Modern Languages" may still be equated, more or less explicitly, with (selected) "European Languages", with separate sections for Asian Studies or Chinese studies.

2.13 The language "charts" – changes, comparisons and conclusions

The history of language learning choices that we have outlined here can, on one level, be summarized briefly. Once the focus widened from Latin, French was the first foreign language. That pattern was repeated in the nineteenth century, when Latin initially enjoyed a central place in the curriculum; when Latin lost ground to modern languages, French was again the winner. In the most recent battle for territory, the introduction of a foreign language as a requirement in primary schools from the age of eight, French has won again, with 77% of schools choosing French. The very existence of an acronym LOTF (languages other than French) in the 1990s to cover German, Italian, Russian and Spanish, confirms that every other foreign language is defined in relation to this first foreign language (Phillips & Filmer-Sankey 1993: 1). Just as there is no contest for the "first" foreign language in the language learning charts, there is similarly little doubt about the next two, German and Spanish, although their relative position has changed (see Table 2.4, showing the stability of these top three at A-level over the 80 years or so, though with Spanish ultimately overtaking German; see also Table 2.3, which shows the ten most popular language combinations at GCSE and confirms the primacy of French, Spanish and German in the early twenty-first century).

German entered the nineteenth century and even the twentieth century with its status as the second foreign language secure, but it ceded that position to Spanish at the turn of the twenty-first century, both in numbers of candidates in GCSE and in the fact that Spanish, not German, was the second most chosen language in primary schools from 2014. (The same pattern is now repeated at universities too.) Spanish, not Italian, was the third language added to the Junior and Senior examinations from 1895, and remained the default third foreign language until it overtook German to gain second place.

If the first three foreign languages are easy to identify with relatively stability over time, the next two places are shared by Italian and Russian. Italian was the third language to enjoy language learning interest in sixteenth-century Britain, and it was also the third language in the examinations for women that Cambridge introduced in 1869. When the new School Certificate was introduced in 1918, Italian and Russian were the two languages added to French, German and Spanish. Even if Muckle (2008a) noted the instability in the history of Russian as a foreign language, the Centre for Information on Language Teaching (CILT) viewed these five – French, German, Spanish, Italian, Russian – as the main languages to focus on in its comprehensive review of O-level (16+) assessment in 1979. Dutch and Portuguese, which each initially enjoyed a modest prominence in Britain, barely have any profile as school language choices. Dutch is due to be dropped as an available GCSE subject after 2018; Portuguese has gained some modest ground, growing as a community language in recent years (CILT 2005: 3). Chinese is growing, but still has a split identity, between community language and (largely) elite foreign language.

It is interesting to compare the ranking of the top five languages just given – French, Spanish, German, Italian and Russian – with other lists that we might expect would influence language choices today and in future, whether at individual or at policy level. The three 'working languages' of the EU for everyday business are French, German and English; the official languages of the United Nations are French, Spanish, English, Russian, Mandarin and Arabic. The most widely spoken languages of the world, ranked by numbers of native speakers, are (1) Mandarin Chinese, (2) Hindi/Hindustani, (3) Spanish, (4) English, (5) Arabic, (6) Portuguese, (7) Bengali, (8) Russian, (9) Japanese and (10) German.

Table 2.4 A-level entries for French, German and Spanish (1938–2010)

Year	1938	1939	1954	1965	1975	1985	1990	1995	2000	2005	2009	2010
French	4,752	4,700	10,342	25,599	24,421	22,140	27,245	27,563	18,341	14,248	14,452	13,850
German	899	873	2,540	7,107	7,810	7,949	9,476	10,632	8,718	5,834	5,810	5,548
Spanish	138	145	660	2,213	2,581	2,615	3,832	4,837	5,702	6,173	7,385	7,629
Italian		12	79									
Russian		0	457									
Total of French, German, Spanish	5,789	5,718	79	34,919	34,812	32,704	40,553	43,032	32,761	26,255	27,647	27,027

(Source: Richard Hudson, Trends in Language Education in England, www.phon.ucl.ac.uk/home/dick/ec/stats.htm#alfg)[29] Data for 1939 and 1954 are from Phillips & Filmer-Sankey (1993: 22); the only years for which data on Italian and Russian are given.

(Including non-native speakers of these languages moves English to second place, puts Russian ahead of Arabic in fifth place and German behind Arabic in seventh place, ahead of Bengali, Portuguese and Japanese.) The sustained strength of French thus makes sense on at least three counts, even if it is not a "top-ten" language by number of speakers: France is a near neighbour, with whom Britain has had close ties over centuries; it also enjoys considerable global status as the official language of both the United Nations and the EU (though Brexit – Britain's planned departure from the EU – might have an effect on the perceived value to Britons of EU working languages), and it is an official language in many parts of Africa. German's loss of ground to Spanish also becomes comprehensible, despite the close ties cultural with Germany since the House of Hanover took the throne in the early eighteenth century, and despite the might of the German economy. Spanish is not a language of the EU, but Spanish, not German, *is* a language of the United Nations, and Spanish is far more widely spoken globally than German, which never gained the ground that Spanish won through colonization; German lost much of its 'linguistic soft power' after World War I, never to regain it (McLelland 2016). On numbers and global status alone, we might expect Russian to hold its own, and we might expect that Mandarin and Hindi, as the two most widely spoken languages, could overtake Italian in popularity. There is some evidence that this growth is already beginning in Mandarin, aided both by China's growing economic clout and by the huge resources poured into Confucius Institutes at many universities in Britain (and around the world) to build China's soft power. The same cannot be said, yet, for Hindi, nor for Arabic and Portuguese. One further important consideration is whether speakers of those languages can themselves communicate in another widely known language – English is used in Indian media and education, with the status of "Associate Language" alongside the official language Hindi and 18 "National Languages"; English is now compulsory in Chinese education (Adamson 2004). English is far less widely learnt in many Arabic speaking countries, so that one might expect Arabic to move up the charts most rapidly of all. However, there is a large gap between classical Arabic and its various colloquial varieties, so that the question of which variety to learn is not straightforward, and the cultural and political distance between many Arabic parts of the world and Britain remains a hurdle. Another consideration remains the cultural bond – Italian is not an EU official language, nor a United Nations language, but Italian vocal music and literature still play a prominent part in Britain's cultural life.

One further general conclusion can be drawn. There are well-founded laments that Britain has too few languages graduates to meet demand, and that numbers of pupils taking languages at GCSE and A-level have been falling. All this is true, and grave. However, taking the long view, the number of languages that are learned by British children and adults has grown steadily since the nineteenth century. Before foreign languages became a formal part of modern language education in the nineteenth century, French, Italian, Spanish, Dutch, Portuguese, German and Russian had all come into the orbit of at least some (but very few) language learners in Britain. (See Chapter 3 on who these learners were.)

However, when modern languages were institutionalized in formal school examinations, initially only two languages were available, French and German, those of our nearest large neighbours. By the end of the nineteenth century, Italian and Spanish had joined them, followed by Russian and Dutch. By 1912, Chinese, Sanskrit or Arabic could also be taken (being substituted for Ancient Greek, in both the examinations of the Joint Matriculation Board, the forerunner of today's AQA, and in the Cambridge Local Examinations). Twenty-four languages were recognized in the National Curriculum in 2004 (Salverda 2004: 357); in 2014, there were 31 modern languages listed. The numbers taking up a language are not as we wish, and above all the numbers taking two foreign languages at GCSE are disappointing (Table 2.3), especially in the light of to the EU's commitment to "1+2" – i.e. that every child should learn two languages in addition to their own mother tongue languages (on the response to this call in Britain, see 6.3.2). And yet, with a modern language currently compulsory in both the primary sector and secondary sector (admittedly only to age 14), languages – and a wider range of languages – enjoy greater visibility than they ever have before.

Strategic interests – geopolitical relationships, war and commerce – have clearly influenced language learning trends in the short term, as the changing fortunes of Chinese, Dutch, German, Italian, Portuguese, and Russian all illustrate. Yet history suggests that it is slower-growing but deeper-rooted cultural relationships that may have a more lasting effect on language learning choices, and that once established, such habits are slow to change.

2.14 Further reading

The contributions in Tyler (2011) offer fascinating insights into early multilingualism in England ca. 800–1250, involving languages including Welsh, English, Latin, Old Norse and, Anglo-Norman French. On the history of teaching and learning Latin in medieval England, see Hunt (1991), and on the place of Latin in the curriculum between 1830 and 1960, see Stray (1998). Hüllen (1999: 79–80) discusses Ælfric Bata's English-Latin colloquia. On the history of Italian teaching in early modern England, see Lawrence (2005), and for its more recent status, Lepschy (1974) and Lepschy and Tamponi (2005). On the history of French learning in England, see Kibbee (1991) and (still useful) Lambley (1920), as well as the bibliography by Alston (1985); Clapton and Stewart (1929) provide a snapshot of the perceived status of French in schools and universities at the time. On the history of ELT, but with much that is applicable to the history of language teaching methods more widely, see Howatt (1984, revised Howatt with Widdowson 2004) and Michael (1987). On the history of German as a foreign language in Britain, see McLelland (2015a, 2015c) and, for the history of German as a foreign language in Europe more widely, Glück (2002, 2013). On the unequal competition between French and German in British schools, see McLelland (2014). For a very rich study of vernacular language learning in early modern England (between 1480 and 1715), see Gallagher (2014), and for an overview of language manuals in sixteenth-century Europe, Sumillera (2014).

Salmon (1996) examines the study of languages in seventeenth-century England, especially Chapter 9. For the history of Dutch learning in England, see references in Salverda (2004), and see Loonen (1991) for the learning of English in the Low Countries. On the history of Russian learning in Britain, see Muckle (2008a, 2008b), and the report by Annan (1962). The history of Spanish learning in Britain remains to be written, but see Martínez (2015, 2017) and references there, including Sánchez Pérez (1992) and Peers (1944); for the early promotion of Spanish in the USA, see Bale (2011, 2017). Likewise, there is little work on the history of Portuguese in Britain, but see Ceu Fonseca (2017) and Sánchez Escribano (2006) and CILT (1982) for a snapshot. Note also the Parry Report (Parry 1965) and Kapcia and Newsom (2014) on Latin American Studies in Britain. A very interesting analysis of an eighteenth-century attempt to explain Hindustani to English speakers is that by Steadman-Jones (2007). For a first foray into the history of Chinese learning in England, see McLelland (2015b), and for the wider history of grammars of Chinese for Europeans, see Chappell and Peyraube (2014); Brockey (2007) has a very readable chapter on Jesuits learning Chinese in the seventeenth century; on Chinese in schools today, see Tinsley and Board (2015). On the history of Europeans learning and describing "exotic" languages, see the survey articles in Auroux et al. (2000, Vol. 1; most of these articles are in German). Fisher (2001) provides a history of an early teacher of Persian at the East India College in the first half of the nineteenth century. See also Salmon (1996), especially Chapters 9 and 10, for the seventeenth-century learning of languages, including Hebrew and Arabic, which were both taught at Westminster School, for example; for the current status of Arabic in schools, see British Council (2015).

A series of publications by CILT in 1980 provide basic statistics on each of French, German, Spanish and Russian in schools; Rodeiro (2009) is a very useful analysis of modern language uptake at GCSE in 2007. Annual "Language Trends" reports prepared since 2003 by CILT and Centre for British Teaching (CfBT) and provide regular snapshots of language learning trends in Britain (see also Chapter 6).

Notes

1 The study of English was not encouraged in Spain until 1759, nearly a century after the first grammar of Spanish for the English (Sumillera 2014: 61).
2 The adjective was for centuries treated as a sub-category of the noun.
3 The tables in this chapter, drawn from disparate sources, are not directly comparable with one another. Table 2.1 provides figures only for the Cambridge Board Examinations (UCLES), rather than national figures, for example (for similar figures for the equivalent Oxford University board, see Ortmanns (1993: 34). There have been considerable increases over the twentieth century in the overall numbers of candidates sitting examinations at 16 and 18, which renders comparisons of raw figures over time meaningless. All statistics given exclude Scotland, which has its own examinations system, but the figures presented by Ortmanns (1993: 204–213) for examinations sat in Scotland in the period 1954–1984 show broadly very similar patterns.

4 Ancient Greek was added to the curriculum of grammar schools as a second language in the sixteenth century, strengthened by its usefulness to Protestant theology as the language of the New Testament. It gained further in prestige in the early nineteenth century: if Latin was the language of education, Greek was associated with "culture" (Stray 1998: 32). As Kirk (2016: 91) puts it,

> Matthew Arnold (1822–1888), son of the eminent reforming headmaster of Rugby Thomas Arnold, summed up the attitude towards Greek prevalent from the mid-century, when he wrote that, 'the power of the Latin classic is in *character*, that of the Greek is *beauty;* and character is capable of being taught, learnt and assimilated; beauty hardly'.
> (Henry Labouchere Taunton 1886: 597; emphasis in the original)

5 My translation from Siepmann's German: *auf den klassischen Sprachen beruht Deine Zukunft. In Rugby wirst Du allerdings auch im Deutschen und im Französischen geprüft, aber das Lat. u. Griech. bilden die Hauptsache* in Siepmann, Letters, vol. 1902–1904, February 1902. See McLelland (2015a: 126).
6 Officially, French only ceased to be the language of the courts in 1731.
7 Much of the following account of the status of French up to 1600 also follows Kibbee (1991).
8 This Anglo-French romance was one of the emerging new romance and verse forms that were making French a literary language in England under the patronage of Eleanor of Aquitaine, who married the English King Henry II in 1152, just as the courtly culture of France spread through much of the rest of Europe too. For example, it seems likely that a version of the Lancelot story was commissioned by the Anglo-Norman noble Hugh de Morville in the late eleventh century. See McLelland (2000: 4–11).
9 See the regulations of the Local Examinations and Lectures Syndicate to the Senate of Cambridge University, Cam.c.11.51, vol. 60.
10 On the campaign for Spanish in the USA, see Bale (2011), and 6.3.4.
11 As the name suggests, Le Mayre may have been of French-speaking background; at any rate, he attended the French rather than Dutch Protestant church in London (Dibbets 1971–72: 4).
12 Thanks to David Appleby (p.c.) for this information.
13 The 1887 edition is labelled the fourth, but this may be because it was loosely based on the third edition (1849) of a textbook by Franz Ahn, in German. On Hoogvliet's biography, see Noordegraaf (1992).
14 Figures combine the July and December figures. Source: "Papers, class lists, reports", Cambridge Library Cam.c.11.51, Vol. 54 (1911).
15 The same A.J. had published a larger (folio) reference text, *A Compleat Account of the Portugueze Language*, in 1701.
16 On the status and role of examination boards, see 5.1.1.
17 These were the counterpart to courses that had been running in Marburg since 1897, when Rippmann had attended the first one, established by Eduard Koschwitz (1851-1904), Professor of French at Marburg, with heavy involvement of the reformer Wilhelm Viëtor from 1898 onwards. On Rippmann, see McLelland (2012).
18 In fact, for those pupils who took German, the allocation of hours was comparable to that for French, and in the "army class" of Public Schools, was actually often higher than for French. See "Language Teaching in Schools", *Educational Times* (1894: 141).
19 See the regulations in Cam.c.11.51. vol. 60.
20 Polish, by contrast, was overwhelmingly taken by candidates in state schools (77%), with only 4% from independent schools, so has the more typical profile of a "community language".

21 See Lorch (2017) for the biography of one such candidate, Thomas Prendergast, who entered the College at the age of 18.
22 One such Visitor was Sir Charles Wilkins (1749–1836), author of a *Grammar of the Sanskrita Language* (1808) and a new edition of Richardson's *A Vocabulary Persian, Arabic, and English* (1810) (books widely used at the College at the time), and creator of the first Bengali typeface.
23 Sebastian Puncher (deputy archivist at Sandhurst), p.c., citing an item about the half yearly exam at Addiscombe in the United Services Magazine.
24 See, e.g., the Cambridge Local Examinations Regulations, Cam.c.11.51 Vol. 67 [1924].
25 The search engine does not capture all courses, however. The School of Oriental and African Studies (SOAS) offers an Urdu pathway within its South Asian Studies programme, for example.
26 Funding was withdrawn from the National Languages Strategy in 2011 by the new Conservative government.
27 For the current state of Arabic in schools, see British Council (2015).
28 Rodeiro (2009: 9) found that only 59.34% of candidates had Mandarin as their mother tongue, but many may have Cantonese or other Chinese background. For the current state of Chinese in British schools, see Tinsley and Board (2015).
29 The figures here for 1985 and 1990 differ slightly from those in Jones (1993: 45), who gives 8358 rather than 7949 for the year 1985, and 9425 rather than 9476 for the year 1990.

3 A sociocultural history of language learning
Why, who, where?

This chapter deals with the *social context* of language learning. Section 3.2 considers language learners from three perspectives: social class, gender, and the special case of adult learners, an important group in the history of language learning, not least because of their sheer numbers compared to school learners. Section 3.3 examines the changing status of language teachers, their qualifications, and the institutions that educated them for their careers as teachers. Finally, Section 3.4 examines language learning opportunities beyond the classroom, including exchanges, pen-friendships, and residence abroad. We begin, however, by considering the history of motivations for language learning. As we shall see, the birth of languages as school subjects in the nineteenth century is just the last in a long list of language learning contexts.

3.1 Reasons for learning languages before compulsory schooling

Today, young people's exposure to foreign language education typically begins as part of their compulsory schooling, and its end-point, at whatever level, is usually some kind of test. Yet the idea of learning a language as a "subject" for some perceived educational benefit is relatively new, an invention of the late eighteenth century. Language *teaching* for specific purposes (such as English for Academic Purposes) is an even newer idea. For example, the first manuals explicitly for teaching German for Commercial Purposes date from the 1880s, and materials for teaching German to scientists, lawyers and other groups appear in the twentieth century (McLelland 2015a: 79–81, 164). However, people have been *learning* languages for very specific needs for centuries. Some of the earliest surviving vernacular language learning materials attest to the perennial immediate needs of travellers in a strange land. Jottings in the margins and spaces of ninth- and tenth-century manuscripts contain word-lists, phrases and short dialogues of the kind to arrange food and accommodation, and to talk to strangers and servants (Jolles 1968, Hellgardt 2001). For travelling players, merchants, diplomats, military personnel and missionaries, at least a little knowledge of a foreign language was a practical necessity, as well as for refugees and migrants of other kinds, but little is known about how these learners learnt. Glück (2014: 54) cites the words of a soldier in Jaroslav Hašek's 1920s novel *The Good Soldier Švejk*, asked by his lieutenant how and where he had learned German: *Tak, sám sebe od* ('Well, just like that, it just happened'). In many cases, we still know little more.

3.1.1 Language learning for trade and commerce

The earliest surviving language learning manuals have their origins in materials produced for merchants. At a time before copyright and before systems of international book distribution, manuals of this kind were endlessly copied, adapted and reprinted. Languages would be added or substituted, resulting in books with multilingual lists of vocabulary and/or dialogues, in parallel columns, replenished or added to over time. The first such materials, pairing two vernacular languages (not Latin), are German-Italian materials used by fifteenth-century Venetian cloth-merchants seeking to learn German for trade with Nuremburg. They spawned a whole family of vocabularies known as the *Introito e porta* (named after the opening words of the first Italian sentence), of which at least 87 editions were published between 1477 and 1636 (see 4.2). A version including English as one of the languages was first published in 1534 (Hüllen 2005: 50–54). A second important family of books, a set of dialogues, was first produced by Noël de Berlaimont (d. 1531), a language teacher in Antwerp, in the Low Countries, at the crossroads of European trading routes. The earliest surviving edition of Berlaimont's *Colloquia et dictionariolum* ("Conversations and a Small Dictionary"), Dutch-French, dates from 1536 (Hüllen 2005: 54). In Britain, an example of a manual based on a text first produced for the Low Countries merchant market is the *Dutch Schoolmaster*, whose author Marten Le Mayre was able to draw on Dutch predecessors (Dibbets 1971–72). Figure 3.1 shows the opening pages of the first dialogue, on buying and selling.

The buying and selling dialogue is a mainstay of early modern language manuals, modelling how to bargain hard, often over cloth. One of four dialogues in the French-Flemish *Livre de Mestiers*, produced in Flanders around 1340, models bargaining for cloth (Kibbee 1991: 79); likewise the English-French dialogues that followed its model, and the fifteenth-century German-Italian materials that gave rise to the *Introito e porta* tradition.[1] The commercial imperative for language learning is a constant throughout the centuries, although late nineteenth-century efforts to promote the teaching of commercial language study in schools were not particularly successful (see 3.2.1 in this volume and McLelland 2015c). In the twentieth century, the Institute of Linguists – first established in 1910–1911, revived in 1924 by a lecturer of Spanish – sought to support "British-born Linguists" in commerce, seeking "1. The fuller recognition of the value of foreign languages in commerce and industry [and] 2. The better remuneration of linguists and foreign correspondents" [i.e. clerks dealing with companies' foreign correspondence] (Smith et al. 2010: 13). It has offered accreditation in languages for many professions ever since, including the police and airline crews, as well as translators and interpreters (Smith et al. 2010: 26, 38). In 2005, it became the *Chartered* Institute of Linguists (thus placing it as an accrediting

Figure 3.1 The Dutch Schoole-Master (*Le Mayre 1606*). Pages unnumbered; the dialogue immediately follows the grammar section. By kind permission of Trinity College Dublin

body alongside the much better-known Institute of Chartered Accountants, for example), which it viewed as an important step "to true recognition of the professional value of language work"; in 2010, it had a membership of around 6,000 (Smith et al. 2010: 66, 70).

3.1.2 Religion and language learning

Religion is another recurrent factor in the history of European language learning. The first manuals for English as a Foreign Language were aimed at French Protestant refugees in England (see 2.8). English speakers' interest in German Protestantism was behind some of the earliest interest in learning German as a foreign language. Prominent reformers such as William Tyndale and Martin Coverdale were proficient in German; some English Protestants fled to Germany and Switzerland during the rule of Queen Mary (1553–1558), including John Knox, who went to Frankfurt am Main. (Blamires 1990). It was religion, too, that motivated many of the first Europeans not only to learn each other's languages, but also non-European languages. The first European grammar of Hebrew was the work of Johannes Reuchlin (*De Rudimentis Hebraicis* 1506), who wanted to make accessible the large parts of the Old Testament originally written in Hebrew, and the Rabbinistic scholarship about them. Later, religious missionaries learned the languages of other continents, especially in Central and South America. As we saw in 2.12, missionaries led the way in the first manuals of Chinese for English speakers; the earliest known manual of German for Chinese learners was produced by a missionary (Teufel 1906; see McLelland 2017a). This rich history of missionary linguistic studies has begun to receive much attention in recent years.[2]

3.1.3 Military language learning

Like trade and religious expansionism, warfare and preparation for it are recurring practical motivations for language learning throughout history. For as long as there have been soldiers, mercenaries and occupying forces, at least some of them have had to learn foreign languages. Yet the history of military language learning in Britain remains largely unresearched, despite rich archival holdings, and despite the importance of multilingualism in the history of European armed forces.[3] In over half of the Habsburg monarchy's regiments, up to five different languages might be spoken (Gräf 2014: 152, n.3), and even if British regiments have been linguistically less mixed, languages were still important. Amongst the British officers serving in the American War of Independence in 1770s, knowledge of French was presumably widespread, for when German troops from Brunswick and Hessen were recruited for the campaign, a knowledge of French, not English, seems to have been the priority (Gräf 2014: 159).

Ordinary soldiers learnt languages too when they could. Cowman (2014) recounts anecdotal evidence of British troops learning French in the trenches of World War I. Learning even a small amount of French "eased essential interactions [and] engagement with the civilian population", and as over a thousand British servicemen married French women during World War I (Cowman 2014: 9), at least some must have got beyond bare necessities and pleasantries. Among the texts published for this large market of soldier language learners was *The Active-Service French Book for Soldiers and Sailors* (Ajax and Harris 1915), a publication costing sixpence. It brought together, in a conveniently waterproof cover, Ajax's 24-page *Soldier's Language Manual, No.1*, and Harris's 32-page *French for the Front*. Harris justified the publication of his *French for the Front* with the pitiful anecdote of soldiers who, separated from their regiment, were fired on by the French and were killed, for they had not had a single word of French to call out, not even *Anglais* "English". By contrast, another group on another occasion had shouted out the only two words they knew (*Du pain!* "some bread"), and this had been enough to give the French soldiers they met time to discover they were English.[4] The subtitle of *French for the Front* promised "A Short Cut to the French Language in Rhyme". Harris presented what had to be learnt in the form of 116 four-line rhymes, and advised, "Copy out a rhyme on a slip of paper, and take it with you on a route march, saying or singing it to the rhythm of the march". Below are three examples; one can imagine how the end rhymes would have helped drum in the phrases chanted while marching along. The topics covered in these examples – from first exchanges ("Understand, do you?") to a matter of life and death ("Fired on by the French"), to mental trauma ("Nerves bad") – are typical of Harris's matter-of-fact coverage of life at the front (Harris 1915:10, 23, 27; Harris used a larger font n to indicate nasal n in the "How to say it" column, replaced here with bold **n**).

French	How to Say It	English
3. UNDERSTAND, DO YOU?	(*Comprenez-vous?*)	
Vous êtes français	voo-za*i*t frah**n**sai	You are French,
Mais vous parlez anglais?	ma*i* voo pahr-leh-zah**n**glai?	But you speak English?
Vous me comprenez,	voo me*r* co**n**preneh	You understand me,
N'est il pas vrai?	na*i*-teel pah vra*i*?	Don't you?
73. FIRED ON BY THE FRENCH	(*Frappés par les Français*)	
Amis! Anglais!	am-ee! ah**n**-gla*i*!	Friends! English!
Nous sommes anglais!	noo som-zah**n**- gla*i*!	We are English
Ne tirez pas!	ne*r* teereh pah!	Don't fire!
Nous sommes alliés!	noo som-zal-yeh!	We are Allies!
97. NERVES BAD	(*Les nerfs malades*)	
Vous avez	voo-zavveh	Your nerves
Les nerfs malades,	la*i* na*i*r malad	Are wrong,
Il vous faut	eel voo fo	You must
Prendre du repos.	prahndr' de*u* re*r*poh.	Rest.

Examinations for military personnel date from 1855, when tests in German were introduced for the Military Academy at Woolwich (see 5.1). Russian became a growing priority from the 1870s, especially for prospective Indian Army Officers, at a time when a Russian attack on India was feared (Muckle 2008a: 32).[5] In 1885, a new regulation allowed naval officers three months' leave to improve their knowledge of French, German, Italian or Spanish. By 1886, officers could present themselves for examination in any European or Oriental language, to be awarded either a "pass" or an "interpreters'" certificate. In 1887, special leave of absence could be granted to some officers to go abroad in order to acquire the necessary proficiency to become interpreters, though not for the major European languages (Muckle 2008a: 33). In 1890, the Army Lists named 49 qualified Russian interpreters, 85 in 1895, 127 in 1909; the Navy Lists for 1907 and 1909 each list around a dozen qualified Russian interpreters (Muckle 2008a: 36). Unfortunately, we do not have comparable figures for the other languages. Not all those who passed the tough interpreters' examination had the opportunity to use their expertise. Robert Spottiswoode (1841–1936) recounted in his memoirs the considerable efforts he made to learn Russian in Moscow during 17 months of leave granted for the purpose. Passing as an interpreter, he was duly rewarded with a cheque for £200, but was then posted by the army to Ireland, where he spent the next 47 years, and never had the chance to use his hard-won knowledge (Muckle 2008a: 34).

44 *A sociocultural history*

The time devoted to language teaching in the army was always at the mercy of other pressures. For example, at Sandhurst it was reduced by two-thirds during the Boer War of 1899–1902, though when it was re-instated in 1902, it included not just French and German, but also Hindustani, as an option for Indian Army cadets (Morton 2014: 5). Similarly, during World War I, when the officer training course as a whole was cut from 18 months to three months in order to "meet the urgent demand for officers on the front line", French and German instruction were temporarily cut entirely, despite their importance for cooperation with the French and Belgian allies and for interrogating German prisoners-of-war (Morton 2014: 14, 29).

While the history of language learning and teaching by British armed forces personnel in World War II is unresearched,[6] the U.S. Army Specialized Training Program (ASTP) in Foreign Languages in an interesting case (Velleman 2008). The ASTP Foreign Languages programme was set up in 1942, building on an Intensive Language Program (ILP) established in 1941 by the American Council of Learned Societies (ACLS) to provide courses in language and area studies of less commonly taught languages. The ILP had been conceived by the Executive Secretary of the ACLS, Mortimer Graves, to harness the skills of linguists, developed in analysing unwritten Amerindian languages, "to do likewise with languages deemed strategically important in the event of the world war which he saw as inevitable" (Velleman 2008: 386). By the summer of 1942, 700 students were enrolled in 56 courses in 26 languages, across 18 universities, "by far the most impressive array of intensive language instruction ever presented in American academic life" (Graves & Cowan 1942: 3, cited by Velleman 2008: 386). The ASTP established approximately 500 intensive speaking courses in over 30 languages in 55 U.S. state universities between April 1943 and April 1944. The original focus was on Arabic, Bengali, Burmese, Chinese, Finnish, Greek, Hindi, Japanese, Malay, Russian, Serbo-Croatian, Swedish and Turkish, but in response to political pressures, other more established languages were added too, including French, Dutch and Spanish, and the number of learners increased greatly from a projected 1,500, so that by the end of April 1943, some 15,000 trainees were studying languages under the programme.[7]

Britain's equivalent of the ASTP was established not during World War II, but after it, during the Cold War. The Joint Services School for Linguists (JSSL) opened in 1951 to supply personnel for interception and interpretation; by the time it closed in 1960, when conscription ended, some 5,000 men had been trained in Russian (cf. Elliott & Shukman 2003: 11; cf. Boiling 2005). Like the U.S. ASTP, it was a very intensive form of language learning, with teaching by a trained linguist, followed by drills in small groups with a native speaker. The experiences of one conscript, who completed his National Service in the RAF signals section in 1957–1958, are recounted in McLelland (2015a: 182–183). Having learnt French and German at school and intending to progress to university, he was selected for eight months of intensive instruction in Russian. Batches of between 300 and 400 uniformed conscripts at a time learned Russian in eight-hour days, alternating between traditional grammar-presentation in classes of about 25 (taught by teachers who were typically English Russianists) and small-group teaching with a native Russian speaker, followed by vocabulary learning in the evenings (500–700 words a week). The conscripts were intended to reach O-level standard in about eight weeks, and A-level in about six months.

Despite how little we know of such cases of language learning in the armed forces, it is an important strand in the history of language education, for three reasons. First, the sheer scale of the armed forces means that at times when language learning has been prioritized, military personnel become the majority of learners, especially of lesser learnt languages. The learning of Russian in the armed forces dwarfed what little teaching there was in the universities before 1914 (Muckle 2008a: 32); likewise, the number of conscripts who passed through the JSSL in the 1950s. To ignore their experience is to ignore much of the language teaching and learning that was going on. Second, such large-scale and high-profile language learning programmes could change wider social attitudes to language learning. Velleman (2008: 407) argues that the ASTP was "instrumental in bringing to the attention of the United States public, for a brief time at last, the importance of foreign language learning". Thomas (2003: 5) wrote that the JSSL

> was created for a practical military purpose [...] but ultimately of far greater significance was that it created a generation of young and influential Britons who had generous, respectful and affectionate feelings for Russia – the eternal Russia of Tolstoy, Pushkin and Pasternak.

Third, and finally, programmes such as the ASTP and the JSSL arguably resulted in a partial democratization of language learning (see also 3.2.1). Admittedly, ASTP trainees already had to have one year of college education; in the JSSL, they had to have a School Certificate in Latin or another foreign language, statistically more likely in those with a grammar school or private school education. Still, relatively large numbers of men who would otherwise have had no opportunity to learn a language to such a high level now did so.

3.1.4 Language learning for social prestige and leisured cultural enrichment

Mastery of French was already a marker of good breeding and prestige in the Middle Ages, but in the course of the Early Modern era, knowledge of other foreign languages also began to carry social prestige. Language learning was a socially desirable "accomplishment" for the nobility, in the same category as fencing, riding or dancing. Being able to speak one or more European languages made it possible to participate in elite polite society, whether on the Grand Tour or in salons at home, in the European-wide phenomenon of the "art" of conversation. Increasingly, though, this language learning was not a mere social necessity. It was, or could be, a leisure activity in itself, providing access to a rich culture, especially literature. Kibbee (1991: 103–104) observes the beginning of this widening of cultural horizons in sixteenth-century manuals for learning French:

> The extra cultural material in the grammars shifts from the 'books of courtesy' (elementary guides to good table manners) in the early part of the century, to religious and moral material in the middle part of the century [...] to brief guides to popular wisdom and European culture at the end of the century.

The growth of a literate and leisured middle class fuelled the market for literary translations, which in turn spurred interest in reading such works in the original. This development is particularly obvious in the case of German. In the preface to his *Elements of German Grammar* (1774), Wendeborn commented, "[T]he Germans have lately made great improvements, both in their language and their manner of writing", so that even the French were now taking an interest, and the English would no doubt follow suit:

> Among the English the German has been hitherto very little known; but there is reason to expect, that within a few years [...] the language and the literature of the Germans will no more be looked upon with indifference.
> (Wendeborn 1774: [1], viii; see Guthke 2011 and
> McLelland 2015a: 58–76 for further discussion)

3.1.5 Academic value and the birth of a school subject

Already from the early seventeenth century onwards, a minority of language learners had been driven by academic interest in analysing the language itself, especially its history and its relationship to other tongues. An early example is John Minsheu's *Guide into Tongues* (1617), a very large 500-page dictionary of 11 languages for those interested in comparing words across languages. While Minsheu claimed the book might serve as a practical guide for merchants "that are in person to traficke in forreien Countreys and Tongues", its audience was clearly a scholarly one, for it had a Latin preface, a certificate from the University of Oxford, and a list of over 400 subscribers that included "most of the illustrious names of the day from King James to John Donne" (Schäfer 1978: v). Despite such (limited) scholarly interest, it was only in the 1830s that French and German were introduced to the curriculum in British grammar and public schools. Language teaching began to acquire the status of a bona fide subject in the schools now catering to the upper and upper-middle class elite, first in German *Gymnasia* (in the late eighteenth century) and, somewhat later, in England, in the rapid expansion during the Victorian period of British "Public Schools" (i.e. fee-paying private schools). The prospectus of University College School (founded as part of University College London, established in 1826), made it clear that boys would learn first French, and then German; five hours a week were allocated to both combined (see Usher et al. 1981: 13). Other schools followed in the

1830s and 1840s, beginning with Shrewsbury, which introduced French in 1836 and German in 1837; French and German were taught at Harrow by 1839, followed by Winchester, King's School Canterbury, Marlborough and Uppingham (Proescholdt 1991: 95; Ortmanns 1993: 28). At Rugby, under Thomas Arnold's headship (1828–1841), French and German were apparently made compulsory for pupils not taking a science (Ortmanns 1993: 27; Hope Simpson 1967: 7).

The status of the languages at these schools was initially somewhat shaky. On the one hand, the textbooks produced make it clear that the goal was mental training through grammatical analysis and intellectual growth through translation of edifying literature (see Chapter 5 and McLelland 2015c). Yet the languages did not always enjoy the status of a full subject. At Uppingham, for example, French and German were first introduced as optional subjects taught in the afternoons (Ortmanns 1993: 28). At Eton, French had been available at least from the 1780s, when Mr. Porny, the author of a *Practical French Grammar* (Porny 1784), was French master there; but in the 1860s, it was still available only as an extra, and was considered impossible to teach as a regular subject in class. The sole French master at Eton was described to the 1864 Clarendon Commission as "a mere objet de luxe" (cited by Cohen 1996: 88). In general, language teachers were more likely to be adjunct part-time appointments, and to be native speakers who were, by definition, from outside the establishment circles, who were not well-respected, and were often ridiculed for their Frenchness (Cohen 1996: 90).

Still, the value of French and German as school subjects was clearly signalled when they were included amongst the subjects for which examinations were offered to school pupils by the Oxford and Cambridge Universities' examination boards, beginning in 1857–1858. As we shall see in Chapters 4 and 5, the status of languages as formal academic subjects led to a radical shift in emphasis in teaching styles and in the expectations of what learners should master. In contrast to the eighteenth century, where conversational fluency was prized, nineteenth-century (boys') school education focussed on linguistic and literary analysis. Oxford Professor for Modern Languages Max Müller's statement on the purpose of foreign language teaching to the Clarendon (Public Schools) Commission in 1864 has been oft-quoted: "I would aim principally at securing an accurate knowledge of grammar and secondly a sufficient amount of reading – but I should not attempt fluency in conversation" (e.g. Proescholdt 1991: 95). Henry Weston Eve, a teacher of French and German and then headmaster at University College School advised the Headmasters' Conference in 1879, "Your first object is to discipline the mind; your second to give a knowledge of French or German" (cf. Hawkins 1987: 113). However, as we shall see in 3.2.2, there were also gender differences in the status of languages as school subjects.

3.2 Learners: who could or should learn a language?

All decision-making about language teaching and learning in Britain, from the individual choice to the level of national strategy, rests on assumptions about who should be able to learn a language; about who should have to; and about who is

48 *A sociocultural history*

best able to do so. The common-sense answers to such questions have undergone considerable change over the last century or so. There are even differing attitudes within the British Isles. For example, the numbers of pupils choosing A-level languages dropped in England and Wales in 2015, but *more* pupils chose languages as Higher subjects in Ireland's Leaving Certificate compared to the previous year. At policy level, too, there are important differences (Chapter 6). Here, we consider the history of who had the opportunity or obligation to learn a language, and why, considering in particular social class and gender, and the experiences of adult language learners.

3.2.1 Social class and language learners: language as an elite accomplishment or languages for employability?

We have seen in 3.1 that language *learning* has taken place in all kinds of contexts, as necessity dictated, amongst people of any age, gender and social status. The same cannot be said of access to language *teaching*, which was much more restricted for most of history, chiefly to a middle-class and upper-class elite.[8] Indeed, the same can be said of access to *any* kind of education, with a general trend of widening access over the past 150 years or so, especially as children's school lives have been extended. The Elementary Education Act of 1870 first made education compulsory for all children in England and Wales up to the age of ten – 80%–85% of pupils who attended elementary schools of various kinds, initially mainly church schools and dame schools, left school at ten. The minority of middle- and upper-class children went through an entirely separate system of education, taught either privately at home, in boarding schools, or in private day schools. Since 1870, the school-leaving age in Britain has been steadily raised: to eleven in 1893, twelve in 1899, 14 in 1918, 15 in 1947, and 16 in 1972.[9] The extension of schooling into teenage years for all pupils created far more scope for wider learning experiences, including languages education.

From the late Middle Ages onwards to the eighteenth century, the pupils of language teachers fall into two categories. The first belonged to the growing middle class: merchants or their sons, and others who needed language skills for their profession, catered to in materials like those discussed in 3.1.1. They would have been taught by private tutors or language masters, or, in some cases, in the private schools catering to the emerging middle classes. French was widely taught in such schools; German seems to have been taught only in the so-called Dissenting Academies of nonconformist Protestant groups in the eighteenth century, where modern languages were taught alongside Latin, Greek, English, mathematics and a science (Ortmanns 1993: 21, following Watson 1921: 694). The number of these and similar schools increased after 1779, when non-conformists were legally allowed to be teachers.

The second group of learners was the nobility. Since the Middle Ages, they generally learnt French, and from the sixteenth century onwards, as fashion dictated, they might also have learnt one or more of Spanish, Italian or German

(Chapter 2). Interest in these languages increased further with the growth, from the second half of the seventeenth century, in "the travel of the young man of rank often in his teens, undertaken as the 'crown' of his liberal education" (Cohen 1996: 54–63; Chaney 1998–63, citation from Cohen 2001: 130). The so-called Grand Tour provided both the justification and the opportunity for learning languages to gentlemen and (rarely) gentlewomen. Indeed Howell's famous guide for travellers (1650), published at the start of the era of the Grand Tour, promised *Instructions for Forreine Travel. Shewing by what cours, and in what compasse of time, one may take an exact Survey of the Kingdomes and States of Christedome, <u>and arrive to the practicall knowledge of the Languages, to a good purpose</u>* (my emphasis). Language masters increasingly catered directly for this Grand Tour market. For instance, in his bilingual manual of German and English (1687) Heinrich Offelen included, in addition to the usual early modern dialogues on practical subjects (e.g. accommodation, food, asking the way, shopping) three dialogues catering to curious gentlemen travellers, in which two "Gentlemen" discuss the laws, customs and peculiarities of "strange Countries", dealing first with France, then England, and finally Germany. They combine practical country-specific information (e.g. post-days, the dangers of French pickpockets) with information about the sights to be seen (including the palace of Versailles, the trade fairs Frankfurt and Leipzig). Thus the trend that Kibbee already observed in French materials of the sixteenth century continued in the seventeenth and eighteenth centuries: more attention was paid to cultural information, initially the kind of everyday culture useful to travellers like the examples just given.

The intended class of the learners is evident in the attention paid to the elaborate rules of polite society. König (1715: 190, 193) shows us how to pay a social call, for example: "Pray make my compliments to him' *Ich bitte euch, meine Complimenten bey ihm abzulegen*". "Sir I come to pay my humble Respect to you. *Ich komme mein Herr, meine unterthänige Aufwartung bey euch abzustatten*", or, sometimes, in warnings to avoid the artifice of excessive politeness of "standing on ceremony" and "making too many compliments" (Sewel 1706: 253–254). The art of making conversation on anodyne topics is also often modelled:

What Weather is it to Day?	Was ist heute für Wetter?
It is the finest Weather in the World.	Es ist das aller schönste Wetter von der Welt.
The Sun shines.	Die Sonne scheint.
Is it windy abroad?	Ist es windig?
No! It is very calm Weather.	Nein, es ist sehr stilles Wetter. Es ist sehr stille.
It will be very hot then this afternoon.	So wird es Nachmittag sehr warm werden.
I believe so; for the Sun is at the highest now.	Ich glaube es, dann die Sonne ist am höchsten nun.

I am afraid we shall have a storm.	Ich fürchte wir mögthen ein Ungewitter haben.
It does not look so.	Es sieht nicht darnach aus.
I beg your Pardon, look those Clouds.	Verzeihet mir; sehet ihr dieses Gewolck?
Well, what signifies that?	Nun gut, was hat das zusagen.
That signifies Thunder.	Das bedeut Donner.
I doubt at least that it will rain.	Zum wenigsten glaube ich es wird regnen.

(König 1715: 192)

As noted in 3.1.4, "high" culture increasingly featured too, for example in collections of proverbs, and extracts from well-known literary authors, to meet the needs of leisured learners, who did not need to earn a living, so wanted not only tools for effective communication but also stimulating reading material to occupy them too.[10] Even once languages were included in formal schooling in the nineteenth century (see 3.1.5), they remained the privilege of the social elite who had access to Public Schools, grammar schools, and the other fee-paying schools that imitated them. These elite beginnings – with an emphasis on edifying literature and, later, grammatical analysis – left their mark on assumptions about what language teaching as school subjects entailed throughout the twentieth century (Chapter 4).

The first attempts to make language learning available to the overwhelming majority of children who did not have access to an elite education began surprisingly early, not long after compulsory elementary education was introduced in 1870, which, for the vast majority of children between 1870 and 1900, was also their entire education.[11] Data from the 1851 census reveal that in elementary education, only 3.8% of public day schools catering for the poorer classes offered a modern language; 2.3% of boys in public day schools and 1% of girls in public day schools were learning a modern language (Bayley 1989: 58). After 1870, however, the elementary curriculum was extended, and in 1875, three categories of subject were established. Alongside "Standard" subjects (the three Rs, compulsory for all), schools were free to teach "Higher" subjects such as geography, elementary science, or English and "Specific" subjects, which could be taken by individual pupils in the higher classes. French was approved as a possible "Specific" subject in 1872, and German by 1880.

In 1895, of 32 "Higher Grade Elementary Schools" or "organized science schools" listed in the Bryce Commission's report on "secondary" education, teaching 22,480 children, French was offered by virtually all; 11 offered German as well as French. In general, it was the schools in larger urban centres that offered languages. For example, the Leeds Central Higher Grade Board School and the Sheffield Central Higher Grade School taught French for "up to three hours" and German for "up to two hours" a week. The Central Higher Grade Board School at Manchester offered French but not German. At Ducie Street School in Manchester, French was taught one an hour a week.

In practice, there were still only tiny numbers taking languages. Only 3% of children in Standards IV–VI, or 90,000 out of an elementary school population of nearly three million, took any 'specific' subjects at all, and geography, grammar and literature accounted for nearly 90% of all the tests taken by such pupils.[12] In Derbyshire, in 1872, for example, 1,077 pupils took geography; only five took French, then a newly approved subject. In 1885, when French had been an approved specific subject for over a decade, and German for at least a few years, there were still only 423 passes in French among the 18,499 children who passed in specific subjects in ten London boroughs; there were none at all in German (Bayley 1989: 61–62).

Yet the schools were under steady pressure from employers and their lobby groups to teach languages, in order to help meet the demand for foreign language clerks in commerce and business. As an article in the *Educational Times* demanded in 1887,

> Why should not Englishmen do the work from which they are [. . .] displaced by foreigners? And the only answer is the very humiliating one, that Englishmen do not receive a schooling to qualify them to do such work.
> (*Educational Times*, December 1, p. 466)

So the 1880s saw efforts to establish the teaching of French and German for commercial purposes. A small flurry of textbooks for teaching "Commercial" French and German were produced, and the Cambridge Local Examinations Syndicate briefly offered a Commercial Certificate with a compulsory foreign language element. However, the language examinations attracted few entrants, and there were even fewer passes (in German, never more than 12 candidates passed, and in one year as few as four), and the certificate was discontinued after five years, in 1893. Examiners, teachers and heads seem to have concluded that it was not feasible to teach a language to a usable commercial standard in the time available (see McLelland 2015a: 80–81).

In 1895, new rules required the teaching of at least one modern language in higher grade and science schools receiving government grants. However, a crucial distinction was made. Languages could be taught alongside shorthand and bookkeeping in the commercial classes, but French or German could also be offered as literary subjects, viewed as a welcome counterbalance to science in the organized science schools. For this kind of language teaching, higher grants were available. From 1904, in the newly defined "secondary schools" (defined as giving "a complete graded course of instruction, of wider scope and more advanced degree than that given in elementary schools"), the curriculum must include at least one language other than English (which could be Latin), but languages could be omitted if a school could show that its English course already provided "adequate linguistic and literary training" ("The Education Act. Regulations for Secondary Schools", as published in *The Tablet*, July 2, 1904: 33). This expectation of "adequate linguistic and literary training" makes clear that foreign languages education in these schools was not to be practically or commercially oriented, but part of a liberal education.

Meanwhile, in the few surviving higher elementary schools, teaching languages was discouraged. In the new junior technical schools, teaching languages was not permitted unless the language could be shown to be of direct value for industrial occupations. However, there were strenuous objections, because the Institute of Mechanics and Electrical Engineers and the Institute of Chemistry required a language for their entrance examinations. The Board of Education finally relented in 1926, and in 1929 two-thirds of the 9,169 pupils in junior technical, junior commercial and junior art schools were taking a modern language (Board of Education 1930b: 7, Table II, cited by Bayley 1989: 68). Restructuring the education system in this way – higher grade schools were phased out, as secondary education was phased in – meant that during the first half of the twentieth century, modern languages, now largely restricted to the secondary schools, were no longer even theoretically available to the vast majority of working-class pupils. Many of them would turn to evening courses to supply the gap, once they had left school (see 3.2.3).

A step change in the availability of language teaching beyond the elite in Britain was the introduction of "comprehensive" state-funded schools from the late 1950s, replacing the post-war tri-partite system of grammar, technical and secondary modern schools. Where full comprehensivizataion was implemented (not everywhere in Britain), this meant the abolition of the so-called 11-plus examinations used to select the most academically able pupils for grammar schools, hitherto the main providers of foreign language teaching. Since then, a language has been, in theory, available to all pupils at secondary school. The optimism about teaching a foreign language to all pupils, of all backgrounds and abilities, is captured in the somewhat patronizing but well-intentioned words of Thimann (1955), reflecting in 1955 on the worth of teaching modern languages in secondary modern schools (albeit from his position as a teacher at Nottingham High School, a private selective boys' school!):

> To my mind, the essential reason for widening the scope of language teaching [i.e. beyond grammar schools] is the breaking-down of isolation [. . .] opening a window on the world. For children who spend almost a lifetime in a small industrial town [. . .] the escape from an environment, the exercise of an imagination – these are surely worth-while experiences. Since there is no magical teaching method, Secondary Modern French may not always be good French: the thrill and triumph of speaking another language may not endure: there may not be the same financial incentive to learn as in many European countries. But the wider outlook that we hope to secure through language teaching – this is, perhaps, the best answer to those who would crowd it out with more English or more Mathematics, simply because these are the stuff of everyday life.
>
> (Thimann 1955: 128)

In 1977, a report on *Modern Languages in Comprehensive Schools* found that roughly three-quarters of all pupils were learning French in the first three years of secondary school. Ten years later, in 1987, the high point of language teaching for all was reached, when a language was made compulsory for all pupils between the ages of 11 and 16. This was a revolution compared to the availability of languages at the start of the century, even if it was a century behind some other parts of northern Europe, where one or even two foreign languages were made compulsory in secondary education in the second half of the nineteenth century (see, e.g., Giesler 2014, Cabau 2014, Kok Escalle 2015 on Germany, Sweden and the Netherlands). In any case, the provision only lasted until 1993, after which pupils merely had to take at least a "short course" in languages (worth half a GCSE). Still, in 1995, languages made up 10% of all subject entries at 16+ examinations in England and Wales. From 2004, it ceased to be compulsory for pupils aged 14–16 to take a language (i.e. at Key Stage 4, leading to GCSE examinations). In the twenty-first century, the modern languages social class division is back again, almost as stark as it was a century ago. In 2007, over half of comprehensive pupils and two-thirds of secondary modern pupils did *not* take a foreign language at all as a GCSE subject (see Table 3.1).[13]

Another new stark class division concerns the opportunity to take more than one foreign language. In 2000, over a third of pupils in independent (fee-paying) schools and a quarter of pupils in grammar schools (academically and therefore to some extent also socially selective) took more than one foreign language. The percentage doing so in secondary modern schools was negligible, at 2.7%, and only 7.5% in comprehensive schools, though the gap narrowed slightly in 2007.[14] Schools in deprived areas have the lowest take-up of a language at GCSE (Vidal Rodeiro 2009: 12). In the most deprived areas, CILT (2007) found that 'the culture of the community is unambitious and modern foreign languages are perceived as difficult' (cited by Rodeiro 2009: 12). Thus, while the structural barriers to language learning across the social spectrum have been removed over the past century, there still remain stark social differences in language learning patterns.

3.2.2 Gender in language learning and teaching

In the early twenty-first century, languages were more likely to be taken by girls than boys; in 2014, girls made up 56% of language candidates at GCSE, boys 44%. At A-level, female candidates outnumbered males by nearly two to one in 2014: 64% of entrants were female, 36% male (CfBT 2015: 30–31). Just 33% of languages students at universities are male (Tinsley/British Academy 2013: 19, citing CILT 2010). The ratio of female-to-male candidates was far less skewed at A-level in 1965, with a female-to-male ratio of 54:46 (CfBT 2015: 31). We cannot fully explore the possible reasons for this change here, but the fact that a higher proportion of boys continue with languages in all-boys' schools than in co-educational settings suggests that social factors, including social gender identities, play a significant role. These same socialization forces probably also help construct the common-sense belief that girls are better at languages than boys, as well as the perception of certain languages as more feminine than others.[15] However, such perceptions are context-specific. Sunderland (2013) suggest boys

Table 3.1 Uptake of combinations of modern foreign languages by school type (percentages of students) (from Rodeiro 2007: 20). "Secondary modern" schools are "schools that normally take children who have failed to gain a grammar school place, in the areas that retain academic selection".

Combination	2000				2006			
	Comprehensive	Grammar	Independent	Secondary modern	Comprehensive	Grammar	Independent	Secondary modern
No foreign languages	21.6	2.7	12.9	31.6	51.4	7.4	12.9	66.9
French	67.3	73.1	81.5	81.5	62.6	63.4	73.2	75.1
German	28.5	38.1	27.8	12.3	26.7	36.3	20.0	9.6
Spanish	8.1	11.5	16.9	6.9	14.1	19.7	24.8	15.3
French and German	4.6	17.1	18.4	0.9	4.0	11.5	9.0	1.4
French and Spanish	1.6	6.0	12.2	1.0	2.8	7.5	14.0	2.1
More than one foreign language	7.5	25.0	34.8	2.7	9.0	21.9	27.0	4.6

may see French as more "feminine", German less so; and we shall see below that French became increasingly feminized in eighteenth-century English discourse. In one school inspected by the Board of Education (1930b: 10), girls were routinely drafted into French, all boys to German. Yet in early twentieth-century Ireland, German was perceived as a subject for girls from the outset, in contrast to French, which was long predominantly perceived as a boys' subject; up to 1917, French was learnt by the vast majority of boys in Ireland, and girls joined them only gradually; the number of female pupils learning German was at times seven times higher than the number of male pupils (Fischer 2000: 465).

If differential take-up and success in language learning is at least in part the result of socially constructed perceptions of the kinds of people that language learners are (or "ought" to be), looking at gendered constructions of social identity in language learning in the past may help us develop greater awareness of today's constructions. In that spirit, this section addresses questions whose answers seem likely to be relevant to male and female preferences about language learning:

- How have genders been represented in language learning materials?
- If some languages and cultures have been perceived as more feminine or masculine than others, how and why has this come about (taking French as our case study)?
- What status has knowing a foreign language had in the social identity of language learners?
- How and why have male and female learners been taught differently?

Representations of gender in language teaching materials

Women's roles in language learning materials of the early modern period reflected their subordinate status in society. Women often appeared as silent, or at least subordinate, often maids and servants; in one dialogue, which recurs in many manuals, a chambermaid fends off the advances of a man in bed feigning illness. If women were allowed outside the domestic sphere, their participation in discourse was limited, often unsuccessful: their efforts are rebuffed, or a male chaperone rescues them from their inadequate efforts. "The female voice is silenced outside of the domestic, unless she has a man to speak for her: the bustling commercial life of male oriented manuals, and the competence which it entails, is denied her" (Gallagher 2014: 88). Gallagher (2014: 100) argues that females often appear even more circumscribed in seventeenth-century language learning manuals than in reality, where some women did have at least some freedom in the domains of commerce. Some Dutch-English manuals show female traders in the market, but in general, as Fleming (1989: 27) observes, "One of the strategies [. . .] to encourage female obedience is to represent women as being already simple, chaste, and obedient". An example of how this "effective tranquilizer" can be worked in to the very fibre of a grammar is Erondell's *The French Garden*

(1605), where "the men have active, scholarly, and sometimes wicked attributes; the women are passive and invariably good (and incidentally often of a lower class)". In the examples that follow, the noun phrases illustrate, for masculine and feminine grammatical gender in turn, what in Latin grammar would be vocative, nominative, genitive, dative, accusative and ablative cases. The men, boys and gentlemen of these example sentences exist largely unfettered, but females are constrained: they are "fair", "wise", "virtuous". The lords go hunting; the ladies are passive, honoured. Male "scholars" are matched by "gentlewomen", whose learning is invisible; the king is not matched by a queen, but by a goddaughter, who can be summoned; likewise, in the last case, the lords appear alongside mere maid-servants.

O man, O boye	o faire maide! o wise woman!
The Lordes be gone a hunting	The Ladies are honoured
I speak of the Gentlemen	I speak of the virtuous Ladies
I have given to the Schollers	I have given to the Gentlewomen
The wicked men have killed him	The maidens have overcom'd him
Where is the King? I see him not.	Where is my goddaughter? Call her.
By or with the Lordes	By or [with] the maiden servantes.

Examples from Erondell (1605), given by Fleming (1989: 27).

This constrained representation of females continued in textbook materials until the late twentieth century. In language materials of the 1970s and 1980s, "gender bias is rife in terms of both relative visibility and occupational and personal stereotyping of female characters". By the 1990s, however, a study of male and female discourse roles in dialogues of three 1990s textbooks of English as a Foreign Language revealed "an encouraging level of gender fairness" (Jones et al. 1997: 469). My own examination of gender in textbooks of German as a foreign language throughout the twentieth century matches this finding. Role stereotyping and implicit subordination of women and girls is widespread until the late twentieth century, but from the 1990s there are concerted efforts to show both males and females in a wider variety of roles, and in some textbooks there are chapters explicitly tackling the question of gender roles in society (see McLelland 2015a: 322–333). In the *Pictorial French Course* (14th ed. 1914, Figure 3.2), even a typical living room scene reveals assumptions about gender roles. We see the mother playing the piano, her middle-class accomplishment. Her daughter, perhaps singing or reading along to the music, is following in her mother's footsteps, while the younger girl, tucked at her grandmother's feet, is fully occupied with her doll, practising for her future role as mother. Her brother, in contrast, is given the space to be active, playing with a ball. While the grandmother sits back from the hearth, the grandfather, as the senior male, has the best seat by the fire. He, with his newspaper, and the father, reading or writing a letter at the table, are both preoccupied with the outside world. At the other end of the twentieth century, *Deutschland hier und jetzt* (Rowlinson et al. 1993), by

Figure 3.2 Lamartine's Pictorial French Course *shows 'The family in the living-room' (14th ed. 1914: 1) The same image was used in the equivalent* Pictorial German Course.

contrast, devotes a chapter to *Frauen in Deutschland* ("Women in Germany"). Besides features on women in all kinds of professions, the chapter includes a feature written by a female fencing champion, celebrating the fact that women are now able to participate in all aspects of elite sport. Thus, while in the past the language classroom reinforced gender roles just as the rest of society did, from the late twentieth century, we see the classroom being used to challenge stereotypes and circumscribed roles.

Femininities and masculinities in language learning

Social gender roles in society have not merely been reinforced in language learning materials. Language learning itself has been gendered for at least four centuries – and not just because access to education was gendered. For a few women, there were opportunities to learn a language (and for some others it might be unavoidable, married off abroad for dynastic reasons), but their language knowledge certainly accorded them no status. A commonplace book of 1633 recounts that when a young woman who could speak and write Latin, Greek, Hebrew, French and Italian, was presented to King James, the King's reply was merely, "But can she spin"? Whether or not the anecdote is true, it signals plainly what was expected of women at the time (Gallagher 2014: 93; Salmon 1996, Ch. 12). However, as access to education widened to include at least an elite minority of females, language learning became recognized as a desirable accomplishment for both men and women. The author of *An Essay in Defense of the Female Sex* was able to assert in 1697 that "there are almost as many Ladies as Gentlemen speaking it [French]" (p. 37, cited by Cohen 1996: 83). Males and females learned in different settings, however. Females were more likely to learn entirely in the home with a governess or visiting tutor, or perhaps in a school with a visiting master. Men were more likely to learn, or at least to perfect their learning, on a "Grand Tour". Travelling to France to perfect one's French accent had a long tradition in England, going back to late medieval courtly practice (see 2.3), and the Grand Tour around Europe built on this tradition, taking young men away from the society of their mothers and sisters to be socialized as gentlemen. Part of the English gentleman's role was to learn to speak French, "a bold and hardy speech", like the French gentry themselves, according to Howell (1650: 19–20). Howell advised that in speaking French, one should "let it come forth confidently whether true or false Sintaxis; for a bold vivacious spirit hath a very great advantage in attaining the French, or indeed any other Language". Young men should return from the Grand Tour ready to display their fluency with a "bold vivacious spirit", even if the grammar ("Sintaxis") was not perfect.

From the outset, there were problems for male social identity lurking in this model of education in French. First, the art of polite conversation, as practised by the French, and imitated by the rest of Western Europe, was a feminized practice. It was believed that ladies' conversation refined men. Men would learn from ladies' natural tendencies the characteristics of "good" conversation: natural, free and easy, showing delicacy and polish. Men would learn to discipline themselves to avoid vulgar speech (Cohen 1996: 18). Men's success in French conversation therefore required a degree of effeminacy, taking on feminine characteristics. Second, not only French conversation but also the French language itself was beginning to be perceived as feminine. English was a strong and masculine tongue, but for some commentators, French, with its soft musicality, had become so polished that it had lost its virility (Cohen 1996: 39). Men who dropped French phrases into their English conversation were ridiculed as fops, criticized for having been 'seduced' by French. Third, whereas Howell had advocated the development of a 'vivacious' fluency ahead of grammatical accuracy, the mere display of fluency began to be disparaged in the later eighteenth century. The London-based French language teacher Lewis Chambaud criticized parents who expected their children to acquire French for display, to "shew in an assembly that they can speak some French"; required by their teachers to speak only French but not taught grammar, these children acquired a mere "glittering Gibberish" (Chambaud 1762: xvi–xvii).

Increasingly this criticism was a gendered one. The perhaps ungrammatical volubility that for Howell was suited to a "bold vivacious spirit" was now a feminine weakness. A gentleman should stand out by his lack of display, by his silent pondering before speaking; "shallow sprightliness", "voluble rashness" and "florid talk" were viewed by Hannah More as particularly female weaknesses in her *Strictures on the Modern System of Female Education* (More 1799, Vol. II: 64–65). "The true gentleman [. . .] displayed neither his foreign clothes nor his foreign tongue. He was expected not to display even his knowledge of languages" (Cohen 1996: 59). In sum, French itself, conversational fluency and display of language ability had, by the end of the eighteenth century, all become feminized, associated with females, and therefore devalued, and unmanly in the eyes of English society.

Teaching girls and boys differently

As more girls were given access to education, whether in the home or, increasingly, in private day or boarding schools, a small market in materials aimed particularly at females developed. In Calbris's *A French Plaidoyer Between Five Young Ladies* (1797), five young noblewomen vye with each other to explain the rules of French syntax clearly and elegantly (cf. Cohen 1996: 87, Beck-Busse 2014 [1999]). Not all the works ostensibly aimed at women were genuinely only for their benefit. Erondell's *French Garden* (1605) covered topics relevant to women that other popular manuals did not, such as a discussion between a lady and a nurse about the care of a young child, or the vocabulary of a lady's intimate toilette, but it has been convincingly argued that the author also had at least half an eye on male readers, offering them "an erotic scrutiny of female domestic privacy" (Fleming 1989: 19). The earliest materials aimed at females specifically were for French (Erondell 1605, Colsoni 1699), followed by Italian (Baretti 1775, Grimani 1788, Cassella 1837). Manuals for girls learning French continued through the nineteenth century – including Gislot (1824), Roche (1833), Cassella (1837), Edgeworth (1868), Witt (1873), Lemercier (1901).[16]

60 *A sociocultural history*

In the nineteenth century, as formal school education in foreign languages became established, the gendering of language competences became more entrenched. Cohen shows this very clearly in her analysis of two important educational reports, those of the Clarendon Commission (which investigated education in ten Public Schools, and reported in 1864), and the Taunton Commission (which examined secondary education outside the Public Schools, and reported in 1868, having investigated 782 grammar schools, plus some proprietary and private schools). In boys' schools, French was not well established and was often taught by a low-ranking Frenchman, open to ridicule for his accent in English. Lacking the declensions of Latin and with a grammar considered simple, it could not discipline the mind. The mere fact that it could be picked up in the home, passed from a nurse to her charge, rather than taught by a qualified teacher, proved its simplicity (de Groot 2013: 37). In girls' schools, by contrast, French was so commonly taught that it was even used as the "means of testing their general linguistic cultivation" (Taunton Commission vol. 7, 403, cited by Cohen 1996: 91). The Taunton commission found that girls "knew French better than boys", had "a correct ear", "quicker perception", and "greater aptitude". These observations explained away girls' higher achievements in spoken French compared to boys. Measured against what it was assumed really mattered, the criteria of mental discipline and grammatical knowledge (i.e. the goals in boys' schools), girls did poorly, and so their attainment was judged overall to be poor (Cohen 1996: 90–92).

Cohen sees this nineteenth-century development as a continuation of gendered constructions of identity in England, but a very similar development can be seen elsewhere in Europe. In Germany, languages education in girls' schools had a much higher profile and set very different priorities compared to boys' schools. While boys were driven down the syllabus to the end-goal of examinations on translation and grammar (see Chapter 5), the educators of girls had more freedom. Girls were largely taught by women, and a "distinctively female" didactic approach emerged in the last third of the nineteenth century (*weiblich geprägte Didaktik*, Doff 2002: 275), which built on the longer tradition of teaching foreign languages to girls, in which written expression, reading of lighter literature, and conversation received the most attention (Doff 2002: 386). For example, guidelines for teaching English in higher girls' schools, agreed at a conference of German education ministers in 1873, show that although coverage of grammar was expected, more emphasis was given to communicative competence:

> French and English: Knowledge of morphology and syntax. Ability to *write* letters and shorter essays quite correctly on things from their immediate world of experience (*Anschauungskreis*) and to be able to *talk* about such things in simple sentences with correct pronunciation; to read an English and a French book with correct understanding. Acquaintance with the chief works of English national literature and with the classical period of French literature.
>
> (Doff 2002: 391, my translation)

In England, when the first Examinations for Women were established by Cambridge in 1870, there were two telling differences compared to the existing examinations. First, there was a choice of three languages – not only French and German but also Italian. Second – at least in the first year, 1869 – the examiners required candidates of the French examination to "Write in French a short essay on *Les Horaces, Le Verre d'Eau*, or *Atala*". This was presumably not deemed a success, since it was not continued, but it shows the expectation that girls, more than boys, might be expected to write freely in the language, something that was not required in the standard school examinations until much later. The methods used in girls' schools to achieve fluency in reading, speaking and writing formed an important reservoir which the language teaching Reformers of the late nineteenth century drew on in their innovations. One influential female figure in language teaching reform was Mary Brebner, a graduate of the Cambridge Training College for Women Teachers, whose report on observing language teaching practices in Germany in 1897, funded by a £50 Travelling Scholarship for Women Teachers, was reprinted many times (Brebner 1898).

3.2.3 Adult language learners

A history of language learning is incomplete without considering the experiences of adult learners, for the very simple reason that there have been large numbers of them. With limited access to languages in compulsory schooling beyond an elite minority until the second half of the twentieth century, self-instruction manuals proliferated from the early decades of the twentieth century onwards. The *Self-Educator in German* (1901), for example, was part of a series aimed at aspirational learners wanting to equip themselves with the kind of education that secondary schooling would have provided. In the *Complete Self-Educator* compendium volume (1939), French was included alongside English, arithmetic, history, geography, economics, biology, chemistry and physics.[17] The *Teach Yourself* series began in 1938 (see McLelland 2015a: 178–180). Linguaphone (established in 1901) catered to the independent learner, as well as running private language schools, as did Berlitz, which had been established by Maximilian Delphinius Berlitz in the USA in 1878, and spread rapidly (see 4.6).

Evening courses in languages offered an opportunity for those who had left school without the chance to learn a language. According to 1911 government figures, there were 422 evening classes in French, at 199 centres; German was offered in 55 centres, Spanish in seven, and Italian in two (Bayley 1989: 68–69). In 1938, there were over 36,000 enrolments for language courses at Evening Colleges in 1938, and just under 57,000 at Evening Institutes (French, German, Spanish, Italian and Russian).[18] With just over 5,700 entries for A-level languages (French, German and Spanish) in that year, the number of adults learning a language in an evening course outnumbered A-level language candidates by a factor of about 16,[19] although of course the final level attained was presumably generally far lower. At this time, colleges and institutes still catered to adults (or teenaged school-leavers) seeking to extend their qualifications; organizations such as the Workers Education Association (WEA) and the Mechanics' Institutes also sometimes included languages in the classes that they offered to artisans and working men and women. However, under the provisions of the 1944 Education Act, the funding for adult education provided through university extra-mural programmes or other responsible bodies such as the WEA explicitly excluded modern languages, which were deemed "vocational" and hence ineligible under the provision of "liberal" adult education, a situation which held for most of the twentieth century (and already criticized by Hicks 1944). Language teaching in adult education since 1944 was, therefore, chiefly in colleges run by Local Education Authorities, and was viewed as an extension or recreational activity. The City Literary Institute in London in 1962, for example, had "a 'cultural' content in most courses and about half are clearly announced as 'literary', a term taken here in its broadest sense" (Hay 1962). In 1961, about 2,250 enrolments – a quarter of the City Literary Institute's 9,000 annual total – were for languages, split between French (46%), Italian (23%), German (14%), Spanish (10%) and Russian (7%), all having met the requirement that they could "understand a short prose 'unseen' at 'O'-level GCE" (Hay 1962). This single London institution, then, saw almost as many post-GCE language enrolments in 1961 as there would be Spanish A-level candidates in 1965, and the equivalent of over 6% of all A-level languages entries in that year (cf. Table 2.6 in Chapter 2). Many, many adults, then, have experienced learning a language – unlike science, maths or history – in a relatively informal setting, and reaching only a fairly elementary stage. We must bear this in mind when considering public perception of modern languages, and their relatively low status in society as subjects or disciplines.

Given the optional, informal nature of adult education courses, it is hard to track the history of modern languages education in them with any certainty, but the *Journal of Adult Education*, founded in 1926, offers some insights into the reality, in particular a 1961–1962 special issue on Modern Languages (vol. 34, 1961–1962, January issue). The lecturer-in-charge of modern languages at Bolton Technical College reported that learners there fell into two groups: "vocational courses catering for a tiny minority" and " 'general interest' courses" (Hargreaves 1961–62: 23). The first smaller group was easy to teach; the second group could present problems of insuperable difficulty; and often both groups were in the same class. Hargreaves summarized the results of a survey undertaken in Bolton Technical College[20]:

> The average student in evening classes in Modern Languages is middle class, prefers a conversational approach to the normal "grammar grind", and studies with tourism as the main incentive. Most students are spinsters under forty. French and German are the favourite languages. Appropriate social activities are popular, particularly when these involve meeting nationals whose languages are being studied. [. . .] They are sensitive to unsatisfactory physical conditions, dislike changes of teacher, and are unenthusiastic about existing text-books.
>
> (Hargreaves 1961–62: 24)[21]

Part-time teachers at such colleges faced a difficult task: "Due often to lack of training, to indifference on the part of administrators, to ignorance of how to effect changes", they could struggle make progress "in the face of mounting student indifference [. . .] No training schemes or short courses are available for them [. . .] No Body or Association speaks for them" (Hargreaves 1961–62: 23). A motion was put to the Modern Languages Association in 1961 to ask the Council

> to consider the problem of teaching modern languages in institutes of further education (other than in full-time courses in colleges and universities) with particular reference to method, content and continuity of courses, examinations (external), recruitment and qualifications of part-time staff.
> (Hargreaves 1961–62: 24)

However, a shortage of facts and figures made it difficult to provide a basis for such a discussion.

How to cater to the diverse student body in adult education classes was a recurring theme, both in method and in the development of suitable materials. However, adult education, like female education in the nineteenth century, provided a space where innovation could take place. Mabel Sculthorp's report on the use of the language laboratory with adult beginners of French at Ealing College (Sculthorp 1961–62) and the intensive courses in Spanish and German whose development she also oversaw there (cf. McLelland 2015a: 185) are examples of early and important trialling of innovations in method and materials. There was particular appetite for such experiments in the adult learning world because, as Hay (1966–67) pointed out, with only 1.5 hours a week for 34 weeks a year, it would take 30 years for these learners to achieve an A-level standard in French. In addition, as Hicks had already pointed out in 1944, adult education provided a space in which a wider *range* of languages than the traditional school foreign languages could be offered. Such experiments could be "more easily made in the less highly-organized work of adult education. It should be encouraged and sympathetically watched" (Hicks 1944: 179). This trajectory – from adult education language to mainstream language – has arguably been followed by Chinese in recent decades (McLelland 2015b).

Adult education also provided a space for experiments in non-traditional styles of encounters with the language and culture. Hicks (1944: 184) singled out the example of Lamb Guildhouse in Cheshire, a college for short-term residential courses, run by a voluntary association of subscribers and hosting courses run by the WEA, Manchester University extra-mural department, and others (Kelly 1950: 86–87). It held "occasional language week-ends, with games, songs and competitions in the foreign language, which were well attended and greatly enjoyed". By the 1950s, there were about 25 such short-term residential colleges, although most folded in the 1970s. At another such college, Attingham, in Shropshire, modern languages began in the 1950s with eight three-day language weekends over the period 1949–1959 (five in French, two for German,

64 *A sociocultural history*

and one for Italian), and grew in the 1960s. Despite the aspirations of these colleges to provide educational opportunities for all, many of the course participants were teachers or university students, though this tendency seems to have reduced somewhat as time went on.[22] Inspired by the Danish *volkshuset* or "People's College" model, these independent short-term residential colleges, where people from abroad could work as volunteers in the kitchens for a period, were also one of the mechanisms for exchanges between continental Europe and England (see 3.3.4).

3.3 The educational infrastructure of language learning – institutionalization, professionalization, and learning beyond the classroom

Having considered who learned languages, we turn now to the history of building the infrastructure that provided them with teachers, and with learning opportunities beyond the classroom (including the emergence of study abroad). We begin with the history of language teachers. Britain's earliest teachers of foreign languages were typically native speakers who found themselves, by force of circumstance, living among English speakers, and whose foreign language knowledge was a marketable commodity that they used to help make ends meet. The Huguenot refugee population – Calvinist Protestants who left Catholic France in waves throughout the sixteenth, seventeenth and eighteenth centuries – provided a reservoir of such French speakers. Claude Hollyband, author of many French textbooks in the sixteenth century, was a refugee who arrived in London in the 1560s; so too was Pierre de Ploiche; both of them ran language schools in London. Several such schools flourished around St Paul's Churchyard (near St. Paul's Cathedral), the centre of the London book trade at the time (Kibbee 1991: 131, 191; Howatt 1984: 20). Some teachers were bilingual by upbringing, like John Florio, who wrote Italian manuals, and François Hillenius, who boasted in his Dutch manual of "having from my very Cradle been acquainted with both these languages of English and Dutch" (cited by Gallagher 2014: 45).

Among the first teachers of German, and authors of materials for English learners, were native speakers of German who also had a university training. We do not know why Martin Aedler, author of the first grammar of German for English speakers, originally came to England, but he taught Hebrew at Cambridge University (Van der Lubbe 2007). Heinrich Offelen signed himself a Doctor in Law in the dedication of his German-English *Double Grammar* (Offelen 1687). By contrast, John König, who dedicated his 1715 grammar of German to King George I, called himself a *Sprachmeister*, the usual German term at the time for a foreign language teacher, and a designation which seems to place language masters on a par with other "masters", of the kind who taught riding, dancing, fencing and other accomplishments, "altogether a different social category from professors" (Hüllen 1995, n. 14). This distinction is probably not applicable before the eighteenth century, however, for John Minsheu, who wrote the polyglot *Guide Into Tongues* (1617), described himself in his Spanish dictionary as a

"Professor of Languages in London" (Percival/Minsheu 1599); *professeur* and hence professor could simply mean "teacher". Such language masters sometimes taught more than one language – Hollyband taught both French and Italian, for example. Higher qualifications did not necessarily mean greater success – Martin Aedler, highly qualified and attached to Cambridge University, ended his life in penury; John Minsheu, though well-connected to judge by the subscribers list of his *Guide into Tongues*, declared himself to be in debt (Minsheu 1617, ed. 1978, p. v).

Women were engaged in language teaching too. The inclusion of a certain Madame Fournier in the list of subscribers to Wanostrocht's *Practical French Grammar* of 1780 suggests that at least one female French teacher may also have bought a copy of the grammar for her teaching. Certainly women taught languages as governesses – Sarah Lennox, born in 1744, daughter of the Duke and Duchess of Richmond, learned French from her French governess (Cohen 1996: 84), and was doubtless one of many. Specific examples of female instructors are more difficult to identify than their male counterparts, however. Until the nineteenth century, they were virtually never the authors of published materials, whose prefaces are often the source of teachers' biographies; even those texts aimed specifically at a female audience were not written by women. In the nineteenth century, governesses were employed not just by the nobility but by the expanding upper middle classes (Hughes 1993), and, in addition to French governesses, German governesses also became more common, after the example set by Queen Victoria, who had a German governess for her children (Hardach-Pinke 2000: 25). These governesses taught their charges languages; Hooper's handbook for "Ladies engaged in tuition" (Hooper 1873) included reading recommendations for French and German grammar and language history (Weber 2013: 235–236). Many candidates in the College of Preceptors language examinations were German females, presumably many of them governesses. Contemporary evidence suggests many of them were miserable, returning to Germany disappointed (Weber 2013: 235). For if the position of the "language master" was a lowly one, then the position of governess was lower still, and there were so many indigent German governesses that an association of German governesses in England was set up (Association of German Governesses 1876), as well as a home for needy female German teachers in London (Weber 2013: 235, n. 15).

The status of nineteenth-century teachers of foreign languages in schools seems to have been scarcely better. Adolf Rambeau, co-editor of the German modern languages journal *Die Neueren Sprachen*, wrote in the journal in 1894:

> Being mostly foreigners, they are, or were at least, most scantily remunerated, nicknamed "couriers" by their colleagues, and looked down upon as second class school masters. The anecdote of a famous lord and general recommending the son of his French cook for a vacant chair of the French language and literature at the military school of Woolwich does not seem to be quite authentic, but is related everywhere and is very significant. It shows clearly and expresses rather correctly the naïve indifference of the average

Briton for higher education and instruction, and his innate contempt of the teacher and, especially, the foreign teacher.

(Rambeau 1894: 265)

3.3.1 Native speakers or non-native speakers?

At various times in Britain's history there have been tensions between migrant labour and native workers, and language teaching is no exception. The earliest surviving evidence of such tensions may be the satirical *Ortho-Epia Gallica*, a French manual by John Eliot, published in 1593, at a time when the number of "aliens" registered in England was close to 10% of the population (Howatt 1984: 12–13). Eliot's manual reflected the "simmering resentment of the native-born teachers [. . .] at what was becoming a foreign monopoly in the language-teaching business" (Howatt 1984: 28). Eliot railed against the French-born teachers who would, he said,

> persuade everyone [they] meet, that my book is a false, feigned, slight, confused, absurd, barbarous, lame, unperfect, single, uncertain, childish piece of work, and not able to teach, and why so? Forsooth because it is not [their] own, but an Englishman's doing.
>
> (Eliot 1593: A3^r, cited by Howatt 1984: 28)

Eliot appears to have had a point, for English-born authors of French manuals do seem to have disappeared from the market of printed French-English conversation manuals by the mid-seventeenth century (Gallagher 2014: 231).

When languages began to be established in schools in the nineteenth century, it seems language teachers were still generally native speakers. Only in the course of the nineteenth century did the place of native speaker teachers begin to be taken, slowly, by English-born teachers with formal training in modern languages. No sooner had English-born teachers begun to emerge than efforts began to establish their value and, indeed, superiority over foreign teachers. Colbeck, in his first lecture at Cambridge on the teaching of languages in schools, came down firmly on the side of the English-born teacher. While allowing for rare, impressive exceptions, he considered that an Englishman stood a better chance of being able to keep order in class than a foreign teacher of the same quality – and in reality, a foreign teacher trying his luck abroad was more likely to be an "inferior man" than the superior kind required to maintain discipline in a language and culture not his own (Colbeck 1887: Lecture 1, pp. 28–31). The concern was not just about male teachers. Very similar concerns were raised about the average French governess in England, in the *Courrier de Londres*, the French newspaper in London, in 1894 (see Thomas 2005: 218–219).

In a paper read to the College of Preceptors in 1885 on "French teachers and teachers of French", a certain S. Barlet was ultimately less negative. True, the first teachers of French in schools had been native speakers who taught "as much by what they were as by their words and deeds", and "they themselves and their teaching were held up to ridicule, if not to contempt" [. . .] "Do what he may, the foreign master remained an alien – I well-nigh said, an enemy!" (Barlet 1885: 11). Such teachers were accused by traditionalists of "I am afraid I must say it – of not being an Englishman! He is not one of them". Arnold and Waren (1900: 243) cited the apparently not unrepresentative view of native French teachers given by one respondent to their survey on modern languages in Preparatory schools: "When I have tried foreign masters, their ignorance of our code of trust [. . .] has been a greater evil than their pronunciation was good".[23] Schools, Barlet recognized, wanted in their French teacher "an educated man and a gentleman". Yet, Barlet argued, "individuality is stronger than nationality, and the foreigner disappears as soon as the man, the gentleman, can be seen" (p. 13, 12). While French-born teachers might still often be found to be unsatisfactory, Barlet was at pains to point out that the reason lay in the poor selection procedures and poor remuneration, rather than in the nature of being French. As the numbers of foreign teachers were now insufficient to do all the teaching required, Barlet welcomed the recognition amongst English masters that they could help foreign teachers, but still feared that matters had gone too far:

> A brake is needed [on] the movement set a foot, I repeat, to oust the foreigner from English schools, and to replace him by Englishmen [. . .] Considering then, on the one side, that the number of foreign masters in a school cannot be indefinitely increased; on the other side, that the English masters are ready and willing, and competent to lend their best help in the school as exponents of modern languages, I would suggest that they should work together, as it is obvious that they cannot but further the educational end they have in view [. . .] French teachers and teachers of French are both necessary, and [. . .] they ought to stand side by side.
> (Barlet 1885: 12, 14, 16)

Barlet urged that the way to improve the status of native French teachers was to improve the standards for recruitment and remuneration. One initiative he noted was the *Société Nationale des Professeurs de Français en Angleterre* (SNPF), founded in 1881, to which only suitably qualified French-born teachers were admitted. It had 87 founder members, 145 by 1887, and 193 by 1914. The SNPF was, however, criticized for representing only those of French nationality – Germans, Poles and Swiss teachers of French in England were not admitted (Thomas 2005: 6). Women members – whose status was lower still than that of the men – were also not always welcomed, and an association for female teachers of French abroad was founded in in London in 1894, followed by an England-specific *Association des Institutrices Françaises en Angleterre* in 1903 (see also Faucher & Lane 2013).

German teachers in England seem generally to have been native-born Germans until the later nineteenth century. Certainly, that is true of the authors of textbooks for English learners over the period 1680–1800 (McLelland 2015a: 19–68). The first English-born author of a German textbook was George Crabb

(1800), followed by John Rowbotham (1824). It is only in the 1870s and 1880s that non-German names become more numerous in the chronological bibliography in McLelland (2015a). One was the Irish-born Augustus Henry Keane (1873), who studied in Germany, and taught English, French, German and Hindustani at the Hartley Institute in Southampton.[24] Through the careers of other names in the bibliography, we can trace the establishment of German in Public Schools and grammar schools: Robert Herbert Quick (1874) was master of Modern Languages at Harrow from 1869 to 1874; Henry Watson Eve (1880) was headmaster of University College School, as well as dean of the College of Preceptors, the first professional body of teachers, from 1884; Benjamin Townson (1886) and Coverley Smith (1892) were both assistant masters at the Nottingham High School; Francis Storr (1891) was a teacher at Merchant Taylors School and became a council member of the College of Preceptors.[25]

As with French, once this class of English-born German teachers emerged, the question of competition with German-born counterparts arose. In the letters pages of the *Educational Times* of 1894, a correspondent under the pseudonym of Grammaticus maintained, "The ideal German grammar is that compiled by an Englishman, for the simple reason that, having learned the language himself, he is better able to appreciate the difficulties his compatriots encounter, and to smooth the path before them". Still, such a book should "be written in collaboration with a native of the country, or at any rate revised by one". Grammaticus concluded, "This is not at all a case of Englishmen versus Germans" (*Educational Times*, March 1894, p. 142). However, the question of German or English teachers of German became considerably more fraught with the outbreak of World War I. The discussion had been launched already in 1913, when a Modern Languages Association (MLA) sub-committee found that only 8 of 23 Modern Languages professors in English universities were British. Its 1916 report recommended that the Modern Languages professoriate should ideally be made up of British-born staff (Bayley 1991: 16–17). The committee's report led to a discussion at the MLA's General Meeting on 11 January 1918 of the same question applied to schoolteachers (reported in *Modern Language Teaching* 14 (1918): 22–25).[26] At the meeting, Mr A. Hargreaves from City of London School had proposed that, "in the interests of education" – including "the formation of character" – it was preferable to have modern languages taught "by persons of British nationality". After all, since Englishmen were not allowed to teach in French and German schools, why should Britain be more welcoming? Further arguments raised against foreign teachers echoed those canvassed by Barlet and Colbeck thirty years earlier: that it was difficult to attract the best candidates, for the best would secure good jobs at home; that they would not stay; and that their qualifications were often no more than being a native speaker. This last point was particularly unwelcome to the local members of the MLA because it meant that native speakers supplanted qualified Englishmen by dint of being cheap.[27] Mr. S.A. Richards from Hackney Downs School argued that "To teach a foreign language efficiently it is necessary for the teacher to have a studied the language analytically. [. . .] To encourage Englishmen seriously to study foreign languages with a view to teaching, we must protect them from unfair foreign competition". Some of the arguments were more jingoistic. Mr. Somerville remarked that "there was risk [. . .] in allowing Germans to teach in our schools of bringing English boys into contact with German morality and ideals", even if in Senior years, at least, a Frenchman could be a valuable assistant in bringing boys "into closer touch with French ideas and atmospheres, and also as a vivifying influence on staff"(!) (p. 23). However, Miss Pope, of Somerville College (Oxford) countered, "One great function of Modern Languages teachers was to widen sympathies of pupils and diminish insularity" and that contact with "the living foreigner" as a member of teaching staff could assist in this. One of the leading figures in modern languages education, Walter Ripman, was firmly opposed to the proposed resolution against foreign teachers. British-born, but of German parents, he had found it advisable to anglicize the spelling of his name from Rippmann, and not surprisingly, he considered the resolution "inopportune" and "likely to cause resentment" (p. 24).

Ultimately, the establishment of minimum qualifications for languages teachers defused the *either-or* question of native speakers vs. non-native speakers. This was in turn part of the process of professionalization of teachers, which had begun across Europe, as we shall see next, as well as the availability of Modern Languages courses at university level.

3.3.2 The professionalization of teachers and the question of qualifications

The final quarter of the nineteenth century saw the establishment across Europe of school language teachers in formal education as a professional group with their own sense of identity and authority in their chosen field. One recognizable step in this process was the establishment of professional journals, analysed by Linn (2017). The lead was taken by language specialists in German universities who founded journals such as the *Zeitschrift für romanische Philologie* (1877) and *Englische Studien* (1877). From the 1880s, journals more narrowly focussed on language teaching in schools emerged: a *Revue d'enseignement des langues vivantes* (RELV) in France (1882), and in Germany, *Phonetische studien*, established in 1888, was renamed in 1894 *Die neueren sprachen: Zeitschrift für den neusprachlichen unterricht* ("Modern languages: journal for teaching modern languages"). Gradually this development spread to England. Germany's *Neuphilologentag*, at which modern language teachers had been meeting biennially since the early 1880s, was watched with interest by their counterparts in Britain,[28] and the Modern Language Association was founded in England in 1892; by 1911 its members exceeded one thousand (see *Modern Language Teaching* 7 (1911): 11). Its journal, the *Modern Language Quarterly*, founded in 1897 and renamed *Modern Language Teaching* in 1905, became "the leading journal for the discussion of modern language problems" (*Modern Language Teaching* 28, 3 [September 1947]: 117),[29] providing an additional outlet for modern language teachers who previously relied on the *Educational Times*, the organ of the College of Preceptors, published since 1846. Reflections on methods for language teaching were regular fixtures in both publications.[30]

One of the explicit aims of the College of Preceptors, which had provided examinations for teachers from 1846 (see *Educational Times* 1887: 254), was to achieve better public recognition for their profession. Language teachers were no exception in seeking to establish the qualifications necessary for their role. As Adolf Rambeau lamented in 1894, the view prevailed that

> the instruction of modern languages may be safely intrusted [sic] to a young man who has not yet finished the elements of his science and never had any experience; to an amateur who knows something about French or German literature and grammatical rules and understands a written text fairly; to a *maître de langue* or *sprachmeister* who may be an excellent private teacher but perhaps quite incompetent in class; to any foreigner who looks like a gentleman and who is supposed to know his mother tongue well enough.
> (Rambeau 1894: 267)

The new generation of modern languages advocates, including Rambeau himself, did not share this view. Rather, whether they emphasized the philological study of languages, the importance of the new science of phonetics, or both, they increasingly shared the view expressed by Barlet in 1885 that modern languages had now been "elevated to a science", and thus required "expert exponents" (Barlet 1885: 11). How to establish the qualifications of these expert exponents, both women and men, became an increasing concern. The College of Preceptors examinations were one such qualification. Its candidates included many women, presumably governesses seeking a formal qualification and thus improved status in their profession (Weber 2013: 235). Queen's College and Bedford College (founded in 1849 and 1849) were also established to provide higher qualifications for women – the pioneering Walter Ripman taught German at both (McLelland 2015a: 119). Modern languages were also given some attention in the training colleges for elementary teachers, including in some institutions for women, though to judge from the time allocated to them, they were offered merely "to add a veneer of cultivation and refinement" (Bayley 1989: 65, based on analysis of the 1888 Cross Commission reports). Women were not, at first, able to take degrees at university, though they were allowed to sit examinations at Cambridge from 1882. Instead, Cambridge introduced an Examination for Women in 1869 – almost all of the 24 successful candidates that year (out of 36 entrants) took languages (Roach 1971: 120).[31]

As for male teachers, it was becoming accepted that they should obtain their education in Modern Languages at university (after a first grounding in school), although Camridge lecturer Karl Breul emphasized that training teachers should not be the *only* purpose of Modern Languages at university, which should also promote the science, and prepare men (sic) for other professions too. In a paper read to the College of Preceptors on "The Training of Teachers of Modern Foreign Languages" (published in the *Educational Times* 1894: 225–231), Breul underlined the importance of training languages students in both philology and phonetics; they would also be taught *realia*, "i.e the outlines of German life and thought, customs and institutions" (p. 229). Rambeau's view of what was needed in the USA was couched in very similar terms: University courses should provide "ample opportunities for studying, beside the historical part of their science, especially *modern* French and German, *spoken* French and German – i.e. practical phonetics – and everything pertaining to the nation life of modern France and Germany (*realien*)" (Rambeau 1894: 268). Breul noted with pleasure that under new regulations at Cambridge there was now a *viva voce* examination in pronunciation. It was not yet compulsory, but "a headmaster should, in the future, not appoint a Cambridge man to a modern-language mastership who has failed to show practical efficiency in this part of the examination" (Breul 1894: 227).

In addition to ensuring that teachers had a qualification in the *language* they were to teach, there was growing concern to ensure prospective teachers were also prepared for their profession as language *teachers*. Generations of language teachers had offered advice in prefaces to their manuals on the best method of teaching or learning a language, but as an audience of interested professional language teachers grew, the first lectures and treatises on teaching foreign languages in schools emerged. In 1887, Colbeck, assistant master at Harrow School, delivered two lectures at the Cambridge Teacher Training Syndicate's request titled *On the Teaching of Modern Languages in Theory and Practice* (Colbeck 1887). Colbeck's approach was fairly traditional. He was much concerned with how to explain and practise grammar and translation; only two pages at the end of his second lecture dealt briefly with dictation, "audition" (i.e. listening) and pronunciation. Colbeck considered that "the power of conversing in a foreign language can be acquired at least as easily late as early; [...] it is *much* less important than translation, and less important than composition" (Colbeck 1887: Lecture 1, p. 16). However, things were changing. In 1882, a now famous pamphlet by Wilhelm Viëtor had decried the poor results of modern language teaching in German schools, calling for new methods to address the problem (Viëtor 1882). Henry Sweet's paper to the Philological Society in 1884 on the "Practical Study of Languages" had introduced the ideas of the German language teaching Reform Movement to Britain (cf. Sweet 1899). So only a year after Colbeck (1887), William H. Widgery, assistant master at University College School, published a pamphlet based on a series of articles in the *Journal of Education* (Widgery 1888), which now reflected many ideas of the Reform Movement across Europe (see Chapter 4). Widgery put the case for the study of languages and of language teaching as a "mental science" in which it was crucial to understand how learners acquired language, invoking pedagogues such as Pestalozzi, and giving the spoken language a far more central place than Colbeck had done – Widgery devoted ten pages to the new science of phonetics and its importance to language teaching.

Women teachers particularly benefited from these early beginnings in language teacher training. In 1895, Karl Breul presented a series of lectures on "the teaching of modern foreign languages" at the Cambridge Training College for Women

Teachers, and repeated it in subsequent years. The lectures were published in 1898 as *The Teaching of Modern Foreign Languages in our Secondary Schools* (1898) and sold out within months, so that a second edition was published the following year. Useful as such language teacher–specific training no doubt was, it was not until 1973 that university graduates *needed* an additional qualification for teaching in state schools, nor was there much incentive for teachers to spend that additional year on a diploma of education of the kind that began to be offered from about 1911 (Thomas 1990: 19), for their salary would be little more than those without such a diploma. In the 1950s, about one-third of graduate teachers in secondary schools were untrained (Patrick & Reid 1980: 7). By contrast, in Germany, teachers in grammar schools had faced an examination since the early nineteenth century; there, the idea of a year's practical training for teachers dates back to the late eighteenth century and became compulsory in the late nineteenth century (cf. Mandel 1989; Christ 2005). In Italy, from 1869 onwards, candidates for language teaching positions had to hold a diploma, which could either be obtained by sitting an examination, or by demonstrating prior knowledge and/or experience. The examination included a compulsory oral element, which, from the late 1880s onwards, also included questions on teaching methods (Mandich 2005). In the Netherlands, from as early as 1806, teachers were required to obtain a so-called Certificate of General Admission, which could also indicate a qualification in a particular subject, including languages; the examination included reading aloud in order to assess pronunciation. Between 1837 and 1857, 613 certificates that included a foreign language qualification were awarded: 268 for French, 206 for German, and 139 for English (Wilhelm 1993: 79).[32]

A special feature of twentieth-century language teacher education in Britain was the role of Local Education Authority language advisors, appointed from the 1960s to support language teachers facing many changes. At its first conference, in 1969, the National Association of Language Advisors boasted 40 members; by 1974, there were more than 150. Local Education Authorities (LEA) advice extended to adult education teachers too: Leicestershire LEA languages advisor Duncan Sidwell authored an adult education language tutors' handbook, published by the National Institute of Adult Continuing Education (Sidwell 1987a, b). The role of LEA advisors declined in the 1980s and 1990s, as more budget was devolved direct to schools, leaving less central funding for shared LEA posts, and short staff development courses for staff were, for some years, offered by the schools inspectorate (Moys 1996). A number of other organizations also provided considerable support, including the Central Bureau for Educational Visits and Exchanges (which merged with the British Council in 1992) and, especially, the very active CILT (Centre for Information on Language Teaching and Research, founded 1966) until its closure in 2011, when it merged with CfBT (originally the Centre for British Teachers).

3.3.3 Languages as a discipline in higher education

A prerequisite for the status of modern languages as a discipline (or as disciplines) was a secure place in the universities, the keepers of knowledge. As Christ (2005: 9) observed, it was the fact that Germany's language teachers had been to university like doctors, lawyers and clerics that gave them a comparable professional status. In Britain, Modern Languages did not win their place in the University easily. There had been language teachers at universities since at least 1800, and the first chairs in modern languages were established in the 1830s, though Trinity College Dublin was somewhat earlier, in 1775 (McLelland 2015a: 81–82; Holmes 2011: 13–14). However, the first attempt to establish a School of Modern Languages at Oxford was defeated in 1887, amid fears that modern languages, being too easy, would draw students away from the study of Latin and Greek. The failure of the motion (with votes tied at 92 on each side) was reported with gleeful relief in the *Educational Times* (1887: 468–469); a clinching argument seems to have been that the examiners had outnumbered the candidates in Modern Languages in 1886–1887. An Honours School was only established in Oxford in 1903 (Muckle 2008a: 4–41), but by 1911, Breul could state in his presidential address to the Modern Language Association that "There are now at all the Universities Honours courses, in which students and future teachers, authors, librarians, diplomatists, civil servants, and others, can go through a highly specialized scientific course of instruction in French, German and other European languages" (*Modern Language Teaching* 7 (1911): 9). The Leathes Report of 1918 was another important step, especially in supporting languages other than French and German at universities. The importance of Spanish, Italian and Russian alongside German and French was accepted, and the committee proposed 55 new university Chairs of Modern Languages, including ten for each of the four LOTF. In the face of strong budget pressures, these grand plans were never implemented, but some universities did extend their range of modern languages, and "at last European languages other than French and German began to emerge as university subjects" (Bayley 1991: 18).

A sceptical view of the status of Modern Languages as a serious subject was still being expressed in 1921 in an article in the *Contemporary Review*, which noted that Modern Languages at university were "usually regarded as a 'soft option'" – a view which the author appeared to endorse; Modern Languages students "never faced and tried to think out problems of philosophy, politics and ethics", unlike their counterparts studying the classical languages, who would be reading great thinkers on logic, philosophy, law, history and ethics. The author dismissed Modern Languages programmes as "little more than nurseries for teachers", for the majority of their students became teachers – 80% of University College London languages students, apparently (Bridge 1921: 807–808). Adolf Rambeau, by contrast, would have viewed this apparently damning statistic with pleasure, as evidence that language teaching was increasingly being staffed by qualified graduates. Rambeau considered that most Modern Languages experts ("neophilologists") now had a clear sense of their discipline:

> Most of the "neophilologists", and, I believe, those belonging to the younger generation almost universally, have now a broader, more exalted and truly 'humanistic' conception of what their science means. We are far

from intending to compete with classical philologists, Sanscrit scholars, Assyriologists, and Egytopologists [. . .] Our principal aim is to study not only the language and literature, but all the complex parts of the present and modern civilization of France, of Germany, of Great Britain [. . .]. We wish to be international mediators, interpreters of foreign tongues, thoughts and sentiments from one nation to another. We desire to teach each nation to respect her own national life and that of her neighours, and to understand the character, qualities, virtues and vices, of her own civilization and those of the civilizations of the other great countries. Thus, we are working and fighting against 'chauvinism', and for an enlightened patriotism, for the peace and progress of mankind.

We are proud of being 'humanists' in this sense of the word. This is the ideal of our philology, an ideal, at the least, as high and as noble as that of any other science.

(Rambeau 1894: 276)

The numbers of graduates in Modern Languages increased from 60 in 1904 to 200 in 1914, and to 600 by 1923 (Bayley 1991: 22), and the expansion continued. In 1963, French could be taken at 38 universities, compared to 106 in 1996. The number of higher education institutions where German and Spanish could be taken also roughly trebled over the same period (see Table 3.2), though much of the increase was due to the founding of new higher education institutions during the 1960s, many of which began to offer vocational courses with "applied languages" (Coleman 1996: 71). More than half of students on language courses in 1996 were on combined courses, rather than Single Honours programmes, and more universities began to follow the example of the former polytechnics in offering a language with other subjects, such as a business-related subject (Nott 1996: 62). Such teaching of languages, sometimes known as "service" teaching, is increasingly offered through University Wide Language Programmes and

Table 3.2 Number of higher education institutions in the UK offering particular languages in 1963 and 1996 (taken from Hawkins 1996: 399; compiled from Stern 1965).

Language	1963 entry	1996 entry
French	38	106
German	37	98
Spanish	27	77
Italian	23	46
Russian	26	39
Japanese	3	32
Portuguese	17	16
Arabic	12	11
Chinese	5	11
Dutch	7	6

A sociocultural history 75

increasingly available at beginners' level, even for those languages traditionally taught in schools. This and the very common patterns of the Joint and Combined Honours languages degree make languages more available, to some extent making up for lack of opportunities in the school sector. However, it has perhaps not improved the status of languages as disciplines at universities, where they are, arguably, increasingly viewed as ancillary (and, for timetablers, extremely inconvenient) subjects.

3.3.4 Language learning beyond the schoolroom: visits and residence abroad, and pen-friendships

A sociocultural history of language learning must give some consideration to the ways in which learning has taken place *outside* the classroom. Throughout the history of language learning, learners have sought more or less formal opportunities to spend time abroad in a country where the target language is spoken. From the late Middle Ages onwards, German merchants and specialized craftsmen sent their sons abroad, where they acquired a foreign language alongside the skills of their trade (Glück 2014: 46–47),[33] and similar exchanges took place between French and English merchant families (see Kibbee 1991: 12, n. 6). As the Grand Tour developed, various academies, more or less short-lived, were established to cater to this market; one such academy, in the village of Richelieu, in the Loire Valley (considered to offer a particularly pure form of French), was specifically intended to attract nobles from northern Europe, and included modern foreign languages in its programme of study – Spanish and Italian as well as French (Bruschi 2017).

As language learning became institutionalized in schools and universities, opportunities for their language learners to spend a prolonged period abroad were, paradoxically, at first reduced. However, as railways made travelling easier, holiday courses aimed at language teachers were established. Walter Ripman was one of 26 teachers from England who attended the first such course at the University of Marburg in 1897 (noteworthy for the involvement of the reformer Wilhelm Viëtor from 1898 onwards: McLelland 2015a: 119). Such courses had begun to spread across Europe since the 1870s, and by the late nineteenth century, there were holiday courses in "practically all the countries of Europe" (Christ 2005: 8, my translation); Walter Ripman taught on one at Queen's College in London; a 1905 letter to *Modern Language Teaching* drew attention to a new holiday course at the University of Edinburgh for teachers, which may have been the first such course in Scotland. *Modern Languages* (12.2 (1930): 56) highlighted a "Spanish week at Liverpool", for Liverpool was an important early centre for the study of Spanish (see 2.5). In France, scholarships were offered to language teachers to attend holiday courses abroad from 1902; there were 50 such scholarships available in 1908 (Rival 2012: 66). The French government was the first to fund an international institution to promote the study of their language abroad by providing courses, including residential holiday courses: the Alliance Française was founded in 1883 (Bruézière 1983); Germany's Goethe

Institute followed half a century later, in 1952. Spain joined in much later with its Instituto Cervantes, founded in 1991.

School trips and exchanges between school-aged children, too, began to develop – the School Journey Association was established in 1911, and while many one-week or two-week journeys were within Britain, by 1929, its vice-chairman reported that "an increasing number of schools [. . .] visit the Continent, out of term-time, in the school holidays" (*Modern Languages* 1930: 111). Out of 512 "modern" schools that were the subject of a 1930 Board of Education report, 75 (about 15%) had arranged "foreign tours" (Board of Education 1930b: 14). In France, a "Société d'échange international" had been established in 1902 to put in touch with each other families who were keen to host a child from another country, and in 1906, the French language teachers' journal *RELV* set up a travel abroad committee which organized two-week summer trips (Mombert 2001: 176–177). The journal *Modern Language Teaching* published appeals for host families for French or German children under the aegis of the International Exchange of Children (Ridley 2014: 55, 79). Britons seem to have been slow off the mark, however – Ridley records that in one unspecified year (between 1905 and 1914), 97 children from Germany took part in exchanges with France, but only 14 English children did so (Ridley 2014: 79, no source given).

Organized educational trips abroad for adults offered by the Co-operative Holiday Association (CHA) – founded in Lancashire in 1894 by Thomas Arthur Leonard, a key figure in the British outdoor movement who also had strong internationalist sentiments – also provided a means of cultural exchange. The CHA organized holidays at centres in Kelkheim, near Frankfurt, and at Dinan, in Brittany, providing an opportunity to try out the language learnt in evening classes. In turn, group visits to CHA centres were organized by the German equivalent association, the *Ferienheimgesellschaft*, from 1910 (see, e.g., the 1910 prospectus in Ridley 2010: 105). The motivations of these initiatives were varied. In the case of the CHA, there were close connections to internationalism, the peace movement, and worker education. The target group for their activities was working people, but German students took advantage of CHA holidays to spend time in England (see Ridley 2014: 60), and presumably, at least some British students did the same in reverse. The CHA was also involved in some school exchanges between Germany and England, including with Manchester Grammar School, though details are sketchy (Ridley 2014). The Institute of Linguists also organized summer schools and trips abroad for its members (Smith et al. 2010: 18, 24).

Another scheme to promote pupils' real use of the language with native speakers was the Scholars' International Correspondence network, set up in 1896 by an enterprising teacher of English in France, Paul Mieille, with the help of a British journalist William T. Stead. The first list of matched pen-friends was published in the *Revue Universitaire* in 1897, with the names of two hundred boys. A Leipzig teacher, Martin Hartmann, added Germany to the scheme in 1897; the USA joined in 1898, with the support of the Modern Language Association of America's International Correspondence Committee. By 1900, already some 57,000 correspondents were involved in the scheme (Schleich 2017). Out of 512 "modern schools" (state-funded secondary schools) and covered by a 1930 report, 127 had "regular correspondence with schools abroad" (Board of Education 1930b: 14). Such schemes have continued ever since, albeit with changing technologies, though concerns expressed by Thimann (1955: 137) about the time needed to administer them and the "enormous wastage", probably remain valid. Even Thimann judged that "though it does not add greatly to their sum total knowledge", foreign correspondence "inspires children to greater efforts", (Thimann 1955: 137).

A crucial development in the history of residence abroad was the establishment of Language Teaching Assistantships, which also marked the beginning of government involvement in promoting cultural encounters beyond the classroom. The French government first put a proposal to the English Board of Education to exchange language assistants in 1904, leading to a formal agreement the following year. A similar arrangement between France and the Prussian government followed in 1905, with other German states following suit (Rival 2013a). The British scheme began by sending young, part-time teachers to conduct reading and conversation lessons in a school while continuing their own studies. Later, it was opened to undergraduate students, generally after completing two years at university. In 1904–1905, 58 English teachers, 17 of whom were women, were placed in French schools. Six went to Prussia, with two of the places reserved for candidates from Scotland (Finkenberger 2005: 70; Wörsching 2012: 123; see also Faucher & Lane 2013). It took until 1909 for girls' schools to be included in the scheme, apparently largely due to reluctance from the independent girls' schools sector in Britain, over which the government could exert little authority, and where the larger schools often already employed a German teacher (Finkenberger 2005: 70). In 1908–1909, 81 French assistants had positions in Prussia, and 64 German assistants in France; about a quarter were female (Rival 2012: 100). Spain and Britain had an assistantship scheme from 1936. Austria and Britain set up a scheme in 1954; Quebec joined in 1990 (Rowles & Rowles 2005: 4).[34]

Until the mid-1970s, there was a rapid annual increase in the number of assistants participating in the programme, which peaked in 1973–1974 at 4,578 Foreign Language Assistants (FLAs). However, in the late 1970s, the number of places available in the UK dropped by 20% as Local Education Authorities (LEAs) – at that time solely responsible for deciding how many assistants to appoint to the authority – faced fierce cuts in overall funding allocations from the national government. Similar budgetary pressures arose in the mid-1990s, by which time funding – and therefore the decision as to whether to appoint FLAs – had been delegated to individual schools. However, in 2005, there were 2,665 FLAs in post in British schools.

The motivations for establishing the assistantship exchanges were mixed. The scheme was intended to equip the countries' future language teachers with first-hand experience of using the language and living the culture that they would teach, a concern that emerged from the Reform Movement. The assistants' presence in schools also provided pupils with real-life encounters with the language and culture they were learning. This was, then, a significant break away from the nineteenth-century emphasis on Modern Languages as a scientific discipline. At the same time, at the level of foreign policy, the initiative coincided with a time when all three countries – France, Germany and Britain – were seeking to increase their soft power through cultural diplomacy abroad.[35]

Already after the first year, the value of the assistantship scheme was recognized in a Board of Education report: "It cannot be doubted that a year spent abroad in this way is of the greatest value to anyone intending to become a teacher of modern languages" (Report of the Board of Education – Scheme for Exchange of Teachers 1905–1906, cited by Rowles & Rowles 2005: 4). As envisaged, those with experience abroad do seem to have become language teachers in many cases. An inspection of 512 "modern schools" in 1929 found that of the 934 language teachers, 260 had resided abroad for six months or more (whether as assistants or under some other scheme is not reported); only 215 had not lived abroad at all (Board of Education 1930b: 12).

Gradually, other ways for university students to spend time abroad began to develop. As early as 1911, the University of Leeds Senate passed a regulation allowing students to spend time abroad during their degree, an initiative credited to Prof. Schueddekopf, who had experienced first-hand the benefits of study at more than one university in his native Germany (Frank Finlay, p.c.). However, it was not until decades later that a period of residence abroad began to be built in to language degrees as a requirement.[36] In Scotland, the Scottish Education Department had required intending language teachers to spend a year abroad since 1906 (Leathes 1918: 15; Bischoff 1939: 197), and as most language students at least wanted to keep that option open, almost all went abroad. Hamish Reid, who studied French and German at Glasgow, spent a year abroad in France 1957–1958 as an assistant, then a semester at the University of Göttingen in 1959, organized by the Glasgow German department and replacing the first semester of the penultimate ("Junior Honours") year.[37] At Nottingham in the 1950s, students of Modern Languages, all on three-year Single Honours degree courses (e.g. German with French as a subsidiary subject), were required to spend the third term of their first year at a university in a country where the language of their main subject was spoken; there was no provision for their subsidiary subject. Students of German were expected to enrol as a *Gasthörer* (auditor) at a university of their choice – most commonly Tübingen, Freiburg, Heidelberg, Vienna or the Free University of Berlin. Most students of French chose to go to Paris. For Russian, too, Paris was the destination, since it was virtually impossible to study in the Soviet Union. Instead, students lived with Russian émigré families in Paris. This was presumably not very satisfactory, for those émigrés who still spoke Russian would generally have been a generation older than the students, but it was perhaps the best that could be done.[38] Students in the degree program in Iberian and Latin American Studies at University College London, which began in 1967, went abroad for a term and summer vacation at the end of their first year. Students were told to go to Spain and sign up for a language course; they were also required to spend a month on a language course in Portugal. There was no regulation from the university, although students' respective LEAs (who provided the grants to study) required proof of attendance at courses abroad.

By the 1960s, some courses required a full year abroad, rather than just a term. According to Nott (1996: 64–65), in 1963–1964, most students of French spent a full year abroad; for German, about half spent a term and the rest a year; in Spanish, most spent a term. (The individual stipulations can gleaned from Stern 1965). By 1972, the year abroad had become an "almost universal requirement" in England (Nott 1996: 65). Some exchange arrangements between British and continental universities have a long history: the University of Birmingham's link with Mainz was established soon after World War II by Joe Horne (originally Hornberger), a Jewish refugee keen to normalize relations with Germany after the war. The EU's Erasmus Programme, established in 1987, provided a structure for these ad hoc agreements, which were often based on personal links between staff. Gradually, especially as it became impossible to survive abroad on LEA grants, work placements – first set up by polytechnics and colleges of advanced technology, but increasingly popular among university students keen to improve their employability – became an alternative to studying or an assistantship. Since 2006–2007, these internships abroad have also been eligible for an EU Erasmus student mobility grant, as are study placements (though the future of such schemes after Britain leaves the EU is far from clear).

There was considerable variation between universities in their attitude to the place of residence abroad in the degree. At the University of Newcastle, a year abroad was fully integrated into a four-year degree by 1964 at the latest; German students, at least, were encouraged to work as language assistants, rather than to attend university. At Manchester University around the same time, a full summer term abroad was required at the end of the second year, and students were also strongly encouraged to apply for the teaching assistant scheme for a full year. Oxford and Cambridge – whose degree content remained entirely literary and philological for longer than many others – were slow to embrace residence abroad. A student at Exeter College (Oxford) who expressed an interest in the assistant scheme in the 1950s was advised instead to take himself on a walking holiday down the Rhine in the summer vacation. Even in the mid-1960s, Oxbridge students expressing an interest in a term or year abroad seem to have been more or less firmly discouraged, though some went anyway. The warmest encouragement reported to me was summed up as follows: "We don't approve of it, but we won't put anything in your way" (to a student at St. John's College, Oxford). There is still considerable variation in the extent to which universities require academic work during the year abroad (in some cases a full dissertation, in others, some kind of reflective report on the experience, or an oral presentation or examination on students' return into final year), and whether these marks are included in the final degree calculation.

In the twenty-first century, the year abroad came under threat with the introduction of full fees for university students in England from 2012, which raised the prospect of universities charging the full £9,000 for the intercalated year. After a

80 *A sociocultural history*

concerted campaign by the University Council of Modern Languages (UCML) and the British Academy (BA), the fee charged to students for the year abroad was capped at 15% of full fees. The campaign was able to draw on a body of evidence about the academic, cultural, intercultural, linguistic, personal and professional benefits of residence abroad (see Coleman & Parker 2001), including the outcomes of three Residence Abroad Matters projects in the 1990s (for details see Coleman 2001).[39] A paper for the BA and UCML in 2012 emphasized the increased employability of students who had been abroad (Coleman 2012). A key point was not only their improved communication skills but also their intercultural competence – a transferable competence not specific to their language of study. According to the paper, 86% of 600 language students surveyed described the year abroad as the "most valuable part of the degree", an assessment which arguably does little for the status of the Modern Languages as disciplines at universities, but certainly helped preserve the year abroad. Its future after "Brexit" remains to be seen (although the capped fee is not restricted to students on EU placements).

3.4 Conclusion: languages for all?

Over the past century, huge changes have made foreign language learning far more accessible to more people than it ever was before. Compulsory schooling is only one – and the most recent – context in which languages have been learned. Often learned simply for practical need – for travel or migration, trade, or military purposes – foreign languages could also be markers of social distinction. Learning languages was a recognized accomplishment, which yielded the ability to participate in the world of a European social elite and, increasingly, also to appreciate a rich literary culture. In the nineteenth century, modern languages became established as school subjects and as disciplines, albeit with differing emphases for males and females; modern languages were, at least in the eyes of their advocates, 'elevated to a science' (Barlet 1885: 111), and their teaching professionalized. In the course of the twentieth century, languages were made widely available to learners across the ability range, in all kinds of schools, to large numbers of adults as well as to children.

In raw figures, vastly more people learn a language to at least some level in Britain now than ever before. Yet languages are still more a female subject than a male subject. Another constant is the wide divergence in attitudes towards modern languages: great respect and loyalty from those who have studied them to a high level, but a tendency in society at large to view their study as of uncertain value. The very availability of language learning in all kinds of settings and in all kinds of degree combinations means that languages have never quite lost their ancillary status. The extremely wide availability of low-level language learning outside universities, and the fact that some of this low-level learning is replicated at university (in semester-long language modules, for example) means that the "discipline" of modern languages remains opaque to many.

3.5 Further reading

Loonen (1991) provides a history of English-Dutch manuals in the context of Anglo-Dutch trade. See Hüllen (2005: 50–54) for the *Introito e porta* tradition, and further references there including Rossebastiano (2000); for editions, see Guistiniani (1987) (German-Italian) and Stegmann (1991) (Catalan-German). For the various editions of the vocabulary part of Berlaimont's language manual, see Niederehe (1994: 441–442) and (1999: 445–446), Peeters-Fontainas (1965: 166–187), Lindemann (1994: 604–606, 615–619) and Pablo Núñez (2010, vol. 2, 202–311). On the history of the ASTP, see besides Velleman (2008) also Keefer (1988, on the ASTP more generally), Matthew (1947), Angiolillo (1947) and Cowan (1991). On the history of language learning and multilingualism in Europe's armed forces, see Glück and Häberlein (2014).

Cohen (1996) is a key study on the history of gender in the history of teaching and learning French; see also Beck-Busse (2014 [1999]) and Fleming (1989). Doff (2002) provides an excellent detailed examination of foreign language teaching in German girls' schools of the nineteenth century. For references on the language teaching Reform Movement, see Further Reading in Chapter 4. Contributions to the history of teach-yourself manuals include Sørensen (2010), McLelland (2015b), and Mairs (2017). Rybak & BBC (1980) examines the motivations, background and experiences of adult language learners on BBC language courses.

Much of the history of languages as university disciplines has yet to be written, but on the history of Russian in universities, see Muckle (2008b); for German, Weber (2006, 2012, 2013), Flood (1999); for French (still seemingly very under-researched), Holmes (2011); for Spanish, Martínez (2014). Stern (1965) offers a snapshot of university languages provision in the 1960s. On the history of teaching modern languages in Dutch universities since the 1840s, on the establishment of the first chairs of modern languages in the 1880s, and their slow rise to the status of university degrees (not until 1919!), see Kok Escalle (2015). The history of modern languages teacher training in Britain has not been systematically described, but see Wringe (1996) and Moys (1996) for in-service training. On the professionalization of language teachers in Europe in the late nineteenth century, see the contributions in Suso López (2005). For language teacher training in the Netherlands, see Wilhem (1993) and Hulshof et al. (2016), and for Germany, see Christ (2005). On assistantships, see besides Rowles & Rowles (2005) and Rival (2012, 2013a, 2013b), Audra (1955a, 1955b) for a 1950s view of exchanges and assistantships. On pen-friendships, besides Schleich (2013, 2015, 2017), see also Barrier (1955). Board of Education (1903–1939) lists "holiday courses on the Continent for instruction in modern languages". Jones (1996) provides a survey of "contacts with the foreign country" available to teachers in 1996. On residence abroad, see Coleman (2013) and Ehrenreich (2008), including the research agenda mapped out by Byram (2008b). Hoffa (2007) and Hoffa and de Paul (2010) offer a history of U.S. study abroad in general.

82 *A sociocultural history*

Notes

1 See Radtke (1994) and McLelland (2004) for examples, and further discussion in McLelland (2016a).
2 See Zwartjes (2012) for an overview. How such missionaries got on when plunged into the unknown as "field workers" is an important strand in the history of how languages were described, taught and learned, which there is no space to explore here (but see Zwartjes 2012).
3 Glück and Häberlein (2014) have recently provided the first collection of studies of military multilingualism, but largely in a German-speaking context.
4 Other such works are *Soldier's Language Manual No. 2* for German (Ajax 1916); a tiny (12×9cm) *Soldier's English-French Conversation Book* (Gallichan 1917); *the Soldier's Manual: Military Expressions in English, French and German: Organization, Material, Personal, Operations, Works, Aero Words, etc.* (Beckwith 1917); a *Vade-mecum for the Use of Officers and Interpreters in the Present Campaign: French and English Technical and Military Terms* (Plumon 1917). *Country Life* magazine also published *Lessons for Soldiers: The Adventures of Corporal Atkins*, "a selection of nine comic playlets with translation and vocabulary" (Cowman 2014: 9).
5 The manuals of Freeth (1886) and Kinloch (1890) were explicitly intended for such learners; Nestor-Schnurmann (1884) also had such pupils.
6 Note, however, the Institute of Linguists involvement in the production of elementary French and German manuals for the forces, *Bill et Tom en France*, and *Bill und Jock in Deutschland*, apparently followed by similar manuals for Spanish, Russian and Arabic (Anon. [1941], Anon. 1942, cf. Smith et al. 2010: 21, see also p. 22).
7 Separate initiatives in languages were the Navy Japanese Language School, the Military Intelligence Service Language School, and the Civil Affairs Training Schools (Velleman 2008: 385–386, note 1, following Matthew (1947).
8 The question of social class is complex, and the boundaries between, and divisions within, social classes are difficult to define, even more so when considered across a period of several centuries, during which the middle class(es) expanded and social mobility also increased. Here I adopt, broadly, Bayley's working definition: the upper class consisted of the "landed aristocracy and gentry"; the middle class of "professionals, industrialists, white-collar workers, small shopkeepers and businessmen"; the lower or working class consisted of "artisans, semi-skilled, and unskilled workers" (Bayley 1989: 57, n. 2).
9 See the Introduction in Hunt (1987) for a good overview of this history up to the late twentieth century. From 2015, young people must remain in some form of education until their eighteenth birthday, though not necessarily in school – an apprenticeship or other training is also acceptable.
10 On the distinction between "high" and "low" culture in the history of language learning, see Risager (2007: 28–29).
11 Despite the increasing use of the label "secondary", there was no natural progression from elementary to secondary education, for, beyond a very few exceptionally bright and fortunate elementary pupils who won scholarships, only the elite continued their education into their teenage years (Hunt 1987: xvi–xviii; Bayley 1989: 57–58). The account below follows Bayley (1989).
12 Admittedly, these figures do not include Standard VII and ex-Standard VII, where French and German were more likely to be taught.
13 Although there is no required minimum or maximum number of GCSE subjects required, 80% of Year 11 pupils took at least eight subjects in 2000 and seven in 2006 (Rodeiro 2007: 6).
14 The drop in entrants from private schools may be explained by increasing use in independent schools of International GCSE and other forms of assessment; see CfBT (2015: 24).

15 There is insufficient evidence of neurological differences that might make girls genuinely "better" at languages than boys, nor can preference be explained by clear differences in learning styles and strategies. Although some gender-related tendencies have been found, "there is no proof that these are innate, or otherwise fixed" (Sunderland 2013: 265). Nevertheless, girls do better than boys at languages in GCSEs, and in some countries, "girls do so much better than boys that entrance requirements are lowered for boys applying to attend English-medium schools" (Sunderland 2013: 265).
16 The apparent lack of such materials for German probably reflects the smaller market for German, too small to be profitable if divided on gender lines.
17 Language learning by correspondence was also a possibility: surely one of the earliest instances must be Ivan Nestor-Schnurmann, who taught Russian by correspondence in the 1880s, charging four shillings a lesson, payable every fourth lesson, for the handwritten materials that he sent out (Nestor Schnurmann 1884; Muckle n.d., accessed 2015).
18 At Colleges, teaching was at a higher level than in the Institutes, according to Ortmanns (1993: 109).
19 That factor was considerably lower by the 1980s. In 1984, there were 64,259 adult students on language classes at some 380 adult education centres (Arthur 1996: 53). Even allowing that this covers only about 60% of possible providers in England and Wales, the total number cannot have been more than three or four times the 32,704 A-level languages candidates in1985 (cf. Table 2.4 on p. 33).
20 The full report of the survey, by Mr C.L.M. Harding, appeared in the *Times Educational Supplement*, 9 Dec 1960, "Wastage widens the gap". See also Harding (1961–1962).
21 Hargreaves went on to review a number of textbooks that he considered suitable, for French, German, Spanish, Italian and Russian, pp. 26–27, 37. He also published his own textbook for adults, *French Once a Week* (reviewed in *Journal of Adult Education* 35: 42).
22 My thanks to Sharon Clancy and her team of volunteers at Attingham for unearthing this information. The courses were not, despite the aspirations of these colleges, very affordable for ordinary working men and women: the cost of two or three pounds for a four-day course would be a quarter or more of a miner's weekly wage, for example (Clancy, p.c.).
23 Preparatory schools are so called because they prepared pupils to sit the entrance examinations to major Public Schools, at the age of 12 or 13.
24 Endowed by Henry Robinson Hartley, the Institute offered day and evening classes to anyone who could attend, and was the forerunner of the University of Southampton. Keane later took up a professorship of Hindustani created for him at University College London.
25 For the works published by these men, see the listings in the bibliography of McLelland (2015a).
26 See also the Leathes Report (1918), pp. 146–151.
27 The relatively low pay and poor career prospects of language teachers were raised as one of the factors "that militate against the efficiency of modern language instruction" in a 1908 Modern Language Association report, which gives details of average salaries (Brereton et al. 1908: 38, 67). Similar concerns about poorly qualified foreigners undermining the status of British-born language specialists, but in businesses rather than schools, also motivated the foundation of the Institute of Linguists in 1910 (see Smith et al. 2010: 12–14).
28 *Educational Times* (1887: 273). See also the report on the tenth event in 1902, reported in *Modern Language Quarterly* (1902: 160). The German modern language teachers' association was the *Allgemeiner Deutscher Neuphilologen-Verband* (ADNV). Note also the reform-minded societies set up elsewhere in Europe. In

the Netherlands, the first *Nederlands Philologen Congres* took place in Amsterdam in 1898 (Kok Escalle 2015: 60). In Scandinavia, the Quousque Tandem Society had been by founded by Otto Jespersen in 1886; the *Association Phonétque Internationale* was established in France by Paul Passy in the same year (Wilhelm 2017: forthcoming). Despite the early establishment of the *Revue de l'enseignement des langues vivantes* in France, a language teachers' association was not established there until 1902, the *Association des professeurs de langues vivantes* (APLV). See Rival (2012: 58–59), following Mombert (2001).

29 It was renamed *Modern Languages* in 1919 and became the *Language Learning Journal* from 1989.
30 In addition to those already noted (e.g. Barlet 1885), see, for example, the discussions of methods reported in the *Educational Times* of 1892 and 1893: "Old and new methods of teaching modern languages" by J.J. Beuzemaker (*Educational Times* 1892: 505–509, canvassing the methods of Comenius, Mulcaster, Ascham, Jacotot, Ollendorff, Prendergast, Otto, and Gouin); Howard Swan on Gouin's Series Method of teaching languages (*Educational Times* 1893: 282–286); and the review of Robson (1929) and Purin (1929) in *Modern Languages* (10 (1930): 20–21). See also Atherton's analysis of R. H. Quick's paper to the College of Preceptors (Quick 1875; Atherton, in prep.).
31 The examinations were re-named Higher examinations from 1878 and made available to both male and female candidates, running until 1883. Examinations specifically for women were not universally welcomed by advocates of education for women, many of whom instead wanted access to the same examinations that men sat. See Roach (1971: 109–120).
32 However, the Netherlands was, like Britain, late to come to formal teacher training; from 1921, it was possible to take a degree whose graduates were also qualified as language teachers; but teacher training institutes were not established in the Netherlands until the 1970s (Wilhelm 1993: 71–76).
33 Research has documented such exchanges for well-to-do merchant families in Augsburg and Nuremberg (see contributions by Kuhn, Lang and Schwanke in Häberlein and Kuhn 2010).
34 In Britain, the programme was administered by the Board of Education and then the Department of Education and Science until 1964, and then by the Central Bureau for Educational Visits & Exchanges until 1992, when the Bureau was integrated into the British Council.
35 For example, in Prussia, the Foreign Office established a dedicated schools section in 1906 (cf. McLelland 2016).
36 The information that follows is based on recollections of various individuals of their own study abroad experiences. My thanks to Paul Coggle, John Flood, David Hill, Bill Jones, Tony Kapcia, Julian Preece, Hamish Reid, Tony Waine, Bruce Watson, Wilfried van der Will and others.
37 The MA course at Glasgow lasted five years (though students started a year younger than in England).
38 However, see Muckle (2008a: 165–167) on organized group trips for teachers of Russian to Soviet Russia.
39 The projects, led by the universities of Lancaster, Oxford Brookes, and Portsmouth, were funded in response to the Teaching Quality Assessment process in 1995–1996, where university teaching was investigated; demonstrating learning from the year abroad was identified as a weak point in many universities (see Coleman 2001).

4 How languages have been taught and learned

4.1 Introduction

We might summarize a layperson's view of how foreign language teaching and learning has changed over time as follows: in the (imprecisely defined) Old Days, language teaching was all about grammar and translation, but nowadays, things are "better", and people learn to speak the language. In this chapter, I shall offer a less simplified history of methods in language teaching. We shall see, for example, that grammar and translation did not dominate all language teaching until the twentieth century, nor was it a new idea to pay attention to the spoken language – not surprisingly, people had been doing that for centuries. A warning: the history that follows deals with methods of teaching European languages in Europe and, occasionally, with Europeans learning non-European languages in other parts of the world. That is the history about which most is known. The history of language learning by speakers of non-European languages is little researched, and so too is the history of how non-European languages were learned – for the curious, there are many research projects waiting to be tackled!

The history of language teaching and learning has been variously divided into periods. Byram and Hu (2012) provide overviews of three periods: the nineteenth century, the period from the Reform Movement (beginning ca. 1880) to 1945, and a period since 1945, characterized by behaviourist, then communicative and task-based approaches (Van Essen 2012, Pennycook 2012). Howatt and Smith (2014) begin a little earlier, with a "classical" period, 1750–1880. I have, by contrast, chosen to start at the beginning, or at least as far back as surviving sources allow us to go (4.2). My second period begins around 1600 (4.3), when grammars of vernacular languages and manuals for learning them began to circulate in large numbers across Europe. Another key innovation emerges in the later eighteenth century – grammars with targeted exercises, a development which went hand in hand with the inclusion of foreign languages in school curricula, albeit still for a tiny elite only, and with a growing interest in teaching literature (4.4). The nineteenth century (up to the 1880s) saw many attempts at innovation alongside a dominant emphasis on teaching grammar and translation (4.5). It was followed by the Reform Period (1880–1920), one of whose defining characteristics was the reformers' new – or rather, renewed – concern with teaching the spoken language (4.6). Howatt and Smith (2014) rightly identify a "scientific period" beginning around 1920, characterized by the concern to establish a scientific basis for language teaching, drawing on insights from psychology and the emerging discipline of applied linguistics (4.7). A caesura comes in the scientific period in the 1960s, with a turn to communicative approaches, later also including task-based learning (4.8). Of course, any periodization is a simplification: older practices persist alongside new methods, approaches and techniques, as I illustrate in 4.9 by examining two texts from 1938 and 1947, which between them point back hundreds of years, *and* forward into the 1990s. Finally, I turn, briefly, to the history of "teaching culture" as part of language teaching (4.10).

As we saw in Chapter 3, much language learning goes on with little or no help from a teacher. In materials used by Italians keen to learn German for the cloth trade with Nuremberg in the later Middle Ages, the suggested reply to the question of "Who taught you?" is "Here, there and everywhere":

> Chanstu icht teutz "Can you speak any German?"
> Jch chan ein wienig "I can a bit"
> Wer hat dichs gelert "Who taught you it?"
> vmb vnd vmb vbar all "Here and there and everywhere".
> (Blusch 1992: 105, from a fifteenth-century manuscript. I have replaced the Italian with my English translation)

A great deal of language learning has always been this kind of on-the-job, sink-or-swim learning of which we have no records at all. Helmut Glück gives some examples – from a Polish princess, who, at the time of her marriage in 1475 to George, son of the Duke of Landshut (in southern Germany), spoke no German at all, to soldiers, migrants, refugees, and travelling entertainers, all of whom presumably picked up the languages they needed as best they could (Glück 2014: 47, 54). A literate minority with the leisure to do so might learn languages by translating texts out of the foreign language, with or without the help of a teacher. Roger Ascham (1515–1568) believed that translation was the best way to learn Latin (Sumillera 2014: 67–70), but the approach was clearly also used for vernacular languages too. The author of *The Dutch Schoolemaster* advised his readers to "provide yourself of a Dutch Dictionary and learne to translate the hardest book you can find" (Le Mayre 1606: to the reader, A2 verso; see Dibbets 1971–72: 4), and there is evidence from eighteenth-century Germany of young women translating from French and Italian in order to improve their knowledge of the language (Brown 2009).

Any history of how languages have been learned thus needs to be bear in mind that most of the history is invisible, below the surface of the iceberg. In what follows, however, I focus on how languages have been *taught* – even if, for the early period, the story is very incomplete, since we are reliant solely on what surviving materials hint about how teaching was done. As Loonen (1991: 2) observed "There is no way for us to sit in on a class taught three hundred years ago, nor can we witness the conditions in which the teaching took place there except in the odd picture or description". It is also important to differentiate between the musings on education of well-known names – such as Roger Ascham and John Locke – cited by Titone (1968), Kelly (1969), Germain (1993), Caravolas (1994), and Hüllen (2007) – and those actually involved in the reality of teaching. We must also distinguish in Europe between learning Latin – the language that a small elite learned for many centuries as their working language – and the history of learning the *vernacular* languages of Europe, the everyday languages of ordinary people. Latin and other foreign languages were, for many centuries, learned in different ways, until methods used in the teaching of each one gradually influenced the teaching of the other, as we shall see below. Despite this, some histories have not made the distinction sufficiently clear (e.g. Kelly 1969, Wheeler 2013). We must also bear in mind that until the late seventeenth century, the teaching of foreign vernaculars was very much "an international affair, a cultural activity in Europe of a homogeneous character which did not alter with the languages taught" (Hüllen 1997: 54). We shall see that there are whole textbook families whose contents – vocabularies and dialogues, especially – were widely shared across Europe and merely adapted to different language combinations. Likewise, the Reform Movement (ca. 1880–1920) was a European phenomenon. A final word of caution: in modern discussions of language pedagogy, it can be useful to distinguish systematically between terms such as methodology, approach, method, and technique, but in the following, I use these terms in a commonsensical, non-technical way.

4.2 Language learning up to around 1600

The earliest written evidence of language learning and teaching consists of bilingual vocabulary lists and bilingual (or plurilingual) model dialogues, in which key communicative events might be modelled, from gossip about the weather or the latest Sunday sermon, to a sales negotiation in a cloth shop. The tradition of model dialogues in European foreign language teaching reaches at least as far back as the so-called *Hermaneumata* of third-century Greece,[1] of which versions survived in medieval manuscripts (see Stevenson 1929: iv–vi for some snippets). We saw an early Anglo-Saxon/Latin example of this in 2.2.

For Latin, teaching grammar and translation also featured from the very beginning. We cannot be sure to what extent the native language was used in class, but Orme deduces from the available evidence that pupils "must have turned pieces of English [i.e. their native language, NMcL] into Latin, or vice versa, and Latin words in glossaries were sometimes provided with English translations" (Orme 2006: 43). There is evidence of just this kind of practice in a manuscript fragment of a school exercise written by an eleventh-century German-speaking pupil. The pupil writes *Verba quae ad me misisti ut tibi exponam, in theodiscam linguam transtuli* ("The words that you sent me for me to explain to you I have translated into the German language") (printed in Müller 1969: 1). There then follows a list of ecclesiastical and liturgical vocabulary in German and Latin, as well as translations of snippets of Donatus's elementary Latin grammar, the *Ars minor*, including attempts at German renderings of the names for the parts of speech, such as *namo* (lit. "name") for noun and *zuoze demo verbo* (lit. 'to-the-*verbum*') for adverb. It was common to tackle texts by proceeding from a more or less complete word-for-word interlinear translation (where perhaps only those Latin words causing difficulties would be annotated) to a more idiomatic rendering – the same method appears to have been applied to reading other texts, such as psalms, as to Donatus's grammar itself (see Henkel 2009); a rather late manuscript example of an *Ars minor* glossed in this way shows the progression from interlinear, word-for-word, to a free translation. In the 1473 manuscript, owned by Konard Bücklin, the Latin is translated into German, but below I have given the translations in English (see McLelland 2004: 210 for an extract; for the full text see Ising 1966, here p. 26).[2]

Text in Latin

Nomen quid est. pars oracionis cum casu corpus aut rem proprie communiter ue significans. proprie vt Roma Tyberis. communiter vt vrbs flumen.

The explanation

Quid *what* est *is* Nomen *the name* [i.e. noun] parsoracionis *a part of speech* cum casu *with a falling voice* [the term case derives from Latin *cadere* to fall] corpus *body* aut *or* rem *the thing* proprie *properly* aut *or* communiter *commonly* significans *meaning* proprie *properly* vt *as* Roma *Rome* Tyberis *Tiber* Communiter *commonly* vt Vrbs *as the city* flumen *as the river*.

The meaning in German

What is the noun? A part of speech with case signifying a body or thing properly or commonly. Properly as in Rome and Tiber. Commonly as in the town and the river.

After mastering the *Ars minor*, pupils would move on to studying more detailed grammatical works which, amongst other things, told them which Latin words belonged to which grammatical categories and which patterns of inflection they followed. Since this was something that native speakers of Latin would have known by intuition, it was not covered by the *Ars Minor*, but had to be painfully learnt by the generations of non-native speakers who went on to learn Latin (see Law 2003: 65–88).

While learners of Latin in the Middle Ages all learned the grammar of the language as a matter of course, learners of foreign vernacular languages in the period did not. For most languages, there simply were no grammars of the vernacular to learn from. The very idea that the vernaculars could be made to fit the fixed rules of grammar seemed fanciful – the German monk Otfried von Weißenburg famously wrote apologetically of his dialect that it was "not accustomed to be held by the reins of grammar" (see, e.g., McLelland 2009: 57; Gardt 1999:

13–20). A small number of exceptions stand out. Aelfric of Eynsham's Latin grammar, written in Anglo-Saxon in the late tenth century, encouraged his pupils to match grammatical concepts to their native Anglo-Saxon (Vineis & Maierù 1994: 185–186; Orme 2006: 43); the Irish *Auraicept na n-Éces* (lit. "the precepts of the poets", written and revised over the seventh to eleventh centuries) and the four *Icelandic Grammatical Treatises* (written in the twelfth and thirteenth centuries) were attempts to apply various aspects of Latin thinking about grammar, spelling and style to Irish and to Icelandic. The *Donatz Proensals* or "Provençal Donatus" by Uc Faidit seems to have been written around 1240 for native speakers of Italian wanting to compose songs in Provençal, the language of the troubadours. In fact, it gives most space to lists of rhyming words, but it is a landmark in its own way, as the first grammar of a vernacular for foreign learners in Europe. It is also unique. (See Vineis & Maierù 1994: 186–189 on these works, also Hayden 2011 for the Irish text).

So, unlike learners of Latin – taught through an explicit curriculum of grammar and reading – learners of vernacular languages were, up until the sixteenth century, never taught the grammar of the language, or at least not explicitly. How they learned can be illustrated by the case of Italian cloth-merchants learning German in Venice in the 1420s from Georg von Nuremberg, the first German as a Foreign Language teacher that we know by name (see Blusch 1992: 299–303; Glück & Morcinek 2006).[3] The materials consist of a substantial section of basic vocabulary, given in Italian and German, loosely grouped by topic, lists of verbs, and some dialogues (see Glück 2006: 42). These 1420s manuscripts may be the earliest surviving materials of this kind, but they cannot be the first, for they already demonstrate a well-thought-out didactic concept (Schröder 2006). For example, there is some implicit focus on form (frequent use of imperatives of verbs, comparative and superlatives of key adjectives like *good* and *bad*, numerals needed for naming prices), and key specialist vocabulary particularly relevant to the cloth trade. Some grammatical patterns may have been presented explicitly, for a large portion of the 1424 manuscript consists of columns that look like complete verb paradigms for about 20 or so high-frequency verbs, and generally in the order that we would expect to find in a grammar: first, second and third person singular, followed by first, second and third person plural (Blusch 1992: 123ff.), and running through the tenses. For about 30 further verbs, the second person imperative, infinitive and past participle are given. There is no explicit grammatical terminology, and there are no generalizations deduced about patterns of verbs, but some rules of thumb would have become obvious – grammar by induction, then, at the very least – and perhaps more. As for the dialogues, the lively exchanges also model the pragmatics of commercial interactions between Germans and Italians, especially the art of haggling over prices (McLelland 2004: 212–215). They embody the precept attributed to Jakob Fugger that the best language to learn is the language of the customer (Glück & Morcinek 2006: 4). Much of the vocabulary of the dialogues has already been presented to learners in the preceding word-lists, where the vocabulary is not only grouped by topic, but also individual entries are often closely associated variations on a theme, including idioms, to help reinforce learning (e.g. words for salt water, clean water, unclean water). However, the presentation of the dialogues suggests that they were not simply for memorizing verbatim (in the way that the *Ars minor* grammar was to be memorized, for example), but could be used as a starting point for practising variations on commercial exchanges (Schröder 2006). In the extract that follows, from a fifteenth-century manuscript (Blusch 1992: 116–117), we see how the agent appointed by the Republic of Venice helps the buyer and seller in their dealings with another.

Wer ist da	Who is there?
Friunt	A friend
Vas wer euch lieb	What would you like?
Jch wolt peter	I'd like [to see] Peter
peter man fragt nach euch	Peter, someone's asking for you
wer fragt nach mir	Who's asking for me?
Der hutig choffman vnd der vnderchöffel [. . .]	The merchant from [earlier?] today and the agent [. . .]
zaig her die tuecher vnd lauss in och sehen	Show the fabrics and let him see too
Jr habt ein vnterchaufel er verstet sich bas druff	You have an agent and he knows better about it
[. . .]	[. . .]
frag in ob im die tücher gefallant oder nit	Ask him if he likes the fabrics or not
Vmb die seiden werd wir wol uberain [. . .]	We'll come to an agreement about the silks, I think [. . .]
Die tücher sind guot genuog	The fabrics are good enough
Jr habt wol si mochtent Jemers nit besser sein fur in	You're right, they could never be better for him
Ez ist die uarheit ich verste mich auch etuas dar auff	It's the truth, I also know something about it

The hope of commercial gain was one major reason for learning a foreign language; religious conviction was another (Chapter 3.1.2). By the sixteenth century, Europeans were no longer just learning each other's languages – missionaries were learning the languages of other continents, especially in Central and South America, and in China and South-East Asia. Looking at how two different Catholic orders tackled learning Chinese in the seventeenth century can give us some insight into the range of ways that such missionaries tackled the challenge. The Jesuits, operating in mainland China, adopted what Klöter (2010) calls an "accommodationist" approach. Highly educated, the Jesuits concentrated on building a relationship with the intellectual elite of the Chinese empire, not least because their mission faced opposition, and relationships with the powerful were a survival strategy. So the Jesuits learnt the elite variety, *guān huà* 官话 (officials' language), Mandarin, often beginning with the same primers that Chinese children used to develop their character recognition and writing skills, such as the *Three Character Classic* (三字经 *San Ze Jing*), so-called because each line consists of three characters, and still used in elementary education in China today.[4] The Jesuit missionaries would then move on to studying the Confucian classics, again in much the same way as a novice Mandarin scholar and civil servant of the empire would have done.

Meanwhile in the Philippines, the Dominican order were also learning a variety of Chinese for their missionary endeavours, but took a very different approach. The Philippines had been made a Spanish colony in 1565, so the Dominicans were much more protected than the Jesuits in China. They were also rather less highly educated; and, in the Philippines, there was no elite Chinese cadre on whom to concentrate their efforts. Rather, their focus was on learning the vernacular spoken by the Chinese traders and fisherman established there, a variety of Hokkien (a Chinese language variety that originated in the Fujian province, 1,500km or so to the north of the Philippines; the name derives from the pronunciation of *Fujian* in this variety: hok^4-$kien^3$). Some clues as to how they went about it can be garnered from the manuscript materials that remain, in particular the *Arte de la lengua chio chiu* (where *chio chiu* is believed to be the city Zhangzhou), dated by Klöter to around 1620 and believed to be the oldest grammar of any Chinese language (see Figure 4.1). As Klöter (2010: 84) points out, Hokkien dialects – with tones, and little inflectional morphology – were ill-suited to the Graeco-Roman approach to describing grammar by going through each part of speech in turn and describing the way the words inflect. The Chio Chiu grammar does use the familiar superstructure of Latin grammar, because that is what the

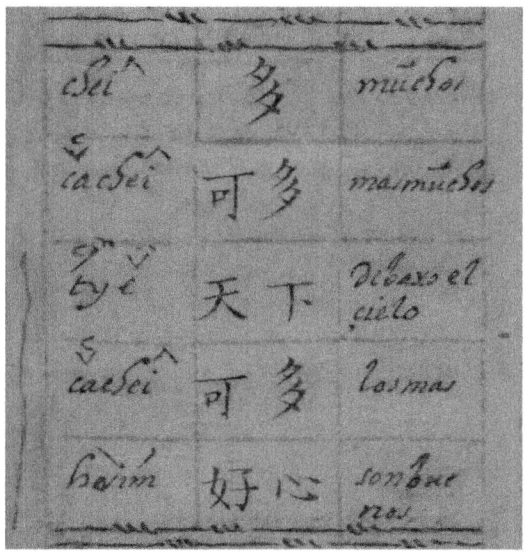

Figure 4.1 *Arte de la lengua chio chiu* (ca. 1620), f. 5r. By kind permission of the University of Barcelona. Note the rendering of Chinese pronunciation (left), the Chinese characters (centre – for the benefit of the native speaker tutor, perhaps?) and the Spanish translation (right); the vertical line on the left of the bottom three entries indicates that they are to be read vertically as a single entity, in this case meaning "Under heaven most [people] are kind"

newly arrived European expected to encounter in a grammar – but from the outset, its applicability to this new language is called into question. For example, the section on pronunciation is followed, as we would expect, by sections on declension and conjugation, but under declension we are told swiftly, "This language does not have different nouns and terms for distinguishing cases", but that there are particles which distinguish cases (p. 189). Similarly we are told under conjugation that the language does not have endings, and does not distinguish persons or mood except by use of particles (Klöter 2010: 99). In general, the grammar has relatively little in the way of explanation, whereas there are "long sections of examples of concrete usage" (p. 89). Alongside sections on pronouncing, on declension, on conjugation of verbs, on adverbs, on other adverbial particles, on conjunctions, and on negations, there are sections on the ways of asking and responding, on modes of composition (i.e. the formation of spoken sentences); on numerals, measure words, time, money and units of measurement. To some extent, the focus is not on what readers needed to *know about* the language, but on what they needed to be able to *do*.

It is clear that the learner was expected to have access to a native speaker for practice. Diacritic marks for the tones are used consistently throughout, but they are not described in detail, so we must assume that they would have been pronounced by a native speaker and then imitated – practice, not the ability to describe the practice, was crucial.

> All these differences will be understood clearly when these and the following examples are pronounced by a Chinese. [. . .] he should be given a Sangley for exercise, although a Father Minister will teach the practice. In order to learn with perfection from the beginning, all tones are indicated in the vocabulary. (Klöter 2010: 187)

It is not fully clear what "practice" and "exercise" are, but Klöter (2010: 189, note) suggests that "practice" refers to language teaching in general including explanations in Spanish, while exercise was done with a native speaker. If that is true, then the method closely resembles that used in intensive World War II army courses centuries later (see 4.7).

So we find two approaches in early European efforts to learn Chinese – amongst the Jesuits, an elite-focussed method that treated the pupil like a native-learning child (a theme that we shall see recurs many times); and, in the Philippines, a practical focus on the everyday vernacular that combined native speaker and non-native speaker instructors.

Meanwhile back in Europe, materials for non-native speakers to learn the European vernaculars were becoming more widespread. In 1477, the German printer Adam von Rotweil had already printed a German-Italian manual based on materials used in Georg von Nuremberg's Venice school, omitting the dialogues and leaving a vocabulary grouped according to topics (e.g. human body, flora, fauna), followed by lists of adjectives with comparative and superlative forms, verbs with infinitive, first person singular and participles and full paradigms of some key verbs. Adam von Rottweil's book (ed. Giustiniani 1987) was the first printed bilingual vocabulary in Europe. Its publication only 25 years after the birth of the printing press in the 1450s is indicative of high demand for such materials. Gradually other languages were added or substituted, yielding vocabularies of up to 7, 8, or 12 languages in parallel, often including Latin. Hüllen (2005: 53) counts at least 87 editions between 1477 and 1636.

While Adam von Rottweil's vocabulary became the most widely disseminated vocabulary, it was complemented by a tradition of bilingual dialogues begun by an Antwerp language master called Noël de Berlaimont (d. 1531). The earliest surviving edition of Berlaimont's *Colloquia et dictionariolum* ("Conversations and a Small Dictionary"), Dutch-French, dates from 1536 (Hüllen 2005: 54). Berlaimont's name, in various spellings, became confused with the word *parlement*, taken to mean "speaking, conversations", and became in time the name of a genre, describing a language learning manual with conversations. Hüllen (1999: 107) counts more than one hundred editions of various language combinations between 1530 and 1703, with up to eight languages at once, across Western, Central and Southern Europe (Loonen 1991: 191–209).[5] Such bilingual (or multilingual) dialogues were versatile – they could be used for private study; the learner could also practise reading them aloud with a tutor or fellow learner to develop fluency; see Figure 3.1 on p. 41 for an example.

4.3 The first foreign language grammars and "full" textbooks (1600–1750)

While two familiar ingredients of language learning – vocabularies, and dialogues – were being widely used across Europe by the sixteenth century, in most cases written grammars of the vernacular languages did not yet exist. In the sixteenth century, that began to change. The rise of towns and associated trade called for increased record keeping; more ordinary people needed to be able to read and write, to manage the administration of their businesses, societies and town councils; and with printing came the possibility of writings in the vernacular reaching wide audiences (Protestant Bibles were key early texts); with rising cultural and linguistic patriotism scholars no longer assumed that their vernacular was inherently inferior to Latin and unworthy of study and cultivation. The circulation of printed texts made people aware of regional variation, and efforts to cultivate and fix the form of the language began, as had been done for Latin centuries earlier. Joachim du Bellay said of French in his *Deffense et illustration de la langue française* (1549), "Our language is not so irregular as people are inclined to say", and others were coming to the same conclusion about their own vernaculars. All of these factors led to the first attempts to write grammars of at least some of the vernaculars: a grammar of Spanish appeared in 1492, French in 1530, Dutch in 1583, English in 1586, and German in 1573 (see Padley 1985, 1988; Tavoni 1998).[6]

These grammars varied in their approach and influence. The 1583 Dutch *Twe-spraak* was largely an orthographic guide (Dibbets 1985, 2000); Nebrija's 1492 grammar of Castellan was, according to Tavoni (1998: 30) "forgotten" soon after it was published, although more recent research suggests it did serve as a model for Spanish missionary linguists (see Klöter 2010). Significantly, though, two of these pioneering works were written for *non*-native speakers of the language, Palsgrave's 1530 grammar of French and Ölinger's 1573 grammar of German. Ölinger's grammar was inspired by his experience of teaching German to young French noblemen (McLelland 2001: 11–12). From the very beginning of the vernacular grammatical tradition, then, explaining the language to non-native speakers was a spur to analysing the grammar of languages. These early grammars had many weaknesses, including a tendency to take Latin grammatical concepts and just make the language fit. For example, since Latin has no articles, Bullokar's *Bref Grammar of English* (1586) treated English articles merely as 'signs' or 'notes' placed before nouns to identify them as nouns (Robins 1994: 137). In German, the first grammarians failed utterly to fathom the distinction between regular and irregular verbs, or between strong and weak verbs – Albertus (1573) only hoped that *volente Deo*, "God willing", he might be able to explain the system later; for now, it could be learnt by practice alone (*solo vsu*) (McLelland 2009: 67).

However, gradually progress was made, and insights from grammarians began to inform foreign language teaching. For example, the first textbook of German for the English, Martin Aedler's *High Dutch Minerva* (1680), drew on the most authoritative grammar of German of the seventeenth century, that of Schottelius (see Van der Lubbe 2007; McLelland 2011). Aedler's manual was a somewhat scholarly grammar, with no model dialogues, but this was unusual for the period. Learners (and teachers) came to expect a combination of materials – the dialogue-and-vocabulary-based approach from the practical vernacular tradition, *and* explicit grammar teaching copied from the model of Latin grammar teaching. So a few years after his grammar of German, Ölinger published a set of twelve dialogues (Ölinger 1587).[7] In the Low Countries, a Dutch speaker wishing to learn a foreign language in the late sixteenth century could draw on pronunciation guides, lists of conjugations, texts to read with parallel translations, and dialogues. Gradually these began to be bundled together, and a sense emerged of what a complete language learning manual should consist of, which remained fairly stable until around 1800. As Loonen (1991: 108) characterized bilingual English-Dutch/Flemish manuals over the period 1500–1800, "A typical textbook would contain: a short preface; a grammar section; idiomatic phrases; dialogues; and personal and commercial letters". Texts might also contain a word-list, proverbs, some texts for reading, and other practice material. A fairly early example of this kind of text is the bilingual *English Schole-Master* (1546), which Loonen considers the first "full" bilingual textbook for learning English to be published in the Low Countries (Loonen 1991: 201, cf, 108). In England, London-based French teacher Claude Mauger's *True Advancement of the French Tongue* (1653) was an early text that combined grammar and dialogues.

4.4 Language teaching 1750–1800: the "practical grammar" and exercises

With grammars of foreign languages now readily available, teachers began to devote greater attention to teaching grammar – it was, after all, one way of marking out their expertise compared to any mere native speaker with whom to practise conversation. It is often said that the shift in Europe to drilling grammar and practising translation began with Johann Valentin Meidinger's 1783 textbook of French for German learners (e.g. Hüllen 2005: 93) and that it was connected to establishment of foreign languages as school subjects in the German state school system. Meidinger's influence was indeed considerable, but his textbook did not come out of nowhere. Already in 1750, Louis Chambaud (d. 1776), a Frenchman teaching in England, was challenging the established method of teaching through a combination of grammar, vocabulary and dialogues. Chambaud wrote witheringly in the preface to his *Grammar of the French Tongue* (1750) of masters who,

> not knowing what to contrive for forwarding their boys, presently begin by making them learn words, dialogues, and phrases, and labour hard to beat into their heads as many common sentences as they can; pretty much after the same manner as parrots are instructed.
>
> (1750: xviii)

He was also critical of forcing learners to use only French in school, a practice which he believed condemned learners either to resentful silence or to "a barbarous broken French" (Chambaud 1750: xviii), and thus made them hate French. Asking pupils to speak French too soon was counterproductive, he believed, for "beginners [. . .] most certainly cannot practise what they have never learnt before" (Chambaud 1750: xxiv). Rather,

> two things are chiefly to be considered in the learning of a language: first, the words; then, using those words conformably to the genius of the language. The one is the object of memory, the other that of judgment and reflection.
>
> (Chambaud 1750: vii, xix)

Crucially, in Chambaud's view, such "judgment and reflection" were best schooled through explicit teaching of grammar, with exercises on each point of grammar in turn, followed by translation and construing – Chambaud was proud to announce that he had "composed a set of Exercises upon the Grammar Rules, which was never attempted before" (Chambaud 1750: viii).

Chambaud points out that no parent would ask a music teacher to teach his son without expecting him to learn the principles and rules of the art, for the boy

> might perhaps learn how to sing some airs, which he had often heard repeated to him; but he could never sing at the opening of a book, for want

of having first learnt the nature, use and power, of the several notes [. . .] that compose Music, make the rules of Harmony, and are the guides to the voice in singing. It is the same with a language. Those who are desirous to learn it, must begin with the principles, proceed by the application, and finish by the practice of them. To act contrarily is to pervert the natural order of things, and attempt impossibilities.

(Chambaud 1750: xxv)

Chambaud's words echo those of the German grammarian Schottelius in 1663, who also used the analogy with music to argue that merely to speak the language is not to be master of it. Reason, not practice alone, were required to master a language (McLelland 2011: 59–61, Schottelius 1663: 10, 67). Schottelius's goal was to get *native* speakers to take as much interest in studying their own language as they did in studying Latin; Chambaud, a century later, wanted learning a *foreign* language to have the same status as learning Latin.

The tussle between those who advocated learning by practising speaking with the aid of dialogues, and those who advocated a more analytical approach, with greater emphasis on explicit grammar practice, was not limited to the study of European languages. British authors writing the first textbooks of Hindi or Urdu for English speakers were similarly divided. John Gilchrist (1798) explicitly sided with Chambaud in advocating language learning as a task for reason, not mere memory and experience, and was critical of George Hadley's preference for the tradition of "familiar dialogues" (Steadman-Jones 2007: 192–208).

In a passage added to the preface in the 1765 edition, Chambaud described his own rational, grammar-based teaching method as follows:

The lesson consists of four or five parts, which ought to keep an equal pace together: the materials of the language, I mean the Vocabulary and Forms of Speech; the way of using them, or the Grammar; the Exercise, which is the practice of the Grammar Rules, and the pronunciation or reading: to which, translating and construing must be added, when the scholar has learnt his Accidence. The lesson must always begin with the pronunciation, and each part always follow in its turn in the same order, for fear of forgetting something. [. . .] As to the first construing book, the scholar must first translate the fable, then construe it.

(Chambaud 1765: vii, xiii)[8]

Note that "construing" is not just a means to ensure that the sentences are understood correctly. Rather, even after translation has been done, construing must follow. For Chambaud, it was apparently a worthwhile task in itself in learning a language, part of "a regular and methodical way of learning" (Chambaud 1750: xxvii). In Chambaud's "set of Exercises upon the Grammar Rules, which was never attempted before" (Chambaud 1750: viii), the first exercise, on the article, begins with a series of unconnected sentences to translate:

The Creator of Heaven and Earth is the God of Christians. The fear of death, and the love of life are natural to men. The horror of vice and the love of virtue are the delight of the wife. Give me the meat. Cut the bread. Bring the mustard.

(Chambaud 1767: 26)

All the elements of what is known as Meidinger's approach are thus arguably given by Chambaud, some thirty years before Meidinger.

The belief that studying the grammar of a foreign language provided a kind of training for the mind gained ground over the following decades. In the neo-humanist curricula of the *Gymnasien* now being set up as the state took control of the school education system in Germany (Landfester 2012), beginning with Prussia in 1794, modern languages were now valued less as practical communicative tools than as a means of "mental training", part of the overarching aim of education to develop pupils' intellectual rigour (Macht 1994; cf. also Macht 1992). As the German writer Jean Paul put it, learning Latin was a form of *geistige Gymnastik* "mental gymnastics", and "so a foreign language, especially Latin, remains the healthiest amongst the early exercises of the power to think" (*Folglich bleibt eine fremde Sprache besonders die lateinische unter den frühern Uebungen der Denkkraft die gesündeste'* Jean Paul 1807: 349, 351, cited by Kirk 2016: 97).

It was in this context that Johann Valentin Meidinger (1756–1822) wrote his so-called practical French grammar (*Practische Französische Grammatik wodurch man diese Sprache auf eine ganz neue und sehr leichte Art in kurzer Zeit gründlich erlernen kann* "by which one can learn a language thoroughly in a short time, in a quite new and very easy way", 1783), which seems to have set a fashion in modern language teaching across Europe.[9] But Meidinger was not the first to use the term "practical grammar" for a text combining grammar and exercises for practice in one volume. That honour perhaps goes to the Flemish teacher Nicolas Wanostrocht for his *Practical grammar of French* published in London in 1780.[10] Wanostrocht explained that "The several parts of speech are arranged in the usual order, and each part is discussed under a separate section. Each rule is followed by a familiar exercise, which the master may use in the place of a dialogue. At the close of every section, a recapitulatory exercise is given upon all the preceding rules" (Wanostrrocht 1780: iii). Figure 4.2 shows Wanostrocht's first exercise, on the use of articles with nouns – like Chambaud, Wanostrocht supplies interlinear vocabulary.

Such "practical" grammars soon proliferated. Fick's *Praktische englische Sprachlehre* (1793) was the first for learning English (discussed in Howatt 1984: 132; Klippel 1994: 142). John Uttiv's *Complete practical German grammar* (1796) was the first for English learners to tackle German, and Uttiv explicitly stated that he had "chiefly followed: and indeed often strictly copi'd" the "truly excellent" method of Meidinger (Uttiv 1796: Preface A2). For example, the first exercises begin: *The father of the master. The proprietor of the garden. The brother of the gardener. the looking-glass of the sister. The chamber of the girl. The daughter of the mother. The sword of the governor* (Uttiv 1796: 28). The exercise was followed by

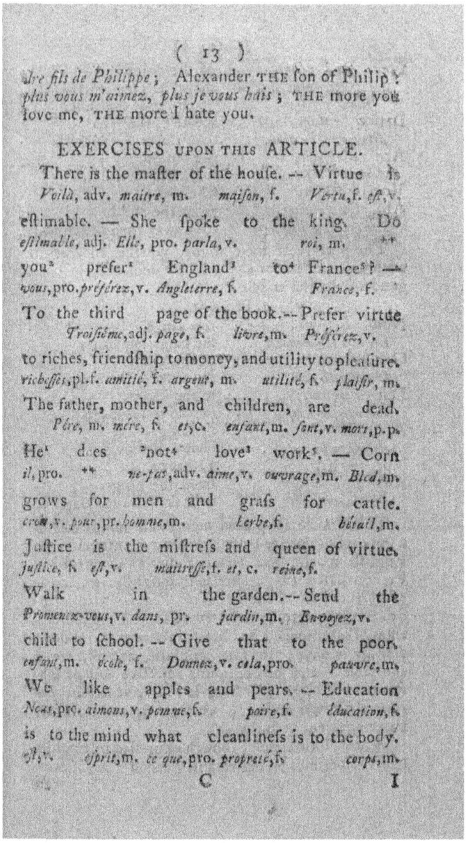

(13)

dre fils de Philippe; Alexander THE ſon of Philip: *plus vous m'aimez, plus je vous hais*; THE more you love me, THE more I hate you.

EXERCISES UPON THIS ARTICLE.

There is the maſter of the houſe. -- Virtue is
Voilà, adv. *maitre*, m. *maiſon*, f. *Vertu*, f. *eſt*, v.
eſtimable. — She ſpoke to the king. Do
eſtimable, adj. *Elle*, pro. *parla*, v. *roi*, m. **
you² prefer¹ England³ to⁴ France⁵? —
vous, pro. *préférez*, v. *Angleterre*, f. *France*, f.
To the third page of the book. -- Prefer virtue
Troiſième, adj. *page*, f. *livre*, m. *Préférez*, v.
to riches, friendſhip to money, and utility to pleaſure.
richeſſes, pl. f. *amitié*, f. *argent*, m. *utilité*, f. *plaiſir*, m.
The father, mother, and children, are dead.
Père, m. *mère*, f. *et*, c. *enfant*, m. *ſont*, v. *mort*, p. p.
He¹ does ²not⁴ love³ work⁵. — Corn
il, pro. ** *ne-pas*, adv. *aime*, v. *ouvrage*, m. *Bled*, m.
grows for men and graſs for cattle.
croit, v. *pour*, pr. *homme*, m. *herbe*, f. *bétail*, m.
Juſtice is the miſtreſs and queen of virtue.
juſtice, f. *eſt*, v. *maitreſſe*, f. *et*, c. *reine*, f.
Walk in the garden. -- Send the
Promenez-vous, v. *dans*, pr. *jardin*, m. *Envoyez*, v.
child to ſchool. -- Give that to the poor.
enfant, m. *école*, f. *Donnez*, v. *cela*, pro. *pauvre*, m.
We like apples and pears. -- Education
Nous, pro. *aimons*, v. *pomme*, f. *poire*, f. *éducation*, f.
is to the mind what cleanlineſs is to the body.
eſt, v. *eſprit*, m. *ce que*, pro. *propreté*, f. *corps*, m.
C I

Figure 4.2 The first exercise in Wanostrocht's *Practical Grammar of French* (London, 1780: 13). By kind permission of Cambridge University Library

the vocabulary needed for translation into German: *The father, der Vater The master, der Lehrer*, etc. Uttiv's exercises were judged by an anonymous reviewer in the *Allgemeine Literarische Zeitung* (Anon. 1797) to be "fade[n]" ("dull"), and "ganz nach dem Meidingerschen Manier" ("completely in the Meidinger manner") – evidence that this "practical" approach had its critics from the very outset.

The title of Gebhard Wendeborn's *Elements of German Grammar*, published in 1774, may have been inspired by Chambaud's similarly named *Elements of the French Language* (1762). Symptomatic of the changing priorities in language teaching, Wendeborn explicitly excluded dialogues and vocabulary, "since they are not constituent parts of grammar", but promised that if his grammar were well received, he would write a short practical grammar with exercises, as Chambaud had done for French (pp. ix–x). Wendeborn did indeed issue a book of exercises in 1797, responding to the "wish of many" for exercises "illustrating his Grammar and giving, to a beginner, an opportunity of putting the rules, which are laid down there, into practice" (Wendeborn 1797: preface, p. 1). Wendeborn regretted that the style of his exercises was not as "neat and elegant", nor as "connected and interesting" as in other types of writing. However, "[t]he author's chief aim was to combine, in each line of an Exercise, as many words as could be well joined, to elucidate the particular rules for which they were intended". As an example, consider his exercise on the definite article, to be translated into German:

> The cunning fox, that killed the hen of the poor woman, who sold the eggs to the wife of the butcher, has been seen near the cottage, which is not far from the meadow, where the cows and the sheep of the farmer are grazing.
> (Wendeborn 1797: 8–9)

Besides requiring eleven definite articles which between them cover all three genders, singular and plural, and all four grammatical cases, the sentence also includes syntactical complexities well beyond any learner at the start of studying the grammar.[11]

Wendeborn's exercises show that the question of grading exercises was initially a challenge. In 1824, John Rowbotham (1793?–1846) criticized existing grammars where "the first exercises begin with long sentences, which require the application of all the rules of syntax, and that, in some instances, more rules are requisite than the writers themselves have given". By contrast, Rowbotham promised his readers,

> In this grammar, every rule or important note is followed by easy exercises, or by suitable examples; the exercises increase in difficulty by regular and almost imperceptible gradations, commencing with the articles and nouns, which are sufficiently difficult for beginners.
> (Rowbotham 1824: iv–v)

By the early nineteenth century, then, the idea of learning foreign languages from a grammar with accompanying graded exercises, including translation into and out of the language, was established. It was this that grew into what was later disparagingly called "the" grammar-translation method. Whatever its later detractors said, its intentions were laudable: to provide both a grammatical foundation *and* appropriate, targeted exercises to allow learners to practise applying the rules as they learnt them, step by step.

4.5 The nineteenth century: grammar and translation, and patented methods – but not "the" grammar-translation method[12]

Nineteenth-century textbook authors who combined grammar, exercises and translation along the lines of Meidinger include Johann Heinrich Friedrich Seidenstücker (1785–1817), Johann Franz Ahn (1796–1865), Heinrich Gottfried

Ollendorff (1803–1865) and Karl Plötz (1819–1881). The names of Seidenstücker and Plötz are rare in texts used in Britain,[13] but Ahn's and Ollendorff's "methods" were extremely widely used, and later fiercely criticized during the Reform Movement by Bahlsen (1905); Kelly (1969: 52) considered them the "best known Grammar-Translation texts". But even amongst this group, considered the prototypical exponents of "the" grammar-translation method and so roundly dismissed by Reform advocates in the late nineteenth century, more recent scholarship has recognized that there was much innovation. For example, while Titone (1968: 27) judged that in Seidenstücker's texts "the sole form of instruction was mechanical translation", Klippel (1994) argued that Seidenstücker's innovation consisted in distinguishing between beginners and advanced, with different methods for each, using an inductive approach for beginners, rather than beginning with explicit grammar teaching from page one (Klippel 1994: 347). Ahn did the same, presenting grammar implicitly to beginners, rather than explicitly, so that this so-called grammar-translation author "uses very little grammatical terminology and in fact has no grammar rules at all" until learners are more advanced (Wheeler 2013: 114). For example, Ahn's German grammar begins as follows (Ahn & Pfeiffer 1868: 5):

1.
Masc.   *der Vater*, the father
Fem.   *die Mutter*, the mother
Neut.   *das Buch*, the book
gut, good; *groß*, tall, big; *klein*, small, little; *ist*, is
2.
Der Vater ist gut. Die Mutter ist gut. Das Buch ist gut. Ist der Vater groß? Ist die Mutter klein? Ist das Buch gut?
3.
The father is tall. The mother is little. The book is good. Is the father good? Is the mother tall? Is the book small?

The learner is first introduced to some vocabulary. Note that the verb form *ist* is introduced simply as an item of vocabulary, *is*; its part in a verb paradigm 'to be' is not dealt with, because the grammatical focus here is on the use of the article. These vocabulary items allow the learner to understand the simple sentences that follow, which model the use of three articles for the three genders, and the formation of a simple Subject-Verb-Complement structure. Having grasped the pattern, the pupils are then expected to generate their own permutations, by translating the given English into German. This is the very method advocated by the reformer Walter Ripman in his *Hints on Teaching German* in the early twentieth century: "How is the grammar to be taught? First let the pupils observe for themselves, lead them to discover the rules, then repeat with as much variation as possible" (Ripman et al. 1917: 13), and Ripman's own *First German Book* begins somewhat similarly to Ahn's. After a list of German names, Ripman's text begins:

Der Vater. Die Mutter.
Das ist der Vater. Der Vater ist ein Mann. Er ist ein Mann.
Das ist die Mutter. Die Mutter ist eine Frau. Sie ist eine Frau.
Wilhelm ist ein Knabe. Hier ist der Knabe.
["The father. The mother.
That is the father. The father is a man. He is a man.
That is the mother. The mother is a woman. She is a woman.
William is a boy. Here is the boy".]

There are important differences between Ahn and Ripman et al. First, Ripman et al. do not use English, and their approach expects more active use of the spoken language in class, for pupils soon learn to ask each other *Bist du ein Knabe?* and to answer *Ja, ich bin ein Knabe* ("Are you a boy? Yes, I am a boy" Ripman et al. 1917: 2). Ripman et al. begin with noun phrases rather than adjectives as complements, and move more swiftly to other sentence patterns (with pronouns and adverbs). However, in their fundamental approach to presenting grammar, Ripman the reformer and Ahn the despised grammar-translation bogeyman are in fact very similar in how they approach beginning learners.

Ollendorff was another prolific textbook author, whose books for the different languages were "essentially translations of each other", with "the same grammar, the same examples, and even the same translation sentences" (Wheeler 2013: 115). In the eyes of later Reformers, he also stood for explicit rote learning of grammar. But he was an innovator too, basing his method on spoken questions and answers, in which most of what learners needed to answer was provided in the question posed, so that they were scaffolded from the known to the unknown (see McLelland 2015a: 87–88; Wheeler 2013: 115–118). Again, there are obvious similarities with the intensive question-and-answer classroom practice advocated by Ripman decades later. Ollendorff's *New method of learning to read, write, and speak a language in six months, adapted to the German, for the use of schools and private teachers* broke down the material into lesson-sized chunks, presented in the Table of Contents as a course over five months, and so presented learners with a course-book rather than a mere grammar. Ollendorff's detailed instructions for the teacher on how to use the book included a clear emphasis on pupils speaking – first imitating the teacher's pronunciation, then answering the questions put by the teacher, with the ultimate goal that pupils would be able to "keep up a conversation in the energetic language which you teach us", as a passage for translation in the final lesson pointed out (Ollendorff 1850: 416; see McLelland 2015a: 87–88)

The supposed dominance of grammar and translation in the nineteenth-century language learning is also undercut by the case of a third nineteenth-century champion of a patented "method", Emil Otto (1813– ?). Otto shared with Ollendorff the emphasis on speaking, following a model pioneered by Thomas Gaspey in his *Englische Konversationsgrammatik* (Gaspey 1851; cf. Klippel 1994:

405). Like Ollendorff, Otto believed that pupils would learn grammar best by learning to apply it not only in writing but also in speaking too:

> The *"German Conversation-Grammar"* [...] combines the grammatical and logical exposition of the German language with the constant application of the different forms and rules to *writing* and *speaking*.
>
> The book is divided into Lessons, each complete in itself, and containing, in a methodical arrangement, a portion of the grammar followed by a German *Reading exercise* in which the different grammatical forms are applied to whole sentences. An *Exercise for translation* into German comes next: the lesson being concluded by an easy *Conversation*, re-embodying the matter introduced in the previous exercises. The most practical method of acquiring and developing the faculty of *speaking* German is for the student to be questioned in German on subjects already familiar to him by translation.
>
> (Otto, revised by Lange 1890: preface, cited McLelland 2015a: 91)

For example, an early exercise begins with written translation into the target language of short sentences drilling the verb 'to have' with the accusative, such as *I have not the stick. The child has the stick.* The next exercise is a *Sprechübung* ("speaking exercise") where pupils are required to put questions and answers, such as *Habe ich die Feder? Ja, du hast die Feder. Hast du has Buch? Nein, ich habe das Buch nicht* "Have I the pen? Yes, you have the pen. Have you the book? No, I do not have the book" (Otto 1864: 22). While not wildly interesting, they do suggest that conversation about the classroom environment was expected.

Otto also produced separate textbooks for practising conversation. He recognized the limits of what was practicable in teaching conversation in schools, but this fact demonstrates that he did intend his books for use in schools (Otto 1864 V, VI.; cf. Klippel 1994: 341). His *German-English Conversations* (Otto 1864) were based on the earlier *Englisch-deutsches Gesprächsbuch* (1864; cf. Klippel 1994: 341; cf. also Otto & Wright 1889). Otto wrote in the preface to his conversation book,

> To learn to speak a foreign language, four elements are required: 1) a store of words; 2) a number of easy short phrases; 3) subjects fit for the purpose; and 4) a series of regular conversations and dialogues in good German.

Note the absence of grammar from this list when the focus in on speaking.

The names of Ahn, Ollendorff and Otto in part became so well-known because they were energetically marketed as "methods". Materials had been recycled and applied to new languages for centuries (as in the case of the vocabularies and Berlaimont dialogues), but now publishers sought to trade on a name. Ahn's method had first been developed for French, but was rapidly translated, adapted to new languages, and imitated. Ahn's original text for Germans learning French (Ahn 1834) had 207 re-editions or reprints over 50 years (Macht 1994: n.p.); by 1885 it had reached its thirtieth edition,[14] and altogether 61 editions over the 81 years from 1856 to 1937 (Klippel 1994: 405–406); I know of eleven editions of his method for English learners of German between 1849 and 1888. Ollendorff's self-proclaimed method was no less popular. His textbook for English learners of German went through 22 issues or editions between 1838 and 1876, and there were also popular versions for English learners of French, Italian, Spanish and Russian. Ollendorff resorted to handwritten numbers and signatures to authenticate his works and to distinguish them from the large numbers of imitators (see McLelland 2015a: 87, n. 62). Editions of Otto's textbooks included dire warnings from the publisher Julian Gross that he owned the "method of Gaspey-Otto-Samer [. . .], having been acquired by purchase from the authors", and that any imitators would be "persecuted according to the law" (see McLelland 2015a: 92). The sheer number of editions of the works by these three authors, Ahn, Ollendoff and Otto, none of which is accurately described as mere grammar and translation, shows that many learners were not faced with grammar and translation only. However, despite Ahn's innovative intentions and the popularity of his works, Macht (1994: n.p.) observes,

> The memories attached to them seem to be mainly unpleasant, probably due to the drudgery of having to learn by heart large numbers of totally unconnected model sentences void of any real meaning, e.g., *You always interrupt me when I am speaking. You were coming from the tailor's as I was going to the shoemaker's. Your nephew is always smoking when we call to see him. While the house was burning, the people were running to fetch water and could not get any* (Ahn 1834: Vol. 1, p. 48).

Bahlsen – who had been taught by Plötz – was no enthusiast, writing of "a barren waste of insipid sentence translating" (Bahlsen 1905: 10).

It probably remains true that school classroom practice often fell short of the ideals envisaged by the authors, especially as far as speaking the language was concerned, and especially once public examinations were introduced from 1858 onwards, catering to the Public Schools and grammar schools that had begun to introduce French and German to their curricula from the 1830s (see Chapter 3).[15] The University of Cambridge Syndicate examinations in French and German were virtually identical to those for Latin and Greek, differing only in the literary texts set for study. For example, the 1858 Cambridge under-16 examination regulations read as follows for French:

> Passages will be given from Voltaire's Charles XII., for translation into English, with questions on the parsing and the historical and geographical allusions:
> Also a passage from some modern French author for translation into English:
> And easy English sentences for translation into French.

The under-18 examination requirements followed a similar format. Given the well-known tendency to teach to the test, it is likely that despite all the evidence of innovation in nineteenth-century textbooks, French and German were indeed often taught in schools according to the formula *reading, translating and grammar*. (See Chapter 5 for the history of languages examinations.)

Two further figures in the nineteenth-century history of language teaching deserve mention. Claude Marcel and Thomas Prendergast both taught adults and had less influence on school teaching practice than the other authors discussed earlier, but they are no less interesting for the history of ideas about language teaching. Claude Marcel (1793–1876), a Frenchman who taught French in Cork, Ireland for four decades or more, was keen to avoid the perceived vice of "mental translation". He published his first reflections on language teaching in 1820, *Practical Method of Teaching the Living Languages, Applied to the French, in which Several Defects of the Old Method are Pointed Out and Remedied*, the year after opening his language school in Cork; his most important work was *Language as a Means of Mental Culture and International Communication* (1853). Despite having virtually no influence at the time, he has been judged, in retrospect, a "major theorist" of the nineteenth century, who drew particularly on educational theory to promote his principles for teaching languages in schools as part of "mental culture" more widely (Smith 2009: 178–179; see also Howatt 1984: 152–156).

Thomas Prendergast (1807–1886), like many before and after him, sought inspiration from how children acquired language, in order to develop what he called the *Mastery* system of learning languages.[16] He took inspiration from his observation that children appeared to be able to produce whole memorized chunks of language fluently, well before they were able to understand the underlying grammatical structures. They then gradually "enlarge their narrow sphere of conversation by interchanges and transpositions of words" (Prendergast 1864: 34). In the same way, then, adult learners should learn the language inductively, not through explicit grammar. They should be presented with sentences which, by dint of repetition, would be thoroughly learned, and so be produced readily, an approach that in some sense anticipates behaviourist sentence pattern drills in the mid-twentieth century. Learners should then be given the means to vary those core sentences by substitution of vocabulary and re-arrangement of elements. A diagram at the back of Prendergast's book showed how two model sentences could be used to generate a further 250 sentences in this way (reproduced in Howatt 1984: 160), an idea that suggests the beginnings of thinking generatively about language, in the way that Chomsky would nearly a century later: finite resources could generate infinite new utterances (Gallardo 2001). It was important to identify the right set of minimal sentences to lead to mastery, and so Prendergast also sought to identify the most frequent words. Although he relied solely on intuition, his list was for English was, Howatt showed, a good effort (Howatt 1984: 158). It seems that there was interest amongst language teachers in Prendergast's approach, including from R. H. Quick, who taught at Harrow, and from the head of the Cheltenham Ladies College (Atherton 2010: 17–18;

Lorch 2017). However, Howatt identified the fatal flaw in Prendergast's method – young children may indeed learn chunks, but they do not learn long convoluted and artificial sentences, deliberately dense with linguistic structures, as in "When the man who brought this parcel for me yesterday evening calls again, give it back to him, and tell him that it is not what I ordered at the shop" (Prendergast 1864: 165, cited by Howatt 1984: 159). Such artificial sentences still stood firmly in the tradition of teaching through explicit grammar and translation.

4.6 The Reform Movement and beyond: reactions against nineteenth-century school language teaching

Despite the constraints of teaching to the test of grammar and translation, we have seen that the nineteenth century witnessed numerous attempts at innovation. Throughout the century, there was ongoing tension – as there had long been – between those who advocated allowing pupils to learn a language as naturally as possible, more or less similarly to acquiring a mother tongue, and those who rejected it. The advocates of so-called natural approaches – such as Thomas Prendergast – pointed to the fact that no number of drills prepared one for real communication; and that there was a big difference between being able to repeat a grammatical rule and being able to speak correctly and fluently. Meanwhile, advocates of teaching grammar explicitly pointed to the poor results of those who had had every opportunity to practise the language but still made little progress – Chambaud (1750 [1797]: xxi) had cited as evidence the experience of French Huguenot refugees in Britain, and of English people who had lived decades in France, but who could not speak the language well at all. In essence the two camps were grappling with the relative importance of two phenomena that applied linguists of the twentieth century would come to view as the distinction between learning and acquisition in Krashen's sense, or between declarative knowledge and procedural knowledge (Johnson 1994).

Outside the boys' school system, there was still scope for innovation, both in private language schools for adults and in the education of girls, who, for most of the century, were much less likely to be working towards formal examinations (see 3.2.2, 3.2.3). In Germany, many of the key figures in the Reform Movement taught (or had taught) in schools for girls, and this may well be true of other parts of Europe. The leading reformer in Britain, Walter Ripman (originally Rippmann), taught at two pioneering women's colleges, Bedford College and Queen's College in London, though another important but somewhat less radical figure, Otto Siepman, taught at the boys' Public School (see McLelland 2012). Advocates of so-called natural methods, with greater emphasis on using the target language, were also to be found in private language schools for adults, as we shall see below. Meanwhile teachers in boys' schools, with an eye to the requirements of final examinations (see Chapter 5), were more likely to stick to the formula of teaching grammar and translation, even if with some innovations of the kind outlined in 4.5. However, by the 1880s, even within this system, there was growing frustration. The resulting Reform Movement in Europe is generally said to have been kick-started by the pamphlet of Wilhem Viëtor (1882), who expressed frustration at the hours and hours devoted to foreign languages in Germany's *Gymnasien* (grammar schools) with so little to show for it.

Growing professionalization of language teachers gave the Reform Movement a collective momentum that had been lacking from previous individuals' efforts at radical change, who – like Marcel and Prendergast – had generally remained somewhat lone figures, even if they had some limited influence. Many adherents of the Reform Movement in Britain, such as William H. Widgery, Otto Siepmann and Louis von Glehn, were teachers in schools, while others such as Henry Sweet and Karl Breul were based in universities; Ripman spanned the two. Between them, in a pattern mirrored across Europe, they drew both on practical classroom teaching experience and on emerging sciences, especially insights from psychology into how learning occurs, and the measurement and analysis of the sounds of a language in the new science of phonetics, and discussed their ideas in the professional fora newly available to them (see 3.3.2). Reformers varied in just how radical were their approaches to overhauling the teaching of modern languages, but two main characteristics can be identified, both of which grew out of new scientific insights of the nineteenth century. First, work in child psychology and pedagogy showed the value of using pictures and real objects (*realia*) from the culture to help children learn. Second, the new linguistic science of phonetics gave reformers the hope of teaching accurate pronunciation in a reliable way, at a time when recordings of native speakers were not yet available. These two sciences together provided credible support to a new generation of teachers who, in effect, only re-asserted what language masters and learners had accepted for centuries until the birth of the "practical" grammar – the importance of practising *speaking* the language. Innovators differed, however, in whether they saw speaking as the prelude to being able to read literature, or as a primary goal in itself. For Ripman, the spoken language was a means to a higher end. He advised the young readers of his *New First German Book*:

> What I want you to learn first is to think in this foreign language, until it almost ceases to be foreign. Do not be afraid to speak in class; for the more you do so, the sooner you will be able to read.
> (Ripman et al. 1917: vi, from 'To my readers')

In other words, for Ripman, giving space to the spoken language did not mean conversation was the sole goal – it was a stage on the way to being able to read, first simple passages, but ultimately literature, which was, after all, the focus of the school examinations of which Ripman was himself an examiner.[17]

Meanwhile, however, private language schools for adults were offering "utilitarian, conversation-based foreign language courses" (Howatt & Smith 2014: 83). In the USA in the 1870s, a German emigrant to the USA, Gottlieb Heness, and his French colleague Lambert Sauveur called the method used in their language school the "Natural Method" (see Finotti 2010, Howatt & Smith 2014: 83), because they expected learners to succeed best when "picking up" the language in the way that a child or a foreigner in a new country would. They relied on teachers using illustrations, actions, or object lessons to make clear the meanings of new words and expressions, without resorting to translation into the mother tongue. Maximilian Berlitz, who set up his first language school in Providence, Rhode Island, in 1878, acknowledged his debt to the "Natural Method" of Heness (Finotti 2010: 18), but called his own method the "Berlitz Method". His language schools proliferated in Europe, and the company remains one of the best-known, language learning "brands" today. It may have been imitators, unable to use the copyrighted "Berlitz" label, who coined the term "Direct Method", which then also began to be used to describe reformed language teaching in schools (e.g. Glehn 1912), especially after the French government used the label when it stipulated that schools should focus on the spoken language (Howatt & Smith 2014: 84; Van Essen 2012: 309). When used of commercial language schools, "Direct Method" tended to mean "no using the first language", but in school classrooms, Direct Method advocates were less rigid about banning the first language. However, translation *into* the language being learnt was, in general, firmly rejected within the Reform Movement as well as by Berlitz.

Classroom communication without recourse to the mother tongue was an aspiration that endured well beyond the Reform Movement generation. Recognizing that not every meaning could be readily conveyed by using a picture or object, in 1950, A. S. Hornby codified his "situational approach": teachers could convey meaning using gestures and actions in the classroom, or indeed be describing an imaginary situation, in which the language structure might be used (Howatt & Smith 2014: 85–87). According to Howatt and Smith (2014: 87), situational language teaching – "whose debt to the Reform Movement, via Harold Palmer, was clear to Hornby himself" – was the "dominant approach" in British teaching of English as a Foreign Language in the 1960s. In Britain's foreign language teaching too, textbooks ordered by grammatical topic, one grammar point per chapter, were gradually replaced by chapters structured around *situations* and the language *functions* appropriate to particular situations (such as greetings, introductions, asking for information, expressing an opinion, giving advice), which still characterize materials today.

4.7 The scientific period I (ca. 1920–1970): the industrialization of language teaching and the goal of "automatic" knowledge

A landmark in the global history of language teaching is the year 1923, when the Institute for Research in English Teaching was founded in Tokyo, Japan, by the English teacher Harold Palmer (1877–1949) and his adherents (Smith 1999: 72). The world's first institution devoted to research in language teaching, it symbolizes the start of a new, scientific period in which ideas about language teaching methodology were increasingly based on scientific research, rather than on intuition or past experience. This first "scientific" period was also a period of beginning *industrialization* of language teaching, characterized by efforts to make language teaching more rational and efficient, according to a replicable method. New technologies – which had always prompted changes in language teaching – were seen as particularly promising in achieving that goal during the period.

4.7.1 Excursus: technology and language teaching innovations, 1500–present

No one would deny the difference that a good teacher makes in the classroom, but changing technology too has had a transformative effect on teaching. In the sixteenth century, printing and the affordability of paper as opposed to vellum meant learners could consult their own copies of books for the first time, and so allowed a major change in methodology away from memorization. The relative affordability of paper also made more pedagogically effective layouts possible. For example, rather than noun declensions or verb conjugations appearing in space-saving running text, they could now be presented in tables, whose layout could help the reader spot patterns; different fonts could be used to highlight forms or to differentiate languages at a glance, as in Latin grammars for German learners already within a few decades of the invention of the printing in the 1450s (Puff 1995: 139, 281–283). Guy Miège wrote in his English grammar for French learners that he would rather use ten pages than five if it made possible "all those advantages of Braces and Columns, which make the Matter both pleasant to the eye, and obvious to the understanding" (Miege 1688: Preface A2 verso, cited by Howatt 1984: 55).

Later, the affordability of illustrations also had a major effect. Comenius had used illustrations in the seventeenth century (examples are given by Howatt 1984: 48 and Reinfried 1992: 55), but his case remained exceptional, for pictures were expensive, both to produce and reproduce. It was not until the late nineteenth century that it became common to use images as a visual teaching aid. In the 1880s, wall posters showing the four seasons, or town and country scenes, initially used in Swiss primary classrooms, were adapted by Reformers to foreign language teaching and were used across Europe (see Reinfried 1992: 110–113, 115, 117, for examples, and McLelland 2015a: 112–113 for their use in England). Gradually, images were included in the textbooks themselves – for example, a picture plate of German coins could substitute for real coins; object lessons could be based on a picture of the object rather than the object itself. In Rees' *Pictorial Courses* for French and German, each lesson begins with a full-page illustration labelling elements of a scene, making it easier for the teacher to introduce new vocabulary without recourse to the first language (see McLelland 2015a: 113–115, 258 for examples of coins, object lessons and detailed labelled scenes; see also Figure 3.2 on p. 57). Initially used as an aid for static description, series of pictures or comic strips began to be used to provide cues for narratives: Koischwitz (1933: 100) already contains a series of four pictures to serve as cues for writing a story in German, an idea that the audiovisual movement later further developed. Illustrations were also very important in representing the culture of the language being learnt (McLelland 2015a: 255–260; see also 4.10).

If the first major technological innovations were for the eye, the next wave were for the benefit of the ear. The science of phonetics was embraced by many reformers, as a way of ensuring that learners were taught to pronounce the language accurately. However, although the use of at least some phonetic notation continues in some textbooks to the present day, the idea of reproducing whole lessons of text in phonetic script (as in Ungoed 1912; see McLelland 2015a: 116) was relatively soon abandoned, though it seems to have been considered useful for French longer than for German, with its more predictable spelling rules. Rather than using symbols as a proxy for the sounds of the foreign language, it became possible to listen to authentic speakers of the language first-hand. The 1920s saw the beginnings of regular radio broadcasts in Britain. School radio broadcasts emerged almost immediately, and already in 1930, an article in *Modern Language Teaching* (pp. 115–117) discussed the value of various radio programmes for language learning. By 1930, a Board of Education report on language teaching in modern schools reported that 196 of the 512 schools surveyed made use of the gramophone, and 67 used the "wireless" (i.e. radio; Board of Education 1930b: 14). Phonetics could not compete. As David John Rees wrote in the preface to Baumann's *Pictorial German Course* in 1910,

> The utter inadequacy of the Phonetic or imitated pronunciation method of representing strange sounds by stranger combinations of symbols, has long struck the writer as being wearisome and ineffective, to say the least. For those who are unable to obtain the services of a native teacher the author has consistently advocated the use of the Phonograph as the next best means, and the fact that thousands of phonographic language records are now being used by private students and even by teachers for their improvement of the pronunciation proves the utility of this mechanical device.[18]

Rees founded Rees Linguaphone Records, pioneering the use of illustrated textbooks, the Rees Pictorial Language series, with accompanying native speaker recordings. Bought in 1901 by Jacques Roston, a translator and language teacher who emigrated from Russia, Linguaphone used mail order marketing and distribution techniques from its office in High Holborn, London, to become a very successful company. Linguaphone succeeded in winning for its recordings some of the leading experts of the day – for German, for example, the speaker of the model pronunciation on the records I have from 1927 was Theodor Siebs, well known as the author of the first ever guide to standard German pronunciation. The records were reviewed favourably in the pages of *Modern Languages*, where the reviewer noted approvingly that female voices were also included (*Modern Languages* 1930: 88; the Italian Linguaphone records also received a positive review). The review noted that Paul Menzerath, responsible for the German records, presented them as "the first attempt to treat colloquial German as a subject of study". For French and English, Linguaphone was apparently able to draw on the services of the equally eminent Paul Passy and Daniel Jones, respectively.

Roston published a new monthly journal *The Linguist*, and its second issue (1927) offered a description of the Linguaphone method:

> A Linguaphone course is composed of a series of records dealing with everyday subjects, situations and needs. Whenever you have a moment to spare, you slip one of these records on your gramophone and follow, in a special pictorial textbook, the speaking of a cultured native teacher. The textbook contains, side-by-side with the printed text, composite pictures illustrating the various persons, objects and actions described in the text.
>
> With the aid of these pictures you learn to associate the appearance of things with the appropriate word sounds. This is the truly natural way of learning a language, a way you first, as a child, learned your own mother tongue. The results of this method are astonishing. Under this tireless tutor, mastery becomes easy. Quite soon you find yourself able to speak fluently, to understand others and also to read and write correctly.

According to the company's own history (www.linguaphonegroup.com/about-us/heritage/), Linguaphone courses were used in training thousands of Allied troops during World War II, as well as with thousands of refugees preparing for resettlement. Meanwhile, HMV produced its own materials – for German, for example, Otto Siepmann produced 24 German language gramophone records in 1932–1933. Foylophone apparently also published language courses (Smith et al. 2010: 22).

From the use of audio recordings, it was a relatively small but significant step to the development of the language laboratory, a classroom where individual learners could not only listen but also, crucially, could respond to recordings at their own pace, doing "pattern drills" not so very different from the kind imagined by Prendergast, to promote automaticity of production (on this goal, see 4.5.2). In Britain, language laboratories first sparked keen interest amongst teachers of adults, as a series of articles in the *Journal of Adult Education* attests (Sculthorp 1961–62; Titmus 1962–63, Whitehouse 1963–64). Whitehouse (1963–1963) considered language laboratories particularly useful for vocational courses where there were military, economic, or financial incentives to speed up the process of learning, but predicted that they could prove their worth in schools too. The first language laboratory in a British school was opened in Salford Grammar School in 1962, and only five years later, there were 200 (Hawkins 1996: 354). Publications offering guidance on their appropriate use accompanied their spread, generally cautioning that bad teaching was just as possible with a language laboratory as without it (e.g. Stack 1960, Dakin 1973). Dakin (1973: 59–60) highlighted the dangers of "meaningless" drills, of learners being lulled by the "tum-te-tum" effect. His concern was scarcely different from that of Viëtor (1905: 23, 34), who had already lambasted exercises that pupils could complete mindlessly and mechanically, only waking briefly each time a new pattern of exercise was introduced.

It was clear that the new audio and visual technologies were here to stay, and a dystopian view of language teaching of the future was presented by Newmark

(1963–64). The use of film, television, wireless and the like simply for "enrichment" of language learning had

> no future. The shortage of teachers alone will compel TV, wireless, and possibly cinema to begin direct teaching. Classes of forty to one hundred children will sit at their desks in large halls, supervised only by ushers with less to do that nursing auxiliaries.
> (Newmark 1963–64: 316)

Teachers would have to work hard to compete with the quality of technology-based teaching:

> Otherwise, TV will take over the main instructional role, leaving teaching-machines (designed both for oral and written work) to set and correct individual exercises. More ambitious compositions and literary essays will be corrected, and discussion and debates (possibly started off by the ushers) monitored from a room in the county or borough offices. [. . .] the teacher may come in to discuss cultural and political questions after the language has been learned [. . .] but perhaps even this will be better done by an electronic computer [. . .] It remains to consider what, if anything, the teacher can do that cannot be done by machines. The threatened teacher will immediately protest: the media instruct, the teacher educates; the most effective teaching is personal, and comes about in a meeting of two minds; each child needs individual attention; the child or teacher produces his best work out of devotion or respect for a good teacher, rather than for a subject; the machines will produce stereotyped rather than creative work in an increasingly automated and mechanical society; education should be human. All this has a partial truth, but it is absurdly unrealistic [. . .] The facts of population, social justice and professionalization may eventually turn language-teaching to a relay of groups of eighty to one hundred pupils operating teaching-machines and attending TV (both media are so compelling that indiscipline is unlikely) and then splitting into sub-groups for classes where children will get far more personal attention from better qualified teachers than they do at present.
> (Newmark 1963–64: 315–319)

Newmark feared a new kind of "mass instruction with minority teaching" because "first-rate teachers are rare but pupils multiply" (p. 319). However, it is in the nature of "new" technologies that for the generation who grow up with them, they are no longer new. They are never, therefore, for long seen as replacements for the teacher, but are simply added to the list of resources that teachers and learners can draw on. And so Newmark's dystopian vision has not yet come to pass.

Still, Newmark was right in seeing that the future would increasingly involve audiovisual materials, and computers too. The Audio Visual Language Association was founded in 1964 (Hawkins 1996: 354). Hickel (1965) already offered a comparative overview of television language teaching materials available in Europe; in Britain, the BBC invested strongly in radio language programmes from the 1950s to 1980s, with programming for learning French, German, Spanish, Italian and Russian (Rowntree 1961–62). In the days before the internet enabled ready access to media outside one's own country, the high production values of the BBC's broadcasts could offer learners an experience "second only to being in the foreign country", for example through interviews with ordinary people and well-known personalities. Television programmes were generally felt to provide "the motivational element", while radio was useful for "solid teaching purposes" (Rybak & BBC 1980: 20, 22).

The audiovisual movement provided the momentum for a Foreign Languages Materials project, which began work in 1963 to develop four audiovisual language courses for French, German, Spanish and Russian, where film-strips combined with audio could supply a rich situational context, in Hornby's sense, for language in use (*En avant, Vorwärts, Adelante, Vyerod* – see 6.3.3 for the background to the project). As one former pupil recalled,

> We learnt from watching [the] adventures on the overhead projector as the teacher turned the handle on the side to produce a very slow moving story and then she'd move it back a scene and we all 'do it again', in other words we read the 'script' in German out loud [. . .] and we plodded our way through stories of going to the park, going to the shops and visiting things and other people.[19]

Written work concluded the lesson. The textbook was entirely in the target language, and virtually every page was richly illustrated with photographs, cartoons, or picture stories (see Figure 4.3 for a French example).

In isolation, a new technology is powerless, and a potential distraction from the core business of the language classroom. However, all these new technologies interacted with changing ideas about how languages were best learnt.[20] During the Reform Movement era, illustrations helped teachers use the language in class with less recourse to translation into the mother tongue, whether or not they were strict adherents of the Direct Method. Recordings and broadcasts made a focus on the spoken language feasible without relying entirely on the teacher as a model and sole expert. The language laboratory was not only a way of building listening work into lessons, but also, more crucially, made possible the intensive practice of language structures that behaviourist approaches to language learning saw as the route to success (see 4.7.2). For example, influence of the behaviourist stimulus-response approach to language learning is evident in the Nuffield courses, with exercises of the following pattern:

Du hörst: Schau! Das ist Hans
Du sagst: Guten Abend, Hans! Wohin gehst du denn?
[*You hear:* Look! That is Hans. *You say:* Good evening, Hans! Where are you off to, then?]

(*Vorwärts*, Nuffield 1974: 46)

Figure 4.3 A picture story from *En Avant* Nuffield Introductory French Course Stage 4b (Nuffield 1971: 17). Reproduced by kind permission of the Nuffield Foundation

One of the benefits of Computer Aided-Language Learning (CALL) was the opportunity to provide learners with instant, appropriate, tailored feedback on their mistake, and an opportunity to try again. Game-like elements could keep learners motivated. Zettersten (1986: 20–41) provides some examples from the relatively early days of CALL, such as a pronouns exercise disguised as a whodunnit (the Great Pronoun Theft, where a sufficiently high score allows learners to guess the culprit); for discussion of more recent developments in CALL since the 1980s, see Davies (2012). A 1992 National Curriculum poster is now an interesting historical document in the history of technology in the classroom, giving many concrete suggestions for "Information Technology-Related Tasks" in language teaching. Examples include the use of database software to compile information gathered from classroom surveys, using word-processing programmes to create gap tests, create the layout for a leaflet, or rewrite an authentic text such as a newspaper article for a new audience (National Curriculum Council 1992).

Technology can also simply facilitate the practical modalities of language learning. For example, inexpensive phone "apps" such as Pleco can now use a very rudimentary attempt of a Chinese character drawn on a phone screen to suggest possible characters; the user simply selects the correct one, and definitions, examples in context, pronunciation and stroke order are all at one's fingertips. This is a revolution compared to the arduous and lengthy task of looking up a new word or character in a printed dictionary, where entries are commonly listed by number of strokes and then by stroke order. Even with the massive infrastructural support of the Chinese government's Confucius Institutes, one might wonder whether the current boom in Chinese language learning globally would have been possible without the existence of such facilitating technologies.

4.7.2 *Scientific descriptions of language and of language learning as the basis for teaching methods: basic vocabulary, behaviourism and contrastive analysis*

Alongside technological efficiencies, efficiencies were also sought in the first scientific period by trying to make sure that learners spent their limited time on the most crucial aspects of the language: on core vocabulary, and on those areas of grammar most likely to cause difficulty, for example. Whereas in the nineteenth century Prendergast had tried to identify the most useful words to teach by introspection, word-frequency studies now sought to identify core vocabularies empirically. Louis (1954) used 1920s word-frequency studies to define the vocabulary which he used as a basis for his German textbook (Morgan 1928; Hauch 1929); French examples include Adams and Knight (1929), Duff (1933) and Tharp (1934); Palmer and Hornby published their *Thousand-Word English* in 1937 (Palmer & Hornby 1937).[21]

So much for vocabulary. But structuralist linguists saw languages as systems into which different words – or sounds with different meanings attached – had to be slotted. How could these grammatical structures be learnt most efficiently? Behaviourist theories of language learning suggested that language, just like any other behaviour, was a collection of habits formed by associating appropriate responses to given stimuli. Harold Palmer's *Principles of Language Study* (1921) had already presented language learning as "habit-forming and habit-adapting" (the title of the eighth chapter of the book; see Wheeler

2013: 161–164). The American structuralist linguist Leonard Bloomfield used the language of behaviourism to describe language communication as stimuli and responses (e.g. Bloomfield 1933: 24), so that learning a language meant acquiring the habit of giving particular responses to particular stimuli. Once a scientific method of teaching according to these principles had been established, it was anticipated that it could be rolled out on a large scale, for any language and any group of learners (just as the Ahn, Ollendorff and Otto "methods" had been widely applied in the nineteenth century), and an intensive programme could make the whole process as efficient as possible. This was precisely the aim of the intensive language courses developed for the USA's ASTP during World War II (see 3.13). The program typically required 15–17 hours of instruction weekly, over nine months (Velleman 2008: 388); the goal was to achieve a command of the colloquial form of the language, including "the ability to speak the language fluently, accurately, and with an acceptable approximation to a native pronunciation" and "a practically perfect auditory comprehension of the language" (Agard et al. 1944: 4, cited by Velleman 2008: 388). The program had the backing of important American linguists – Leonard Bloomfield himself was responsible for the *Spoken Dutch* manuals (Bloomfield 1944–1945). However, the implication in excitable press reports that the method of these "scientific linguists" was able to achieve in weeks what traditional instructors in schools and colleges could not manage in years, made them very unpopular among much of the language teaching establishment. One genuine problem was the recruitment of native speaker assistants (known as "guides"), many of whom were unqualified as teachers, and not all of whom, it became clear, even spoke the standard variety being taught. The program, with its heavy focus on spoken and listening proficiency, was also criticized for being "anti-cultural, anti-writing, anti-reading and anti-grammar, and hence anti-academic", as Velleman summarizes (2008: 391).

The ASTP was abruptly discontinued when the need for troops on the ground became too pressing. But, short-lived though it was, the ASTP methods and materials had some lasting effects on civilian language instruction. Some universities introduced moderately intensive language pathways with eight to ten hours teaching a week, for example. Some of the ASTP's basic tenets were also revived in what became known as the audiolingual method, including habit formation and error correction through drills; an ordered four-skills approach (listening, speaking, reading and writing); and contrastive analysis as a basis for sequencing materials (Velleman 2008: 396–397). The audiolingual method also made use of the new technology of the language laboratory, in which every learner could be presented with identical stimuli, but individually, to practise giving their own response, through imitating, memorizing and overlearning, until their responses became *automatic* (Byram 2012). This was the automatic production that Prendergast had already aspired to for his learners in the nineteenth century, and that Palmer also saw as achievable through habits (Palmer 1921: 98) – but now there was both a scientific justification and the technology to support the process.

Stack (1971) gives numerous examples of the kinds of repetitive, or, in Prendergast's terms, "reiterative" drills (Prendergast 1864: 33–34) that could now be practised with the help of the language laboratory, including imitation, repetition, substitution and transformation drills. For example, a substitution drill for object pronouns might give the stimulus *Robert voit la maison* "Robert sees the house". The student's task is to speak the sentence but to substitute the noun with the correct object pronoun: *Robert la voit* "Robert sees it". After a suitable pause, for the learner to record their response, the correct response is played (Stack 1971: 142). Exercises would consist of a whole series of such drills on the same pattern. Transformation drills required a change of word order or grammatical structure – e.g. changing the given stimulus from present to future tense, *Ich gehe nach Hause* > *ich werde nach Hause gehen* "I will go home", or negating an affirmative sentence, *Je travaille* > *Je ne travaille pas* "I do not work". Chain transformation drills required the initial sentence be transformed progressively. For example, the basic utterance given might be *He doesn't study*. Learners would then respond to single-word cues on the recording in turn (*She, we, they* etc.) to produce the utterance in turn with different pronouns, and then again substituting the verb (*read* rather than *study*, say), and so on (examples from Stack 1971: 147, 149, 158).

After World War II, a whole new field of second language acquisition research was born.[22] In contrast to centuries of earlier reflections on language learning, the field now started from the premise that second language learning was *not* the same as learning a first language, so that "natural" approaches seeking to mimic the child language acquisition would not necessarily yield the best results. After all, the very existence of a first language as a starting point was a crucial difference. One early outcome was contrastive linguistics. As Charles Fries put it in 1945, "The most efficient materials are those that are based in a scientific description of the language to be learned, carefully compared with a parallel description of the native language of the learner" (Fries 1945: 9). The systematic comparison of the language would identify likely areas of error and so, in behaviourist terms, prevent the transfer of habits from the learner's own language to the new one being learnt, that might yield incorrect utterances (Lado 1957). A flurry of contrastive grammars resulted, as well as guidance on how to determine which learner errors could be attributed to interference from the first language. In Britain, the Centre for Language Teaching Research commissioned a whole series of contrastive analysis and error analysis bibliographies for English in contrast with French, German, Spanish, Italian and Russian (Language Teaching Library et al. 1980, 1982, 1983, 1984a, 1984b).[23]

Contrastive accounts of languages have continued to flourish, more recently often also with a discourse-focussed or text linguistics approach, rather than limited to grammatical structures. But already by the 1970s, it was becoming abundantly clear that not every learner error could be explained simply as interference of the first language in a system that could otherwise be learned perfectly by imitation. Rather, it was realized that learners had to build their own language system as they progressed, from simple words or unanalysed chunks to more complex structures, and that non-target-like utterances were a normal part of that process. This yielded new research foci, in particular on the best kind of "input" and, in turn, new teaching methods.

4.8 The scientific period II: 1965–2000 and beyond: the communicative period and the four skills

Howatt and Smith (2014) date the start of the "communicative" period in language teaching to around 1970, but it arguably began already in the 1960s. In Britain, a 1963 pamphlet, produced by a working party of teachers already argued that "communication" should be recognized as the main aim of Foreign Language study:

> Now that we are no longer mesmerised by the necessity to imitate the Latin text-books [. . .] we can see that languages are for us to use, for the purpose of *communication*. This is an aim which requires no justification to young minds whose natural curiosity can willingly be harnessed to the study of a foreign language. The fact that some pupils often fail to reach a high standard of accomplishment is no reason for giving up the attempt. As much might be said of many other subjects. It is worth noting that real ability to communicate is quickly and drastically tested by the most exacting of examinations – as soon as the pupil meets a foreigner. [. . .] This puts a great responsibility on modern language teachers.
> (Incorporated Association of Head Masters 1963: 13)[24]

Thus, the group argued, "The aim of communication should underlie discussion of method, teacher training, etc. [. . .] This will help us define the kind of language we teach and the nature of the tests we use in assessing progress" (Incorporated Association of Head Masters 1963: 50). We shall see in Chapter 5 that, while it took some time, this is exactly what happened – school language examinations now assess all four communicative skills explicitly and separately. The desire to focus on communication as the goal of language learning was also supported by developments in research which suggested that it was communication itself – and not the forming of habits through copious repetition – that promoted successful learning. Skinner's *Verbal Behaviour* (1957), the most famous application of behaviourism to language learning, was equally famously attacked by Noam Chomsky in a 1959 review, arguing that language learning proceeds not by imitation, but by a process of creative construction. Research on language acquisition within a broadly Chomskyan framework showed from the 1970s onwards that just as in first language acquisition, second language learners appear to progress through relatively fixed stages of morphological and syntactical development in their spontaneous production, regardless of whether or not they "know" the grammar explicitly. Acquisition, as opposed to learning, seemed to take place in some as yet imperfectly understood way, in response to appropriate input in the target language; and, as learners progressed through stages, their language (or "interlanguage", their emergent, developing version of the target language) would be characterized by predictable non-target like utterances. To take an example from German word order, research by Pienemann and others (e.g. Pienemann 1984) showed that learners regularly and predictably acquire the ability to "front" constituents such as adverbs into first position in main clauses *before* they acquire the rule that the main verb must come second. This leads inevitably to ungrammatical utterances of the form *Heute ich arbeite* ("Today I'm working") rather than *Heute arbeite ich*, with the verb *arbeite* in the required second position. While non-target-like, such utterances were *both* successful as communication *and*, despite being faulty, a step in the acquisition process. If that is the case, and if the primary aim of language instruction is to enable communication, then there seemed little point in placing heavy emphasis on grammar because, even once the rule for a structure is "learnt", many or most students will not be able to produce it in spontaneous speech until much later anyway.

Communicative language teaching thus made logical sense, with grammar playing a part, but "neither the primary goal of a beginning foreign language course nor a prerequisite for developing communicative proficiency", to quote the authors of *Kontakte. A communicative approach*, for students beginning German at university (Terrell et al. 1992: xix). Terrell et al.'s textbook is an interesting example for us because the authors were unusually explicit about the research basis for their teaching rationale. They accepted the distinction proposed by Stephen Krashen between *learning* – conscious knowledge that could be consciously applied, for example in carefully planned writing – and *acquired* knowledge, "normally used unconsciously and automatically to understand and produce language" (Terrell et al. 1992: xviii). As Terrell et al. explained in their advice "To the student", "Learned knowledge [as opposed to acquired knowledge, NMcL] is useful when we are writing, or when we have time to prepare ahead of time what we want to say", but in most communicative situations, there would not be sufficient time to draw on and apply knowledge as well as thinking about the content of what to say (p. xxiii).

Language acquisition and language teaching research therefore began to tackle the question of the best kind of language input to promote successful communication. Language laboratory exercises had given every learner more class time to practise speaking, but they did not give practice in real communication. They were replaced by small-group and partner work, which maximized learners' opportunities to practise communication with others. What is more, learners were not just "learning to communicate", but rather, "communicating to learn" (Howatt & Smith 2014: 91), for it seemed that it was precisely such successful communicative experiences that helped promote acquisition. As Terrell et al. explained to their prospective students, "The interesting thing about acquisition is that it seems to take place best when you listen to a speaker and understand what is said". This view gave added justification to the ideal – rediscovered from the Reform Movement – of using the target language in the classroom: "That is why your instructor will always speak German to you" (Terrell et al. 1992: xxiii). Task-based learning activities – such as information gap tasks – were designed to promote communication, since they required careful listening and negotiating of information, especially if pair-work partners were each provided with only part of the necessary information to complete the task, so that they had a genuine problem to resolve.

4.8.1 The four communicative skills

Hand in hand with the view formulated in the 1960s that the goal of language teaching was communication, came the tendency to conceptualize communication as consisting of four skills. An awareness of different language skills is anything but new. Already in the first century CE, Quintilian seemed to view teaching as requiring "the interrelation of four activities: reading, writing, speaking, and listening. No one was more important than the others", although he was in fact less explicit about the importance of listening (Murphy 2000: 485, referring to *Institutio Oratoria*, preface to Book I, para. 27, and Book 10 10.1.1). More recently, Claude Marcel, in one of the most thoughtful nineteenth-century theoretical reflections on language teaching in the British Isles, distinguished between spoken and written language, and *impression* (receptive skills), which precedes *expression* (production), thus explicitly identifying four branches of language study (Howatt 1984: 153; Marcel 1853: I, 335). But it was only in the 1960s that teaching that catered to all four skills – and distinguished receptive and productive skills – became an orthodoxy. The 1962 Annan Report on the teaching of Russian wrote, "The student should hear, speak, read, write – in that order – in mastering new work. For recognition must come before active use, and hearing a modern language is the surest foundation for successful study of the language" (Annan 1962: 38). The German textbook *Sprich Mal Deutsch* (Rowlinson 1967) – whose title *Speak German*, or, with the colloquial particle *mal*, perhaps *Go, on, speak German!* was programmatic – is an early example of a textbook that presents the task of language teaching as developing four, implicitly equally weighted "skills":

> This three-book course aims to teach the skills of understanding, speaking, reading and writing German, in that order, to twelve- to fourteen-year-old beginners. [. . .] The course aims above all to be lively and stimulating, encouraging the pupil's interest in Germany and at the same time teaching him to understand and communicate in German.
>
> (Rowlinson 1967: 5)

Explicit grammatical knowledge, while covered in explanations that "have purposely been kept as simple and non-technical as possible", was not one of the stated goals of the textbook at all.

As we shall see in Chapter 5, the view of language teaching as teaching four skills has determined the assessment patterns of the last half century in Britain. Other language-related skills, such as translation, commentary, and the ability to describe the grammar of the language, once prominent in examinations, have largely disappeared.

4.9 The old alongside the new

The chronological overview given in this chapter has been a simplification, for older practices persist alongside new methods, approaches and techniques. To illustrate this, I shall examine two language learning textbooks in the same series, *Teach Yourself*, one for German and one Chinese, published within a decade of each other, but many decades apart in their approach and between them pointing both back hundreds of years, and forward into the 1990s. The author of *Teach Yourself German* (1938), Sydney Wells, had already produced texts of French, German, Italian and even a phrasebook of Dutch. With publications including School Certificate Test Papers in German (Wells 1938) he was clearly part of establishment, mainstream school language teaching. Wells observed in his preface that

> it used to be quite common [...] for a well-educated man to turn out a creditable essay in French or German on the fossil iguanadon, yet to be distressingly inarticulate when called upon to order a second-class railway ticket or a dinner [...] Most of the difficulties of forty years ago were due to an undue importance given to grammar and Classical subject-matter: the teaching did not help the practical man who wanted to travel.
>
> (Wells 1938: vii)

Wells accordingly drew on recent innovations in language pedagogy intended to address these shortcomings. He used phonetic script and sought to explain the pronunciation of the sounds precisely, with illustrations of the position of the lips for the vowels (Wells 1938: 18). In other ways, however, Wells was still heavily indebted to the "grammar and translation" teaching methods of nineteenth and early twentieth-century schools. The title of every one of his lessons presents explicit grammar as the main point of instruction – e.g. "The simple sentence", "Order of words". A typical lesson in the book begins with an explanation in English about the grammar point to be studied, followed by a list of new vocabulary, then exercises to "Read and then turn into English", and finally exercises for translation into German. Despite the apparent focus on "the practical man who wanted to travel", the sentences for translation are drills constructed around the grammar point, with dubious real-world applicability – for example, "Are the gardens long and beautiful? They are beautiful, but not long. Is the tailor always honest? Yes, he is always honest" (Wells 1938: 33).

By contrast with Wells, Wilkinson, having come to the Chinese language as a missionary, adopts neither the traditional school grammar-translation approach, nor newer developments in teaching pronunciation. Though published nearly a decade after Wells's book, Williamson's *Teach Yourself Chinese* contains dialogues with parallel translation that perpetuate a model going back hundreds of years. Many of the dialogue topics are even highly similar to those in seventeenth- and eighteenth-century European manuals. For example, a seventeenth-century manual of German for English speakers also has, like Williamson, dialogues on modes of transport, on buying cloth, consulting a tailor, at the shoemaker's, dealing with laundry, a consultation with a doctor, and discussion of food (Offelen 1687). Williamson urged his readers, "The main purpose [. . .] should be to memorise the dialogues, sentence by sentence, phrase by phrase. If that is done the rules of grammar will be unconsciously acquired" (Williamson 1947: 4–5). His emphasis is on speaking rather than on drilling grammar; while there are brief "Grammar notes" (pp. 425–436), there are no exercises of any kind. One might consider this an early version of a "communicative" approach, except for Williamson's insistence on memorizing the dialogues word for word. In fact, his advice coincides with that given to learners contained in a typical early eighteenth-century language manual, "First learn the vocabulary. Then the short familiar phrases. Afterwards the proverbs and familiar dialogues" (Beiler 1731: 287). Williamson's manual was reprinted in 1979, so that until Scurfield's new edition in 1991 (Scurfield 1991), *Teach Yourself Chinese* offered learners a method that owed much to centuries-old traditions of practical hands-on language learning, and nothing at all to twentieth-century language pedagogy, at least judged by European norms.

4.10 Cultural knowledge

This chapter has so far been concerned with the teaching of language. I conclude with a very brief history of teaching (about) culture – for more detailed histories of teaching culture in foreign language learning, see Risager (2007) and, for a history illustrated with numerous examples from twentieth-century textbooks of German for English learners, McLelland (2015a, Chapter 6), as well as Wegner's illuminating comparative study of how German culture was represented to French and English learners in the twentieth century (Wegner 2017, based on her 1999 study). Wegner shows that, beyond certain similarities between England and France, in part "teaching and learning have been determined by national rather than common European concerns" and "reflect the differences in political and ideological standpoints", as well as in pedagogical approach (Wegner 2017: forthcoming). For example, in France, "the aim of developing a *culture générale* was closely connected to literary studies", presenting the German *patrimoine national*, but also giving a "(pseudo)historical" portrayal of the German national character as a traditional enemy. By contrast, Wegner finds German language teaching in England was "more focussed on communicative skills", and "based on an orientation towards individual needs, the country's economic interests, and overcoming *insularity*" (Wegner 2017: forthcoming).

Most teachers are aware of their methods and goals when teaching language, but the passing on of cultural knowledge is often less explicit and less conscious. For many centuries, language learners acquired cultural knowledge more or less "by the by". The dialogues that were typical of nearly all manuals up to about 1800 often implicitly gave rules of thumb about acceptable behaviour – how to pay a call in another country and make polite conversation, or how to negotiate a purchase or a sale, for example (McLelland 2017b). Manuals might also contain more or less detailed practical information about travel and life in the foreign country. For example, Offelen's English-German *Double Grammar* (1687) provided information about English habits of smoking, and drinking tea, coffee and chocolate, and popular pastimes ("There's Tennis, Bowling, Billiards, Ninepins, Tables, Cards, and Dice", Offelen 1687: 216), as well as about sights worth a tourist's visit. From the eighteenth century onwards, anthologies, "set books" for examinations, and selections of material for translation also gave an insight into the culture of a language, especially its "high" culture.[25] However, it was not until the later nineteenth century that reform-minded teachers began to think more explicitly about teaching cultural information. Recognizing that few school pupils would have direct experience of the country whose language they were learning, teachers sought to bring the everyday culture into the classroom, using *realia*, defined as "illustrative facts and studies, comprising a study of foreign life and thought, customs and institutions at different periods, to be partly acquired by personal examination" (Breul, cited by Mary Brebner 1898: 34). That is, teaching *realia* meant teaching facts about the culture (its basic geography and history, for example), but also encouraging inspection of *real objects* from everyday culture, where possible – coins were a popular prop for teaching, as Brebner reported from her visit to German schools in the 1890s (see McLelland 2015a: 114–115).

Teaching of culture took another turn in the 1930s. The originally German *Kulturkunde* movement (lit. "knowledge of culture", hence loosely, "cultural studies") was in part a reaction to the shortcomings perceived in the *realia* approach, in particular the danger of imparting only very superficial and fragmentary cultural knowledge; one must seek instead to understand the underlying essence of a people, their national culture and character. While earnestly meant, this could lead to sweeping generalizations about "the Germans", "the French" and the like. For example, Bithell (1932: 17) attributed "unmitigated honesty" to all Germans – less positive stereotypes were of course equally possible. World War II and the Holocaust, justified by Nazi doctrine claiming the superior characteristics of all Aryan Germans and the supposed inferiority of all Jews, swiftly discredited this approach, however.

Since World War II, British textbooks have typically concentrated on creating sympathetic encounters with the foreign culture, looking at the everyday life of young people like the learners themselves, for example following the experiences of an exchange student in the country (e.g. *John erlebt Deutschland* "John experiences Germany", the title of a 1955 textbook, for example), or with chapters following the lives of the members of a family, as they attend school, pursue their hobbies, celebrate major festivals, and so on. Topics at A-level tended to emphasize concerns shared by learners' own culture and the culture of the language, rather than focussing on culturally specific features that

Kulturkunde had sought to identify. For example, the 1988 German A-level textbook *Neue Perspektiven* "New Perspectives" explored topics including relationships, work, inter-generational tensions, advertising and consumers, the media, and the environment (Della Gana 1988). Significantly, there was also a chapter specifically devoted to *Vorurteile* "prejudices" against foreigners. Similarly, Sidwell and Capoore's 1983 textbook for younger pupils, *Deutsch Heute* "German Today" included "Discussing stereotypes" as a communicative goal in one of its chapters. The National Curriculum (1991, revised 2004: 21) presented as good practice "learning environments in which [. . .] stereotypical views are challenged and pupils learn to appreciate and view positively differences in others".

By the 1990s, *cultural awareness* – a knowledge and acceptance of similarities and differences between one's own culture and that of the language being learned – was sufficiently important that it became an explicit part of the Programme of Study of the 1992 National Curriculum. Pupils should "consider and discuss the similarities and differences between their own culture and those of the countries and communities where the target language is spoken", and "identify with [. . .] the perspectives of people in these countries and communities" (e.g. in role play or creative writing; National Curriculum 1992). Over the course of the twentieth century, then, the ultimate goal had changed from that of teaching culture-specific *information*, to developing a transferable *skill* of intercultural competence, the ability to relate to and mediate in communication with strangers and foreigners (Byram 1997; Guilherme 2012), a goal which, in its very openness, nevertheless reflects a particular world-view.

Another marked change in the history of teaching culture is the representation of women and their place in society. McLelland (2015a: 322–333) illustrates a shift throughout the twentieth century teaching of German from gender stereotyping to conscious inclusion of girls and women in non-traditional roles (and see 3.2.2). We should bear in mind, however, that such cultural representations are still neither neutral nor necessarily realistic – they may reflect modern British ideologies, but not necessarily social norms, either of British or the culture of the language being taught. Teaching culture is never neutral.

4.11 Conclusion

It has been suggested that the history of foreign language teaching is one of "change without progress" (Van Els et al. 1984, cited by Loonen 1991: 272), as a pendulum swing from one extreme to the other, from teaching grammar explicitly and analytically, to relying on sheer exposure to the language for success. In time with the swings of that pendulum go related tendencies – towards more or less use of the first language in the classroom, towards more or less emphasis on authentic language, for example. We have seen that there is some truth in this. In particular, the turn to communicative language teaching of the last half-century or so is not, as it is sometimes portrayed, the first moment of enlightenment, emerging from the darkness of grammar and translation. Rather, it is in some ways merely a return to how things were before. After all, it was not until the seventeenth century that foreign language learners even had the option to learn grammar explicitly, for it was only in the late sixteenth century that the vernacular languages began to be paid the same analytical attention that had been devoted to Latin for centuries. Not until the late eighteenth century did exercises become readily available to help learners apply their grammatical knowledge systematically. The nineteenth-century focus on explicit grammar in schools can, then, in part be read as an enthusiastic embracing of new techniques that promised to make language learning easier. The twentieth century was perhaps no more than a correction to that overenthusiastic embrace.

It is important to remember, however, that once studying grammar became a possibility, to do so became a marker of prestige: for teachers, for pupils, and for the very subject. For Chambaud, teaching French in London, knowledge of grammar was a way to differentiate well-taught pupils from those who "picked up" a language from less expert teachers. In the same way, in nineteenth-century schools, where teachers had to establish the credentials of languages as worthy subjects, grammatical analysis, together with translation, placed the demands of foreign languages on a level with Latin and Greek, all helping to meet the wider educational goal of developing pupils' mental rigour. This differentiated these subjects from the less prestigious teaching of language with the primary goal of communication, that continued throughout the century – in girls' education, in private colleges – and limited the impact of a whole parade of individual teaching innovators. Even if, in line with changing theories of language learning, the more recent focus has been on successful, rather than on formally perfect, communication, we must remember that mastery of the standard language carries prestige in most cultures, and deviations from it are stigmatized. So accuracy in foreign language learning does matter, but we have changed our expectations of how our pupils can arrive at it, and we have learnt to differentiate different skills in which different levels of accuracy may be achievable – between speaking and writing, for example.

In the twentieth century, initial optimism that new scientific techniques would quickly and reliably yield learners who could produce the grammatical structures of the language with perfect fluency was disappointed. The unconscious automaticity that generations of teachers sought remained elusive. But even if the new second language acquisition researchers were proved wrong in some of their initial assumptions, they showed that learning a foreign language is not the same as learning one's first, and founded a whole field of empirical research which continues to inform and underpin developments in language teaching. This is a step change and the major contribution of the twentieth century to the history of language teaching. A further source of real change in language teaching is technological innovation. Disruptive at the time, prompting false starts and creating anxieties – as we saw in Newmark's dystopian predictions in the 1960s – they have in general settled down to offer improved and richer opportunities to learn, from paper, to pictures, to PCs.

As the example of new technologies shows, much change in language teaching is driven by factors that have, in themselves, nothing to do with theories of how languages are best learned: technological, but also cultural and social, political and educational change. We considered the role of social factors on language teaching in the previous chapter. In the next chapter, we turn to assessment, for every teacher knows the power of that carrot and/or stick over what they do – as we noted already in the case of nineteenth-century grammar and translation testing. Finally, in Chapter 6, we turn to the impact of educational and other policy and advocacy on language teaching.

Notes

1 The name comes from Greek *hermeneuma*, plural – *ata*, meaning "interpretation, explanation, making comprehensible".
2 This translation procedure has ghosted through the history of language learning ever since – for example, see De Gasperin (2017) on Baretti's use of literal translation to teach Italian in the seventeenth century and Howatt and Smith (2014: 81) for Hamilton's interlinear translation system (Hamilton 1829); by contrast, contrast Fenwick de Porquet (1830), who believed in instant translation into the target language.
3 In particular, his learners aspired to become *unterkäuffel*, officials whose job it was both to assist German merchants in Venice, and to monitor their trade, to ensure they paid customs duties, etc. See Glück and Morcinek (2006: 1).
4 This method of beginning with materials suitable for young native-speaker learners has echoes down the centuries: an early twentieth-century *Chinese Made Easy* manual still used it for teaching Chinese (in this case Cantonese) to English-speaking readers. See McLelland (2015b), esp. the Figure on p. 93.
5 For the various editions of the vocabulary part of Berlaimont, see Niederehe (1994: 441–442, and 1999: 445–446), Peeters-Fontainas (1965: 166–187), Lindemann (1994: 604–606, 615–619) and Pablo Núñez (2010, vol. 2, 202–311); see also Viémon (2017) on the dissemination of the pronunciation guide, and on the dialogues, see Villoria and Suso Lopez (2017). For the *Introito e porta*, see Hüllen (1999: 331–346).
6 For other languages, the tradition begins much later: the first grammar of Russian appeared only in 1696, Ludolf's *Grammatica russica*.
7 They were originally French-Latin, translated by Ölinger into German, presumably a version of the dialogues for schoolboys, *Linguae Latinae Exercitatio* (1538) of the Spaniard Juan Luis Vivès (1492–1540); see Caravolas (1994: 267–284).
8 I take "construing" here to be synonymous with parsing, which Chambaud defines as follows: "Parse, that is, account for the construction of every word of his lesson, and show how each governs or is governed by another in the sentence" (Chambaud 1765: xiii).
9 On Meidinger, see Kuiper (1961: 73–118).
10 Wanostrocht had come to England in the 1770s to teach the children of Henry Bathurst, second Earl Bathurst, at Cirencester Park. He later founded a school known as the Alfred House Academy in Camberwell, a location, according to the prospectus, "very convenient on account of the coaches going to and from London every hour". He wrote a number of textbooks on French language, grammar, and syntax, mostly for children's use. With his wife, Sarah (*d.* 1820), he compiled *Le livre des enfans* (4th edn, 1808). The school itself was ahead of its time in

encouraging the teaching of French rather than the classics and in its civilized approach to both discipline and leisure (Secombe 2004).
11 Wendeborn's first exercise for translation into German was similarly demanding – see McLelland (2015a: 70). Another example of the practical grammar with exercises to learn German was William Render's *Concise practical grammar of the German tongue* (1799) (see McLelland 2015: 71).
12 This section is an abridged and slightly reworked version of McLelland (2015a: 84–96).
13 Eve lamented in the preface to his German *Grammar for Schools*, "I have not been able to meet with any book by a non-German which does for German what Holder, Plötz, Bernhard Schmitz & c. do for French." (Eve 1880: v). Plötz's epitome of history, first published in English in 1883, appears to have been much more widely known in Britain and the USA than his language textbooks, to judge by the many copies held on COPAC and Hathi Trust. It is Plötz whom Kelly (1969: 53, 220) chiefly blames for the poor reputation of the grammar-translation method.
14 A typographical error means that McLelland (2015a: 87) erroneously gives the figure as 40 rather than 30.
15 The Grammar Schools Act first allowed grammar schools funded through endowments to use their fund for purposes other than the teaching of classical languages (Walford 2006: 81).
16 On Prendergast's biography see Lorch (2017). The most detailed discussion of his method is Atherton (2010); see also Howatt (1984: 156–161).
17 Ripman is listed as an UCLES examiner for the years 1898 and 1899.
18 The page is unnumbered. See Ashby and Przedlacka (2017) for some of the more extraordinary devices for studying the sounds of languages in the early twentieth century.
19 The comment was posted under the name Biblins on a Sausage.net Nostalgia forum on August 22, 2005: www.sausagenet.org/nph-YaBB.pl?num=1124735531 (accessed October 2011).
20 Zettersten (1986) offers a thoughtful exploration of the relationship between new technologies and competing views of language learning that variously emphasized fluency or accuracy. On the history of technology in language teaching, see also Willis (2003).
21 Others sought to establish new versions of languages with limited vocabularies which would make them learnable within a matter of weeks. Examples are Ogden's Basic English (see Wheeler 2013: 167–172), Baumann's *Welt-Deutsch* and Schwörer's *Kolonial-Deutsch* (see Mühleisen 2009, discussed briefly in McLelland 2016).
22 On the history of applied linguistics, see Smith (2016).
23 See 6.4 for the history of the Centre of Language Teaching Research.
24 The working group behind this report included Eric Hawkins (cf. Hawkins 1987, Hawkins 1996).
25 See Klippel (1994: 95) on such anthologies for German learners of English; for German literature presented to English learners, see Guthke (2011, reworked as Guthke 2015).

5 Assessment

5.1 Introduction

Since the first external examinations were established in England in the 1850s, teachers have, to a greater or lesser extent, been teaching to the test – the so-called washback effect (Weir 2013: xvii; noted as early as Brereton et al. 1908: 67–68). This chapter is about who has done the testing, what they have been testing, and to what end. It is not a technical history of the instruments of testing, but in intended to "contextualize the practice of language testing as a socially constructed and interpreted phenomenon" (Taylor 2009: 29, cited by Weir 2013: 1). As Weir (2013: 2) noted, a history of language assessment in the UK is still lacking – Weir's own volume (with contributions from Vidaković and Galaczi) is an important step in this direction, but its 600 pages discuss only the history of English language testing, carried out by just one assessment body, Cambridge University's testing arm (now known as Cambridge Assessment), 1913–2012. So it would be a vast undertaking to give a full history of multiple modern languages across several testing bodies (some with more than one syllabus for the same qualification), at multiple levels and sometimes two tiers (e.g. the less demanding Certificate of Secondary Education (CSE) alongside the GCE, Foundation and Higher tiers at GCSE, and Scholarship or Special papers alongside A-levels). This chapter merely offers a thematic overview of foreign language assessment in Britain (in effect, in England) since the 1850s. A focus on the examinations at age 18 might have been valuable for international comparisions,[1] but I concentrate largely on the under-16 examinations because relatively few pupils continue to an A-level language. It may help readers to know that in England the original Junior and Senior examinations for under 16s and under 18s were succeeded by the School Certificate and Higher School Certificate in 1918; these were in turn replaced by a General Certificate of Education Ordinary Level (O-level) and Advanced Level (A-level) in 1951; in 1965, the less academic CSE was introduced for those not catered for by O-levels. A-levels still remain, but CSE and O-levels were replaced in 1988 by the GCSE, with two tiers, a Foundation tier and a Higher tier.

I begin by considering who tests, and why – who were the testing bodies, for whom were the results intended, and by whom were they used? Sections 5.2 to

5.4 consider what has been tested, beginning in 5.2 with the earliest test forms (translation in and out of the language, grammar questions, and dictation), then turning to the four skills (5.3) and, finally, non-language knowledge and skills (such as the ability to write in English on literary or other cultural topics (5.4). 5.5 deals with changes in assessment criteria, especially the development of attainment targets across a full range of achievement, as seen in the Graded Objectives movement in Britain, and in the Common European Framework of Reference. Since seeing an examination is better than thousands of words of description, 5.7 presents a selection of modern foreign language examinations in England since 1858 (just as Weir (2013) has done for English).The papers are available online at www.routledge.com/9781138651289.

5.1.1 Who tests, how and for whom?

The history of public examinations begins in the 1850s. The College of Preceptors (since 1998 the College of Teachers) was established by Royal Charter in 1849; it was one of the first bodies to provide formal examinations for pupils, from 1851 (as well as for teachers, from 1846). Oxford and Cambridge universities both set up their examination boards for school pupils in 1857–1858, with examinations offered at two levels, for those under the age of 16 (Junior), and for those under 18 (Senior) (see Roach 1971; Raban 2008; Watts 2008). French and German were included from the outset as optional subjects. Other school examination boards followed. At the same time, competitive examinations for admission to certain professions emerged. In 1849 an examination was introduced which required a knowledge of a language (alongside other subjects) before purchasing a commission as an officer in the British Army, although it was apparently "not a severe test" (Roach 1971: 24). These examinations were taken over by the Council of Military Education in 1858 and then the director general of Military Education from 1870 to the turn of the nineteenth century.[2] Woolwich Military Academy had introduced tests for admission in 1855 which included French and German, and examinations in French and German could be taken by candidates for admission to Sandhurst from at least 1859. Today, the armed forces continue to test and accredit language skills of its members, both identifying heritage speakers and training learners, currently at its Defence Centre for Language and Culture at Shrivenham, the site of the Defence Academy of the UK, using a testing system known as STANAG 6001, a set of language proficiency levels agreed by NATO members through the NATO Standardization Agency.

The Indian Civil Service introduced examinations for appointments in 1853, and the Civil Service Commission, in limited form, from 1855 (Roach 1971: 24, 201–203). Individual departments had their own requirements, but, for example, the Treasury required a translation chosen among Latin, French, German and Italian (Roach 1971: 202). Under the combined scheme operated by the Commission from 1858, French, German or Italian (more precisely "the language, literature and history" of France, Germany and Italy), as well as Sanskrit or Arabic language and literature, were each only worth half the marks (375) of either Latin or Greek alone (750), while English and mathematics were awarded 1,500 and 1,000 marks, respectively, and sciences and philosophy each 500 (Roach 1971: 196). Even the best candidates were not expected to get more than half the notionally available 6,875 marks overall, so examinations could afford to be quite stiff, something we should bear in mind when looking at papers from this era – candidates would not need to satisfy the examiners in all elements. From 1870, the Civil Service Commission took on the administration of both the Woolwich and Sandhurst military academies' entrance examinations, in which French and German were among the eleven subjects available, from which candidates could choose at most four.[3]

In examinations for adults not tied to particular professions, the Society of Arts (from 1907 known as the Royal Society of Arts) set up examinations to cater to the Mechanics' Institutes that had spread around the country since the 1820s to provide practical education for working men.[4] The Society's examinations were first instituted in 1856, and continued until its Examinations Board became a separate company in 1987, was sold in 1997, and merged with the Oxford and Cambridge Examinations Boards to form OCR; the RSA's own last papers were set in 1994. The Society first examined 62 candidates in 1856, including eleven certificates awarded for French and four for German (Roach 1971: 62). Prizes of ten guineas were awarded in each subject to the best candidate, both of whom had attended Crosby Hall Evening Classes (Examination Papers of the Society of Arts: 1856–1870 PR.ED/100/17/1). The first examiners were Professors of French and German at King's College London, Adolphus Bernays and A. Marriette.[5] By the 1870s, papers in Commercial Correspondence for French and German had emerged, initially alongside the standard papers in French, German, Spanish and Italian, but – by the 1880s – all the papers were under the heading of Commercial Knowledge. A choice between Commercial and Literary papers (or sections within the same paper) returned in the 1930s (see RSA 1933).[6] The London Chamber of Commerce, set up in 1881, apparently also offered examinations.[7] The Institute of Linguists, founded in 1910, had, as one of its aims, to provide examinations which would "test a practical knowledge of the spoken languages: the ability of the candidate to read at sight and understand the language offered, whether written or spoken, and to express himself or herself both orally and in writing" (Smith et al. 2010: 11, citing the 1936 recollections of the Institute's founder, W. Lacon Threlford). Literary knowledge was not to be tested. The examinations were set and marked by the University of London,[8] and in the first year, ten out of 21 candidates who sat papers in French and German passed, but the examinations do not seem to have been run again after 1911 until the Institute was revived in the 1920s. The Institute of Linguists' Preliminary Certificate examinations, established in 1969, are noteworthy because they offered a qualification not only for the most common but also for less widely taught languages, "thus providing a qualification in community languages that was often not available from any other source" (Smith et al. 2010: 54).[9] Finally, it should be noted that many individual countries run examinations for their own languages: Germany offers its Goethe-Zertifikat at various levels, China its HSK

Chinese Proficiency Test, etc. The Association of Language Testers in Europe brings together these national testing bodies in Europe.

Returning to our main focus, school examinations, other universities joined Oxford and Cambridge in setting up their own school examination boards; Durham did so already in 1858, although its records from this early period do not survive. The University of London followed somewhat later, in 1902 (although it set Matriculation examinations earlier than this). In 1903, the universities of Manchester, Leeds and Liverpool (later joined by Birmingham and Sheffield) combined to establish the Joint Matriculation Board (JMB). The AEB (Allied Examination Board) was founded in 1953. In 1970, CILT (1970: 6) listed nine boards examining the GCE (General Certificate of Education, O-level and A-level), and a further 15 regional boards examining the CSE. Various mergers and changes over time have left three examination boards in England: Edexcel (the result of the University of London's mergers with other boards, and now run by Pearson Education), AQA (run as an educational charity, the result of the Manchester-Leeds-Liverpool JMB merging with other boards, including the vocational City & Guilds board) and OCR (i.e. Oxford, Cambridge and RSA Examinations, still owned and run by the University of Cambridge through its Cambridge Assessment division). This means that school examinations in England are variously run by a company, a charity and a university.[10] In addition to these three boards, there are Welsh and Northern Irish boards (not technically restricted to their own regions, but in practice largely so) and Cambridge International Examinations, originally intended for students at international schools but now also taken by pupils in British schools too. In the International Baccalaureate, begun in Switzerland as a school-leaving qualification for pupils in international schools, a foreign language is compulsory – it is increasingly available in British independent schools and even some state schools and sixth-form colleges.

In sum, then, the history of language examinations in schools and elsewhere is multi-faceted and complex, and a comprehensive overview, either longitudinally, or even in cross-section at one point in time across all examination types, is not possible here. After all, the comparison of 16+ examinations by Moys et al. (1980), which considers five languages at just one examination point, runs to nearly 300 pages. The development of language testing methodologies is also a large and complex field – for useful overviews, see Brunfaut and Clapham (2012) and Council of Europe (2001) and Weir (2013), with its very comprehensive bibliography. The history of assessment presented here remains largely non-technical; the nuts and bolts of detailed marking schemes are not discussed.[11]

5.1.2 Validity, reliability and comparability

Weir (2013: 4, 10) outlines three kinds of validity – i.e. the extent to which an assessment measures what it is believed to measure:

1   Cognitive validity – are the cognitive processes required to complete the test sufficiently similar to and representative of those required in real-life behaviour?

2   Context validity – is the task an "adequate and comprehensive representation" of what would be encountered in a real-life context?
3   Scoring validity – are the criteria used for evaluation appropriate, and are they calibrated to the level of proficiency of the learner being evaluated? Scoring validity includes *reliability* – i.e. the extent to which the results can be relied upon, whether as a measure of *achievement*, of the work done, or as a *prognostic*, a predictor for future performance. For example, are the results comparable for similar candidates in examinations at the same level set in different years, or by different examination boards or for different languages? What about rater reliability (i.e. do markers evaluating comparable work give comparable scores?)

For the first century or so of language examinations, relatively little thought was given to the design of examinations and whether they measured reliably what they were thought to measure. Marking criteria and the weighting of elements in an examination were opaque, and difficult to trace today. Sandhurst Military Academy published a relatively transparent marking scheme for its examinations in French: out of a total of 1,200 possible marks, the dictation was worth 100; the grammatical questions were worth 200, translation from French 500, and the remaining 500 were allotted to translation into French and free writing ([Sandhurst] 1859: 19). However, the school boards do not seem to have offered the same level of transparency until much later. For example, we read statements like "without a fair knowledge of Accidence, a Candidate cannot pass" (University of Cambridge Local Examinations Syndicate [UCLES] 1885 regulations, p. 3); "In order to obtain the mark of distinction students will be expected to do fairly well in this part of the paper" [i.e. translation into English]; "A student can not obtain the mark of distinction without satisfying the Examiners in this part of the paper" [i.e. translation into the language]. In 1912, things were unchanged: the UCLES Senior regulations of 1912 specified,

> In order to pass in French or German candidates must reach a certain standard in the subject as a whole. They may be rejected for weakness in any one of the three parts of the paper. In order to gain the mark of distinction they must reach a higher standard in the subject as a whole, and must also reach a certain standard in 2. and 3. [i.e. translation out of and into the language].

However, the "certain standard" and "weakness" remained undefined.

For many decades, the examiners' most immediate concern seems to have been a particular kind of "consequential validity" (Weir 2013: 10), that is, the question of to what use the test results will be put in society. Initially public examinations were seen as "an excellent testimony to [candidates'] general ability" (Roach 1971: 57). As long as the examination discriminated overall between the very able and the less able, that was sufficient. Providing detailed information about candidates' achievement in particular aspects of linguistic competence in the candidates assessed was unimportant. This is the reason why, for decades, language examinations typically required a translation (and, later, dictation), composite tests which assessed the ability to combine everything learnt – vocabulary, grammar, sensitivity to style – in new contexts. As we shall see, the history of language testing throughout the twentieth century is the story of the move away from this, towards differentiation of skills to be assessed explicitly and individually. The assessment of the four skills separately is taken to its logical conclusion in NATO's STANAG language rating scheme for military personnel, which provides separate scores for each of listening, speaking, reading and writing, from Level 0 ("no proficiency") and Level 1 ("survival") to Level 4 ("Expert") and Level 5 ("Highly articulate native"). For example, a score of 3321 can be read at a glance as level 3 in listening, level 3 in speaking, level 2 in reading and level 1 in writing. Although other testing agencies likewise assess the skills separately, they do not customarily report them quite so transparently.

From 1919 onwards, there were some efforts to ensure comparability across boards and subjects. Since 1919 the Secondary Schools Examinations Council and its successor the Schools Council oversaw the work of examining boards. Their subject committees had access to syllabuses, question papers, mark schemes and scripts; detailed comparative statistics were are prepared annually with an eye to highlighting anomalies and discrepancies that might need further investigation (Otter 1970: 48). By the 1950s, the Incorporated Association of Assistant Masters was beginning to reflect on quirks of examination design that could affect validity (IAAM 1952: 292–295; see Whitehead 1996: 199). The AQA archive contains *O-level Latin, French and Biology. An enquiry conducted by the University of London School Examinations Council and the Joint Matriculation Board into examination standards*, where French was reviewed after a drop in the JMB number of passes in the early 1960s. Two examiners from each board were asked to evaluate work produced by candidates from other boards; it was tentatively concluded that JMB might have set a slightly harsher standard, though, since oral work could not be included in the cross-checking, it was hard to be sure.

At the time, Otter (1970: 48) observed "a general opinion, supported by research, that the problems of reliability in the marking of language papers are smaller than those of other subjects". In recent years, however, there has been a wider perception of both unreliable marking (especially in oral examinations) and of severe grading of modern foreign languages at GCSE and A-level, in particular at the boundary between the very best A* and A grade pupils, and when compared to other subjects with a similarly high academic entry profile (see, for example, QCA 2008: paragraphs 11–15), although the problem has persisted beyond the date of that 2008 report.

The twentieth century is also the history of increasing weight given to cognitive validity and context validity. Of course, cognitive validity – whether assessments are similar to and representative of those required in real life – depends on how "real life" is understood. If "real life" is seen as a post requiring general intelligence and knowledge that one might expect of some (idealized) well-educated person, then a language examination that does no more than contribute to an overall assessment of general ability is fine. For many years, this was the case, at least as far as school examinations were concerned. By contrast, we have already noted examinations in commercial correspondence set by the RSA from the 1870s onwards. Increasingly, however, both cognitive validity and context validity have been judged according to what people might actually need to do with the language – by 1980 Moys et al. (1980) were scathing of translation tests that bore no resemblance to the kind of text a non-native speaker was likely to need to translate in real life. Similarly, the National Foundation for Educational Research, when designing its battery of tests for 13-year-olds in French, German and Spanish as a first foreign language over the years 1983–1985 in England Wales and Northern Ireland, intended to provide a "national picture of performance" across "the whole range of ability", took as a guiding principle that "test content should relate to real-life language activities", "relevant to the pupils' experience" (Dickson 1986: 1, 5). In oral examinations, the transactor role (see 5.3.2) introduced in 1990s examinations is another example of a test intended to mimic real-life situations of language learners interacting with native speakers.

5.2 Test constructs, or what to measure

For much of the history of language examinations,

> we have no direct evidence as to what test developers thought the underlying language construct(s) they intended to measure were. In the first half of our history [i.e. up to the 1960s] there is little documentary evidence available on the underlying basis for test construction, no suggestion of systematic post hoc analysis of test outcomes, nor any evident concern with the use made of test results in society.
>
> (Weir 2013: 4–5)

Although *explicitly* defining these "test constructs" – abilities or capacities of learners that can be measured – began only in the 1980s (Weir 2013: 5), in sections 5.3 and 5.4, I consider what examinations were intended to measure, both in terms of what end users wanted from them, and how they related to the curriculum and syllabus. For practical reasons, I restrict discussion largely to school examinations. Occasional comparisons with other examinations in other settings are also instructive, however, such as the greater emphasis on spoken skills in the examinations set by the Institute of Linguists (see Table 5.1 for a comparative overview of testing regimes in some school and non-school examinations in 1970), or the requirement for free writing in Sandhurst examinations much earlier than in the UCLES examinations. The discussion is based on consultation of the Cambridge Assessment archives (formerly UCLES, with holdings both in Cambridge University Library and in Cambridge Assessment) and the archives of AQA (formerly JMB), as well as those of the Royal Society of Arts and published sources.[12] I discuss the test constructs in the approximate chronological order in which they emerged. While the "four skills" make up current language testing orthodoxy, the IAAM's discussion of test-types in 1952 – published just after the new O-level and A-level examinations had been introduced – is an important historical document, weighing up the competing advantages of the "modern" kinds of tests "which encourage the pupil to use the foreign language without translation" against the

Table 5.1 An overview of test requirements in some non-school and school examinations in 1970, adapted from Adam (1970: 36), with the addition of information from Page and Shortt (1970) on the O-level and A-level boards[14]

	Institute of Linguists					London Chamber of Commerce						Royal Society of Arts					O-level (JMB only)		A-level				
						Single subject			Languages for industry and commerce			Single subject			Bilingual secretarial								
	Prelim.	I	II	Int.	Final	Elem.	Int.	Adv.	Elem.	Int.	Adv.	Elem.	Int.	Adv.	Cert.	Dip.	traditional	alternative	AEB	Cambridge	JMB	London	Oxford
Oral																							
Summarize in French a speech in French			x																				
Summarize in English a text in French				x											x								
Read a French text aloud	x	x					x	x		x	x	x	x	x			x	x	x	x	x	x	x
Translate at sight a text into French			x							x	x												
Converse with one person	x	x	x		x		x	x	x	x	x	x	x		x	x	x	x	x	x	x	x	x
Converse in Fr. in a practical situation	x								x	x		x			x								
Prepared speech in Fr.		x	x		x			x			x					x	x						
Unprepared speech in French	x								x														
Dictation	x	x				x	x				x						x			x	x	x	x

Table 5.2 Relative weightings of test components at O-level/GCSE 16 (IAAM, JMB and AEB data from Whitehead (1996: 200)

	UCLES (first alternative)[15]	IAAM recommendation (1952)	JMB 1965	AEB 1965	First GCSEs set (1988)
Prose translation (into the language)	One passages	20%	20%	*Not set*	*Not set*
Translation out of the language (called "version" by IAAM)	Two passages	20%	30%	30%	*Not set*
Composition	One (outline story for expansion)	13%	17%	17.5%	25%
Reading comprehension	One passage	10%	8%	20%	25%
Dictation	(optional as part of oral examination)	17%	8%	7.5%	*Not set*
Reading aloud	(optional as part of oral examination)	10%	3%	Included in oral examination	*Not set*
Oral examination	(optional, achievement recorded separately)	10%	7%	25%	25%
Aural comprehension	–	–	7%	*Not set*	25%
		100%	100%	100%	100%

"traditional" tests of translation and dictation, as well as grammatical questions (IAAM 1952: 288–343, citation p. 307).[13] The changing emphasis in modern language examinations since the 1950s is evident from Table 5.2, which compares the relative weighting of various possible test constructs, from the IAAM's recommendations in 1952, to the first National Curriculum in 1992.

5.2.1 Translation into the target language (often known as "prose composition")

From the very beginnings of examination boards, translation into the target language was considered a reliable test of good all-round ability, and for the IAAM in 1952, it still seemed "indisputable that translation tests, if wisely set, are of validity unsurpassed" (IAAM 1952: 305). For example, the UCLES Senior German paper of December 1858 required pupils to translate a passage from the philosopher John Locke (see Table 5.3). At Junior level (Higher paper), pupils were required to translate more or less disconnected sentences dreamed up by the examiners to test specific grammatical points – the French paper required translation of phrases and sentences including

> give him some; do not give him any [. . .] I am going to speak; I have just spoken; I am to go; I ought to go [. . .] France is the oldest monarchy in Europe; the longer the day, the shorter the night; is it wine you are drinking?
> (UCLES 1858/2008: 42)[16]

However, we must remember that by 1878 the regulations for both Junior and Senior age groups specified that it was not necessary to pass the translation into the target language; only, a distinction could not be obtained without it. In other words, the passage for translation into the language was seen as a discriminator between merely passable and very good candidates – it was not expected to be

Table 5.3 Opening sentences of the passage for translation into German in Senior/Higher/A-level examinations for selected years, 1858–1994, from UCLES/Cambridge Assessment (taken from McLelland 2015a: 176; see discussion there)

1858 Seniors:	"He that would seriously set upon the search of truth ought in the first place to prepare his mind with a love of it: for he that loves it not, will not take much pains to get it, nor be much concerned when he misses it".
1916 Seniors:	"At last the condition of affairs became so intolerable that the German princes assembled to elect a new emperor who would restore the peace of the Empire".
1919 Seniors:[17]	"King William the Third being on a march, for some secret undertaking, was asked by a general to tell him what his purpose was".
1948 Higher School Certificate:	"A few months after my great-grandfather had gone to Germany, the neighbouring farmers began to complain about inexplicable losses of sheep from among the flocks browsing in the quiet meadows".
1967 A-level:	"Mary opened her handbag and made sure that her handkerchief, purse, keys and all the other important things were in it".
1970 A-level:	"Richard and his wife were travelling along the motorway from Frankfurt to Munich".
1987 A-level:	"It was a fine evening in May when the station taxi drove her to the gate of the house".
1994 A-level:	"When we reopened conversation we talked about what we had done since school".[18]

achievable by all, even at a time when these examinations were taken by a small elite of pupils. By 1970, with comprehensivation of education, far more pupils were likely to be able to take a language (generally French). The need to set papers that also discriminated between pupils at the lower ability range grew accordingly, and alternatives to the difficult task of translation into the language were increasingly offered. Page and Shortt noted a wide range of alternatives across the different examination boards at O-level, including free composition, a written comprehension test, and a "much enlarged oral/aural test" (Page & Shortt 1970: 14). Page took the view that at O-level, "the abolition of translation has produced a distinct improvement in the authenticity of written French. Anglicisms still occur, but the habit of thinking it all out in English first is dying" (Page & Shortt 1970: 11). Shortt remained an advocate of prose composition at A-level as "a valid test for the university aspirant", but acknowledged the argument often made that for many learners "it is of doubtful value as a means of learning the foreign language, and preparing for it wastes too much valuable time that could be better spent in building up experience" (Page & Shortt 1970: 18). By 1980, Moys et al. (1980: 253) noted that the prose composition, once "the mainstay of most language examinations", now played a much smaller part. Two English boards, as well as the Northern Irish and Scottish boards, no longer included it at all at O-level; in all the others except the Welsh board, it had become optional. However, "it is still true that the majority of teachers choose to enter their pupils for prose translation and it remains undoubtedly the most demanding task facing the majority of candidates". Moys et al. were unenthusiastic about translation at this level, however: "On the whole, the texts remain the pieces of deathless prose they always were: events of mind-deadening triteness heavily contrived to include the grammatical points the examiners wish to test" (Moys et al. 1980: 252–253). Table 5.3 shows the evolution in the kind of passage set between 1858 and the 1990s in one examination board. Moys et al. noted considerable variations between the boards, both in the inherent level of difficulty, and in the length of text and the time allowed for its translation. For example, they contrasted a "straightforward text of 150 words" to be tackled in 30 minutes (JMB French O-level, 1978) with a "complicated passage of 252 words" to be translated in 66 minutes (O & C Italian O-level, 1978). The Welsh board had the most generous time allowance of all – 53 minutes for a relatively simple passage of only 125 words. For many years, translation into the foreign language – while still used as a test of all-round mastery of the language in some university undergraduate degrees – all but disappeared from school language learning. In the Council of Europe's CEFR, translation rates a single mention in over 250 pages (Council of Europe 2001: 99) – but in 2016, translation of short sentences into the target language returned in the newly revised GCSEs, under the heading of "writing and grammar".

5.2.2 Translation from the target language into English

Translation from the foreign language into English was a basic requirement from the outset, and – unlike translation *into* the language – pupils were required to pass it in order to pass the subject. For example, the UCLES regulations for 1878 specified that

> one or more easy passages not contained in the books named will be set for translation from the language into English, a vocabulary of the less familiar words being given. A student can not pass in the language without satisfying the Examiners in this part of the paper.
> (Cam.c.11.51.20: 3)

In the UCLES examinations, papers contained two passages for translation into English – the first a "seen" passage (i.e. taken from one of the set books that pupils had been studying), the second an "unseen". The seen passage was the easier of the two tasks, but as an examiners' report on the German Juniors examination lamented in 1896,

> The translation by many candidates of a sentence not included in the paper, though occurring in the immediate context of one of the extracts set, shewed [sic] that the preparation of these candidates had been of a bad mechanical type.
> (UCLES December 1896. Report and supplementary tables 1896, p. xxxix)

In other words, candidates regurgitated a memorized translation. Translation into English was not merely a test of basic comprehension, but also of the skill of rendering the sense in idiomatic English. A 1920 examiners' report was critical of "un-English translations" in the Junior French examination, where candidates had apparently been prepared "without being trained to express themselves in idiomatic English" (UCLES 1920 report, Juniors, p, 10. 11). Translation into English continued to be set right up to the 1980s, at both A-level and O-level (where it was required by all boards except in two "alternative" syllabuses; Moys 1980: 253–254) – see, for example, the 1980 Spanish O-level paper given in 5.7. However Moys et al. (1980: 253) queried the value of the translation test, once reading comprehension had become "an assessable and acceptable skill to test at O level and CSE", given that the only point tested by translation and not also tested by these comprehension tests was "how well they can express themselves in English". Most candidates were

> not capable of 'translating' in any real sense of the word. They are occupied only in an exercise which requires them to replace those 'units of meaning' they understand in the foreign language with a more or less adequate version [. . .] Precise translation as a written skill is a demanding skill which it is unrealistic to expect at this stage.
> (Moys et al. 1980: 253)

Moys et al. were, incidentally, also highly critical of the low cognitive validity and low context validity of the texts chosen. The survey by Moys et al. found 17 passages of narrative prose "varying only in degrees of remoteness from the candidates' sense of the world" (Moys et al. 1980: 253). They would have preferred a test based on the kind of material "which might normally require translation in real life" (a letter, recipe, or assembly instructions, for example).

Over the twentieth century, then, translation into English, viewed initially as a straightforward comprehension test – with the advantage, for those who were up to it, of showing understanding of nuance, as well as basic factual understanding – came to be viewed as a skill quite distinct from today's four core skills. This perception has arguably become all the stronger in recent decades with the emergence of the field of Translation Studies, and the development of undergraduate and postgraduate degrees with a named Translation element. However, translation into English has re-appeared in the new GCSEs from 2016, as part of the assessment of reading.

5.2.3 Grammatical knowledge

The only component of the first generation of school language examinations that was not a test of multiple skills simultaneously was that of questions on grammar, which were universal in the first 60 years, until the 1920s. In general, they required pupils to demonstrate explicit metalinguistic knowledge, both of the grammatical forms themselves and of the language used to describe them – for example by declining or conjugating given items from memory, or stating the rules for use of verbs or prepositions, but without the additional challenge of applying the rules to new contexts in free writing. For example, the UCLES Higher tier German paper for Senior (under 18) candidates in December 1858 – the highest level – asked candidates, "What cases are respectively governed by the following verbs: *reuen, ärgern, träumen, pflegen, zahlen, bezahlen, lehren*? and what by the following prepositions: *um, mit, nach, ohne, nebst, zu, in, auf, halben, wegen*?" (UCLES 1858/Cambridge Assessment 2008: 96). The UCLES Lower-tier French paper at Senior level asked questions such as "*ne trouve rien*. When does *rien* not require *ne* before the verb?" or "*dans*. What distinction is made in the use of the prepositions *en* and *dans*?" (UCLES 1858/Cambridge Assessment 2008: 91). At the lowest level, in the Lower-tier Junior (under 16) French paper, the grammatical questions – all based on words contained in the passage for translation – included questions such as: "*eux*: What are the rules for the use of the pronouns *moi, toi, soi, lui, nous, vous, eux*" or "*cette petite troupe fut entourée*. Write this sentence in the plural" (see 5.7; UCLES 1858//Cambridge Assessment 2008: 41). In German we find questions such as the following in the Lower-tier Junior paper: "Give the cases of the following words in the above fables, and account for them [. . .]" or "What is the force of the following particles, as compounded with verbs: *ab, an; be; ein; ent; miss; um; ver; vor; weg; zer; auf*?" (Actually, a rather open-ended and far from straightforward question – whole dissertations have been written on the topic) (UCLES 1858/2008: 44).[19]

Similar questions were also set in non-school examinations for admission to professions. For example, the German examination for admission to Sandhurst Military College in 1881 included the question "Write down the first person singular of all the tenses of the verb *wollen*" and "Decline in both numbers: *mein neues Messer; grüne Wand; diejenige Arbeit*" (Rühle 1884: 21). In some years, the Sandhurst admission examinations were set by Max Müller, Professor of Modern Languages at Oxford, and his philologist's fascination with grammatical details and exceptions is perhaps evident in a question such as "Write ten German words which have a different meaning according to the gender in which they are used" (December 1859), although other questions were more elementary, such as "Decline *Er, Sie, Es*". The UCLES Examinations for Women, later renamed Higher Examinations (i.e. higher in level than the Senior examinations) and opened to both men and women, required knowledge of philology as well as grammar. For example, in 1871, questions included the following: *To what principal channels may modern Teutonic dialects be traced back? State Grimm's Law, and illustrate it by examples of cognate English and German words. Explain "Umlaut" and "Ablaut" and give examples of each* (Cam.c.11.51.26, p. 36). Prospective candidates were encouraged to consult Max Müller's *Lectures on the Science of Language* (1861–64) in preparation.

IAAM (1952: 304) considered grammar questions to be of pedagogical value in that they "force the pupil to concentrate on reproducing facts which he has learnt"; but they soon induced "weariness" in the able, "frustration" in the less able. Despite the disappearance of questions testing explicit grammatical knowledge, lack of grammatical accuracy has remained a constant complaint in examiners' reports, a "sempiternal similarity" between 1858 and 2008 (Humberstone in Cambridge Assessment 2008: 9). The apparent lack of attention paid to grammar by teachers was bemoaned in a 1920 Juniors report:

> errors in tense forms and concords in the work of pupils at school should be treated by teachers with greater severity than appears to be the case at present: elementary errors of this nature often seriously marred what might otherwise have been quite satisfactory work.
> (UCLES Junior report for French 1920, p. 7)

A 1949 UCLES report on French again noted "Elementary grammar was often at fault" (UCLES 1950 Report on the Work in School Certificate French, July 1949, p. 2 of report) and again, in 1987, on the A-level, "On the whole it would be true to say that grammatical errors of the most basic kind prevented many candidates from achieving reasonable marks" (UCLES 1987: 30). On the German O-level of the same year, the examiners wrote that "the written German produced this year showed a marked ignorance of the basics: cases, agreement, verb conjugations and particularly word order. The candidates who correctly used subordinate clauses sending the verb to the end, separable verbs, compound tenses and "interesting phrases" stood out, but they were few in number" (UCLES 1987: 9).

Questions about explicit grammatical knowledge disappeared from the UCLES School Certificate regulations some time between 1930 and 1940, a change in accord with the prioritization of context validity and cognitive validity in recent decades. It might be argued that questions testing memorized grammatical knowledge are on the same cognitive level, as, say, being able to write out words or short phrases from memory in writing tasks, which feature prominently in the National Curriculum attainment targets. One might argue that such mechanical knowledge is a necessary precursor to being able to *apply* that knowledge in production (no less than being able to reproduce memorized vocabulary in highly constrained contexts) and therefore merits being tested explicitly. One might also assert that giving it explicit value would help candidates recognize its importance. However, the low context validity – the fact that producing grammatical forms will never be required in "real-life" communicative situations – has ruled it out under the prevailing orthodoxy. Grammar did not cease to be accorded weight – in the composition section of the 1977 JMB O-level syllabus B (worth 35% of the examination as a whole), marks were equally awarded for grammatical accuracy, variety of structure, appropriate idiom and vocabulary, and for subject matter. However, there is clearly a lowered expectation regarding grammatical forms. Some syllabi sought to specify what grammatical structures were expected. For example, the AQA 1988 syllabus specified the grammatical structures listed in Table 5.4. Despite the total absence of verbal morphology of any kind, the specification assured its readers that "It will be possible to complete all the tasks set, and to earn maximum marks, by the correct use of the structures contained in the list at the level indicated" (p. 48). Note too, that there was no expectation that pupils would be able to handle the associated grammatical terminology (as in papers up to the 1930s).

In the CEFR, grammatical competence is included as one of several "general competences" which learners "draw upon" in order to "carry out the task and activities required to deal with the communicative situations in which they are involved"[20] (Council of Europe 2001: 101). However, unsurprisingly, "it is not considered possible to produce a scale for progression in respect of grammatical structure which would be applicable across all languages" (p. 113). Rather, grammatical accuracy is expected merely to improve from A1 to C2, with "reasonable accuracy in familiar contexts" expected at B1, and "consistent grammatical control of complex language" by C2 (p. 114).

5.2.4 Dictation

Dictation was the earliest way of testing familiarity with the spoken language. It made its earliest appearance in 1859 for those candidates taking French or German for admission to Sandhurst Military College ([Sandhurst] 1859: 19), in a section headed "Speaking and Reading". It was included in what were called "oral" or "spoken" language tests set by school examination boards from the early twentieth century onwards. However, dictation is not *just* a measure of comprehension of the spoken language, nor is it a *direct* measure (see Weir 2013: 350–353). It is quite possible to comprehend perfectly a passage heard and yet achieve no marks at all in written dictation (French and Dutch children exposed to the Dictée as an exercise could confirm this!). Dictation is, like translation, a

Table 5.4 Grammatical structures required in the French GCSE (1988, AQA specification, pp. 48–50)

"The structures which the candidate will be expected to understand and produce are shown below. The structures expected at Higher Level include those shown, together with the structures expected at Basic level" (p. 49). "(L.R.)" indicates that the item need only be understood in reading or listening comprehension; productive use is not expected.

Basic Level

1. Nouns: Gender, singular and plural, including common irregulars – e.g. *yeux, journaux*
2. Articles: All forms of definite, indefinite and partitive articles, including the distinction between *il boit du vin, il ne boit pas de vin, and il boit beaucoup de vin*. The use of *de* before an adjective which precedes the noun is encouraged, but the use of *des* in such circumstances will be accepted.
3. Adjectives and Adverbs:
    a. Regular formation and position of adjectives (masc., fem., plural) and adverbs. Common irregular adjectives and adverbs
    b. Demonstrative adjectives: *ce, cet, cette, ces, -ci, (là* L.R.)
    c. Possessive adjectives *mon, ma, mes, ton, ta, tes, son, sa, ses, notre, nos, votre, vos, leur, leurs, (mon, ton, son* before a fem. noun L.R.)
    d. Indefinite adjectives/adverbs: *autre, tout, même, (chaque, quelque(s)* L.R.)
    e. Regular comparatives of adjectives and adverbs (*plus, aussi, moins*) + adjective/adverb (*mieux, meilleur* L.R.)
    f. Regular superlatives: *le plus, le moins,* + adjective/adverb; (*le mieux/le meilleur* L.R.)
    g. Quantifiers: *très, assez, peu, trop* + adjective/adverb, *beaucoup, pas beaucoup, un peu*
    h. Interrogative adverbs *combien, comment, où, pourquoi, quand*
4. Pronouns:
    a. All subject pronouns, including *on.*
    b. Direct and indirect object pronouns used with imperatives, negatives and affirmatives, before and after a verb, e.g. *regarde-moi, (ne me regarde pas* L.R.) – apart from certain set phrases as exemplified in tasks section – e.g. *Je peux vous aider?*
    c. (The use of *en* as a pronoun, the use of *y* in the sense of "there" – e.g. *il en prend, il y va* L.R.)

Higher Level

Irregular adjectives and adverbs as in the vocabulary list
mon, ton, son before a fem.
(*chaque, quelque(s), plusieurs, n'importe quel, qui, comment, où,* etc. L.R.)
Superlatives
le mieux, le meilleur
(*le pire* L.R.)
tout à fait, bien, presque, si; (*tout, tellement* L.R.), (*que/comme* L.R. as in *que/comme je suis fatigué*)
Productive use of (b) as defined at Basic, and in addition: Use of two or more pronouns before and after a verb (L.R.) – e.g. *il me l'a dit, donnez-m'en.*
Productive use of (c) as defined at Basic.

composite test of skills: aural comprehension, spelling, and grammatical knowledge (especially in a language like French where, for example, correct spelling of past participles depends on being able to mark their agreement, which in turn requires a sophisticated grasp of the grammar of the sentence). Dictation was introduced to UCLES examinations from 1901, and was still a feature of French A-level in the 1980s.

It is worth noting that another indirect measure of spoken language knowledge, phonetics, was included for some years as an element in the Cambridge Certificate of Proficiency in English, established in 1913 (Weir 2013: 13). However, it was never tried in the conventional school examinations.

Below, I give three specimens of the dictation passages set at the UCLES Higher School Certificate of July 1930 (taken from Cam.c.11.51.73, p. 72, 76, 78, and reproduced by kind permission of Cambridge Assessment Group Archives), which might provide a useful point of comparison with the sample of English passages from the Cambridge Certificate of Proficiency in English given by Weir (2013: 375–380).

UCLES Higher School Certificate French, July 1930, specimen dictation passage

THE ASTROLOGER

Le roi Louis XI, | sur la parole de son astrologue, | qui lui avait prédit le beau temps, | était allé chasser ce cerf. | Quand il fut au bois, | il recontra un pauvre homme | qui conduisait devant lui | son âne chargé de charbon. | On lui demanda s'il ferait beau, | et il annonça qu'il pleuvrait assurément. | Lorsque le roi fut rentré tout trempé, | il fit venir le charbonnier. | "D'où vient, | dit-il, | que tu es plus savant | que mon astrologue? | – Sire, dit celui-ci, | ce n'est pas moi, | c'est mon âne. | Quand je le vois se gatter | et secouer les oreilles, | c'est un signe certain | qu'il tombera de l'eau". | Cet incident fut, | par la suite, | un sujet de plaisanterie pour le roi, | qui reprochait à son astrologue | d'en savoir moins qu'un âne. |

[*Astrologue* to be written on the blackboard.]

UCLES Higher School Certificate Spanish, July 1930, specimen dictation passage

[No title is given for the passage]

Los pájaros | que viven en climas fríos | construyen sus nidos en los huecos | de los edificios antiguos, | dentro de los campanarios | y las torres de las iglesias, | y, en fin, | siempre al abrigo del aire. | Después que han construido | su nido con los materiales | que les convienen más | o que encuentran con mayor facilidad, | comprendiendo | que el calor es necesario | para la vida de sus hijos, | tapizan y alfombran | por dentro su casa | con su propio plumón | o con la lana, algodón | o pelo de algún animal | según los paises. | Luego la hembra | pone dentro del nido | unos cuatro o cinco huevos, | y los abriga | con su propío cuerpo | hasta que nacen los polluelos, | que necesitan también | el calor del nido | para poder vivir y desarrollarse.

UCLES Higher School Certificate German, July 1930, specimen dictation passage

CHANGING PLACES WITH A DONKEY

Zwei Studenten gingen | an einem Walde vorbei; | da lag ein Bauer, | der hatte seinen Arm | in die Halsterleine | seines Esels gesteckt | und schlief. | Der eine Student | zäumte den Esel ab | und trieb ihn davon; | der andere aber | legte sich den Halster an, | und blieb | an des Esels Platze stehen. | Endlich erwachte der Bauer | und war nicht wenig verwundert | als er einen Studenten | am Halster hielt. | Der Student bat ihn flehentlich, | er möchte ihn | weiter ziehen lassen und erzählte, | er sein ein so wilder Bursche gewesen, | daß sein Vater ihn aus Zorn | in einen Esel | verwünscht habe; | jetzt wäre aber | die Zeit der Verwünschung um, | und da sei er wieder | ein Student geworden.

5.3 The four skills

When school examinations began in the 1850s, none of the "four skills" around which all assessment criteria have been structured for the past half-century or so was directly and uniquely tested. Reading comprehension was tested by translation into English, which also required, however, the skill of rendering what had been understood into idiomatic English of an appropriate register. Writing was tested by prose composition – i.e. translation into the foreign language. Speaking and listening were initially not tested at all. Yet by the end of the twentieth century, the four skills of reading, writing, speaking and listening were all explicitly tested, and were weighted equally. In particular, the productive skills of speaking and free writing – the former initially completely unassessed, the latter only via translation – became much more prominent. In the approving words of Page and Shortt (1970: 10), "What used to be considered 'frills' are now 'real work', i.e. what the examiners want". For a brief period in the early twenty-first century (e.g. the AQA GCSE 2010 specification), the productive skills of speaking and writing were even weighted more heavily than the receptive skills, each worth 30%, together the majority of the paper; reading and listening comprehension were each weighted at 20%. Below, we survey the development of assessment for each of the four skills at in turn, but do not consider changes in weighting or detailed marking criteria.

5.3.1 Assessing reading comprehension

The reading comprehension test was first introduced as a replacement for translation into English – it was seen as measuring understanding by one means rather than another (an interesting view of the purpose of the translation into English). For example, the UCLES regulations for the School Certificate specified in 1940 that part of Paper 1 for French and German required candidates to answer questions on a passage "instead of translating it" (Cam.c.11.51.83, p. 11). The passages for comprehension could be literary, including verse (see the 1940 German paper in 5.7.7 for an example). Pupils were required to answer the set questions in the foreign language, and, as a 1949 report noted, "Many candidates who knew the answers were unable to express them in correct French" (UCLES 1949: 11). For, as Moys et al. (1980: 250) pointed out 30 years later in their review of 1979 O-level reading comprehensions, answering questions in the target language is "a test of production as well as of comprehension, so the candidate already has two substantial tasks". Nevertheless, this format of answering in the target language remained quite stable; it was still used in the new O-level examinations set in 1951, and continued to be used into the 1970s. Between the 1950s and 1970s, this format vied with the précis in English, as in the 1951 and 1970 O-level examinations given in 5.7.7 and 5.7.8. The précis had the advantage that pupils were not hamstrung by writing in the target languages; however, the art of condensing material is a difficult one, which goes well beyond basic comprehension.

By 1980, the Cambridge examinations had switched to multiple-choice questions, a format which tested candidates' comprehension without requiring them to produce language themselves. Comprehension questions requiring written answers tended "to fall back on straightforward comprehension of factual content – What time did the train leave? How did the man get across the river?" (Moys 1980: 25), thus not testing "implications, interpretations, even the mood or bias of the writer or characters" (which might have been easier to judge in the older comprehension test requiring a good translation into English). But well-designed multiple choice questions could ensure pupils were not simply regurgitating a relevant piece of text from a given passage, for example by requiring candidates to choose the most appropriate remark for a given situation, or choose the most appropriate word to complete a sentence (e.g. the UCLES 1980 German GCSE paper). Multiple-choice questions allowed scope for testing the more subtle kind of understanding referred to by Moys too. Later examinations included a combination of multiple choice answers in the target language and questions in English (e.g. the 1999 GCSE test given in 5.7 as well as in A-level papers), still avoiding confounding comprehension with productive skills.

5.3.2 Assessing speaking

Competence in the spoken language was the first to be identified as a distinct skill, to be tested separately from the remainder of the language test. The earliest appearance of conversation in an examination is by proxy. In a paper for admission to Sandhurst in June 1868, set by Max Müller, candidates were told that "Those who are able may write a conversation in German between a soldier and a beggar" – that is, they were invited to produce conversational German, but not yet to speak themselves.[21] In the short-lived Commercial Certificate examinations offered by UCLES in the 1880s – where a modern language was compulsory, but there were no "set books", so the focus was strictly on the language itself – an optional conversation test was offered, but many did not sit it, and of those who did, many did not pass it (see McLelland 2015a: 80–81). This may be because a very high standard was set – when the RSA introduced oral examinations in 1902, its examiners reported with satisfaction that although the take-up was initially low, examiners "were able to maintain a decidedly high standard. It is believed that no candidate has been awarded a certificate who does not possess a knowledge of the foreign language such as would render him of considerable use in any business occupation in the country in question" – a very high threshold indeed! (RSA 1902–1906: 68).

There remained a tension between the desires of commercial interests to have a measure of spoken fluency – with no concern about knowledge of literature – and the academic inclinations of the examiners (generally university men) and teachers. In the *Educational Times* of January 1, 1897, a certain R.J.D. represented the academic view:

> For the majority of students, ability to read German fluently is the great object. A man who never leaves his native country, but keeps abreast with German thought, is far more cosmopolitan than one who perhaps spends every summer chattering at German spas, but has read nothing.

Nevertheless, with growing recognition of the importance of the spoken language, the UCLES board introduced an optional examination in the spoken language to its school examinations in 1901, consisting of reading aloud, writing a dictation, and holding a short conversation, which would be related to one of the set books for the written examinations.[22] However, the examination cost extra, and it did not contribute towards the final mark unless the candidate would not obtain a distinction without it. Some commentators considered conversational competence an impractical expectation, in the face of a shortage of teachers willing to teach according to new methods; "they cannot speak themselves, and therefore cannot teach others to speak" (Brigstocke 1905: 110). Still, Brigstocke continued, in the *Modern Language Teaching* journal, it was the duty of all to work towards a time when "all who take up modern languages *must* work for proficiency in *a real and conscientious* oral test [...] to persuade the rising generation that *viva voce* work is absolutely necessary" (p. 111).

In 1912, the UCLES regulations included, for the first time, a separate section on "Spoken French" or "Spoken German" (though not yet for the other languages available, Dutch and Spanish). The examinations still required an additional fee. At Preliminary level (i.e. approx. age 14), candidates were required to read a passage aloud, and to engage in a short conversation with the examiner. At Junior and Senior levels, candidates were additionally required to write from dictation; and the conversation was to be based in part on a set book selected by the school, of not less than 10,000 words in length. Reporting on these spoken examinations for the first time, the examiners considered the French results at Preliminary level "promising", as most of the 207 candidates (about 7% of those taking the written papers) read "clearly and with a creditably pure accent", and for some, "conversation was easy and correct"; a "satisfactory proportion" of candidates understood the questions put to them. At Junior level (1,038 candidates, about 13% of those taking the written papers), reading was "fairly good", although grammatical errors and misuse of tenses was a problem (pp. xxx–xxxi); the report on the Senior examinations (992 candidates, under 20% of all those taking the written papers) was similar. Comments on the spoken German examinations were broadly similar to those in French, though it appears that at all levels a handful of candidates had excellent German thanks to residence abroad or other "special opportunities of speaking" (p. xxxiii). The requirement to base the conversation on a set book was evidently a challenge, and by 1918, the regulations for the School Certificate now made the set book for conversation optional, and its minimum length had been reduced to 6,000 words. Senior candidates no longer had to pay a fee for the spoken examination, though the examiner's travel expenses had still to be met by the school. By 1925, oral examinations were also available for Spanish and Italian.

In the 1930s, the Committee on Education for Salesmanship reiterated the importance of oral examinations, considering "effective oral tests imperative", whatever the practical difficulties (Board of Education 1931: 118). The JMB ran compulsory oral examinations for the first time in 1932, consisting of reading, dictation and conversation, in which "Candidates will be required to answer orally in the language concerned questions set upon the passage to be read aloud", to be conducted by the school teaching staff. Feedback in the board's report for that year indicated that "nearly all schools welcomed it" – nearly all candidates read fluently, though often with a poor accent. In UCLES, meanwhile, languages were listed in 1930 both under their own heading and under the grouping of "Modern Studies" along with history, geography and English, where pupils were required to take two or three of the available subjects (see 6.4 on this concept of "Modern Studies"). Under "Modern Studies", the regulations stated that "An oral test also forms an integral part of each subject; candidates must pass in this, in each of the language papers" (Cam.c.11.51.73, p. 8). This was a turning point in the history of school language examinations: the oral examination needed to be passed in order to pass in the language. However, it only applied to languages when taken under the heading of Modern Studies. In the UCLES 1940 School Certificate, the oral test remained optional, and failure in it would not "prejudice the result"; this was still the case in 1950. By 1960, Cambridge's regulations for O-level at least specified that candidates must attend the oral examination, and that the marks from it would count towards the mark in the subject, although it did not have to be passed in order to pass the subject (Cam.c.11.51.116: 31–32). A sea-change can be detected in the 1960s: JMB's 1966 report noted with pleasure that "there were plenty of candidates keen to talk and to please" (p. 24), with (in Spanish) "welcome evidence of increased attention to oral work". The increased weight given to oral skills was emphasized by the JMB examiners in their report on the French A-level of 1977, who pointed out that the reading and conversation tests were now worth 1% more than translation into English, and only 1% less than prose composition (i.e. translation into the language). Still, progress was uneven:

> Examiners frequently report that there are enormous differences in achievement from centre to centre which they believe clearly result from a deliberate policy in some centres severely to limit the amount of time and practice devoted to the productive oral skills.
> (JMB 1977 report, p. 34)

By 1994, oral skills had become worth a quarter of available marks at GCSE, and the tasks required candidates to perform in a number of roles, rather than simply to survive a "conversation": as a "transactor" (in the situation of an English person "having to cope with an authentic situation when confronted by a French person"), as an interviewee (answering questions about themselves in at least five topic areas), and as narrator (reporting on an incident witnessed) (Cambridge Assessment 1994: 6). The CEFR similarly acknowledges the range of ways in which spoken competence may be required, differentiating both "spoken interaction" (e.g. interviews, discussions, obtaining goods and services) and "spoken production" (e.g. sustained narrative; addressing an audience).

In non-school examinations, the increased emphasis on oral skills came much earlier, in line with the demands already urged by the Committee on Education for Salesmanship. The Institute of Linguists' new syllabus introduced in 1934 made oral examinations compulsory at all stages, and the weighting for the oral examination at Associate and Final levels was set at a substantial 30% of the marks (Smith et al. 2010: 16). It took until the 1970s – when the JMB Syllabus B weighted conversation at 30% – for this to be matched in school examinations; oral production was again briefly weighted at 30% in GCSEs in the early twenty-first century, but in general, it has been weighted at 25%, equal with the other skills, for most of the twenty-first century.

5.3.3 Assessing writing

Writing in the target language has always been required in examinations, but, for the first half century, it was generally in the form of translation from English into the language. Although this task has almost no context validity – for it is rare indeed to be required to translate out of one's native language professionally – this "prose composition" was (and still is, at university level) considered a good holistic measure of competence, since it requires candidates to tackle a wide range of structures and to have a wide vocabulary, without the option of taking evasive action in the face of difficulties. Free composition, by comparison was judged by the IAAM (1952) to have only moderate validity, but opinions had shifted:

> Our predecessors of 1929 [i.e. IAAM 1929] pointed out the danger of injustice in this test, yet it has tremendous educational value, not least of which is its encouragement to think in the foreign tongue, and we cannot possibly contemplate its exclusion from the papers.
> (IAAM 1952: 323)

The very first emergence of free writing in German is in the Society of Arts regulations for its 1857 examinations, which specified that for a first-class certificate, candidates must be able to write an essay on literature "in good German".[23] In June 1859, the examination for admission to Sandhurst set candidates the task of free composition: "Write in French a letter containing a brief account of your purpose in acquiring a language so widely spread and illustrated by so many writers". This kind of question remained a staple in these examinations, albeit with some variation depending on the examiner.[24] In the equivalent German examination (which seems generally to have been at a somewhat lower level than that for French), a composition seems to have been less often expected. Free composition continued to be a feature into the 1880s, also in the military Staff College and Indian Civil Service examinations. It seems to have been usual to offer a choice of two topics, one more historical, political or military in focus (e.g. the significance of the Mediterranean in past and present; a biographical sketch of Wellington), one more general (e.g. the influence of school on the character of a boy; the journey from London to Bombay – these examples are from the papers in Rühle 1884: 24, 70, 74).

In the UCLES examinations, a free composition question only made its appearance in 1869, and only in the first year of the Examination for Women; the experiment was not repeated. By 1910, a subject for free composition was offered in the Junior examinations as an alternative to translation from English into the language (UCLES 1912 regulations: 10), but the report on the 1911 Juniors was not encouraging. Few chose the free composition, and "the productions of these were largely worthless", even if a few wrote "admirable little essays" (Cam.c.11.51.54: xxx). However, when the new School Certificate was introduced in 1918, JMB required a "Free composition (to be based on the selected works)"; UCLES offered free composition as an alternative to translation. From the 1920s, JMB's topic ceased to be related to a set book. Candidates for French were asked to write about 100 words on topics such as the duties of parents to their children; a sailor's life; or an ideal holiday; or they could follow a skeleton narrative outline given in the form of phrases in French, a model that continued into the 1930s. As examples, the cues for writing in the 1930 UCLES School

Certificate German and Italian were as follows (reproduced by kind permission of Cambridge Assessment Group Archives):

> Write in GERMAN a narrative of not more than 150 words based on the following outline:
>
> *Ein Ausflug auf das Land oder an die See.*
> (Ein Brief).
> Früh aufstehen – Zweirad (Motorrad, Motor-Omnibus) – mit Geschwistern (Freunden) – schöner Morgen – was wir auf dem Wege sahen – Ankunft in einem Walde (an der See) – Mittagsmahl – Ruhen (Wandern, Rudern, Spielen) – Blumen (Muscheln) – Flugzeug über uns – Tee – Rückkehr – Sonnenuntergang – herrlicher Tag.

> Write in ITALIAN a narrative of not more than 150 words based on the following outline:
>
> *The Death of Julius Caesar*
> Guilio Cesare – pervenuto al culmine della sua grandezza – sospetto da Bruto e Cassio ed altri repubblicani – congiura – Cesare trucidato in mezzo al Senato – "Tu quoque, Brute"

In Spanish and German, topics included writing about an aeroplane flight; "the content of a poem that you have read"; "A Christmas tree"; "The Car"; or, again, pupils could follow a given outline. The topics for Russian were comparatively challenging: "any Russian story you know"; "War and Peace"; "The League of Nations". A JMB report on German in the 1932 School Certificate Examiners' reports found that most did well in their writing: "The essays were mainly amusing and original", although it was pointed out that paragraphs learnt by heart and "dragged in by the heels" would not score marks (1932 JMB report on the School Certificate, p. 16). The report on French essays was less positive: "the Essay brought out a weakness of vocabulary very surprising since candidates wrote mainly about events of daily life at home or school" – vocabulary gaps noted were 'bedroom, French lesson, examination, to take, news, game, illness'.

By the mid-1960s, guided narrative writing following an outline in the target language was well established at O-level, but there was a good degree of variation between subjects. French, Spanish, Italian and Russian examinations all contained a free composition based on a printed outline, or set of pictures (in the case of French only), or continuing a story begun in translation sentences. German, by contrast, had a reproductive test, which combined (or confounded) listening comprehension with writing, as pupils would hear a story and were asked to retell it in their own words in writing with aid of printed outline. The JMB report on French O-level examinations in 1966 observed, "There were some excellent essays as well as many very poor ones"; most candidates chose the picture question (of which the Spanish 1980 examination in 5.7 contains an example) (JMB report on 1966 French O-level examinations, p. 22).

Until the 1980s, the essay topics seem to have been quite variable, though with emphasis still on the narrative. At A-level, meanwhile, candidates were required to write more (250–350 words by 1970), and with a growing tendency to set topics requiring candidates to present a view or argue a case – e.g. "the value of examinations" (UCLES French, 1970), "'The student protests have only anarchy as their goal' – what is your view of this statement?" (UCLES German, 1970), "Would it be good for France and Great Britain to have the same political and social institutions?" (UCLES French, 1980). However, since then, the criteria for attainment in writing show a greater explicit differentiation of text-types (a form, letter, narrative piece, presentation of a controversial topic) and a tendency to match them to different attainment levels (see 5.5). Early examiners barely differentiated between narrative, a personal letter and presenting an argument. For example, in an 1880 Sandhurst German examination for the Staff College, candidates were given a choice of very different kinds of writing task – either a narrative account of "one of the great battles of the Franco-German war in 1879" or "a letter to a friend, describing the neighbourhood you live in"; the following year, the choice was between "army discipline" (presumably at least in part an opinion piece) and a letter to a friend providing a narrative of "your doings during the last two or three years" (Rühle 1884: 25, 27).[25] By contrast, one of the notable features common to the CEFR (self-)assessment criteria (Table 5.5 in section 5.5) and the attainment targets of the National Curriculum (Table 5.6) is the progression through text-types – from the highly constrained text-types such as a postcard or form (A1), to a short note (A2), to descriptive and narrative writing (B1), to making a case in writing (B2). (The prominence of the now moribund text-type of the "letter" (at B1) is arguably a flaw in the context validity of these criteria.) Likewise, mastery of a wider repertoire of registers is also recognized in the progression through the levels.

Assessment of writing in modern languages also illustrates how global changes to GCSE assessment regimes affect how modern languages are assessed. In recent years, both coursework and controlled assessments were introduced alongside examinations – under controlled assessment, introduced in 2010, students were able to work through guided steps towards a final piece, produced under controlled conditions for assessment.[26] The latest GCSEs revert to examination-only assessment, however.

5.3.4 Assessing listening comprehension

Listening comprehension was first tested, indirectly, as part of dictation tests, which were introduced in school examinations at the beginning of the twentieth century. However, it was the last of the "four skills" for which specific tests were developed, half a century later, and it remains, according to Weir (2013: 347) the most neglected in the classroom and the least researched, partly because of the greater practical complexities involved. (For a fuller history, see Weir 2013: 355–371). Listening tests emerged in the JMB 1952 O-level syllabi, where each of the two alternative syllabi required an aural test with listening comprehension.

An aural test was introduced at O-level by the UCLES "first alternative" syllabus in 1959, requiring the reproduction in writing of a story heard, with credit being given both for comprehension and for the "quality" of the candidate's language (Cam.c.11.51.116, p. 26). The following is an example of this task taken from the 1970 German UCLES O-level (Syllabus A, paper II), which was expected to take candidates about 30 minutes (reproduced by kind permission of Cambridge Assessment Group Archives).[27]

> Re-tell in German in 150–200 words the story which will be read to you and of which a summary is printed below. You are not expected to try to reproduce the story word for word, but you should give the principal points of it, and you should not introduce into your answer material which is not in the story read to you. The story contains about 200 words.
>
> *[The story to be read, "in a natural way", with changes of voice to convey dialogue permitted, but not explanatory gestures, was as follows. It would be heard twice – once right through; and a second time with a short pause at the end of the first and second paragraphs.]*
>
> *Meanness rewarded*
>
> Ein berühmter Londoner Maler wurde einmal von einem reichen, aber sehr geizigen Lord eingeladen, ein Wandbild für die Halle seines vornehmen Schlosses zu malen. Das Gemälde sollte zeigen, wie die Kinder Israels, verfolgt von Pharaos Armee, durchs Rote Meer zogen. Der Maler verlangte hundert Pfund für seine Arbeit, aber der geizige Lord wollte ihm nur zwanzig geben.
>
> Da der Maler gerade Geld brauchte, beschloß er, die zwanzig Pfund anzunehmen und ließ sich auch sofort bezahlen. Am nächsten Morgen erschien er sehr früh. Er kam aber nicht allein, sondern mit einem Hausanstreicher, der einen Eimer mit roter Farbe und einen riesengroßen Pinsel trug. Noch bevor der Lord von seinem Bett aufgestanden war, hatte der Anstreicher die ganze Wand mit blutigem Rot bedeckt.
>
> Der Maler prüfte sein Werk und ließ dann den Herrn des Hauses rufen. Als dieser die Halle betrat, sagter der Maler: "Es ist fertig!" "Was ist fertig?" fragte der Lord erstaunt und ahnte nichts Gutes. "Das Rote Meer!" antwortete der Maler mit ernster Miene. "Aber wo ist der Pharao? Und wo sind seine Soldaten?" "Ertrunken, Mylord!" kam die Antwort. "Und wo sind die Kinder Israels?"
>
> Der Maler verbeugte sich höflich und erwiderte: "Die haben schon das andere Ufer erreicht".
>
> *Meanness rewarded*
>
> Londoner Maler bekommt eine Einladung – der geizige Lord – die Kinder Israels – Pharaos Armee – das Rote Meer – nur zwanzig Pfund – annehmen –

Hausanstreicher mit Eimer, Farbe und Pinsel – der Herr des Hauses erstaunt – wo ist Pharao? – das andere Ufer.

In the 1960s, testers were still feeling their way. JMB's French, Spanish and Italian O-level all had a listening test with questions to be answered in English after hearing a passage. Russian did not yet have such a test at all. Initially the format of the test required candidates to answer questions after listening, but this was found challenging (not surprising given the additional cognitive load needed to connect written questions to aural input – Weir 2013: 349). Still, even after adjustments were made, the JMB report on the 1966 French O-level examinations noted, "It had been hoped that the revised aural test, with less left to memory, would bring better performances. In fact scoring this year was poor" (p. 23). In 1976 JMB experimented with requiring a summary in the foreign language of a spoken passage, but this discontinued after 1978, perhaps because, as the Board's annual report noted in 1977, "quite a larger number" of candidates obtained full marks – a failure to discriminate which no amount of scaling or normalization across the cohort can fix (JMB 1977 report, p. 34). JMB's aural test was weighted at 15% of the total examination in its 1977 GCSE Syllabus B, a syllabus where the aim was to reduce the use of English to a minimum. By 1980, Oxford's board was the only one where a listening comprehension was merely optional (Moys 1980: 246). In the first National Curriculum (1992), the aural examination was weighted equally with the other components, at 25%, and – excepting a brief reduction to 20% in the early twenty-first century – has remained so.[28]

5.4 Non-language knowledge and skills

One considerable change over the history of language examinations is the diminishing prominence of non-language knowledge and of skills not related to proficiency in the foreign language. One of these is the requirement to be able to write well in English, whether in translations or in an English précis to test comprehension (see the 1951 French paper in 5.7 for an example). We noted in 5.2 that writing idiomatically and in the appropriate register created difficulties in translation into English. Good written English was (and is) obviously also necessary in answering questions on literature, history or geography at A-level. As one examiners' report noted of A-level Italian, "It was evident that candidates who had clearly had the advantage of residence abroad or Italian parentage and thereby showed facility in prose composition, were ill-prepared to write relevantly in English on their set texts" (JMB 1966 report on A-level, p. 91). The recognition of a category of candidates of this kind in the UCLES languages examinations – non-native speakers of English – may indeed have prompted the establishment of the now hugely influential Cambridge Certificate of Proficiency in English in 1913 (see Weir 2013: 15). The high point in assessing the ability to write in English as part of a language examination was probably the optional dissertation of between two and three thousand words in English on a topic concerned with contemporary French civilization, available for example in the JMB French A-level in the

1970s. However, it was only weighted as the equivalent of a single essay question in an examination, and this apparently led candidates to spend too little time on it (JMB regulations for 1977, p. 131).

Literature was a mainstay of the syllabus for most of the nineteenth century, at both Junior and Senior levels. Indeed, the syllabus was largely defined by the "set books". The set books would provide the "seen" passage for translation into English, whose language would also provide the inspiration for grammatical questions and requests to explain "the historical and geographical allusions". In the first year, 1858, the UCLES French pupils were faced with Voltaire's *Charles XII*, while German candidates tackled Lessing's fables. Voltaire, along with La Fontaine and Lamartine, remained a frequent fixture on the French Junior syllabus until 1900; at Senior level, Corneille, Racine and Molière were frequent. In German, Schiller and Hauff made frequent appearances; at Senior level too, Schiller, Lessing, as well as Goethe, were frequent. There is a noticeable tendency to include texts featuring historical figures, presumably in an effort to furnish a historical as well as literary education – Schiller's *History of the Revolt of the Netherlands* and *History of the Thirty Years War* were early favourites.[29]

The stranglehold of literature on the syllabus loosened gradually from the 1890s to 1918. In 1891, UCLES allowed for the setting of alternative papers "for students who prefer to be examined in the language generally and not in any set book", at both Junior and Senior levels (Cam.ca.11.51.4, 1891 Regulations, p. 3, note C); the Commercial Certificate (1888–1894) had also been a pure language syllabus. Set books had become optional at Junior level by 1912, and disappeared from the under-16 syllabus with the introduction of the School Certificate in 1918.

As noted in 5.3.2, a short-lived experiment in the Cambridge Board was the inclusion of languages in a subject grouping called Modern Studies in the Higher School Certificate, along with history, geography and English. This grouping – where candidates were required to take two or three subjects – implicitly linked the study of modern languages to the history and geography that had been at least a minor feature of the earliest language examinations (which had required candidates to explain the "historical and geographical allusions" in the given text). Presumably related to this hope that French and German would be seen as necessary complements to history and geography, a subsidiary subject paper on "the geography of Germany and France" briefly appeared in the 1930s, whose regulations stipulated the study of "the geographical setting for France and Germany (to be studied in relation to Europe as a whole)", "the main elements of the racial and cultural geography", and "the modern Economic and Political Geography of France and Germany (to be particularly studied in relation to the changes effected by the Peace Treaties)" (Cam.c.11.51.73: 21–22).[30] While the Modern Studies model did not survive, Higher School Certificate French in 1940 still included a compulsory paper with "A choice of straightforward questions on the twentieth-century history and social and political institutions of France [. . .] A choice of straightforward questions, physical and economic, on the geography of France" (Cam.c.11.51.83: 9–10). The new 1951 A-level syllabus also included, as one of three required papers, one on "Prescribed texts, history, geography, life and institutions". It was also possible, at least in the Cambridge Board, to take this A-level paper in lieu of the language papers for O-level. With answers to be written entirely in English, this was not deemed a language paper, but still yielded a pass in the subject of French or German. This alternative (no longer available) is an eloquent expression of the long-running tension between two competing conceptualizations of modern languages at school. Should taking a language at school – like the majority of non-school examinations (RSA, Institute of Linguists, STANAG 6001) – simply lead to a test of linguistic proficiency, in essence an assessment of how close the learner can come to the attainment expected of a literate native speaker or full bilingual? To what extent is it legitimate to expect a school language subject, alongside English, history and the like, to train candidates, and test them, in critical thinking on topic areas related to the culture being studied?

5.5 Specifying levels of attainment

Just as language testing constructs began to be made more explicit in the later twentieth century, so too were the criteria by which to measure them.[31] Furthermore, from the 1970s onwards there was a growing desire to recognize achievement at all levels – not just those levels of achievement that, when taken together, happened to earn the award of pass as part of the national school examinations system taken at 16 or 18. Valette and Disick (1972: vii) observed a growing desire to develop what they called "performance objectives – carefully worded statements describing the desired outcomes of instruction in terms of student behaviour". Descriptors, specifying what the learner can do, have since become standard, as in the CEFR (e.g. B2 writing: "I can write clear, detailed text on a wide range of subjects related to my interests"). Such objectives, it was believed, made it possible to give each learning activity a clear purpose, both motivating the learner and making teachers accountable to stakeholders for what their instruction achieved. They also made it possible to individualize targets, so that learners could "be freed to learn at their own pace" (Valette & Disick 1972: 4).

In Britain, the so-called Graded Objectives movement began in opposition to planned changes to the 16+ examinations. Despite the fact that 90% of the school population now took a foreign language, Harding et al. (1980: 2) noted an apparent "failure to get much that is worthwhile taught to the majority", and a tendency, after only one or two years of language instruction, to weed out pupils unlikely to pass a CSE or GCE O-level. This in effect led to "a large number of pupils being set unsuitable tasks at which they not surprisingly fail". They argued instead for "goals which more pupils can reach and by doing so experience success in language learning" (Harding et al. 1980: 3). Learners who did not proceed to O-level would thus still have accreditation for their learning, and a sense of achievement. In formulating objectives, context validity was an important consideration: "the most worthwhile objectives would seem to be the ability to use the language for realistic purposes rather than, for example, the ability to describe the language or use it for purposes which the actual user would rarely need to employ". The emphasis was on "communicative competence in practical situations" (Harding et al. 1980: 4). The objectives would not be pinned to a particular school stage or ability range, but would be available to learners of all ages, including adult learners. Providing accreditation for shorter courses of study might also, it was hoped, promote the learning of a wider range of languages. The first syllabuses based on Graded Objectives were trialled in York and Oxfordshire in the 1970s (Buckby/Schools Council 1981).[32] Meanwhile the Council of Europe's Modern Language Project was yielding similar reflections on assessment, initially primarily for adults (Trim 1978). Starting from Jan van Ek's "Threshold Level", which sought to define the level required to live and work in an English-speaking country (Van Ek 1976), a series of levels was developed for language learning more widely (Van Ek 1986, 1987, Van Ek & Trim 1998), leading ultimately to the *Common European Framework of Reference for Languages: Learning, teaching, assessment* (CEFR, Council of Europe 2001). These assessment criteria – backed up by the European Language Portfolio and European Language Passport (Little et al. 2011; Dobson 2012) have had tremendous influence both within Europe and beyond (including, for example, the HSK or *Hànyǔ Shuǐpíng Kǎoshì* 汉语水平考试 levels for Mandarin Chinese).

In Britain, however, the original aspiration of a unified set of attainment for all learner types remained a mirage, despite multiple attempts. A set of National Language Standards were published in 1993 by a "Languages Lead Body" with its secretariat based in CILT, the Centre for Information on Language Teaching (on CILT, see Chapter 6). The Standards specified "performance criteria" and guidance for assessment for Listening, Speaking, Reading and Writing, at five levels (the highest level requiring, for example, the ability to "exchange highly specialized and complex correspondence", or "produce texts for public consumption"). The standards were intended to "relate to the use of foreign languages at work. For providers of language training the standards will become the basis of new courses and national vocational qualifications (NVQs/SVQs)"[33] (Languages Lead Body 1993: 1). However, the Languages Lead Body seems to have been short-lived, and there is no evidence that the scheme was widely adopted, as had been hoped. A scheme similarly intended to be widely applicable, but only at lower ability levels, was Asset Languages, set up as part of the National Languages Strategy in 2005 (see Chapter 6). It was intended to provide language learning accreditation at all 17 grades, conceived as rungs on a so-called Languages Ladder from beginner level to mastery (DCFS 2007), just as the proponents of Graded Objectives had envisaged in the 1970s and 1980s. The scheme was likened to music grades, in that levels were not linked to age, and were intended to motivate learners in the early stages by achieving short-term goals. The first three grades described stages lower than A1 in the CEFR; Grade 4 was equated with A1, Grade 5 with the upper end of A1. They were intended for use not only in in primary and secondary schools but also in further and adult education. The Languages Ladder was considered by its advocates to be particularly valuable in providing accreditation where existing GCSEs were not intended for foreign language learners but for those who spoke the language at home – e.g. Arabic (Tinsley 2012). By 2010, Asset Languages accreditation, operated by Cambridge Assessment, was in place for 25 languages, including many less commonly taught languages, but never at all levels in all languages. The scheme was highly flexible, so that learners could gain accreditation in each of the four skills (reading, writing, listening and speaking) separately and at different levels as appropriate – in this sense, it resembled the military STANAG scheme. Despite high hopes, however, the Asset Languages accreditation scheme was discontinued in 2012.

All of these accreditation schemes assess reading, writing, speaking and listening separately. Like the National Curriculum until its most recent version, they all also focus on language skills *only*.[34] This contrasts markedly with the (purely implicit) criteria for school languages attainment for much of the twentieth century, which placed considerable emphasis on cultural and/or literary knowledge of various kinds. That kind of knowledge had also been in the minds of some among earlier generations reflecting on describing attainment. Valette and Disick's handbook on Modern Language Performance Objectives, published in 1972, included not only the four skills with which we are familiar, but also "Way-of-Life Culture", "Civilization" and "Literature" under the wider heading of "Knowledge Testing". For literature, for example, Valette and Disick distinguished student behaviours that could be measured from the most mechanical (e.g. the memorizing of a poem) to the recall of factual information (e.g. knowledge of figures of speech, stating the main ideas of works studied), to analysis and evaluation of a literary work (e.g. analysing the use of figures of speech in an unfamiliar text). Under "Attitudes, Feelings and Values" they conflated attitudes to the target language culture and attitudes to the value of language learning more widely. Under "Gestures", the ultimate goal was "to train an individual to be bicultural". For example, "when the student describes a large fish he caught, he would use one gesture when speaking English and another when speaking French" (Valette & Disick 1972: 181).[35] Such "knowledge testing" has never featured in the National Curriculum, nor in GCSEs, although the National Curriculum did specify "the content of the modern foreign language curriculum" as "Areas of Experience", "to be explored "through the target language" (NCC 1991: 38). These "Areas of Experience" included *Everyday Activities; Personal and Social Life; the World around Us, the World of Education, Training and Work; the World of Communication; the International World; the World of Imagination and Creativity. The International World* provided an opportunity to deal with national stereotypes;[36] the *World of Imagination and Creativity* could include media, cinema, short stories and poems. However, there was no explicit "knowledge testing" of these areas of experience.

The National Curriculum of 1992 marked the high point of separately defined language attainment targets, with its 102 attainment targets across the four skills, each specified for ten levels.[37] By contrast, the 2013 National Curriculum looks like a return to earlier habits in three ways. First, as in all the subjects, brief outlines replace detailed definitions of levels (see Table 5.5). Second, the reading of literary texts makes a return to the core curriculum below A-level after a break of a century (see 5.4): pupils will "read literary texts in the language [such as stories, songs, poems and letters]".[38] Third, translation into the target language likewise makes a return, having becoming optional at GCSE by the 1970s and then disappearing altogether. It remains to be seen how this curriculum content will translate into detailed assessment criteria.

Table 5.5 Writing assessment criteria in various schemes

STANAG 6001 (used by NATO)	CEFR 2001	National Language Standards (1993)	Languages Ladder (2007)	GCSE and A-level equivalencies (?)[39]
0+ memorized phrases The candidate can write letters, numbers, dates, personal names, address, nationality, etc. in a registration form. Can write memorized words and phrases, often with some mistakes. Cannot express ideas clearly at sentence level.			**Grade 1**: I can write or copy simple words or symbols correctly	
		Level 1 (deal with predictable everyday tasks) Produce written information to deal with predictable day-to-day activities. Produce familiar information in standard formats	**Grade 2**: I can write one or two short sentences to a model and fill in the words on a simple form.	
			Grade 3: I can write a few short sentences, with support, using expressions which I have already learnt.	
1 Survival (similar to CEFR A1 /A2) Can write lists, short notes, phone messages to meet immediate personal needs. Can complete forms.	**A1 (Breakthrough or beginner):** I can write a short, simple postcard, for example sending holiday greetings. I can fill in forms with personal details, for example entering my name, nationality and address on a hotel registration form.	**Level 2 (deal with varied daily activities)** Produce written information to deal with routine and daily activities. Construct everyday texts using set phrases and structures. Produce notes and short messages to fulfil every day requirements	**Grade 4 [=Breakthrough]**: I can write a short text on a familiar topic, adapting language which I have already learnt. **Grade 5**: I can write a short text on a range of familiar topics, using simple sentences.	
	A2 (Waystage or elementary): I can write short, simple notes and messages relating to matters in areas of immediate need. I can write a very simple personal letter, for example thanking someone for something.			GCSE Lower Tier

2 Functional (equated with B1) Can write with some precision simple personal correspondence and routine workplace correspondence and related documents, including brief reports	B1 (Threshold or intermediate): I can write simple connected text on topics which are familiar or of personal interest. I can write personal letters describing experiences and impressions		GCSE Higher Tier
3 Minimal professional (equated with B2 and lower C1) Can write effective formal and informal correspondence and other documents on practical, social and professional topics and special fields of competence.	B2 (Vantage or upper intermediate): I can write clear, detailed text on a wide range of subjects related to my interests. I can write an essay or report, passing on information or giving reasons in support of or against a particular point of view. I can write letters highlighting the personal significance of events and experiences.	Level 3 (deal with key work tasks) Produce written materials to deal with a variety of work tasks Produce written texts to fulfil routine work requirements	A-level
4 Full professional (upper C1/C2) Can write the language precisely and accurately and can draft all levels of prose pertinent to professional needs.	C1 (Effective operational proficiency or advanced): I can express myself in clear, well-structured text, expressing points of view at some length. I can write about complex subjects in a letter, an essay or a report, underlining what I consider to be the salient issues. I can select style appropriate to the reader in mind.	Level 4 (deal with complex work tasks) Produce written materials to deal with complex tasks Produce technical texts Exchange complex correspondence Convey information, ideas and opinions in written form	

(*Continued*)

Table 5.5 (Continued)

STANAG 6001 (used by NATO)	CEFR 2001	National Language Standards (1993)	Languages Ladder (2007)	GCSE and A-level equivalencies (?)[39]
	C2 (Mastery or proficiency): I can write clear, smoothly flowing text in an appropriate style. I can write complex letters, reports or articles which present a case with an effective logical structure which helps the recipient to notice and remember significant points. I can write summaries and reviews of professional or literary works.	**Level 5 (deal with highly specialised tasks)** Produce written materials to deal with highly specialized tasks Produce highly specialised texts Exchange highly specialised and complex correspondence Present and debate arguments on complex matters in written form Produce texts intended for public consumption		
5 Native/bilingual				

Table 5.6 Attainment targets for writing in the National Curriculum, 1992–present

1992 National Curriculum Levels	National Curriculum (NCC 1991: 32–35); levels 5–6 expected for majority of pupils at end of Key Stage 3, i.e. aged 14	National Curriculum Programme of Study Key Stage 3, 2004 revision, = QCA 2004)	Languages Programme of Study (QCA 2007)	National Curriculum 2013	GCSE Specification AQA (2016) for GCSEs sat from 2018 onwards
Level 1*	copy familiar words correctly	copy single familiar words correctly. They [i.e. pupils] label items and select appropriate words to complete short phrases or sentences.	[unchanged from 2004, see left]	"By the end of key stage 3, pupils are expected to know, apply and understand the matters, skills and processes specified in the programme of study". For writing, the relevant specifications are: • express and develop ideas clearly and with increasing accuracy […] in writing;	Students are expected to be able to: • communicate effectively in writing for a variety of purposes across a range of specified contexts • write short texts, using simple sentences and familiar language accurately to convey meaning and exchange information. • produce clear and coherent text of extended length to present facts and express ideas and opinions appropriately for different purposes and in different settings.
Level 2	copy familiar short phrases correctly; write individual words from memory	copy familiar short phrases correctly. They write or word process items [for example, simple signs and instructions] and set phrases used regularly in class. When they write familiar words from memory their spelling may be approximate.	write one or two short sentences, following a model, and fill in the words on a simple form. They label items and write familiar short phrases correctly. When they write familiar words from memory, their spelling may be approximate.		

(Continued)

Table 5.6 (Continued)

1992 National Curriculum Levels	National Curriculum (NCC 1991: 32–35); levels 5–6 expected for majority of pupils at end of Key Stage 3, i.e. aged 14	National Curriculum Programme of Study Key Stage 3, 2004 revision, = QCA 2004)	Languages Programme of Study (QCA 2007)	National Curriculum 2013	GCSE Specification AQA (2016) for GCSEs sat from 2018 onwards
Level 3	write short sentences to convey simple, factual information; write short phrases from memory	write two or three short sentences on familiar topics, using aids [for example, textbooks, wallcharts and their own written work]. They express personal responses [for example, likes, dislikes and feelings]. They write short phrases from memory and their spelling is readily understandable	write a few short sentences, with support, using expressions that they have already learnt. They express personal responses. They write short phrases from memory and their spelling is readily understandable.	• write prose using an increasingly wide range of grammar and vocabulary, write creatively to express their own ideas and opinions, and translate short written text accurately into the foreign language. (The multiple levels, as specified above, had been used in all subjects, have been removed in all subjects.)	• make accurate use of a variety of vocabulary and grammatical structures, including some more complex forms, to describe and narrate with reference to past, present and future events. • manipulate the language, using and adapting a variety of structures and vocabulary with increasing accuracy and fluency for new purposes, including using appropriate style and register. • make independent, creative and more complex use of the language, as appropriate, to note down key points, express and justify individual thoughts and points of view, in order to interest, inform or convince.

Level 4	write a small number of related sentences from memory to find out and convey simple information and feelings; adapt a simple text by substituting individual words and set phrases	write individual paragraphs of about three or four simple sentences, drawing largely on memorised language. They are beginning to use their knowledge of grammar to adapt and substitute individual words and set phrases. They are beginning to use dictionaries or glossaries to check words they have learnt.	[unchanged from 2004, see left]	translate sentences and short texts from English into the assessed language to convey key messages accurately and to apply grammatical knowledge of language and structures in context
Level 5	produce a short piece of continuous writing, consisting of simple sentences, to seek and convey personal information, feelings and opinions; adapt a simple model text by substituting phrases and simple sentences of their own; apply	produce short pieces of writing, in simple sentences, that seek and convey information and opinions. They refer to recent experiences or future plans, as well as to everyday activities.	write short texts on a range of familiar topics, using simple sentences. They refer to recent experiences or future plans, as well as to everyday activities.	

(*Continued*)

Table 5.6 (Continued)

1992 National Curriculum Levels	National Curriculum (NCC 1991: 32–35); levels 5–6 expected for majority of pupils at end of Key Stage 3, i.e. aged 14	National Curriculum Programme of Study Key Stage 3, 2004 revision, = QCA 2004)	Languages Programme of Study (QCA 2007)	National Curriculum 2013	GCSE Specification AQA (2016) for GCSEs sat from 2018 onwards
	basic elements of grammar concepts and generally adopt correct word order	Although there may be some mistakes, the meaning can be understood with little or no difficulty. They use dictionaries or glossaries to check words they have learnt and to look up unknown words.	Although there may be some mistakes, the meaning can be understood with little or no difficulty. They use dictionaries or glossaries to check words they have learnt and to look up unknown words.		
Level 6	use simple descriptive language to write about familiar topics and experiences, including future and past events	write in paragraphs, using simple descriptive language, and refer to past, present and future actions and events. They apply grammar in new contexts. Although there may be a few mistakes, the meaning is usually clear	write texts giving and seeking information and opinions. They use descriptive language and a variety of structures. They apply grammar in new contexts. Although there may be a few mistakes, the meaning is usually clear.		

Level 7	write a number of simple, discrete statements to explain how something is done or give clear instructions; produce a short piece of continuous writing, real or imaginary, linking sentences and paragraphs and structuring links; redraft writing tasks already given, achieving greater accuracy, precision and variety of expression	Pupils produce pieces of writing of varying lengths on real and imaginary subjects, using an appropriate register. They link sentences and paragraphs, structure ideas and adapt previously learnt language for their own purposes. They edit and redraft their work, using reference sources to improve their accuracy, precision and variety of expression. Although there may be occasional mistakes, the meaning is clear.	Pupils write articles or stories of varying lengths, conveying opinions and points of view. They write about real and imaginary subjects and use an appropriate register. They link sentences and paragraphs, structure ideas and adapt previously learnt language for their own purposes. They edit
Level 8	write an imaginative text, responding to and developing the content of something read, seen or heard; express	express and justify ideas, opinions or personal points of view, and seek the views of others.	produce formal and informal texts in an appropriate style on familiar topics. They

(*Continued*)

Table 5.6 (Continued)

1992 National Curriculum Levels	National Curriculum (NCC 1991: 32–35); levels 5–6 expected for majority of pupils at end of Key Stage 3, i.e. aged 14	National Curriculum Programme of Study Key Stage 3, 2004 revision, = QCA 2004)	Languages Programme of Study (QCA 2007)	National Curriculum 2013	GCSE Specification AQA (2016) for GCSEs sat from 2018 onwards
	ideas, opinions or a personal point of view, with reasons, on a familiar topic; seek information or the views of others on a matter of personal significance	They develop the content of what they have read, seen or heard. Their spelling and grammar are generally accurate, and the style is appropriate to the content. They use reference materials to extend their range of language and improve their accuracy.	express and justify ideas, opinions or personal points of view and seek the views of others. They develop the content of what they have read, seen or heard. Their spelling and grammar are generally accurate. They use reference materials to extend their range of language and improve their accuracy.		
Level 9	express a range of responses and attitudes to events, issues and opinions; develop an argument giving reasons in	Exceptional Performance: Pupils write coherently and accurately about a wide range	Exceptional Performance: Pupils communicate ideas accurately and in an		

	support of or against a particular point of view; complete a range of written tasks, both factual and imaginative, adapting length and style to match purpose and reader	of factual and imaginative topics. They choose the appropriate form of writing for a particular task, and use resources to help them vary the style and scope of their writing.	appropriate style over a range of familiar topics, both factual and imaginative. They write coherently and accurately. They use resources to help them vary the style and scope of their writing.
Level 10	adopt different ways of writing on the same subject in order to change the impact on the reader; choose the appropriate form of writing for a particular task, organising content and ideas to produce a coherent and largely accurate piece of writing; write independently on a range of factual and imaginative topics with little or no use of reference materials		

*I have not included the additional attainment targets at Levels 1–4 for pupils learning Chinese and Japanese (e.g. Level 1: copy simply characters correctly with correct stroke order).

5.6 Conclusions

The history of language assessment since the 1850s has seen substantial change. First, there has been a marked increase in the importance accorded to the productive skills in school examinations (from none at all in 1900 to a 25% weighting for each currently at GCSE), making school examinations more like those used by other bodies such as the Institute of Linguists, the Royal Society of Arts, and the Armed Forced (STANAG). Second, the "four skills" emerged as explicit test constructs – listening comprehension was the last of these, 50 years later than oral production. Another tendency has been an increasing desire to measure attainment in the four skills discretely, avoiding confounding factors. Meanwhile test formats which clearly require a combination of skills – especially translation into the language – disappeared (at least until the most recent version of the National Curriculum). As test-setters gave growing importance to context validity, assessments were designed to measure how pupils might be expected to perform in a real situation, rather that testing mere knowledge (for example, explicit knowledge of grammatical rules). Another consistent development over time – and one that does not seem in any danger of being reversed – is the increasing provision of assessment that caters to and discriminates between pupils at all ability levels. This is an achievement without which much recent policy development – with the focus on language learning experience for all – would not have been possible.

This chapter has not considered the roads *not* travelled in the history of assessment, but they too are worthy of our attention. For example, we should note that the orthodoxy that languages should be assessed through discrete tests of the four skills (reflected in the CEFR, STANAG and the National Curriculum) did not go completely unchallenged. Some advocates of Graded Objectives devised criteria for the assessment of integrated skills in the 1980s. Mindful of the washback effect, such advocates feared that that if skills are tested separately, they are likely to be taught separately, yielding a highly artificial and perhaps therefore less conducive environment for language acquisition. They therefore proposed a so-called Mode 3 GCSE assessment scheme including the testing of integrated skills, which was not, however, accepted. Plans for a languages "Diploma" at A-level – which would have encouraged the study of two languages at A-level, as part of a wider proposed overhaul in the early twenty-first century of assessment at that stage – also came to naught.

Nor have we considered in any detail the relative weighting of components – whether overtly, in the percentage allocated to each of the assessment types, or less visibly, but crucially, in the detailed marking criteria (such as a statement in the 1977 French O-level that in the writing tasks, marks would be equally awarded for grammatical accuracy, variety of structure, appropriate idiom and vocabulary, and for subject matter (JMB 1977 specification, p. 124)). Yet the weighting of individual components can have invidious washback effects – for example, when writing and oral skills were, briefly, weighted more heavily than the receptive skills in the early twenty-first century, an unintended consequence was the reduction of class time devoted to those receptive skills, which in turn tended to reduce the amount of input from which pupils could learn. Nor have we considered the details of marking reliability and validity, which are currently widely perceived as a problem for languages, with consequences not only for individual pupils to whom an injustice may be done, but also for the status of languages if able pupils are advised against a "risky" subject. The devil is in the detail.

At the time of writing, new specifications for both GCSE and A-levels have just been published, but the first pupils will not sit those papers until 2018. It remains to be seen how the goals articulated in the new National Curriculum, the details of syllabus content and assessment criteria derived from it by the examination boards under the guidance of Ofqual (the Office of Qualifications and Examinations Regulation) will translate in to teaching pupils, and the details of how those pupils will in turn will be assessed.

5.7 150 years of examinations

To help illustrate some of the trends discussed in Chapter 5, this section, available online at www.routledge.com/9781138651289, offers a selection of examination papers since 1858. Two examination boards are represented: University of Cambridge Local Examinations Syndicate (i.e. the UCLES) and AQA (originally the Assessment and Qualifications Alliance, the result of mergers of a number of other boards). Section 5.7.1 presents UCLES Junior French papers from the first year in which UCLES set examinations, 1858 (a Senior German paper from the same year is published in McLelland 2015a: 98–99); 5.7.2 presents the UCLES Junior Spanish paper from 1900. No papers from the 1930s are provided, but see 5.2.5 for dictation passages from 1930 and 5.3.3 for examples of guided writing tasks from 1930. The 1940 German paper in 5.7.3 contains an early instance of reading comprehension, based (unusually) on a passage of verse. In 5.7.4, a UCLES O-level French paper is given from 1951, the first year of O-levels ('Ordinary' levels). Section 5.7.5 provides a UCLES Spanish O-level paper from 1980, including a listening and reading comprehension. Finally, in 5.7.6, papers from the AQA GCSE French examinations of 1999 are given, illustrating the standard expected at Foundation and Higher tiers of the GCSE qualification. See also notes 11 and 12 on p. 169 for other past examinations available online.

Note that early examinations give very little information on how relative components are weighted. At best, they indicate which elements need to be passed. For example, the 1940 UCLES Higher School Certificate examination regulations in French, German and Spanish stipulated merely that "the first two papers and the oral test together carry about two-thirds of the total marks" (Cam.c.11.51.83: 9). Note too that the mere appearance of a task on an examination paper did not always entail an expectation that all candidates would be able to pass it. For example, the UCLES regulations for 1912 listed six sections in the Junior French and German examinations, but for a pass, pupils were required only to reach a satisfactory standard in the section of questions on grammar and on one of the two sections containing unprepared translations into English. The remaining sections – translation into English of passages from "set books", translation into the language, or free composition – need not be passed at all, though for a distinction, a suitable standard in translation into the language or free composition was necessary.

Notes

1 For example, note Christ's investigation of examination standards in the history of the German *Abitur* (Christ 2005).
2 Their reports are published on the House of Commons website. I am grateful to Sebastian Puncher for this information.
3 These examinations can be accessed via the Bodleian Library's catalogue, by searching for Sandhurst examinations. Thanks to Sebastian Puncher for pointing out this resource to me.
4 On the earlier history of the RSA see also Menzies and Wood (1935), Sanderson (1913).
5 On Bernays, see Flood (1999), Glass (1996).
6 The RSA also set examinations for many British Prisoners of War in 1942, through the British Red Cross Society and Order of St. John of Jerusalem Prisoners of War Department. Not surprisingly, perhaps, the greatest number of passes in the language examinations was for German: 225, compared to 85 for French, 45 for Spanish, 26 for Italian and 19 for Russian – perhaps the first and only context in language learning history where German took the place of French as most-studied language. Candidates quite often sat for more than Stage (I, II and III) at the same time. Other bodies also made their examinations available to Prisoners of War, but with only one or two candidates each: the Institute of Linguists, the London Chamber of Commerce, the Chartered Institute of Secretaries and the College of Preceptors all had candidates successful in French, at various levels; the East Midland Educational Union passed two candidates in Spanish. (RSA PR.ED/100/10/9, Part I, pp. 7, 12–16).
7 There is no published history of the Chamber, and I have not consulted its archives. The examinations were apparently originally produced by the Birmingham Camber of Commerce in response to demands from industry, especially in the Midlands, for a test of oral fluency. In 1970, the examination was described as "akin to the oral sections of the Institute of Linguists' examinations. Pictures and photographs, previously prepared topics of personal interest, situations, recorded conversations and sight translations into English are used, as well as discussing in the language of the candidate's special expertise" (Adam 1970: 33).
8 Cloudsley Brereton seems to have been a key figure in the committee which devised the syllabi (compare his reports on the state of modern language teaching, Brereton et al. 1908, Brereton 1930).
9 A useful overview of patterns of assessment in the non-school examining bodies like the RSA and Institute of Linguists at one moment in time is provided by Adam (1970: 36). On examinations for adults in the 1990s, see also Arthur (1996: 57–58).
10 The question of who the markers are is also worth noting. For the 1965 summer examinations the Joint Matriculation Board reported that, of 1438 examiners at O-level, 65% were practising school teachers; 9% were university staff; 11% worked at Colleges of Education and Technical colleges. At A-level, of 535 examiners, 41% were practising teachers, 42% university teachers, and 9% at colleges. The hidden history of examinations setters and markers is one that I cannot pursue here – King's College professor Adolphus Bernays was involved in the setting of the first RSA examinations; Karl Breul appeared on the list of UCLES examiners for the first time in 1885; Walter Ripman examined alongside him in 1898; Beresford Webb (a textbook author himself: see McLelland 2015a: 256, 361) is listed as an examiner alongside Breul in 1901.

11 For a history of language testing formats from a tester's perspective, see Weir (2013). An example of a detailed mark scheme, used by Cambridge Assessment for the 1994 French GCSE, is available on their website, together with the corresponding syllabus and question paper: www.cambridgeassessment.org.uk/our-research/archives-service/past-exam-material/french/.

12 Unfortunately, the Institute of Linguists (since 2005 the Chartered Institute of Linguists) has not kept an archive of examinations material through its somewhat chequered history. In the 150th year of Cambridge Local examinations, Cambridge Assessment published a facsimile volume of the 1858 examination papers including French and German. It has also made available a small selection of French syllabi and examination papers since 1857: www.cambridgeassessment.org.uk/our-research/archives-service/past-exam-material/french/. Lawnswood High School also has a small number of French papers on its website (www.lawnswoodhighschool.com/lhs/, or follow the links http://dickhudson.com/history-of-fl-in-uk/. Many of Sandhurst's examinations, held by the Bodleian, have been digitized and are available online through the SOLO catalogue. Contemporary collections of 'past papers', such as those by Rühle (1881, 1884), are also useful sources. For other such collections for German, see McLelland (2015a: 175).

13 IAAM (1952:309–316) is also a valuable source for specimen tests for use at the end of first year and second year in French and German.

14 Not all the categories included by Adam are listed here. Some additional requirements at the Institute of Linguists and RSA examinations are as follows: Final examination requires consecutive interpretation, and an English summary of a French text; Intermediate level requires interpretation of a conversation between French and English speakers; Level II requires translation at sight into French; RSA bilingual secretary Certificate requires written answer in French on a text in English.

15 No mark scheme is given in the regulations, which state only that Paper I (translation into English plus comprehension) has more marks allocated to it than Paper II. See also 5.7.7 for an example of a 1951 paper.

16 Lower-tier papers did not require any translation into the language (see the 1858 paper in 5.7). For comparison, for admission to Sandhurst in 1881, candidates sitting the preliminary German paper also had to translate a few phrases and short sentences into German: "half-past three; the day before yesterday; I was writing a letter when my friend called; they went out as he arrived" (Rühle 1884: 21).

17 This examination also contained, as a separate task, some short, non-literary sentences for translation, "Did you know that Ford is my cousin? Do you know him? Yes, I have known him for two years."

18 This is the opening of the fourth paragraph for translation, rather than the start of the passage. It is cited in the 1995 examiners' report, p. 86.

19 In one case only (a Sandhurst examination in December 1879) – not repeated as far as I am aware – candidates were asked to spot the grammatical mistake in given sentences.

20 It features alongside lexical, semantic, phonological, orthographic and orthoepic competences; other general competences are knowledge of the world and sociocultural knowledge, sociolinguistic and pragmatic competences.

21 In 1869, however, in the equivalent paper, this time set by a Rev. C. Schoell rather than Müller, a more standard essay topic was set, "Country Life". In the equivalent French paper that year, no composition was required.

22 For comparison, Christ (2005: 21) finds the earliest mention of oral competence in the German *Abitur* in Brunswick in 1861, although this was not yet the norm – "C'est seulement à la fin du siècle, que l'on s'intéresse vraiment pour les capacités orales" (Christ 2005: 21–22).

172 *Assessment*

23 For second and third class, candidates could write their answers in English, but still "must be able to translate a piece of easy prose into German" (RSA 1857–1870: 77).
24 The paper cited was set by a M. Alphonse Esquiros; the December paper of the same year, set by M. Savoye, did not include a composition.
25 The earliest requirement for a letter is that set in the December 1859 French examination of the class for commissions: "Write to a friend a short letter in which you will point out, in a familiar way, some of the advantages which would be offered to an English officer by a thorough and practical knowledge of the French language" ([Sandhurst] 1859: 18).
26 See the "Exemplar Material: Controlled Assessment Writing" for Spanish produced as part of an AQA Teacher Resource Bank (2010) for an example of how this worked in practice: http://filestore.aqa.org.uk/subjects/AQA-4695-W-TRB-EMC-2010–2003.PDF
27 Navy, army and air force candidates were *required* to take the paper that included this test (see Cam.c.11.51.116, Pamphlet *Special Arrangements for Members of HM Forces*. Published March 1958). Besides the aural comprehension task, Paper II included a passage for translation into the target language; the whole paper took one and a quarter hours. Paper I, as already in 1940, still consisted of two passages for translation and one passage as a comprehension test, with questions to be answered in the target language. The equivalent Paper II in 1940 had contained a passage for English for translation into the language, and an outline in the language of a story for expansion (as in 5.3.3).
28 In the non-school sector, the RSA's examination in French for catering students, offered in the mid-1990s, consisted entirely of a thirty-minute listening paper, with all questions and answers to be written in English – e.g. understanding instructions from an *aboyeur* (who passes orders from the dining room to the kitchen) (RSA 1994).
29 In the USA, the primacy of literature was similarly taken for granted. The Committee of Twelve recommended in its 1900 report that an intermediate school or college German course should involve reading some 400 pages of "moderately difficult prose and poetry" (Modern Language Association of America 1901: 1419); for French the expectation was 400–600 pages, with about 1,000 pages to be aimed for in an advanced course.
30 Even in the standard language subjects, in the second of the two literature papers, there was also some focus on "the social and literary history of the period; some knowledge of this history will be expected". Cam.c.11.51.73: 8).
31 In the twenty-first century, and likewise intended to increase transparency of assessment, a detailed "Exemplification of standards" was also undertaken, by teachers working with the Qualifcations and Curriculum Development Agency (QCDA), providing exemplars of performance at each level. These disappeared into the archive with the change of government in 2010: see http://webarchive.nationalarchives.gov.uk/20110914130015/http:/curriculum.qcda.gov.uk/key-stages-3-and-4/subjects/key-stage-3/modern-foreign-languages/assessing-mfl/exemplification/index.aspx for the web archive, with real-life examples of pupil attainment at various levels.
32 Clark & Hamilton (1984) is an example of a syllabus for German based on a "graded communicative approach" to school language learning in Scotland.
33 NVQs are National Vocational Qualifications; SVQs are the Scottish equivalent, Scottish Vocational Qualifications. In languages, an NVQ Level 2 is roughly equivalent to a GCSE pass.
34 To be precise, the National Curriculum draft of 1991 did include "developing cultural awareness" as one of six additional skills to be developed (the others

broadly concern generic learning skills – e.g. "developing the ability to learn independently", p. 45), but this did not translate into dedicated attainment targets. By the 2004 version of the National Curriculum, cultural awareness was simply mentioned twice briefly (pp. 6, 16).

35 In the same year, Clark (1972) similarly included "Culture Testing" and "Literature Testing".
36 In this context, essay questions set in the first half of the history of language examinations are instructive. A December 1859 examination of the Sandhurst class for commissions included a passage from translation on the topic "English and French politeness contrasted", by Oliver Goldsmith; at the 1920 Senior School Certificate French examination, pupils were invited to write 250–300 words on the topic *Quant au caractère, l'Allemand est sérieux, l'Anglais est doux, le Français gai* ('In their character, the German is serious, the Englishman gentle, the Frenchman gay'). For discussion of intercultural awareness see 4.10 and, specifically for German, McLelland (2015, Chapter 6).
37 This was a reduction from 144 in an earlier draft (National Curriculum Council 1991: letter to Secretary of State for Education, no page number]).
38 See DfE (2015: 4). Admittedly, many schools already had schemes of learning which incorporated aspects of literature, poetry and film at Key Stages 3 and 4.
39 These equivalencies are suggested by Milton (2007), but he presents them only in order to challenge them. Looking at vocabulary knowledge in particular, Milton finds that while the Lower Tier GCSE might just about be matched with A1, GCSE learners fall well short of the B1 Threshold level of 2,000 words (and 80% coverage of normal text) and it would appear they are well short of the level needed to be independent users. "A-level" students, with under 2,000 words on average, look like they are just hitting the vocabulary levels needed for gist understanding which would place them at B1 rather than B2 level. Elsewhere (e.g. in informal guidance in choosing the right level of Language Centre course at University), A-level is now sometimes presented as spanning B1 and B2, with GCSE Higher spanning A2/B1.
40 I have not included the additional attainment targets given at Levels 1–4 for pupils learning Chinese and Japanese (e.g. Level 1: copy simply characters correctly with correct stroke order).

6 Making the case for languages
A history of advocacy and policy

6.1 Introduction

Chapter 1 of this book examined the history of language teaching and learning "from below", tracing the emergence of different language learning choices and patterns over time. This final chapter now examines that history "from above": the history of efforts to drive language teaching and learning in particular directions through advocacy, lobbying and policymaking in the twentieth and early twenty-first centuries. What have those with power, or at least those Modern Languages advocates seeking to influence power, claimed that language learning and teaching is actually for, and about how it is best achieved? As Cooper (1989) asked, "What actors attempt to influence what behaviours of which people for what ends under what conditions by what means through what decision-making process with what effect?" (Cooper 1989: 98, summarized by Hornberger 2006: 24).

A comprehensive history of advocacy and policy is beyond the scope of this short chapter. Such a history might seek to evaluate the success or failure of campaigning in affecting policy, and of policymaking in achieving desired outcomes. However, we still lack the raw archives-based research of individual policy decisions that would form the basis of such a history.[1] For example, some key documents – such as the National Curriculum documents discussed in 6.4 – are anonymous in their published form, so that much of their history can only be traced through archival work and/ or oral history methods.[2] Languages education has also been characterized by "policy busyness" over the last quarter of a century (see the chronological bibliography of key advocacy and policy documents in 6.6); it is impossible to do justice to the complexity of that development in this chapter, which does no more than offer a broad overview of certain themes. We should note too that languages policy is not only a matter for those interested in school and university education. For example, the Ministry of Defence has its own history of language policies and priorities, which I cannot go into here (e.g. Ministry of Defence 2013; see also 3.1.3).

Nearly half a century ago, the Committee on Research and Development in Modern Languages (CDRML) noted, "There still remain large gaps in our knowledge of ascertainable facts on such matters as: which foreign languages are being taught to how many, by how many, for how long, for what purpose and to what level of competence?" (CRDML 1971: 9). Regular *Language Trends* surveys (produced since 2003 first by CILT, then by CfBT) have gone some way to addressing this need. But a characteristic of British languages education policy is its lack of centralization, which makes it difficult to survey and evaluate policies across all four 'home nations'. Within Britain, Scotland has its own education system, and Wales also has autonomy in some relevant ways. England, Wales and Northern Ireland have multiple Local Education Authorities (LEAs), and, several different examining boards (originally regional, but all offering examinations to schools nationwide). There are differences too between state schools and independent school provision (the latter accounting for about 5% of pupils). The National Curriculum, introduced in 1988, is an attempt to provide at least some uniformity, but it applies only in England, and only in state schools. The crucial question of how much *time* to devote to each subject in the curriculum is also unregulated, and is left to individual schools to decide.

These conditions are very different to those in some other parts of Europe (e.g. France, Italy, Poland); France has "a highly centralized system", with "rigid curricula allowing little flexibility" (King et al. 2011: 22), and this has long been the case (on the imposition of a specified "eclectic" method nationally in France 1920–1960, see Puren 1994). At the other extreme is the Republic of Ireland, which – aside from policies on the Irish language – was reported in 2011 to have no general languages policy, no national curriculum, and only three compulsory school subjects (Irish, English, mathematics); there, "foreign languages survive in post-primary schools because the National University of Ireland requires a foreign language for matriculation" (David Little, reported in King et al. 2011: 24). A comparative international history of foreign language education policy across such different jurisdictions is a desideratum – drawing comparisons across Europe, but also with other English-speaking countries – but it is not yet possible to write that history. For all these reasons, then, this chapter largely concentrates on the case of England.

A full history of languages policy processes would differentiate decision making at different levels: at national level, within LEA, and in individual schools. It would also need to take account of the fact that it is not only *languages* education policymaking that determines language teaching and learning realities. Wider educational policies or policies from other arenas also have intended or unintended consequences for school-level policy decisions about languages education too, such as health and safety and child protection legislation rendering school exchanges more difficult. A single educational policy decision can have considerable impact. For example the decision in 2010 to include a modern foreign language in the English Baccalaureate, a new award for pupils who achieve five good GCSEs in any one of English, mathematics, two sciences, a foreign language and history or geography, sent a strong signal that a modern language was considered a "core" subject.[3] Developments in the tertiary sector, seeking to influence university students' subject choices, also affect languages in schools, not least the availability of graduates to become teachers. The decision to categorize languages at university level as Strategically Important and Vulnerable subjects in 2005 (HEFCE 2005) was a positive step; the decision of some universities to close their modern languages units – most recently Salford, the University of Ulster, and Northumbria – is not. Policy initiatives driven by goals outside education altogether may also intervene – the ASTP and JSSL show the effect that defence policies can have, with the money behind them to implement large-scale language programmes quickly (see 3.1.3); the support for foreign languages (along with science, mathematics, and technology) in the USA's National Defense Education Act of 1958 is a similar case (see 6.3.3; see also Roeming 1967; Watzke 2002: 46–51).

The fact that language planning never occurs in a vacuum means that "It is rarely simple to determine the degree to which a given planning goal has been met. It is usually far harder to determine what factors contributed to that outcome. It is harder still to determine the relative contribution of each factor to the outcome" (Cooper 1989: 163). This chapter does not, therefore, seek to answer the question of "what works?", or even just "what has worked in the past?", questions that might be posed by a "rationalist" approach to policy learning, where a policy perceived as successful in one context may be seen as transferable to new contexts.[4] Rather, like Watzke's historical study of twentieth-century foreign languages in USA education policy (Watzke 2002), it is an attempt to identify continuities and discontinuities, and to draw some conclusions from them. It concentrates on only the first and most fundamental of the policy goals in language acquisition planning identified by Kaplan and Baldauf (1997: 127–140): deciding what languages should be taught where within the curriculum, including to which pupils, and at what stages in their careers.[5] While policy analysis generally identifies distinct stages in the process of policymaking,[6] my approach here is thematic. After an overview of the actors involved in languages advocacy and policy planning (6.2), I consider in 6.3 the history of key questions in languages education: Who should learn? How many languages should pupils learn? When should they begin? Which languages should be offered? In 6.4, I then investigate the changing rationales that have been used to make the case for languages education. After a brief conclusion (6.5), 6.6 provides a chronological – but not comprehensive – bibliography of key documents in the history of languages advocacy and policy. (Other literature referred to in this chapter is listed in the main bibliography.)

6.2 Who sets the agenda? A brief history of actors in languages education advocacy and policy

As the chronological bibliography of reports and policy documents given in 6.7 shows, since the late nineteenth century onwards, government and professional associations' reports have repeatedly turned their attention to the status of modern languages teaching in schools, or of the position of particular languages. To begin with, those seeking to shape professional, public and government opinion on modern languages and their teaching fell into three categories. A first and very important group, in the early stages, was a small number of charismatic individuals, involved themselves in teaching or teacher training, who led by example, and who were also often prominent in their professional associations. Some of those individuals were noted in Chapter 3: Henry Weston Eve, Robert H. Quick, Karl Breul and Walter Ripman; it is still true today that certain key individuals drive much languages advocacy. A second group were the professional teacher associations: the College of Preceptors, with its publication the *Educational Times*; the Headmasters' Conference, founded with 13 members in 1869, of which Eve was President for a period; and the Modern Language Association (founded in 1892), with its journal, the *Modern Language Quarterly*. The discussions over whether teachers of modern languages should be British-born or native speakers is one example of an early policy debate carried out in these fora (see 3.3.1). The Modern Language Association continues today as the Association for Language Learning,[7] alongside the Independent Schools Modern Language Association. The Association of Assistant Masters (founded in 1891, incorporated in 1901) also produced overviews of modern languages teaching at irregular intervals: IAAM 1929, 1949, 1956, 1967). In recent years, university-level associations have also become involved, including the British Academy (established in 1902) and the University Council of Modern Languages, established in 1993 (e.g. Mulkerne & Graham 2011).

A third and powerful voice from the early twentieth century onwards were the government-commissioned reports, whether specific to modern languages (such as the Leathes Report of 1918) or not. Some of the most oft-quoted statements on modern languages and on how they should be taught came from reports with a different, or broader focus than modern languages specifically, beginning with the first two major education reports of the nineteenth centuries, the Clarendon Report and the Taunton Report (1864, 1968), both of which gave views on the place of modern languages in the schools that they investigated (see 3.1.5, 3.2.2). Likewise, the *Second Interim Report of the committee of education for Salesmanship* (Board of Education 1930d: 343) was devoted entirely to Modern Languages and contained the most detailed comparative study to date of languages education in Europe, with notes on the teaching of modern languages in Denmark, Germany, Holland, Sweden and Switzerland.

Gradually, from the 1960s onwards, the voices of professional language teacher trainers joined the discussions (on this history, see Johnstone & Trim 1996, Johnstone 2014). Already in the late nineteenth century, there had been publications intended to support teacher training. For example, Mary Brebner's report on *The Method of Teaching Modern Languages in Germany* (1898, reprinted until 1909), based on her observations on a travelling scholarship in Germany, may well make her the most influential woman in the early history of modern language teaching in Britain. From the 1960s onwards, purpose-written works by modern language education researchers replaced the earlier, sometimes idiosyncratic ruminations on teaching languages by teacher-practitioners.[8] Their authors sought to articulate a coherent vision of the purpose and methods, and assessment of modern languages education. (e.g. Wringe 1976, 1989, 1996; Stern 1983; Hawkins 1987; see also Chapter 5). These modern language education researchers, based in higher education, played an increasingly important role in language policy discussions. For example, Michael Byram's work on foreign language education

178 *Making the case for languages*

as intercultural education has had an impact on curriculum content and on the formulation of rationales for language learning (see Byram 2008a, Chapter 5, and 6.3.3, 6.4). Another new voice, in the 1970s and 1980s, was that of Language Advisors appointed to lead language teachers' professional development in their in Local Education Authorities (see 3.2.2). Their National Association of Language Advisors became a voice in discussions about language teaching in the 1970s and 1980s, but there are now considerably fewer language advisors, and those that survive tend to combine the role with a wide portfolio of duties.

A unique voice – and a crucial development for the support and advocacy of modern foreign languages – was the Centre for Information on Language Teaching (CILT) established in 1966 (see 6.4). From 1966 to 2011, CILT supported language teaching by promoting and disseminating research, producing sample materials and curriculum guides, and monitoring trends in language teaching (e.g. Perren 1978, Moys 1984), also supporting policy work of the National Congress on Languages in Education (NCLE); CILT's second director John Trim was also a powerful voice in European language teaching policy, including the formulation of the CEFR (see Chapter 5). CILT was merged in 2001 with the Languages National Training Organization, a body concerned with standards in languages for vocational purposes,[9] and again in 2011 with CfBT (Centre for British Teaching), which has continued to produce important policy briefings, such as the annual *Language Trends* surveys and a review of international primary languages provision (Tinsley & Comfort 2012; see 6.3.3). In Scotland, Northern Ireland, and Wales, Northern Ireland CILT (NICILT), CILT Cymru and Scottish CILT (SCILT) continue, although CILT Cymru has had much-reduced funding since 2014.[10] The British Council – which took charge of Assistantship schemes in 1992 (see 3.3.4, n. 34) – has increasingly also had a voice in foreign language education advocacy, commissioning reports on Britain's language needs, including more specialized studies such as those on Arabic and Chinese in British Schools (British Council 2013, 2015, Board & Tinsley 2015). The British Council also serves as the secretariat to the All-Parliamentary Group for Modern Languages, established in 2008.

An important feature of British languages education advocacy and policy is the prominence of charitable foundations, in particular the Nuffield Foundation and the National Foundation for Educational Research (NFER). The NFER, established in 1946, is perhaps best known in modern languages research for its deputy director Claire Burstall's evaluation of the Primary Languages pilot in the 1970s (see 6.3.3). The Nuffield Foundation, established in 1943, has funded various important projects in modern languages education, including the primary languages pilot just mentioned. The Nuffield Foreign Languages Materials Project funded the development of a series of audiovisual materials for younger pupils in several languages in the 1960s and 1970s, as well as intensive courses for adults, in response to the needs identified by the CRDML (see McLelland 2015a: 185 for the course in German; see Muckle 2008a: 154–156 on materials for Russian). Nuffield also funded enquiries and position papers;[11] in 2000, the Nuffield Languages Enquiry formed the background for the government's National Languages Strategy published two years later (Nuffield 2000, DfES 2002).

Languages policy development has long taken place in a wider than national context. The Reform Movement begun was a European phenomenon, with modern languages experts already looking cross-nationally from the late nineteenth century onwards. For example, Arnold and Waren (1900) reported a trial of "the German reform method" in an English preparatory school, in which the German Rossmann and Schmidt's *Lehrbuch der französischen Sprache* was used as a basis for teaching throughout, together with the Swede K.E. Palmgren's collection of songs in French and other languages (Arnold & Waren 1900: 245). In the USA, the Committee of Twelve's 1901 report, including discussion of the "phonetic" method, is evidence of reception of reform ideas beyond Europe too. Modern language teaching was the topic of an international UNESCO seminar in Ceylon in 1953, also attended by UK delegates (cf. UNESCO 1953: 13–14; UNESCO 1955). The Audio-Visual Language Association also promoted audiovisual and audiolingual methods – whose origins lie on the continent (see Reinfried 2012) – amongst "progressive" teachers in Britain from the 1960s onwards. Even before Britain joined the EU in 1973, the CRDML noted the "important resolutions bearing on modern languages" passed by European Ministers of Education in 1961 and 1962 (CRDML 1968: 1). Indeed, the European ministers' emphasis on "the desirability of encouraging [. . .] linguistic and psychological research with a view to improving and expanding the teaching of materials" is echoed strongly in the framing of the CRDML's own terms of reference, "to examine the need for research and development in modern languages [. . .] and, where necessary, to stimulate research and development" (CRDML 1968: vi). Likewise, the European Ministers' focus at the time on the need to expand language teaching for adults as well as in schools clearly informed the opening section on "The Language Scene" in CRDML's first report, which noted "the importance of practical skills [. . .] and the need for courses to teach such skills to adults quickly" (CRDML 1968: 1).

The EU and the larger Council of Europe have continued to be very active in issuing reports, comparative studies, guidelines and charters which are relevant to policy developments in Britain too.[12] King et al. (2011: 30) identify five threads in European "policy/policies" on languages since about 1985: 1. a focus on communication skills for worker mobility; 2. a focus on the "acquisition of competences"; 3. a recognition of the equality in principle of all languages (though the reality may be more nuanced, and with the status of "'non-European' immigrant or world languages" less clear); 4. a belief that learning languages and understanding other cultures will lead to better understanding, greater tolerance, mutual respect, and 5. "the creation of a multi-faceted 'European' identity"; and multilingualism as facilitating trade and contributing to "Europe's competitiveness and prosperity". Key EU initiatives include the funding of Comenius, Erasmus and Leonardo da Vinci mobility programmes (for school pupils and teachers, for university students and staff, and for staff in vocational education, respectively). The Council of Europe's Language Policy Unit was established in Strasbourg in 1954, and its European Centre for Modern Languages in Graz, Austria, in 1994 (www.ecml.at/; Martyniuk & Slivensky 2012), with the mission "to encourage excellence and innovation in language teaching and to help Europeans learn languages more efficiently" (www.ecml.at/). The Council of Europe's Charter for Regional or Minority Languages came in to force in 1998, drawing attention to linguistic diversity in Europe (www.coe.int/t/dg4/education/minlang/aboutcharter/default_en.asp). The EU's 2005 Framework Strategy on Multilingualism put forward a view of "multilingualism as a competence which supports both economic growth (trade, competitiveness) and social cohesion (mutual understanding and respect) as well as individual fulfilment and growth" (King et al. 2011: 12). We shall see in 6.4 that these twin emphases have become features of British languages advocacy too – economic growth has been a constant in languages advocacy since the 1918 Leathes Report; social cohesion is a more recent consideration.

The European Year of Languages (2001) was a major joint initiative of the EU and the Council of Europe to raise awareness of linguistic diversity and of language learning; since then, this awareness-raising agenda has been continued through the European Day of Languages held annually each September 26 (http://edl.ecml.at/). The European Language Portfolio was developed to "to support the development of learner autonomy, plurilingualism and intercultural awareness and competence" (www.coe.int/t/dg4/education/elp/; see also McLagan 2006; Dobson 2012). Most influential of all, for language learning worldwide, is without doubt the elaboration of the Council of Europe's Common European Framework of Reference for Languages (CEFR), whose levels are now used across the world in accrediting courses of study and in badging teaching materials (see Chapter 5).

6.3 Changes in policy direction: which languages, how many languages, when?

Having considered *who* has participated in modern languages lobbying and policymaking, we turn in this section to *what* they have advocated and decided, focussing on questions that have recurred throughout the twentieth century. The sections that follow consider the questions of how many languages to encourage pupils to learn (3.2.2), when pupils should start their foreign language learning (3.2.3) and which languages to offer (3.2.4). We begin, however, with a question whose answer changed radically in the course of the twentieth century: whether learning a language should be available, or indeed obligatory, for all.

6.3.1 Languages for all?

Probably the most dramatic and yet least contentious change in languages education policy over the past hundred years has been its democratization: the shift from viewing foreign languages as having a place only in the curricula of more able pupils (and of a social elite, see Chapter 3.2.1), to the attitude summed up in the title of the 2002 National Languages Strategy (2002), "Languages for All". As we saw in Chapter 3, "comprehensive" schools for all pupils began to replace the tri-partite system of grammar, secondary modern and technical schools in many parts of Britain from the 1950s onwards. The number of pupils attending comprehensive schools rose rapidly in the 1960s, especially after the Labour government came to power in 1964, and continued to rise even after the Conservatives took over in 1970 and effectively reversed the policy that had required LEAs to reorganize their provision (Crook 2002). French, let alone any other language, had only rarely been taught in secondary modern schools, but now a grammar school–type education, including a foreign language, became a possibility for all pupils in comprehensive schools. The Newsom Report on education for average and lesser ability pupils, *Half Our Future* (1963), argued strongly that pupils of all abilities should have the opportunity to learn a foreign language.[13] This dramatic change in languages provision was not, as far as I can see, prefaced by long years of campaigning by modern language advocates. Yet, with the exception of the recent introduction of primary languages provision, it is probably the most significant change in the history of foreign languages education.

Far from seeking to reach out to all abilities, earlier writers had generally done no more than digress briefly on how to deal with "the non-linguistic pupil" (IAAM 1929: 67–70, see also IAAM 1949: 266–271) or "the national problem" of the bottom form of a grammar school, a "kind of grammar-school proletariat" (Thimann 1955: 65). From the 1960s onwards, however, teachers and teacher educators began to reflect seriously on how to meet the needs of 'average', 'lesser ability' or 'mixed ability' language learners (e.g. CILT 1972; Varnava 1975; Richards 1976; Hawkins 1987: 46–60; Lee et al. 1998; Ainslie et al. 2001); alternative syllabuses were introduced in the 16+ O-level examinations (see Chapter 5).[14]

By 1984, 61% of girls and 43% of boys were studying a modern foreign language at GCSE level. These figures rose to a high point of 82% and 73%, respectively, in 1997, boosted by the fact that the National Curriculum, introduced in 1988, made a language a compulsory 'foundation subject' for pupils up to the age of 16, with effect from 1996 (Dearing & King/DfES 2007: 8). The trend has reversed since a foreign language ceased to be a required subject at Key Stage 4 (ages 14–16), and in 2007, only 53% of girls and 42% of boys were studying a modern foreign language at GCSE level (Rodeiro 2009: 2). Languages remain an "entitlement" for all pupils in the National Curriculum, but in 2010 fewer than 40% of schools had a majority of pupils taking a GCSE in a language; only 21% had three-quarters of pupils doing so, although in the independent sector a language is compulsory in nine out of ten schools (CILT 2010: 1). The compulsory language requirement was dropped in order to "offer a curriculum that would engage more pupils in effective learning, for example, in vocationally oriented programmes, and thus motivate them to stay on in education after sixteen". This was an important consideration at a time when the UK did poorly compared to other developed nations on the measure of young people staying in education after 17 (Dearing & King 2007: 9). However, the current lack of compulsion – only slightly counteracted by the inclusion of a language in the English Baccalaureate (see 6.1) – is the biggest difference between languages provision in England and many other parts of Europe, as we shall see in 6.3.3.

6.3.2 How many languages should pupils learn?

Another recurring question in the history of language learning debates is that of how many languages individual pupils should learn. The Leathes Report on Modern Studies considered that "We can never by school teaching provide for all the language needs of the nation". Given the limited time available in school, then, attaining a high level in one language at school was preferable to learning "two or more languages badly", for success in one language showed the pupils "that it can be done and how it is done". Learning additional languages in later life would then be embraced as "a pleasing adventure", whereas pupils who "have tried to learn two or more languages and [have] failed in all, [. . .] will assume that [they have] no gift for language and abandon hope of success" (Leathes 1918: 90–91, 208). While firmly of the view that all pupils should learn one language, and if only one, then a modern language rather than Latin and Greek, Leathes (1918: 129) took the view that "Three languages are too many for the majority; two languages are too many for a considerable proportion". Leathes also advised emphatically against starting a second language too soon after the first. At least two years should elapse, which would allow time "to discover whether the pupil shows aptitude for language at all" – if not, pupils should "be confined to the one, or abandon the study of foreign languages altogether" (Leathes 1918: 91).

It was those outside the field of modern languages education, but with an eye on language needs in trade, who were historically more likely to call enthusiastically for two or more languages. The final report of the Committee on Education for Salesmanship (Board of Education 1931: 117) suggested that for those pupils who remained at school still 18 (still a minority at the time), "there is no doubt that some of those who intend to enter commerce [. . .] would do well to study thoroughly at least two modern languages, and some even, if possible, to obtain a grounding in a third". In 1943, the Norwood Report on secondary school curricula and examinations took the view that

> the agent or representative of firms abroad needs other qualifications than ease in the language: besides personal qualities such as initiative and enterprise, he needs sympathy with ideas and an outlook different from those with which he is familiar at home; he must be alive to modes of thought and expression which are not like his own. We [. . .] hold that the best means to develop such sensitiveness is a wide knowledge of foreign languages. We should therefore consider a pupil to be best equipped if he had experience also of at least one language other than that of the country in which he proposed to take up occupation.
>
> (Norwood 1943: 115)

Thus "pupils who show promise should start a second language almost at once", and "once a language has been begun it ought not to be given up within two years" (Norwood 1943: 118).

Given the comparatively low numbers of pupils taking even *one* language to a significant standard in England in recent years, it is perhaps not surprising that the question of learning one, two or more foreign languages has received relatively little attention. One notable exception was a project funded by the Esmée Fairbairn Foundation and run in nine primary schools by the Association of School and College Leaders in 2005 and 2006 (see Barton & Bragg 2010). The project advocated giving pupils experience of a range of languages over the four years of Key Stage 2, drawn from different language families: Romance (French/Spanish), Germanic (German), Eastern European (Russian/Polish), Eastern (Japanese/Chinese) and Indian (Punjabi/Urdu). It was strongly recommended that one of the languages be Latin; some schools taught Esperanto. The project advocated a "multilingual language awareness model". However, the Rose Review of primary education (2009: 102–103) considered that "more sustained attention should be given to one or two languages to ensure that children make progress over four years in keeping with the expectations of the programme of learning".

As for the number of languages learned to an accredited level, where the topic has been raised, it is often to note it as a marker of social class. For example, Vidal Rodeiro (2007: 20) pointed out that over a third of pupils in fee-paying schools took more than one foreign language at GCSE, whereas in comprehensive schools, only 7.5% did (see 3.2.1). At European level, there has been much more policy interest in the question. The EU published in 2003 an Action Plan (2004–2006) for *Promoting Language Learning and Linguistic Diversity* which affirmed that "Every European citizen should have meaningful communicative competence in at least two other languages in addition to his or her mother tongue. This is an ambitious goal, but the progress already made by several Member States shows that it is perfectly attainable" (Commission of the European Communities 2003: 24). The initiative was at least partly intended to preserve foreign language learning diversity, on the grounds that "Learning one lingua franca alone is not enough" (Commission of the European Communities 2003: 24); it was widely recognized that the "Mother tongue plus two" (MT+2) expectation generally meant "Mother tongue plus English plus 1" (King et al. 2011: 34). The question of whether or not it is possible for the majority of pupils to attain some measure of success in learning two languages – the concern of Leathes (1918) – was not even posed in the document. France, Germany, and most European educational systems currently provide for starting a second foreign language either in upper primary or the first few years of secondary school. Within Britain, Scotland undertook in 2012 to implement the MT+2 policy, accepting in full all but three of the Scottish Government Languages Working Group's 35 recommendations to this effect, and the policy is now in the early stages of implementation. In Wales, Welsh is compulsory to the age of 16 in English-medium schools. A compulsory 20-hour foreign language module that forms half of a core unit in the Welsh Baccalaureate (a qualification alongside GCSEs and A-levels) is at best a mere taster, at worst a very misleading signal of what meaningful language learning involves. However, a new "Bilingualism plus 1" strategy announced in 2015 seeks to promote (but not require) the study of a foreign language for all Welsh pupils from primary school to examination level (Welsh Government 2015).

6.3.3 When to start?

The authors of a 2012 international review of primary education for CfBT observed that "perhaps the most compelling rationale for starting early is that it allows for more time for language learning overall and that this sustained experience has the potential to lead to higher levels of proficiency at the end of secondary school" (Tinsley & Comfort 2012: 5). There is currently a strong policy consensus, across Europe and internationally, in favour of starting language learning "early" – i.e. already in primary school.[15] In their report, Tinsley and Comfort (2012) listed 18 jurisdictions where language learning begins on starting school (typically around age six), 13 where it begins around age eight, six where it begins around age nine, and four where it begins later in primary education. Twelve countries had lowered the starting age in the last decade by at least three years, including France (age reduced to six in 2005) and China (age reduced to eight in 2001) (Tinsley & Comfort 2012: 29–30). The EU's view was that

> it is a priority for Member States to ensure that language learning in kindergarten and primary school is effective, for it is here that key attitudes towards other languages and cultures are formed, and the foundations for later language learning are laid.
> (Commission of the European Communities 2003: 7)

In England, although the Council of Europe's MT+2 recommendation was not adopted, the recommendation to start languages in primary school was implemented from 2014; in Scotland, primary languages will be taught from age five (working to full implementation by 2020); in Wales, a recently released plan envisages a foreign language from Year 5 of primary school. Yet, despite this current widespread consensus in favour of early language learning, the question of whether to introduce a foreign language prior to secondary school has been one of the most frequently debated of all in Britain over the last century or so.[16]

In the late nineteenth and early twentieth centuries, we find a rather contradictory state of affairs. On the one hand, French was very widely taught in British preparatory schools from a young age. On the other hand, educators consistently advised waiting until the age of 11 or 12 to begin a language. In 1900, the earliest investigation of the place of language learning among primary-age pupils in Britain found that French was taught in all 124 Preparatory Schools that responded to the survey;[17] 73 schools also offered German, but it was generally taken by a much smaller number of pupils (Arnold & Waren 1900: 232).

While Arnold and Waren were gathering their data on languages in English primary schools, in the USA, the Modern Language Association's Committee of Twelve was formulating its views on the teaching of languages to younger children. The committee elected to make no recommendation on the question at all: it would be "futile" to attempt a general answer, because choices would always depend on local conditions. However, they were sufficiently doubtful of its benefits to stipulate that any language offered should only be optional: "This point seems to require no argument" because "the value of the study is at best so uncertain" (Committee of Twelve 1901: 1406). Their discussion went on to canvass questions that were to be raised again and again in later discussions about primary language teaching: Is it worth starting a language if there is no prospect of it being continued in secondary school? How much can be achieved, really (their view was that even at its best, primary languages teaching is "good for nothing except as a foundation")? What size classes and what kind of specialist teachers would be needed? They concluded that "one who wishes to acquire a modern language thoroughly will always do well to begin in childhood" and that "The later period of youth is distinctly a bad time to begin". However, it is evident from their discussion that "childhood" meant around the age of 12 (Committee of Twelve 1901: 1407). Similarly, in Britain, Widgery (1888: 6–7 [first ed. 1888]), one of the earliest advocates of the reform movement, recommended starting French at the age of 11, followed by German at 12 and a half. The Leathes Committee was similarly cautious in 1918. Despite the well-established practice of teaching a modern language (nearly always French) to primary aged pupils in Britain's private Preparatory Schools, the Leathes Committee, like the Committee of Twelve, was "inclined to believe that the average pupil is not ready to begin the first language at school much before the age of twelve" (Leathes 1918: 117). "It appears to the majority of us far from certain that the early beginning of foreign languages at school is advantageous to their study in general" (Leathes 1918: 114).

A decade later, the first report on Modern Languages teaching by the Incorporated Association of Assistant Masters in Secondary Schools (1929) was highly critical of the teaching of French in Preparatory Schools – the standard reached in French was often "so low as to constitute a severe handicap to the boys themselves and to the schools which admit them" [i.e. the Public Schools to which they progressed] (IAAM 1929: 217). The IAAM attributed the poor outcomes to the lack of expert teachers, as well as to the lack of time devoted to the subject, considering five periods of 40–45 minutes a week the minimum. Despite their misgivings, and despite the fact that the IAAM's ideal time allocation has probably rarely been reached, teaching a modern language to primary aged pupils seems to have continued in private schools throughout the twentieth century. One of the key arguments advanced by the 2002 government report that recommended introducing languages in all state primary schools was the question of social equity: "In the independent sector almost all preparatory schools offer a second language to their 5–11 year olds. The maintained sector must do the same" (DfES 2002: 1).

These negative views on existing primary languages provision – already signalling concerns about teacher expertise and transition to the secondary school – may make the developments over the second half of the twentieth century and beyond surprising. However, there had always been some who advocated an early start for language learning. For example, the age at which to begin a language was one of six points on which a dissenting view was recorded by four members of the Leathes Committee. In the report's "Reservations" section, they argued that French vocabulary and simple grammar "can be and are learned and understood at an early age" (Leathes 1918: 237); pronunciation was indeed *more* easily learned by younger children, and "this difficult and tedious process should be got through at an early age, when time can best be spared for it" (Leathes 1918: 237). So

> we should appeal to the overwhelming amount of experience both in this and in other countries that at least a large number of pupils, both boys and girls, have in fact made substantial progress in languages before the age of 12, and that the knowledge gained at this early stage forms a valuable foundation on which further advance can be made.
> (Leathes 1918: 236)[18]

Internationally, pockets of experiments in primary languages had continued. In the USA, language teaching in elementary schools began with the teaching of German to German migrant children (as an alternative to full German-medium education in schools founded by immigrants), but it continued after World War I with a small number of programmes offering French and Spanish, and with a renewed wave of interest beginning in 1952 (Andersson 1955: 182–183; Johnston 1957). Local trials of Foreign Languages in the Elementary School (FLES) were also funded by the National Defense Education Act (1958) (Simpson 1961; Eriksson et al. 1964; Roeming 1967, Watzke 2002: 46–51). There was interest in the topic at the 1953 UNESCO modern languages seminar in Ceylon; (see UNESCO 1955), it was debated by UNESCO's Advisory Committee on the School Curriculum in 1958, and a meeting of international researchers on the topic was commissioned, held at the UNESCO Institute for Education in Hamburg in 1962, to plan a programme of research on "the psychological and pedagogical aspects of the problem of teaching foreign languages in the primary stage" (leading to Stern 1963, revised ed. 1967, here p. ix). In Britain, the first CRDML report noted in 1968 that "in the last six or seven years many maintained primary schools have introduced a language, usually French, into their curriculum, the children beginning the course most frequently at the age of eight" (CRDML 1968: 2). In Scotland, there had also been considerable expansion, from 25 primary schools offering a language in 1962 to 850 in 1967. The CDRML report cited one (unnamed) English county where 111 of 176 primary schools now had a foreign language, whereas only half a dozen had done a few years earlier. In England, the impetus for introducing a language came in many cases not "from above", from the Local Education Authority, nor from any national initiative, but "from below", on the ground, in schools themselves (Hoy 1977: 3).

In the context of this national and international momentum, and in keeping with the new aspirations to ensure that language teaching policy and practice was research-based, substantial funding was awarded by the Nuffield Foundation to a ten-year pilot project on the teaching of French in primary schools, beginning in 1964. Eighty out of 146 English and Wales LEAs were willing to participate in the pilot; 13 pilot areas were eventually chosen, with 125 primary schools involved, beginning in September 1964. Many other areas followed suit, not officially participating in the pilot but adhering to its principles. The Nuffield Foundation also funded a materials project to produce teaching materials for pupils aged 8–13, for French, as well as German, Spanish and Russian. Halfway through the project, there seems to have been a strong sense that the pilot would become normal provision. One observer wrote in 1969, "it is only a matter of time before the teaching of French in primary schools is generalised all over the United Kingdom" (Hall 1970, cited by Hoy 1977: 7). Yet that is not what happened.

Here, then, was an initiative that had garnered support from above and below, and that had benefited from considerable investment in research, in training, and in materials. So what went wrong? The key document was Burstall's final evaluation of the ten-year project, *Primary French in the Balance* (Burstall 1974). Its credentials as an analysis of a substantial longitudinal study were unassailable, and yet Burstall's interpretation of the results yielded what many considered to be the "wrong" answer, albeit tentatively formulated: "It is hard to resist the conclusion that the weight of the evidence has combined to tip the scales against a possible expansion of the teaching of French in primary schools" (Burstall 1974: 246). Uproar followed (summarized by Hoy 1977: 24–27), as well as cogently argued rebuttals. The National Association of Language Advisors passed a resolution affirming their belief "that there are considerable advantages to be derived from school-based provision of early foreign language study". Many stakeholders accepted the *findings* presented – for example, that there were problems with the transition to secondary school, or that some pupils experienced a sense of failure early on – but not the *conclusions* drawn from them. For example, while the test results suggested that early starters of French did not out-perform later starters significantly, there were many explanations other than the conclusion drawn, that starting young was *per se* a bad idea (Hawkins 1987: 187–188). Other important considerations were the fact that secondary school starters, with whom the primary starters were compared, were generally taught by trained French language teachers, rather than by teachers with only an O-level in French (as was the case for 50% of primary French pilot area teachers). Primary French teachers had often only had short-course training in language teaching, and were using newly developed materials which required technologies with which they were not always familiar; another important factor was the amount of time devoted to French, something which the pilot did not control.

Countering Burstall's overall conclusion against primary languages, Hoy (1977) re-stated the case in its favour. In identifying difficulties, he argued, the project had done exactly what it had been commissioned to do: "ascertain on what conditions it would be feasible to contemplate the general introduction of a modern language into the primary school curriculum" (Schools Council 1966, cited by Hoy 1977: 14). Not surprisingly, given that this was the first attempt to teach all pupils in primary schools, across the whole ability range, using new materials, and with newly or in some cases insufficiently qualified teachers, the study had identified matters that would need to be tackled; but there was nothing in principle against starting early. Rather, doing so increased the time available overall for language learning; successful teaching aroused "great zest and delight" in the children, and early experiences of success could increase confidence in starting a new language, and so prepare pupils for a polyglot world (Hoy 1977: 61–62). However, it is worth noting that Hoy conceded that "Even if Burstall (1974) had urged the expansion of primary French, the implementation of such advice would have been prevented by financial constraints and by the acute shortage of primary teachers who are competent in French" (Hoy 1977: 25). Empirical data was not enough without careful resource planning, especially the preparation of teachers.

Whether one accepts Burstall's reasoning or that of the committee behind Hoy's 1977 report, it seemed in the 1970s that primary languages education had been tried and rejected. In the USA too, the experimental FLES schemes introduced under the National Defense Education Act had produced similarly disappointing results; here too major obstacles were yet again the shortage of qualified teachers, and the transition to secondary school (with pupils marking time while non-FLES students were taught from scratch) (Hawkins 1987: 181). The fact that 40 years later, in 2014, primary languages were introduced nationally in England for pupils aged seven and above might be seen as the triumph of hope over experience. Nevertheless, the 2014 date was this time preceded by almost two decades of preparing the policy ground. By the late 1990s, Driscoll and Frost (1999) felt able to affirm that "any review of our languages capability must surely conclude that the official neglect of modern foreign languages in the primary school is completely unacceptable". Taking it for granted "that the arguments for primary MFL are unassailable and the value of such programmes is obvious",[19] their collection of papers was intended for policymakers and local decision makers to "draw them into a discussion about the issues they will need to consider" *when* implementing primary languages (not if!) (Driscoll & Frost 1999: "Introduction", p. 2, 3). For example, a paper in their volume by Lesley Low (1999), the author of a pilot study of primary languages in Scotland that began in 1989 (Low 1995), pointed out that introducing primary languages had knock-on effects for policy in "virtually every sector from primary through secondary education to the initial and continuing education of teachers themselves" (Low 1999: 54). Many of those points had already been noted by CRDML in the 1960s (CRDML 1968: 3): what age to begin, how much time to devote to the language, and what impact it might have on the rest of the curriculum and wider life of the school. Should all pupils learn a language, and should teaching be given by class teachers or semi-specialist teachers? How should transition to secondary schools be managed?[20] The desire to provide a sound research basis for these key policy decisions led to considerable state investment in teacher development, curriculum and materials development, as well as pilot projects in 19 so-called Pathfinder LEAs in the first decade of the twenty-first century, evaluated very positively by Muijs et al. (2005) in their report for the Department for Education and Skills (DfES). Dearing and King summed up with considerable optimism in their 2007 *Languages Review* for the DfES:

By 2005 over 2000 new primary teachers with a languages specialism had been trained and Continuing Professional Development was available in all Local Authorities, supported by a training trainers programme run by CILT, the National Centre for Languages. An innovative KS2 Framework for Languages was published in 2005 in print and on line [i.e. DfES 2005], [...] New networks have been established, including 75 Regional Support Groups for languages. The National Advisory Centre for Early Language Learning information service has been enhanced and developed and work is proceeding on the production of national schemes of work in French, German and Spanish. Most Local Authorities are now on course to meet the end of decade commitment.[21]

As we have seen, a crucial recurring theme over the decades, as well as in international comparisons, has been the need for adequately trained primary language teachers, from Leathes (1918: 77) to CfBT's international review (Tinsley & Comfort 2012: 8). Indeed, the projected shortage of qualified teachers in England was even presented as a reason for removing the compulsion to take a language at Key Stage 4 (aged 14–16): it would " free up scarce teaching resources" for languages in earlier school years (DfES 2002: 4), the policy relying instead on "inspiring those learning languages in primary schools and at Key Stage 3 to continue to study languages" (DfES 2002: 6).[22] This decision, which took effect from 2004, had an unintended catastrophic effect on languages uptake at GCSE (see Chapter 2). This in turn affected A-level uptake and uptake of languages at university too, thus ironically further reducing the pool of available language experts from whom to recruit teachers. In intention, however, it was at least an attempt to square up to the problem of shortages of qualified teachers that had been a constant theme in a century's discussion of primary languages.

A further fundamental question raised by almost all the reports on primary languages, but not always explicitly, is that of the rationale for language teaching – and for primary language learning specifically. Tinsley and Comfort (2012) tackled this question directly and found that internationally, a frequent reason for early language teaching was the importance of English as a global language to a country's "international aspirations" (Tinsley & Comfort 2012: 6). Where the first foreign language taught is English, language learning in the primary school, whatever else it might achieve, must provide the foundation for continued compulsory learning of English in secondary school. For Anglophone countries, the case for learning one particular throughout schooling was less clear, and other rationales might be sought. In Australia, for example, "the rationale is based on the need for intercultural awareness and understanding in order for Australia to act in relation to changes stemming from globalization and internationalization" (Liddicoat 2007: 10, cited by Tinsley & Comfort 2012: 31). Other rationales noted by Tinsley and Comfort (2012) included insight into other cultures and sensitization to multilingualism in society. It is an open question to what extent greater policy emphasis on such "soft" outcomes, rather than on particular targets for language acquisition (like the A1-level expected at the end of primary school in France),[23] might translate into different teaching practice and outcomes.

The overriding motivation for primary language teaching is still not as clear as it could be; as recently as 2014, Johnstone (2014: 15) was calling for "a clearer and better-grounded rationale for doing it [i.e. primary languages]". To judge from the rationales given leading up to the policy's implementation, one rationale was simply to respond to parent demand; an educational rationale was to "enhance literacy, citizenship and intercultural tolerance" (Nuffield 2000: 6). The comprehensive Key Stage 2 Framework for Languages (DfES 2005), developed to support primary languages, listed four explicit rationales. The first of these was new: to stimulate children's creativity. The others were more familiar: exploring their own and others' cultural identities; supporting oracy and literacy;[24] and supporting learning across the curriculum: "Through the conscious development of language learning they are also learning how to learn" (DfES 2005: 4). A relatively recent addition to the list of arguments for language learning, also in primary schools, is the claim of cognitive benefits to bilingual speakers, including foreign language learners (Tinsley & Comfort 2012: 19). An additional practical rationale given at the time was the simple point "that learning another language needs to start earlier if the next generation is to achieve higher standards" (Nuffield 2000: 6). Implicit in this statement is the expectation that many pupils will continue with their primary school language in secondary school, and this raises the second problem that has recurred repeatedly for over a hundred years: transition from primary to secondary schools. Given that most schools have chosen French as their primary language (77%), followed by Spanish (20%) (see Chapter 2.3, 2.5), the result could be a generation of pupils predominantly learning French or Spanish *only*. Indeed, Low (1999) warned that the Scottish primary languages policy was turning out to be "severely undermining the previous policy on language diversification in Scotland". Even where pupils had learnt a language other than French in primary school, Low noted a "strong Scottish parental preference for French" in secondary school, probably because French was the language they themselves had learnt and that they therefore associated with foreign language learning (Low 1999: 59). It may be that the only way to ensure meaningful transition to secondary school and to maintain at least some diversity is to accept an MT+2 entitlement as policy in England after all. Certainly, the social equity case in its favour is as strong as it was for primary languages, that what is available in private schools should be available to all pupils. Its viability is another matter. For now, it is too early to evaluate the success or otherwise of the primary languages entitlement as a policy, but we may recall the words of John Trim (1997), who suggested that "In practice, national attitudes to early learning are a fairly sensitive indicator of the value placed on foreign language proficiency in the society concerned" (Trim, in Doyé & Hurrell 1997: preface, p. 6). If that is the case, then we might have cause to be cautiously optimistic about a positive change in public attitudes to language learning.

6.3.4 Which languages? The utilitarian case for Spanish and Spanish growth – cause and effect?

Watzke (2002: xii) has observed "a trend over time for one language to dominate and influence how foreign language teaching contributes to the general curriculum". In the USA, that dominant language has been Spanish; in Britain, it is French. Leathes (1918: 92) considered French "beyond question the most important". Not all schools needed to start with French, Leathes conceded – others might choose Italian, German, or Spanish as first foreign language, as long as these schools remained "a minority introducing a healthy diversity" (Leathes 1918: 92). Since then French has remained de facto the first language, with general acknowledgement that this need not be the case in every school. There have been ongoing efforts at diversification (Department of Education and Welsh Office 1973, Schools Council 1981, 1982, HMI 1991, Phillips & Filmer-Sankey 1993), and special attention has been paid to other languages at various times (e.g. Norwood 1943: 117).[25] Russian was given special consideration during the 1950s and 1960s – it was taught to a high standard to a relatively large number of adults in the JSSL in the 1950s, and the Annan report (1962) made the case for expanding the teaching of Russian in schools "in proportion to the importance of the Soviet Union in the world today": "the main effort ought to be made in our schools", and the "immediate objective should be to bring the numbers studying Russian up to the numbers at present learning German" (Annan 1962: 7, 6, 7). Arabic and Chinese have repeatedly been named in more recent reports such as the Worton Report (2009); the British Council (2015: 3) recently placed Arabic "in second place after Spanish" amongst "the languages most needed by the UK in the next twenty years". At the time of writing, the survival of several lesser-taught languages (e.g. Polish, Greek, Dutch) at GCSE and A-level is under threat – while the current government is keen for their maintenance, the autonomous awarding bodies, for whom examinations with few entrants are a costly proposition, are not.

The history of factors influencing the growth of the various languages in British schools was considered in Chapter 2. Here I shall consider just one case, that of Spanish, which offers an interesting historical case study, because we can trace both its advocacy and the growth in English schools over nearly a century. The question is: can we attribute the strong position of Spanish today, as second foreign language in schools, to successful advocacy? The potential importance of Spanish for trade, especially with South America, was already asserted by Leathes (1918: 24–25), for "We were told that the distributing trade of South America had largely passed from English to German firms, even where British goods were concerned, and this because the Germans took the pains to learn Spanish". The Incorporated Association of Assistant Masters was "strongly of the opinion that Spanish could, with advantage, be introduced into the Curriculum of many schools that do not offer it at present" (IAAM 1929: 72). After all, a Board of Education report urged, Spanish was unusually easy (Board of Education Memorandum 1930b: 33–34;

see also Board of Education 1956). The usefulness of Spanish was reiterated by the Committee on Salesmanship (Board of Education 1931: 117): "Spanish is becoming increasingly valuable with the growth of the South American markets", and the Norwood Report on Curriculum and Examinations in Secondary Schools recommended "Spanish should become a chief language in some schools and particularly in areas where commerce has special ties with Spanish-speaking countries" (Norwood 1943: 117). Commercial grounds continued to dominate in making the case for Spanish, far more than for French or German: Allison Peers, an early advocate of the subject, even lamented in 1944 that " 'Commercial' Spanish is [. . .] spoken of as if it were the main end of our teaching, to which we are applying a superficial coating of regard for culture" (Peers 1944: 1–2, cited by Phillips & Filmer-Sankey (1993: 14), and it was an uphill struggle to suggest that Spanish was more than merely "useful". It was only in the 1960s, however, that the so-called Parry Report on Latin America Studies (1965) yielded a concrete policy outcome in support of Spanish: the creation of five specialist university centres for Latin American studies, as well as a system of postgraduate scholarships, which helped to create a generation of researchers across the country.[26] Even after this initiative, in the 1980s, Spanish was still being taken by only about a quarter of the number of pupils who sat German, the second foreign language after French, in their General Certificate Examination (GCE); Spanish overtook German only in 2001 (see 2.5). If we were to attribute this ultimate Spanish success to the advocacy in its favour, then we would have to add the caveat that to achieve success, such advocacy must be sustained for about 80 years.

The conclusions drawn by Bale (2011) from his historical analysis of an earlier campaign for Spanish in the USA certainly suggest caution is called for in connecting the growth of Spanish with advocacy based on its value for trade. Bale analysed three kinds of arguments put to promote Spanish in the USA in the early twentieth century: first, claims for the "High Culture" value of Spanish; second, claims of an affinity between "Spanish American" and "American" populations based on the common experience of having fought for independence; and, finally, the economic case for trade with South America, to harness its purchasing power. Bale (2011) cites Harvard professor Frederick Bliss Luquiens's deft presentation of the economic case for teaching Spanish in the USA in 1915:

> There is a familiar rhyme about an old woman whose pig wouldn't jump over the stile until water quenched fire, and fire burned stick, and stick beat dog, and dog bit pig – whereupon all turned out as it should. In like manner we may achieve success in our South American trade through a series of agencies. It will come through machinery [of trade], markets, and money, which will come through public opinion, which will come through Spanish, which will come through our educators and our teachers of Spanish. Upon them rests the ultimate responsibility.
> (Luquiens 1915, writing in the *Yale Review*, 1915: 711, cited by Bale 2011: 138)

The distinct steps in the strategic and economic case for a foreign language as the road to prosperity – from teachers to "markets and money" – have, as Bale notes, rarely been put so concisely or so explicitly. Yet Bale (2011: 147) concludes, "There is no evidence, however, that actual realization of US economic interests depended on any such language capacity at all". Rather, the USA had demonstrably already established its economic interests *without* the wide teaching of Spanish that was being advocated as necessary at this time. This is, perhaps, a salutary warning against believing our own rhetoric about the economic case for languages. Indeed, despite several recent attempts to make not just a rhetorical but now also an evidence-based economic case for language teaching,[27] a 2011 *Languages in Europe* report admitted candidly that "we have not been able to articulate a very clear and convincing 'business case' [for increased multilingualism], even in the seminar devoted mainly to that question [. . .] the response from employers (especially outside the state and public sectors) to languages remains ambiguous", a fact which "leads us at least to question current orthodoxy in this area" (King et al. 2011: 34).

Bale also asked whether "linking language education advocacy to such [economic] interests has been a practical, effective strategy for expanding multilingual practice and education" – that is, whether, irrespective of its truth value, the economic rationale was an effective advocacy tool for Spanish in the early twentieth century. Bale's conclusion is in the negative:

> Quite the contrary, dominant economic and political interests over-determined the ways in which language education should serve as a resource. As I have demonstrated, the actual realization of those interests across Latin American in fact required no significant Spanish language proficiency, while the expansion of those interests generally constricted social space for multilingual practice and education. Consequently, the gap between the stated rationales behind Spanish language education advocacy and the actual development of the field suggests that linking Spanish language education to putative national interests was neither pragmatic nor politically realistic, but rather romantic and unsuccessful at bolstering study of or proficiency in that language.

This, at the very least, is food for thought for those engaged in making a largely utilitarian case for language learning.

6.4 Changing values, changing legitimacies: making the case of languages from the Leathes Report (1918) to the National Languages Strategy (2002)

Having outlined briefly the key voices in debates about foreign languages education policy, I turn now to analysing how the case for language teaching and learning has been made. Policy actors may choose to present multiple rationales to policymakers and to the wider community, selecting or foregrounding arguments pragmatically in the light of the prevailing socio-political climate (Bale 2011: 140). Rather than looking at success or failure of advocacy (briefly considered for Spanish in 6.3), my focus is on the different rationales chosen by policy actors to advocate foreign languages. Amongst the wealth of reports and position papers on modern languages education in Britain over a century or so, I shall compare three key points in the history of making the case for languages since 1900: the Leathes Report of 1918; the two reports of the Committee on Research and Development in Modern Languages 50 years later (CRDML 1968, 1971); and the presentation of languages education around the turn of the twenty-first century, in the 1999 version of the National Curriculum and in the National Languages Strategy of 2002.[28]

The so-called Leathes Report of 1918, named after its chair, Stanley Leathes, was the first detailed examination of modern languages in British education. One of four reports commissioned – the others tackled classics, English, and natural science – its full title was "The Report of the Committee Appointed by the Prime Minister to Enquire into the Position of Modern Languages in the Educational System of Great Britain". Over its 261 pages, the Leathes Report was detailed and thorough, but some of its recommendations merely confirmed existing practice or the recommendations of earlier reports. Relatively few of its new recommendations were implemented, partly due to the lack of money to finance them, although there was some expansion of modern languages in universities (Bayley 1991: 19–20). Likewise, the National Languages Strategy (DfES 2002) was "a major initiative", whose ground has been carefully prepared (Nuffield 2002, DfES 2002), and whose early achievements were feted by the Modern Languages Team of the Department of Education (DfES 2005); "yet where is it now?", Johnstone (2014: 9) asked dryly after its funding was withdrawn in 2011. Both are thus salutary reminders of the transience of even the most ambitious and well-supported policy proposals. Our interest here, however, is less on what they and the CRDML achieved, than on the changes in the value they set on modern languages.

A perhaps depressing constant from 1918 to 2002 is the repeated conviction that a revolution in public attitudes to modern languages is needed. Leathes (1918: 21) observed that "The prospects of Modern Studies depend on the esteem of the public. All classes and almost all sections of the public have rated them below their true value". At the other end of the century, the report that preceded the National Languages Strategy, *Language Learning* (DfES 2002: 3), observed that "as a country we do not value languages [. . .] We need to challenge this attitude and inspire people of all ages to learn a language". *Language Trends* (CfBT 2010: 4) cited a teacher's view that "More support is needed from society as a whole. We need to give kudos to learning languages not just within the school but nationally". The National Languages Strategy was intended "to change perceptions and raise awareness amongst young people and the wider public of language competence as a key contemporary life skill" (Languages National Steering Group 2002: 2). Arguably the only substantial difference between 1918 and 2002 is that in 2002 the problem had existed long enough for it to be now considered a historic one: "Our record in teaching modern foreign languages has historically not been good enough" (DfES 2002: 3). Another continuity is the recognition that the global reach of English diminishes the perception of the need "to know foreign peoples and foreign lands". Leathes already observed that "the very general use of English throughout the world is an actual impediment to them [Britons] in the acquisition of such knowledge. This impediment can only be removed by the systematic development of Modern Studies" (Leathes 1918: 210). However, there are also important differences; as we shall see, in the course of the twentieth century, the priorities for language learning not only changed; they were reversed.

The Leathes Committee had been commissioned

> to enquire into the position occupied by the study of Modern Languages in the education system of Great Britain, especially in Secondary Schools and Universities, and to advise what measures are required to promote their study, *regard being had to the requirements of a liberal education, including an appreciation of the history, literature and civilisation of other countries, and to the interests of commerce and public service.*
>
> (Leathes 1918: vi, my emphasis)

This view of the rightful place of languages within a liberal education expressed by Leathes in 1918 is similar to the view articulated by the USA Modern Language Association's Committee of Twelve earlier in the century:

> Aside from the general disciplinary value common to all linguistics and literary studies, the study of French and German in the secondary schools is profitable in three ways: first, as an introduction to the life and literature of France and Germany; secondly, as a preparation for intellectual pursuits that require the ability to read French and German; thirdly, as the foundation of an accomplishment that may become useful in business and travel.
>
> (Committee of Twelve 1901: 1393)

In both cases, a nod was given to practical needs ('commerce and public service', or 'business and travel'), but these were listed last; the weight lay squarely on "disciplinary value", the place of languages in a "liberal education". Thus the Committee of Twelve emphasized, "If we teach a foreign language in our schools it should be for the sake of its general educational value" (1901: 1396); Leathes (1918: 87) stated, "Languages teaching in schools has and should have a disciplinary and educative aim. It should train the mind, the taste, and the character [. . .] language training has not only a logical and intellectual value; it has an aesthetic and artistic value".

Let us jump forward half a century to the CRDML, whose activities continued for six years, from 1964 until 1970.[29] Its two reports, published in 1968 and 1971, together total only some 70 pages, compared to the 261 pages of the Leathes Report, but the committee's work was arguably the more epoch-making (including the founding of CILT – see 6.2). Its very title indicated an important shift in thinking: language teaching was now conceived of as a field that required specialized research. While a few pioneers had reported on teaching "experiments" as early as the 1880s (Klippel 2015), in the mid-twentieth century a field of languages education research was now becoming established, and great hopes were held of it. The need felt for such "research and development" was in turn the result of a change in the perceived goals of language teaching. While languages had been taught until the Second World War for their "general formative or cultural value", the committee now believed that "the war showed the importance of practical skills in languages (and, in particular, oral skill), and the need for courses to teach such skills to adults quickly" (CRDML 1968: 1; see 6.1). CDRML asserted that different ultimate goals could be met by the same kind of teaching: "Whatever use language may be put to, there need be no clash between the immediate practical aims of language teaching on the one hand and any ultimate cultural ones on the other". This was not new. In the USA, the Committee of Twelve had also started from the premise that the teaching of modern languages in secondary schools should not differ, regardless of whether "the pupil is, or is not, preparing for college" (Committee of Twelve 1901: 1393). However, the conclusions drawn were very different. In the view of the Committee of Twelve, all pupils should read a good deal of literature – "150–200 pages of literature in the form of easy stories and plays" was envisaged for the second year of a school German course, for example (Committee of Twelve 1901: 1410). After all,

> One who has received the best training that the secondary school can give may not be able to speak his modern language with facility for the practical purposes of life, but he will have been started in the right way; will have obtained a good general knowledge of the language, and will have had some practice in speaking. If then, after leaving school, he needs to be able to speak the language, he has an excellent foundation on which to build. Proficiency will come rapidly with practice.
> (Committee of Twelve 1901: 1396)

The Leathes Report reflects a slight shift in attitude compared to the Committee of Twelve. It fully shared the Committee of Twelve's emphasis on reading good literature, but it also expected at least some attention to be paid to spoken fluency, now listed first amongst the requirements for "adequate" knowledge:

> Adequate progress in a living language may be said to have been made when the pupil is able to speak the language with accuracy and fluency on familiar topics, to read the best authors easily and with pleasure, and to write satisfactory exercises of any simple type.
> (Leathes 1918: 90)

Speaking with accuracy and fluency was now considered fundamental, but it remained only the merest first step, for "Languages are a means, and not an end in themselves" (Leathes 1918: 210). The will and self-discipline of the pupil could only be maintained by a "compelling interest", which "can only be aroused when the language is recognised as a means to higher ends" (Leathes 1918: 89).

CRDML went much further than Leathes had done in its rating of practical skills, so far that it now took exactly the reverse position to that of the Committee of Twelve. Practical proficiency, which the Committee of Twelve had acknowledged only as a possible long-term need, had now become the "immediate practical aims". The exposure to culture through reading, had been considered by the Committee of Twelve "an excellent foundation" for learners of whatever ultimate destiny, on which to build later spoken proficiency if required, and was still considered essential by Leathes to the "full discipline of language" (Leathes 1918: 89). But for the CRDML it became merely a possible "ultimate" cultural aim, for some learners only: "Practical skills must [however] first be realised and for many persons practical aims will be more important" (CRDML 1968: 1–2).

CRDML thus dissolved the hard-won link between language learning and intellectual or aesthetic education of young minds – a link which had first given Modern Languages their disciplinary status alongside subjects such as the classics and English – and so relegated language learning with one fell swoop to the status that it had had until at least the sixteenth century: a practical necessity for some. The only material difference was that increasing international contacts – trade, travel, war – meant that this practical need was likely to be felt by a larger number of people than previously. Government was now formulating policy to encourage such learning, encouraged by the experiences of wartime language teaching (see Chapter 3.1.3).

This change in the stated goals of language teaching went hand in hand with an important change in legitimization strategy. Previously, language teaching had gained its legitimacy from its role in furnishing the key to cultural and intellectual enrichment. As Leathes (1918: 28) noted, "no language attains its full disciplinary value until the initial stages have been passed". Even Walter Ripman, the most radical of language teaching reformers in early twentieth-century Britain, and who led the way in giving primacy to practical, oral training in language teaching, assured his learners that learning a language was

> the key to a vast treasure-house with many beautiful and precious things, which great and good men and women have been gathering for hundreds of years, that each of us may take thereof as much as he pleases, and rejoice.
> (Rippman et al. 1917: vi; see McLelland 2012)

Now, however, the legitimacy of language teaching and language learning was sought in the *research* which underpinned it – or which was yet needed in order to underpin it – and which it was the task of the CRDML to oversee. This was not a uniquely British development. Although Britain did not join the EU until 1973, CILT was founded in the context of resolutions by European Ministers of Education urging "linguistic and psychological research with a view to improving and expanding the teaching of languages" (CRDML 1968: 1).

This new legitimizing strategy for Modern Languages was arguably at best a half-mixed blessing. For language *teachers*, it meant no loss of prestige, and if anything, an increase in status. It recognized that specialized knowledge – both fundamental and more applied research – was needed to develop language learning materials and to teach languages more effectively, with different requirements for different groups and different settings (e.g. children vs. adults, different ability ranges). But for the task of language *learning*, there was an immediate loss of status. Language learning was no longer viewed as the first steps towards a laudable and high-prestige enrichment of the mind, which developed valuable qualities of character; even at quite advanced levels, it merely supplied workers equipped with certain 'skills' to meet the requirements of others in the workplace.

The change in emphasis is partly explained by the increase in the number and kinds of languages covered by CRDML compared to Leathes and the Committee of Twelve. In the early twentieth century, Leathes and his colleagues had in mind a handful of European languages, led by French; in the USA, the Committee of Twelve's 1901 report had been concerned only with French and German. Leathes' report covered both secondary and university languages provision, and his term "Modern Studies" was a pitch for a new field, designed to secure a few key modern languages a place within it; Modern Studies would be "an interdependent whole" covering history, geography, literature and languages, complementing two other "natural" subject groupings of classical humanities, and maths and science (Leathes 1918: 82). The remit of the CDRML was much wider, encompassing both English as a Second Language and "the less usual languages which are not taught in schools and are unlikely to be taught in them to any great extent for some years to come". The National Curriculum and the National Languages Strategy encompassed a wider range still, explicitly including community languages. Not all of these languages had a secure place as subjects in either school or university curricula in which Leathes saw the full discipline of the languages. Recourse had to be had to what could be claimed for all of them: that knowing another language promoted awareness of other perspectives. The recognition of community languages as a valuable resource also addressed a wider policy goal of social cohesion:

> The ability to understand and communicate in other languages is increasingly important in our society and in the global economy. *Languages contribute to the cultural and linguistic richness of our society, to personal fulfilment, mutual understanding*, commercial success and international trade and global citizenship.
> (Languages National Steering Group 2002: 4, Foreword, my emphasis)[30]

Intercultural understanding, a concept developed in modern languages education research (see, e.g., Byram 2008a), was now claimed to be crucial to modern citizenship in the national Languages Strategy:

> Language competence and intercultural understanding are not optional extras, they are an essential part of being a citizen.
>
> (Languages National Steering Group 2002: 5)

Worthy though these goals are – and it is hard to disagree with them – it is difficult for them to compete rhetorically with the "treasure-house" or "compelling interest" that earlier advocates of modern languages presented as the heart of the subject, the "full discipline" (Leathes 1918: 89). One might argue that this is unimportant for the audience of policy documents. Yet even the National Curriculum, the document intended to inform language teaching practice, had little to inspire learners in its 1999 formulation:

> Through the study of a foreign language, pupils understand and appreciate different countries, cultures, people and communities – and as they do so, begin to think of themselves as citizens of the world as well as of the United Kingdom. Pupils also learn about the basic structures of language. They explore similarities and differences between the foreign language they are learning and English or another language, and learn how language can be manipulated and applied in different ways. Their listening, reading and memory skills improve, and their speaking and writing become more accurate. The development of these skills, together with pupils' knowledge and understanding of the structure of language, lay the foundations for future study of other languages.
>
> (DfEE and QCA 1999a: 14)[31]

While this statement might be a fair reflection of what the curriculum covered, it does little to articulate the excitement of the subject. That, to be fair, was better articulated in the original 1992 version, which did make explicit mention of "enjoyment" and "intellectual stimulation" (National Curriculum Council 1992: B1; see also the 1990 *Initial Advice* document). In the 1999 version, however, a page of statements by prominent public figures about the importance of languages also lacks verve: footballer Gary Lineker needed to learn languages when he moved abroad (*not* the anticipated future of most pupils); businessman Sir Peter Parker suggests vaguely that languages 'make the civilized world go around'; for journalist Sir Trevor McDonald, speaking another language is 'polite, demonstrates commitment – and in today's world is absolutely necessary'. John Cleese at least claimed a mild cognitive benefit for language learning, making "our minds stronger and more flexible" (DfEE and QCA 1999: 15). But these are pitifully weak articulations of what one might get out of learning a language, with not a hint of the "key to treasures" that Ripman and others promised a century earlier, or the "intellectual stimulation" of the 1992 document. One might accept this loss as being in the nature of highly constrained National Curriculum documents, or ascribe it to the fact that languages were by 1999 no longer the preserve of an able elite, but an entitlement for all pupils.

But here a comparison with the equivalent 1999 National Curriculum for mathematics is salutary, a subject taught to all pupils, of all abilities. That document speaks of "a creative discipline" that "transcends cultural boundaries" and yields "moments of pleasure and wonder" – surely a more eloquent description of what language learning could be than that in the 1999 Modern Languages document itself (DfEE and QCA 1999b: 14). Where the mathematics document was not afraid to assert "Mathematics is not just a collection of skills, it is a way of thinking" (DfEE and QCA 1999b: 17), the Modern Languages document limited the scope of modern languages to measurable skills. Only its first sentence suggests pupils might develop meaningfully, aspiring to an ideal of "citizenship of the world".[32] One cannot help but recall the view articulated in the Leathes Report (1918: xiv, 207): "Practical ends have been considered first, but the ideal cannot be ignored. [. . .] We do not underrate, we may even be held by some to have unduly emphasised the practical value of Modern Studies [. . .]. But no department of knowledge can obtain its highest development unless it be inspired by an ideal". That "ideal" – so eloquently articulated in the mathematics National Curriculum – was lost in 1999 curriculum for Modern Languages.

Policy documents are written strategically, pragmatically, with different rationales articulated for different audiences. Since the 1960s, articulations of the value of language teaching have focussed on language-as-resource (Ruiz 1984) in meeting economic and strategic goals and, more recently, on intercultural understanding as a means of promoting social cohesion. For example, the 2013 appointment of Bernardette Holmes as director of *Speak to the Future* was announced on the campaign's website with her soundbite, "Language capability is crucial for economic recovery and for social cohesion" (www.speaktothefuture.org/about/, accessed October 2015).[33] These instrumental rationales predominate across Europe, and they speak to government priorities, even if King et al. (2011: 31) warn that "such clearly instrumental arguments have rather less resonance with native speakers of English". However, the 1999 National Curriculum, a document laying the foundation for children's school language learning, was so joyless compared both to previous articulations of the subject, and compared to other subjects, that it begs the question: Was it merely the strategic rehearsal of a rationale for particular audience, or did modern languages advocates lose sight of the "compelling interest" of their subject, in the rush to demonstrate useful skills? Fortunately, the latest version of the National Curriculum does better. There, learning a foreign language is "a liberation from insularity" that "should foster pupils' curiosity", and allow them to "learn new ways of thinking" (Department of Education 2013: 1).[34]

6.5 Conclusion: modern languages advocacy and policymaking

There are both continuities and discontinuities in the history of modern languages advocacy and policymaking over the past century or so. One continuity, already noted in the introduction to this chapter, is the lack of centralization of all aspects of educational policy, so that when recommendations are issued by lobbyists, it is often far from clear through what channels they can be implemented, although since 1988 the National Curriculum, for state schools in England, is one such avenue. Another continuity is the lack of consistency in the infrastructure for languages policy formulation and implementation, which had its heyday in the 1960s and 1970s, when the CRDML (1964–1971), CILT, language advisors, teaching materials development, and research projects together provided excellent infrastructure for developing and improving language teaching. The National Languages Strategy for England (2002–2011) and the appointment of Lid King as a national director for languages in 2003 was a return to the ambition of the CRDML, but its funding was withdrawn in 2011, the same year in which CILT was forced to merge with CfBT; only two years later, the loss of direction was evident in the leading recommendation of the British Academy report *Lost for Words*: "There needs to be a cross-government strategy for language capacity that identifies the language capabilities and requirements of government, and supports the development of these skills" (British Academy 2013: 9; the need is evident in the fact that it was far from clear to whom in government this recommendation was addressed). Nevertheless, the history of primary languages in England demonstrates that language policy formulation has become better founded on research and planning: from intuitive statements about early language learning in the early twentieth century, to a well-planned programme of research in the 1960s, to a greater focus on policy planning backed by extensive research in the late twentieth and early twenty-first century.

A second continuity over the past century is a process of democratization, an expansion in the expectations of who should have the opportunity to learn languages. As Watkze observed with respect to the USA system, initiatives that address the overall aim of widening opportunities in education seem more likely to be implemented (Watzke 2002; see note 13). Amongst the plethora of rationales for primary languages, a key consideration appears to have been social equity: what was available in the private sector should be offered to all pupils. This same rationale also drove the previous biggest ever expansion of language learning, a result of the introduction of comprehensive schools. Might the same rationale be used in future to argue for an entitlement to learn two languages, currently far more widely available in independent schools than in the state sector?

A third continuity throughout the twentieth century is a growing emphasis on the practical value of languages, on the acquisition of skills, hand in hand with ever stronger assertions of the economic rationale for supporting language learning, to facilitate trade and economic growth. Around the turn of the twenty-first century, that rationale was joined (in Britain as well as in Europe and elsewhere) by a rationale centring on the wider policy goal of social cohesion, through creating tolerant, interculturally understanding citizens, sensitized to a multilingual world. This additional instrumental rationale is important to modern languages advocates, given the suggestion from recent work (Bale 2011, in his historical study of Spanish in the USA, and King et al. (2011) with respect to contemporary efforts) that in Anglophone countries especially, the much-vaunted economic rationale may not stand up to close scrutiny.

202 *Making the case for languages*

A still more recent addition to the rationales advanced (and the focus of ongoing research) is the claim of demonstrable cognitive benefit to foreign language learners (Tinsley & Comfort 2012: 19). This rationale has filled an important strategic gap in making the case for languages not to government, but to language learners themselves: what is in it for them? For that question perhaps became more difficult to answer, as the "higher" ideals of the subject lost prominence. They are still there: whether or not pupils read 150–200 pages of literature, as the Committee of Twelve envisaged in 1901, or a bare minimum of "great literature" (as the 2013 curriculum envisages), or indeed no literature at all, language learning surely still involves many "moments of pleasure and wonder", but twentieth-century modern language advocates seem to have become more hesitant about saying so publicly.

A proliferation of rationales is useful when collecting ammunition to make the case for modern languages. It is less useful for policy planning, when a decision needs to made about which of the many competing rationales should take priority in curriculum planning and teacher training, a concern noted by Johnstone (2014: 15) with regard to the future of primary languages. Finally, we must remember that in making the case for languages, we have multiple audiences. One of those audiences is learners themselves. Prominent amongst all the rationales presented to them must surely be the many "moments of pleasure and wonder", when, at whatever level of achievement, the incomprehensible becomes comprehensible, and the unsayable, sayable.

6.6 Chronological bibliography of reports and policy documents in modern languages education, 1890–2015

1864   Clarendon, George. *Clarendon Report on Colleges & Schools 1864. Report of Her Majesty's Commissioners appointed to inquire into the management of certain colleges and schools and the studies pursued and instruction given therein with an appendix and evidence* (Two vols: Vol. I: report and appendix. Vol. II: evidence). London: HMSO.

1868   Taunton, Henry Labouchere. *The Taunton Report.* Report of the Schools Inquiry Commission. London: HMSO.

1893   Committee of Ten. *Report of the Committee on Secondary School Studies. Sub-Committee 4. Other Modern Languages [i.e. apart from English].* Washington, DC: U.S. Government Printing Office.

1894   *Report of the committee appointed to enquire into the entrance examinations (in non-military subjects) of candidates for commissions in the Army (1894).* Presented to both Houses of Parliament by Command of Her Majesty. C-7373. London: HMSO.

1895   Bryce, James, et al. (Great Britain. Royal Commission on Secondary, Education). *Report of the commissioners on secondary education.* London: HMSO.

1900	Arnold, E. P. and Fabian Waren. The teaching of modern languages in preparatory schools. In *Special Reports on Educational Subjects, Vol. 6: Preparatory Schools for Boys: Their Place in English Secondary Education*. Presented to both Houses of Parliament by Command of Her Majesty, Cd. 418. Board of Education. London: HMSO, 231–247.
1901	Committee of Twelve. *Report of the Committee of Twelve of the Modern Language Association of America*. Boston: D. C. Heath.
1907	Great Britain. Scottish Education, Department. *Examination of candidates for recognition as qualified teachers of modern languages: training of teachers*. London: Printed for HMSO by Wyman & Sons.
1908	Brereton, Cloudsley, et al. Report on the conditions of modern (foreign) language instruction in secondary schools. *Modern Language Teaching* 4: 33–38, 65–68.
1909	Civil Service Commission. *Examination of officers of the Army in modern foreign languages* (held under "regulations relating to the study of foreign languages" issued with Army orders dated 1st June 1907), April, 1909. London: HMSO.
1912	Board of Education. *Circular No. 797. Modern languages* (re-issued 1925). London: HMSO.
1912	Board of Education. *Memoranda on teaching and organisation in secondary schools: modern languages*. London: HMSO.
1918	(2nd ed. 1928). Leathes, Stanley, et al. *Modern Studies. Being the report of the committee on the position of modern languages in the educational system of Great Britain*, Cmd 9036, 2nd ed. (Leathes Report), 1928.
1919	Ministry of Reconstruction. *Modern languages in British education*. London: HMSO.
1919	Secondary School Examinations Council. *Reports of the investigators appointed in accordance with the Resolution of the Council passed on 8th. June, 1918, to inquire into the methods and standards of award in the seven approved First Examinations held in July 1918. Subject Reports. Group II – 1. Classics – 2. Modern Languages [and] – 3. Joint Report on Classics and Modern Languages*. [S.l.]: HMSO.
1928	Board of Education. *Report on the position of French in the First School Certificate Examinations*. London: HMSO.
1929	Board of Education. *Position of German in grant-aided Secondary Schools in England*. Educational Pamphlets, No. 77. London: HMSO.
1929	IAAM (Incorporated Association of Assistant Masters in Secondary Schools). *Memorandum on the teaching of modern languages*. London: University of London Press.
1930	Board of Education. *Memorandum on the teaching of foreign languages in certain types of schools*. Educational Pamphlets, No. 82. London: HMSO.
1930	Board of Education. *Second Interim Report of the committee of education for Salesmanship. Modern Languages*. London: HMSO.

1930 Brereton, Cloudsley. *Modern Language teaching in day and evening schools with special reference to London.* London: University of London Press.

1931 Board of Education. *Final report of the committee on education for salesmanship.* London: HMSO.

1934 Collins, H. F. Modern languages. *The Yearbook of Education 1934*, ed. Eustace Percy and M. P. Former. London: Evans, 417–428.

1943 Norwood, Cyril. *The Norwood Report. Curriculum and examinations in secondary schools. Report of the Committee of the Secondary School Examinations Council appointed by the President of the Board of Education in 1941.* London: HMSO.

1945 Peers, E. Allison. *"New" tongues: or, Modern language teaching of the future.* London: Sir I. Pitman & sons, ltd.

1949 Incorporated Association of Assistant Masters. *The teaching of modern languages.* 2nd ed. London: University of London Press.

1950 Scottish Education Department. *Modern languages in secondary schools.* London: HMSO.

1953 Andersson, Theodore. *The Teaching of foreign languages in the elementary school.* Boston: Heath.

1953 UNESCO. *An account of the international seminar on the contribution of the teaching of modern languages towards education for living in a world community.* Paris: UNESCO.

1955 UNESCO. *The Teaching of modern languages: a volume of studies deriving from the International Seminar organized by the Secretariat of UNESCO at Nuwara Eliya, Ceylon, in August, 1953.* Paris: UNESCO.

1956 Incorporated Association of Assistant Masters. *The teaching of modern languages.* London: University of London.

1956 Board of Education (Great Britain). *Modern languages.* London: HMSO.

1957 Johnston, Marjorie Cecil, and United States Office of Education. *References on foreign languages in the elementary school.* Washington, DC: US Department of Health, Education, and Welfare, Office of Education.

1961 Scottish Education Department. *Teaching of modern languages in secondary schools: an extract from the Report of the Secretary of State for Scotland on Education in Scotland, 1960 (Cmmd. 1359).* Edinburgh: HMSO.

1961 Hayter, Sir William, et al. University Grants Committee. *Report of the Sub-Committee on Oriental, Slavonic, East European and African studies.* London: HMSO.

1961 Simpson, Roy E. at al. *Looking ahead in foreign languages: a report of the Production Seminar and Conference on the Improvement of Foreign Language Education in the Elementary School, January 11–16, 1960.* Sacramento: California State Department of Education.

1962 Ministry of Education, Noel Gilroy Annan (Baron Annan) and Scottish Education Department. *The teaching of Russian: report of the Committee* appointed by the Minister of Education and the Secretary of State for Scotland in September, 1960. London: HMSO.

1963 revised ed. 1966. Incorporated Association of Head Masters. *Modern languages in the grammar school: report of a Working Party of Division XII (Lancashire and Cheshire) of I.A.H.M.* London: Incorporated Association of Head Masters.

1963 Newsom, John. *The Newsom Report. Half our future. A report of the Central Advisory Council for Education (England).* London: HMSO.

1964 Eriksson, Marguerite, Ilse Forest, and Ruth Mulhauser. *Foreign languages in the elementary school.* Englewood Cliffs, NJ: Prentice-Hall.

1964 Federation of British Industries. *Foreign Language Needs of Industry. Report of a Working Party in 1964.* [S.l.]: Federation of British Industries.

1965 Parry, J. H. *Report of the Committee on Latin American Studies (chairman: J.H. Parry).* London: HMSO.

1966 Schools Council. *French in the Primary School: The Joint Schools Council.* Nuffield Foundation pilot scheme, London: HMSO.

1967 Incorporated Association of Assistant Masters. *The Teaching of modern languages.* (Fourth edition). London: University of London Press.

1968 CRDML. *Committee on Research and Development in Modern Languages: First report.* London: HMSO.

1970 Baschiera, Karl, and Council of Europe. *The teaching of modern languages in secondary vocational and commercial schools.* Strasbourg: AIDELA.

1970 Cunningham, W., and Scottish Education Department. *Modern languages in further education: report of a Working Party.* Edinburgh: HMSO.

1970 Nuffield Foreign Languages Teaching Materials Project and Schools Council Modern Languages Project. *The regional conferences: a report on a series of conferences held to support the teaching of German, Russian and Spanish.* York: Schools Council Modern Languages Project.

1970 Schools Council (Great Britain). *New patterns in sixth form modern language studies.* London: Evans.

1970a National Steering Committee for Modern Languages and and Scottish Education Department. *Modern languages in SI and SII of the comprehensive school: report of the National Steering Committee for Modern Languages.* Edinburgh: HMSO.

1970b National Steering Committee for Modern Languages and Scottish Education Department. *Modern languages and the less able pupil: second report of the National Steering Committee for Modern Languages.* Edinburgh: HMSO.

1971 British Association for Applied Linguistics, et al. *Science and technology in a second language* [. . .]. London: CILT.

1971 CRDML. *Committee on Research and Development in Modern Languages: Second report.* London: HMSO.

1971 National Steering Committee for Modern Languages and Scottish Education Department. *Alternatives to French as a first foreign language in secondary schools: third report of the National Steering Committee for Modern Languages.* Edinburgh: HMSO.
1972 CILT. *Teaching modern languages across the ability range [. . .].* London: CILT.
1972 Scottish Central Committee for Modern Languages and Scottish Education Department. *The place and aims of modern language teaching in secondary schools: fourth report of the Scottish Central Committee for Modern Languages.* Edinburgh: HMSO.
1973 Welsh Education Office. *Modern languages other than French in secondary schools.* Cardiff: HMSO.
1974 Burstall, Claire, et al. *Primary French in the Balance.* London: NFER.
1976 CILT, ed. *Bilingualism and British education: the dimensions of diversity [. . .].* London: CILT.
1976 CILT, ed. *German in the United Kingdom: problems and prospects.* London: CILT.
1977 Department of Education. *Modern languages in comprehensive schools: a discussion paper by some members of H.M. Inspectorate of schools based on a survey of 83 schools in 1975–1976: H.M.I. series: matters for discussion 3.* [S.l.], Dept. of Education and Science: HMSO.
1977 Hoy, P. *The early teaching of modern languages. A report on the place of language teaching in primary schools by a Nuffield Foundation Committee.* London: The Nuffield Foundation.
1978 Schools Council. Modern Languages, Committee. *Modern languages in secondary schools.* London: Schools Council.
1979 British Overseas Trade Board. *Foreign languages for overseas trade.* London: British Overseas Trade Board.
1979 Perren, George E., ed. *Foreign languages in education.* London: CILT (NCLE [National Congress on Languages in Education] papers and reports 1).
1980 Department of Education and H. M. Inspectorate. *Modern languages in further education (16–18).* London: HMSO.
1981 Davidson, J. M. C., ed. *Issues in language education: papers arising from the second assembly of the National Congress on Languages in Education, 1978–1980.* London: CILT.
1981 Schools Council, Modern Languages Committee, C. G. Hadley. *Languages other than French in the secondary school: an exploratory study of other languages as first or equal first foreign language, a report from the working party of the Schools Council Modern Languages Committee.* London: Schools Council.
1982 Sanderson, David, et al. *Modern language teachers in action: a report for the Language Teaching Research Project, Language Teaching Centre, University of York.* [York]: Language Materials Development Unit of the University of York.

1982 Schools Council. Modern Languages Committee. *The second foreign language in secondary schools: a question of survival.* London: Schools Council.

1983 Inspectorate of Schools. *A survey of modern languages in the secondary schools of Wales: a report.* Cardiff, Welsh Office: HMSO.

1984 Reid, Euan, ed. *Minority community languages in school: the first of two volumes from working parties for the Third Assembly of the National Congress on Languages in Education, Nottingham, 1982.* London: CILT.

1987 Department of Education and Science & Inspectorate of Schools Great Britain. *Modern foreign languages to 16.* Curriculum Matters 8. London: HMSO.

1987 Graham, Colin. *Industry and foreign languages: a study of IC (Language and Communication Services) Ltd, Aston Science Park, Birmingham: undertaken for the Department of Education and Science.* London: Department of Education and Science.

1987 Marland, Michael, et al. *Multilingual Britain: the educational challenge.* London: CILT.

1988 Department of Education & Science, and the Welsh Office. *Modern languages in the school curriculum: a statement of policy.* London: HMSO.

1990 Department of Education and Science and the Welsh Office. *National Curriculum Modern Foreign Languages Working Group: Initial advice.* (The Harris Report). London: DfES.

1990 Scottish Education Department. Inspectors of Schools. *Effective learning and teaching in Scottish secondary schools. Modern Languages.* [Edinburgh]: HMSO.

1991 Department of Education & Science, and the Welsh Office. *Modern foreign languages in the National Curriculum: provisions relating to attainment targets and programmes of study for key stages 3 and 4 only.* London: HMSO.

1991 HMI (Her Majesty's Inspectorate). *Diversification of the first modern foreign language in a sample of secondary schools. A report by HMI, London.* London: HMI.

1991 National Curriculum Council. *National Curriculum Council Consultation Report. Modern foreign languages in the national curriculum.* York: National Curriculum Council.

1992 National Curriculum Council. *Modern foreign languages: non-statutory guidance.* York: National Curriculum Council.

1993 Department for Education, HMI and Ofsted. *Modern foreign languages: key stage 3: first year, 1992–1993. The implementation of the curricular requirements of the Education Reform Act.* London: Office for Standards in Education, HMSO.

1994 Ainslie, Susan, Joanne Bond, & CILT. *Mixed ability teaching: meeting learners' needs.* London: CILT.

1995 Department for Education and Welsh Office. *Modern foreign languages in the National Curriculum.* London: HMSO.

1995 Low, Lesley, et al. *Foreign languages in primary schools: evaluation of the Scottish pilot projects 1993–1995: final report.* Stirling: Scottish CILT.

1995 Office for Standards in Education and Ofsted. *Modern foreign languages: a review of inspection findings 1993/94.* London: HMSO.

1996 Edelenbos, P., & Richard M. Johnstone. *Researching languages at primary school: some European perspectives.* London: CILT in collaboration with Scottish CILT (University of Stirling) and GION (University of Groningen).

1998 Scottish Office, Department of Education and Industry. *Standards and quality in primary and secondary schools 1994–1998: modern languages: a report.* Edinburgh: HMSO.

1998 Moys, Alan, ed. *Where are we going with languages? (Consultative report of the Nuffield Languages Inquiry).* London: Nuffield Foundation.

1999 Burgess, Donald, & Lesley Low. *Proceedings of the national seminars arising from HM Inspectors' report on standards and quality: modern languages, 1994–1998.* Stirling: Scottish CILT.

2000 Nuffield Foundation. *Languages: the next generation: the final report and recommendations of the Nuffield Languages Inquiry.* London: Nuffield Foundation.

2001 Coleman, Jim, et al. *Language learning futures: issues and strategies for modern languages provision in higher education.* London: CILT.

2002 CILT. *A new landscape for languages.* London: CILT.

2002 Department for Education and Skills. *Language learning.* London: HMSO.

2002 Johnstone, Richard, and Scottish CILT. *Evaluation report: early partial immersion in French at Walker Road Primary School, Aberdeen: the first two years, 2000/1 and 2001/2.* Stirling: Scottish CILT.

2002 Languages National Steering Group. *Languages for all: languages for life: a strategy for England.* London: Department for Education and Skills. Now available online at www.languagescompany.co.uk/images/stories/docs/policy/the-national-languages-strategy-for-england.pdf.

2002 McColl, Hilary, Joanna McPake, & Loy Picozzi. *Modern languages in special schools and mainstream units in Scotland 2002.* Stirling: Scottish CILT.

2003 CILT. *Language Trends 2003.* London: CILT. Available online at: www.alcantaracoms.com/wp-content/uploads/2014/05/trends-2003_KS4_report.pdf.

2003 Commission of the European Communities. *Promoting language learning and linguistic diversity. An action plan 2004–2006.* (COM(2003) 449). Brussels. Available from the EUR-Lex website: http://eur-lex.europa.eu/legal-content/EN/TXT/?uri=celex:52003DC0449.

2003 Datta, Manjula, & Cathy Pomphrey. *A world of languages: developing children's love of languages.* London: CILT.

2003	Department for Education and Skills. *Improving modern foreign languages in Key Stage 3: support and guidance from the National Strategy.* London: Department for Education and Skills.
2003	Department for Education and Skills. *Framework for teaching modern foreign languages: Years 7, 8 and 9.* London: DfES.
2003	Head, David, CILT, UCML, & LLAS Subject Centre. *Setting the agenda for languages in higher education.* London: CILT.
2004	CILT. *Language Trends 2004. Languages in Key Stage 4.* London: CILT. Available online at: www.alcantaracoms.com/wp-content/uploads/2014/05/trends2004_KS4_final-report.pdf.
2004	De Silva, June, & Peter Satchwell. *A flying start!: introducing early language learning.* London: Centre for Information on Language Teaching and Research.
2004	Martin, Cynthia, & Anne Farren. *Working together: native speaker assistants in the primary school.* London: CILT.
2004	Sewell, Cherry. *Language learning for work in a multilingual world.* London: CILT.
2005	Department for Education and Skills. *Key Stage 2 framework for languages.*
2005	Bevis, Rosemary, & Ann Gregory. *Mind the gap!: improving transition between Key Stage 2 and 3.* London: CILT.
2005	CILT. *Language trends 2005: Community language learning in England, Wales and Scotland.* London: CILT.
2005	CILT. *National language standards (revised 2005).* London: CILT.
2005	Collins, Carol, & Maggie Greenwood. *Modern foreign languages in a vocational context: an effective way to deliver the National Languages Strategy?* London: Learning and Skills Development Agency.
2005	Department for Education and Skills, & Modern Foreign Languages Team. *A boost for modern foreign languages: how the National Languages Strategy is transforming the languages capability of the nation.* London: DfES.
2005	Department for Education and Skills. *KS2 Framework for Languages* (published in three parts). London: HMSO.
2005	Footitt, Hilary, et al. *The National Languages Strategy in higher education.* Nottingham: DfES Publications.
2005	HEFCE (Higher Education Funding Council for England). *Strategically important and vulnerable subjects. Final report of the Advisory Group.* London: HEFCE.
2005	Muijs, Daniel et al. *Evaluation of the Key Stage 2 language learning pathfinders.* London: DfES (Research Report RR692).
2005	Parker, Linda, & Teresa Tinsley. *Making the case for languages at Key Stage 4.* London: CILT.
2006	CILT. *Language Trends 2006. Languages in Key Stage 4.* London: CILT. Available online at: www.alcantaracoms.com/wp-content/uploads/2014/05/trends2006_ks4_final-report.pdf.

2006	CILT. *Positively plurilingual: the contribution of community languages to UK education and society.* London: CILT.
2006	Klapper, John. *Understanding and developing good practice: language teaching in higher education.* London: CILT, The National Centre for Languages.
2006	McPake, Joanna, & Scottish CILT. *Provision for community language learning in Scotland.* Edinburgh: Scottish Executive.
2007	Canning, John. *Five years on. The language landscape in 2007.* CILT: London.
2007	CILT. *Language Trends 2007: languages in secondary schools.* London: CILT.
2007	Dearing, Ron Sir, Lid King, & Department for Education and Skills. *Languages review.* Nottingham: DfES Publications.
2007	Liddicoat, Anthony, et al. *An investigation of the state and nature of languages in Australian schools.* Adelaide: Research Centre for Languages and Cultures Education, University of South Australia.
2008	CILT. *Language Trends 2008. Languages in secondary schools.* London: CILT. Available online at: www.alcantaracoms.com/wp-content/uploads/2014/05/Language-Trends-2008.pdf.
2009	Cable, Carrie, et al. *Languages learning at Key Stage 2 a longitudinal study: final report.* London: Department for Children, Schools and Familes (Research Report DCFS-RR 198).
2009	CILT. *Language Trends 2009.* London: CILT. Available online at: www.alcantaracoms.com/wp-content/uploads/2014/05/Language-Trends-2009_final-report.pdf.
2009	Clinton, Bernadette, & Marion Vincent. *Leading the way: co-ordinating primary languages.* London: CILT.
2009	Evans, Michael, & Linda Fisher. *Language learning at Key Stage 3: the impact of the Key Stage 3 modern foreign languages framework and changes to the curriculum on provision and practice* London: Department for Children, Schools and Families (DCSF-RR091).
2009	Rose, Sir Jim. *Independent review of the primary curriculum: final report (known as the Rose Review).* Nottingham: DCSF (Department of Children, Schools and Families) Publications.
2009	Vidal Rodeiro, Carmen L. *Some issues on the uptake of Modern Foreign Languages at GCSE. Statistics.* Cambridge: Cambridge Assessment. Online at www.cambridgeassessment.org.uk/ca/digitalAssets/181126_Uptake_of_Modern_Foreign_Languages_-_Stats_Report_No_10.pdf.
2009	Wade, Pauline, Helen Marshall & Sharon O'Donnell. *Primary modern foreign languages: longitudinal survey of implementation of national entitlement to language learning at Key Stage 2: final report.* [London]: Department for Children, Schools and Families (DCSF RR127).
2009	Welsh Assembly Government. *Making languages count: a national modern foreign languages strategy: consultation.* Cardiff: Curriculum

	Support Branch, Department for Children, Education, Lifelong Learning and Skills, Welsh Assembly Government.
2009	Worton, Michael. *Review of Modern Foreign Languages provision in higher education in England.* London: HEFCE.
2010	Alexander, Robin, ed. *Children, their world, their education: final report and recommendations of the Cambridge Primary Review.* London: Routledge.
2010	CILT. *Language Trends 2010.* London: CILT. Available online at www.alcantaracoms.com/wp-content/uploads/2014/05/Language-Trends-2010_Final-Report.pdf.
2010	Maylor, Uvanney, et al. *Impact of supplementary schools on pupils' attainment. An investigation into what factors contribute to educational improvements. Research report DCSF-RR210.* London: London Metropolitan University/Department for Children, Schools and Families.
2011	European Commission. *Languages for jobs: providing multilingual communication skills for the labour market.* European Commission. Available online at: http://ec.europa.eu/languages/policy/strategic-framework/documents/languages-for-jobs-report_en.pdf.
2011	Mulkerne, Sean, Anne Marie Graham, & UCML. *Labour market intelligence on languages and intercultural skills in higher education.* UCML. Available online at: www.ucml.ac.uk/sites/default/files/shapingthefuture/101/17%20-%20Anne%20Marie%20Graham%20emp%20resource%20template_0.pdf.
2011	King, Lid, et al. *Languages in Europe. Towards 2020. Analysis and proposals from the LETPP consultation and review.* (LETPP = Languages in Europe. Theory, Policy, Practice). [Great Britain]: The Languages Company.
2011	Ofsted (Office for Standards in Education, Children's Services and Skills). *Modern languages: Achievement and challenge 2007–2010.* London: Ofsted.
2011	Royal Irish Academy. National Committee for Modern Language, Literary and Studies Cultural. *National languages strategy.* Dublin: RIA.
2011a	CfBT. *The economic case for language learning and the role of employer engagement,* published by CfBT in association with the Education and Employers Taskforce, Business for New Europe and the Association of School and College Leaders. Reading: CfBT.
2011b	CfBT. *Language learning in the FE sector. A survey with FE colleges in 2011.* Reading: CfBT. Available online at http://alcantaracoms.com/wp/wp-content/uploads/FE-Trends-survey-2011.pdf.
2012	CfBT (Tinsley, Teresa, & Youping Han). *Language learning in secondary schools in England: findings from the 2011 Language Trends survey: research report.* Reading, Berkshire: CfBT Education Trust. Available online at: www.cfbt.com/en-GB/Research/Research-library/2012/r-language-learning-in-secondary-schools-in-england-language-trends-2012.

2012 European Commission. *First European survey on language competences. Final Report.* Available at http://ec.europa.eu/languages/policy/strategic-framework/documents/language-survey-final-report_en.pdf.

2012 Martyniuk, Waldemar, & Susanna Slivensky. European Centre for Modern Languages (ECML). In: *Routledge Encyclopaedia of language teaching and learning. 2nd ed.*, ed. Michael Byram and Adelheid Hu. London: Routledge, p. 231 (single page).

2012 Tinsley, Teresa, and Therese Comfort. *Lessons from abroad: international review of primary languages: research report.* Reading, Berkshire: CfBT.

2012a Scottish Government. *Talking the talk, so that Scotland can walk the walk; a rapid review of the evidence of impact on Scottish business of a monolingual workforce.* Available online at: www.gov.scot/Resource/0039/00393436.pdf.

2012b Scottish Government. *Language learning in Scotland. A 1+2 approach. Scottish Government Languages Working Group. Report and recommendations.* Available online at: www.gov.scot/Resource/0039/00393435.pdf.

2012c Scottish Government. *Language learning in Scotland: A 1+2 approach. The Scottish Government's response to the report of the Languages Working Group* Available online at: www.gov.scot/Topics/Education/Schools/curriculum/ACE/LanguageLearning/SGResponse-Revised.

2013 British Academy (report prepared by Teresa Tinsley). *Languages: the State of the Nation.* London: British Academy. Available online at: www.britac.ac.uk/policy/State_of_the_Nation_2013.cfm (accessed May 2013).

2013 British Academy. *Lost for words. The need for languages in UK diplomacy and security.* London: British Academy.

2013 British Council. *Languages for the future. Which languages the UK needs most and why.* London: British Council. Available online at: www.britishcouncil.org/sites/default/files/languages-for-the-future-report.pdf.

2013 Ministry of Defence. *Joint Doctrine Note 1/13. Linguistic Support to Operations.* Shrivenham, Swindon: Development, Concepts and Doctrine Centre: www.gov.uk/government/uploads/system/uploads/attachment_data/file/180778/20131315-JDN113_Linguistic_Support.pdf.

2013 Tinsley, Teresa, Kathryn Board and CfBT. *Language learning in primary and secondary schools in England: findings from the 2012 Language Trends survey: research report.* Reading, Berkshire: CfBT Education Trust.

2014 All-Party Parliamentary Group. *Manifesto for languages.* Online at: www.britishcouncil.org/sites/default/files/manifesto_for_languages.pdf.

2014 Board, Kathryn, Teresa Tinsley, CfBT, & British Council. *Language trends 2013/14: the state of language learning in primary and secondary schools in England.* Reading, Berkshire: CfBT.

2014 British Academy. *Born Global [- Rethinking Language Policy for 21st Century Britain. A policy research project into the extent and nature of language needs in the labour market]. A summary of interim findings.* London: British Academy.

2014 Kapcia, Antony, & Linda Newsom. *Report on the state of UK-based research on Latin America and the Caribbean.* London: Institute of Latin American Studies, School of Advanced Study, University of London.

2015 Board, Kathryn, & Teresa Tinsley. *Language Trends 2014/15. The state of language learning in primary and secondary schools in England.* London: CfBT. Online at www.cfbt.com/en-GB/Research/Research-library/2015/r-language-trends-2015.

2015 Board, Kathryn, Teresa Tinsley, British Council Wales & CfBT. *Modern Foreign Languages in secondary schools in Wales. Findings from the Language Trends survey 2014/15.*

2015 British Council. *The teaching of Arabic language and culture in UK schools.* London: British Council. Online at www.britishcouncil.org/sites/default/files/arabic_report_2015.pdf.

2015 Tinsley, Teresa, & Kathryn Board. *The teaching of Chinese in the UK. Research report*, Alcantra Communications. Available through the British Council website: www.britishcouncil.org/sites/default/files/alcantara_full_report_jun15.pdf.

2015 Welsh Government. *Global futures. A plan to improve and promote modern foreign languages in Wales 2015–2020,* Welsh Government. Available online at: http://gov.wales/docs/dcells/publications/151019-global-futures-en.pdf.

2016 British Academy. *Born global: a British Academy Project on languages and employability.* Online at: www.britac.ac.uk/policy/Born_Global.cfm.

Notes

1 For the USA, Watzke (2002) is an important attempt at just such an analysis, with an attempt at "establishing the persistence of trends that will influence reform efforts" (Watkze 2002: xvi). In Britain, only the Leathes Report has been the subject of serious historical analysis (Bayley 1991, Byram 2014).
2 To take one example, the current director of the Speak to the Future Campaign (see 6.4), Bernardette Holmes, a well-known advocate for languages in Britain, was awarded an MBE (Membership of the British Empire) in 2015 for her services to languages education, but much of her input, and that of many others – e.g. in teacher development and curriculum development at national level, as well as in languages policy and advocacy – is not always acknowledged by name.
3 At the time of writing, late in 2015, the status of this decision is far from secure, however.
4 Raffe & Spours (2007: 6) identify a "rationalist" approach to policy learning, which they distinguish from "collaborative" and "politicised". The National Languages Strategy adopted, as one of three over-arching principles, the rationalist desire "to learn from what works" (Languages National Steering Group 2002: 8).
5 Other key decisions identified by Kaplan and Baldauf (1997: 127–140) are the amount and quality of teacher training (see Chapter 3.2.2), involvement of local communities, materials that will be used and how they will be incorporated into

214 *Making the case for languages*

     the syllabi (see Chapter 4), establishment of local and state assessment systems to monitor progress (see Chapter 5), and determination of financial costs.
6. Common models of the policy process distinguish stages of problem identification, agenda setting, policy formulation/selection, implementation, and evaluation, while emphasizing that the process is cyclical: evaluation will lead to renewed problem identification.
7. ALL also absorbed the British Association for Language Teaching, originally founded in 1964 as the self-consciously modernizing Audio-Visual Language Association.
8. One such personal memoir, *Teaching Languages. A Notebook of Suggestions and Recollections* (Thimann 1955), is cited in 6.3.1 on the subject of teaching less academic pupils.
9. It was at this point that CILT became known as "CILT the National Centre for Languages", rather than its earlier incarnation as the National Centre for Language Teaching and Research (originally the Centre for Information on Language Teaching, from which the acronym stems).
10. An extremely informative reference for the history of this language teaching and research infrastructure in its heyday, including the role of Language Advisors, is Hawkins (1996). The substantial teaching materials of the London CILT library moved to the CfBT in Reading, but its research library remains boxed in the Academy of English at the University of Oldenburg in Germany. Although my focus here is not on university languages education, note too the establishment of the Subject Centre for Languages, Linguistics and Area Studies (LLAS) in 2000, somewhat analogous to CILT, but with a particular remit for higher education, and the Routes into Languages scheme (2006–2016) funded by HEFCE (Higher Education Funding Council for England).
11. See for example Sanderson (1982), noted by Hawkins (1987: 25).
12. The Council of Europe, founded in 1949 and funded by its members, now has 47 member states; it is distinct from the 28-member EU, although no country has joined the EU without first joining the Council of Europe. The Council describes itself as "the continent's leading human rights organization"; all its members have signed up to the European Convention on Human Rights (www.coe.int/en/web/about-us/who-we-are).
13. See Phillips and Filmer-Sankey (1993: 24). The opening up of language learning to pupils across the ability range mirrors developments in the USA, where Watzke (2002: xii) notes the "increased ability of the educational system to provide learning opportunities for all students to formally study a foreign language" has likewise been part of a wider democratization of educational opportunities (see also Watzke 2002: 53–55). Such moves were encouraged by positive accounts of the U.S. Armed Forces language training programmes, where large numbers of learners were apparently successful (see Chapter 3.1.3 and references there).
14. For brief discussion of how this affected materials development for German, see McLelland (2015: 170–173).
15. Nevertheless, although asked specifically to consider whether language learning should start at age seven or age nine in England, the authors felt unable to provide a clear answer on the basis of available data (Tinsley & Comfort 2012: 4).
16. This section deals only with policy development, rather than with research on the age factor itself in language acquisition, but for a recent research review, see Munoz and Singleton (2011).
17. Preparatory Schools prepared their pupils to sit the entrance examinations of the Public Schools at the age of 12 or 13.
18. The arguments come under two headings, "Age at which Foreign Languages should be begun", and "Preparatory Schools" (Leathes 1918: 235–241).

19 Driscoll (1999: 9) indeed noted strong interest in the idea expressed in a series of government commissioned reports. Note also the European comparative study by Edelenbos and Johnston (1996).
20 On the question of transition, see Bevis and Gregory (2005).
21 In fact, the introduction of primary languages – expected by the sector to start in 2010, as is clear from Dearing and King's words here (likewise Rose 2009: 106) – was delayed after a Conservative/Liberal Democrat Coalition, replacing the Labour government that had been in power from 1997 to 2010, decided to the review the decision. It was, however, implemented from September 2014.
22 See, however, 6.3.1.
23 France expects pupils to achieve the level of A1 in CEFR in a foreign language by the end of primary school. See www.education.gouv.fr/cid206/les-langues-vivantes-etrangeres.html.
24 The benefit to literacy across the curriculum was repeated in the Rose Review of the Primary Curriculum (2009: 101); enhanced creativity was noted as a benefit perceived by schools in the Cambridge Primary Review (Alexander 2010: 232).
25 See Phillips and Filmer-Sankey (1993) for a historical overview, especially Chapters 1 and 2.
26 The five so-called Parry Centres at the Universities of Cambridge, Glasgow, Liverpool, London and Oxford were followed by a sixth at Essex, established with Nuffield Foundation funds in 1968, and specialising in Latin American politics. The postgraduate awards were also known as "Parry awards" (Kapcia & Newsom 2014: 17).
27 See *ELAN: Effects on the European Economy of Shortages of Foreign Language Skills in Enterprise* (CILT 2006), *Languages for Jobs: Providing Multilingual Communication Skills for the Labour Market* (European Commission 2011); *Labour Market Intelligence on Languages and Intercultural Skills in Higher Education* (Mulkerne & Graham [UCML] 2011), *The Economic Case for Language Learning and the Role of Employer Engagement* (CfBT [2011]), *Talking the Talk, so that Scotland Can Walk the Walk; A Rapid Review of the Evidence of Impact on Scottish Business of a Monolingual Workforce* (Scottish Government 2012a), *Lost for Words. The Need for Languages in UK Security and Diplomacy* (British Academy 2013), the All-Parliamentary Group on Modern Language's *Manifesto for Languages* (July 2014).
28 The evolution of the National Curriculum from 1992 to 2014 and beyond is complex, and the 1999 document is felt by many in the profession to be weaker than the original 1992 document. However, it is cited here as the latest twentieth-century articulation of the language learning curriculum.
29 It had been established as a result of discussions in the aftermath of the Hayter Report on Oriental, Slavonic, East European and African studies (Hayter 1961) and the Annan Report on Russian (Annan 1962), and the Federation of British Industries' Committee on Foreign Languages and Industry. It was intended to meet a perceived need for "a central body to co-ordinate activities and to promote research and development in the field of modern languages" (CRDML 1968: vi). Set up by the Education Secretary of State and the Scottish Secretary of State, its other sponsors were the Nuffield Foundation, the University Grants Committee, the British Council, and the Confederation of British Industry (the new name of the Federation of British Industries).
30 See also the publications by CILT on the theme of languages and social cohesion: Reid (1984), Marland (1987), CILT (2005, 2006); also McPake (2006).
31 Cited by Mitchell (2014: 206), who also outlines the work on earlier versions that led up to this formulation.

32 This is not to deny the potential value of intercultural education, but to criticize its poor articulation in the document; after all, in the German standards for the first foreign language (Kultusministerkonferenz 2004: 16), intercultural competence at least hints at developing personal qualities that can drive excitement in discovering the world: "insight" and "curiosity".
33 The campaign, established in 2012, is supported by the British Academy, the Independent Schools Modern Languages Association, and university-level bodies (the Centre for Languages, Linguistics and Area Studies (LLAS) and Routes into Languages), amongst others, including some commercial sponsors.
34 More controversially, given the wealth of cultural products that might be studied, pupils are also expected to "read great literature in the original language" (Department of Education 2013: 1).

7 Conclusions – applying lessons from the past to the present and future

Several strands in the history of language teaching and learning have featured in the preceding chapters – language choices, the social context of language learning, methods, assessment, and advocacy and policy[1] – but together they illustrate how continuities or changes in practice in turn reflect continuities or changes in fundamental assumptions, beliefs and values. Let us return, then, to the six fundamental questions about language learning and teaching presented in the Introduction.

7.1 Why do we teach languages?

Charles Colbeck told trainee teachers in 1887:

> We teach Modern Languages, firstly because they are so supremely useful. [. . .] Secondly, we teach Modern Languages because they are, comparatively, so easy that our teaching does not run to waste. [. . .] Thirdly, we teach Modern Languages for the sake of the culture which they afford. [. . .] Fourthly, we teach Modern Languages as a branch of science and research.
> (Colbeck 1887:4–9)

The oldest surviving materials reveal that the earliest learners of foreign languages were chiefly motivated by Colbeck's first reason, the usefulness of the language in practical undertakings, for example in trade or in specialist domains such as law. The argument of utility for the workplace is today often the first argument presented – whether to governments in the hope of securing support; to school management teams to fight for space in the curriculum; or to parents, pupils and students to influence language learning choices. Yet history offers more than one case where using arguments based on utility to motivate uptake in language learning has failed. The experiment in a Commercial Certificate with a languages element in the 1880s, intended to meet a need for commercial clerks with good language skills, failed, as few candidates entered, and even fewer met the standard expected (Chapter 4). The Institute of Linguists, whose mission was to accredit language skills in the workplace, has spent much of its history fighting for its existence; and the early twentieth-century efforts, on both sides of the Atlantic, to increase the popularity of Spanish on the grounds of its usefulness in trade also failed, even if Spanish has since flourished (Chapter 6). More recent representations of languages as useful have also failed to stem the decline in language uptake at higher levels.[2]

Colbeck's second argument, the relative easiness of languages as subjects at school, is diametrically opposed to the view of many in Britain today, where language subjects have been perceived as disproportionately difficult to do well in, and where a language is currently considered a risky choice, even for able pupils. Colbeck presented French and German as "easy" by comparison with Latin and Greek, the yardstick for a good education. The classics ceased to be the yardstick in the twentieth century, and the history of that century is a history of optimism about the value of making modern language learning accessible to more learners than ever before, across a wider ability range. Such decisions reflect an assumption that languages are at any rate no more difficult than the new yardstick of core subjects like English Language and Literature and Maths, subjects that are taken, at different levels, by all pupils, and that fall within the reach of the vast majority. The evidence of many other parts of the world today, where English is a compulsory foreign language for virtually all pupils, also suggests that the fear in Britain that "languages are difficult" is probably more a fear about assessment, and differentiation, than about intrinsic difficulty.

Paradoxically, languages have also suffered from the perception that, once boiled down to communicative skills, languages are *too* "easy", for fluency can be picked up without devoting serious curriculum time to them. Reduced to a set of skills, languages come to resemble other skills such as typing or driving, whose utility is far easier to demonstrate, but which do not merit a place in the core curriculum. Yet, although languages can, like any school subject, be made accessible to all ability ranges, the advanced study of a language and its cultural productions is far more than a set of skills; it is, as Colbeck put it, "a branch of science and research".

Two factors not addressed by Colbeck in the passage earlier, but frequently cited by others in the nineteenth century, are the intellectual rigour believed to be developed by linguistic analysis, and the cultural and moral development encouraged by studying literature and other cultural productions with care and attention. Those beliefs are reflected in the social standing of languages and in the methods of teaching and assessing them in the nineteenth and early twentieth centuries, as we saw in Chapters 3, 4 and 5. With the shift towards language skills in school teaching of the later twentieth century, such arguments faded from prominence in public discourse, but they have recently resurfaced in slightly different forms. As we saw in Chapter 6, languages are again being presented as "good for the brain", but now on the basis of research suggesting bilinguals enjoy certain cognitive benefits. Meanwhile, the cultural argument has resurfaced couched not in the elitist terms of encountering great literature ("the culture that they afford", as Colbeck put it), but – in keeping with the democratization of languages teaching – in research to underpin the lay observation that "learning a language changes you", promoting the development of an *intercultural* awareness and respect that can be transferred to new contexts. In both cases, it is striking that in these modern variants of older arguments, the beneficial changes are believed to take place in learners not through effortful application, but inevitably, without learners necessarily being aware of it (although intercultural approaches certainly do also encourage explicit reflection).

Colbeck's list of reasons for language learning passes over one further crucial reason. As Chapter 3 showed, the *social status* associated with knowledge of a prestige language has been a major factor in language study for centuries, at least since the seventeenth and eighteenth centuries, the era of the Grand Tour and of growing interest in reading and discussing the literature of Europe. The importance of prestige was recognized by the first generation of professional school language teachers in the nineteenth century too, who never tired of arguing that modern languages should rank no lower than Greek or Latin in importance. That conviction was reflected in the first formal assessments of modern languages, which mimicked the assessment of the classical languages. But we should note, too, the distinction made today by sociolinguists between the status and the prestige of languages. Status refers, very broadly, to a language's utility: In what contexts in society can it or must it be used? Prestige, though related to actual status, refers to perceptions of languages, for example their associations with power, economic opportunity and upward social mobility. Research suggests that in the absence of prestige, changing status – making a language more useful or necessary, as recent legislation has done for French in Quebec – does not necessarily make those whom we want to learn it, do so (Kircher 2016). The distinction is useful to language learning advocates too, who should perhaps think not only about arguing in terms of utility (a status argument) but also about re-creating the prestige of language study, perhaps by drawing greater attention in our public engagement to Colbeck's higher level "science and research subject".

7.2 What determines choices about which languages to learn?

As for the choice of *which particular* language to learn, Chapter 2 again showed the importance of prestige since the beginning. French first began to be taught in Britain as a result of social anxieties of the Anglo-Norman elite, concerned that their children did not speak the prestigious French of Paris. The way in which other languages such as Italian, Spanish, Dutch and Russian grew and faded in popularity shows how political, commercial, and military imperatives all play a role too. But German arguably became the second foreign language in the eighteenth century as a result of the growing reputation of Germany's literature and intellectual endeavours, further bolstered by the social status of a language spoken by the ruling house of Hanover and by the resulting strong cultural ties to Germany.

The cultural diplomacy of other countries keen to promote their "soft power" through promoting their language has played a role in shaping language learning too. In Chapter 3 we noted the growth of such cultural diplomacy from around 1900 onwards – both in bilateral assistantship schemes, and in the establishment of institutions such as the Alliance Française, founded 1883, Germany's Goethe Institute, founded 1952, and the Instituto Cervantes, founded in 1991 (while the British Council was founded in 1934 to promote English abroad). China launched its hugely energetic Confucius Institutes programme in 2004, and in the twenty-first century, the growth of Mandarin Chinese has certainly been encouraged by that massive investment. However, the growth in Chinese is so far most marked in the private school sector, whose pupils (or their parents) are arguably most likely to be most attuned to associations of Mandarin Chinese with economic power and hence social status. And that growth is still dwarfed by the growth of Spanish, seemingly not primarily in response to utilitarian arguments, since that case had been made for decades without success, but driven by what sociolinguists call "solidarity" (feelings of attachment and belonging), as more British people have developed cultural ties with Spain as a holiday destination, much as German benefited from cultural ties in the eighteenth century (and then suffered globally after both World Wars; see, e.g., McLelland 2016).

The fact that Spanish has recently ousted German, after more than a century, from its position as second foreign language demonstrates that (apparently) profound changes to language learning habits are possible. Less certain from the history examined here is whether it is ever possible to direct such change from above in the absence of an appetite in the wider population. Government-funded programmes in the light of perceived defence needs in the USA and Britain have shown rapid results in the short term; but with little long-term shift in perceptions, the effect tended not to outlast the duration of the funding. Certainly, the status-utility argument alone does not seem to work.

7.3 Are English speakers a special case when it comes to language learning?

Worldwide there are millions of learners of English, motivated by a powerful combination of status, prestige and solidarity factors (see Linn 2016). Meanwhile, English speakers have a reputation as reluctant language learners, poor language learners, or both. Their lack of interest is often explained as natural enough among those who already speak the world's dominant language today, but there is at least anecdotal evidence that the lack of enthusiasm pre-dates the global dominance of English. John Florio, who taught Italian in sixteenth-century England, had a speaker lament in one of his language learning dialogues:

> Fewe of these English men delight to haue their children learne diuers languages, whiche thinge displeaseth me. When I first arriued in London, I coulde not speake Englishe and I met aboue fiue hundred persons, afore I coulde find one that could tel me in Italian, or French, where the Post dwelt. [. . .] I see certain Gentlemen [. . .] that begin to learne to speake Italian, French, and Spanish, and when they have learned two woords of French, and foure words of Italian, they thinke they have yenough, they wyll study no more.
>
> (Florio 1578: N iii r-v, cited by Kibbee 1991: 101–102)

Four hundred years later, Rambeau (1894: 264) was scathing of attitudes to languages as school subjects in the USA:

> Of course the instruction in French and German could not be dispensed with, but was introduced into schools and colleges unwillingly and only for the utilitarian value of these languages and, consequently, held in very slight esteem. It is still in a worse condition than in any other country of Europe.
> (Rambeau 1894: 264)

Today, as we saw in Chapter 6, Britain's language learning is still perceived to be in crisis despite valiant efforts to promote languages in recent years, largely on the basis of the utility argument already despised by Rambeau in nineteenth-century America.[3]

So are English speakers a special case? Whether in Britain, North America or Australasia, they live in large states where – notwithstanding the strong presence of many other languages, some of them with well-protected status – their situation is not that different from that of Britons for centuries, as an island nation with relatively little 'passing traffic' of other languages. Historically, despite recent patterns of migration, globalization and work mobility, much of Britain, and especially its most populous part, England, has arguably been endemically monolingual in a way that is unlike many other (though certainly not all) parts of the world. Even when members of such English-speaking communities do need to interact with speakers of other languages, English is very often – and increasingly – enough. Another language can confer an *advantage* in business and in leisure (for relationship building, for cultural sensitivity), but it is not, for *most* English speakers, *most* of the time, necessary. The utility argument recently given so much weight in advocacy is, then, at the level of the *individual* at best an overstatement, at worst a fiction, even if not at the level of national commercial and politics interests.

The utility fallacy and a long history of majority monolingualism together mean that the challenge facing language teachers and language advocates in Britain – and probably other English-speaking countries – is indeed particularly great. One might suggest that the challenge is threefold: to establish languages as core, prestige subjects, whilst still accessible to all; to help pupils, but also the wider population, aspire to a multilingual identity as a normal and desirable part of what it means to be human; and to bolster language learners all the more strongly, where their society and family are less well equipped to provide that support from their own experience. England has introduced a compulsory language from primary school to age 14; Welsh policy aspires to a "Bilingual plus 1" nation (Welsh Government 2015). Scotland is in the process of introducing its own policy for learning two foreign languages at school that comes closest to the European Council's goal of "mother tongue + 2".[4] These are big changes, but the lack of widespread language learning in previous generations may make such changes harder to implement. First, assuming that attitudes to language learning – like other educational habits and attitudes – are passed down from generation to generation, parents who are not comfortable and successful language learners themselves are less able to support their children as language learners in the same way that many would do in, say, literacy and maths. Second, we saw in examining experiments with primary French in the 1970s that a lack of language learning in previous generations creates problems of teacher supply that are potentially fatal to the success of such initiatives. It remains to be seen what histories written in a few decades' time will make of today's efforts to bring about radical change.

7.4 What is the right kind of learner, the right kind of teacher?

Although they underlie the decisions made about language teaching methods, assessment and advocacy, the reasons both for learning a language, and for choosing to learn or teach a certain language, are often barely articulated by those taking the decisions. The same is true of the more or less explicit beliefs held about who language learning is for, and by whom language teaching should be done. Chapter 3 traced the changing answers to those questions implicit in the institutionalization and professionalization of languages as school and university subjects, and in the setting of qualifications and standards for their specialists – all efforts to establish languages as "proper" disciplines, as the province of qualified experts. Already in the eighteenth century, teachers such as Chambaud differentiated their expertise in teaching the "principles" of the language, its grammar, from those who merely taught children to chatter on ungrammatically in "glittering gibberish" (Chambaud 1750: xxv; 1762: xvi–xvii). By the nineteenth century, in formal boys' education, though not in all educational settings, the ability to converse in the language was increasingly devalued. Language teachers were instead expected to discipline the mind through language analysis. Their status as experts was under constant threat, however, from native speakers who might lack formal training but who had the fluency that Britain's teachers often lacked, and who were often cheaper to employ. As we saw, the development in the 1880s, across Europe, of summer courses for language teachers, and, later, the gradual institutionalization of the year abroad, helped equip a newly emerging class of home-grown language teachers with the fluency to compete with native speakers. It is worth noting that debates from Britain around a century ago about the relative suitability of native and non-native speakers as teachers have echoes today, for example in the field of Chinese as a Foreign Language – where "home-grown" specialists are still in relatively short supply – and in discourse about language teaching in Russia (Protassova 2017).

We also saw in Chapter 3 how the gendering of language learning may go hand in hand with devaluing language skills. Despite the common perception in recent decades that girls are more successful foreign language learners, at other points in history what girls did well was accorded less status, a pattern familiar from studies of feminized professions. Above all, however, Chapter 3 showed how opportunities for language learning have been democratized over the past century. Once an elite pursuit, language learning – at least to a modest level – is now, like basic literacy and numeracy, believed to be accessible to all, and in many kinds of settings.

7.5 What affects what goes on in the languages classroom?

Pioneers of new (or revived) teaching methods and techniques have in part been responding to changes in the social context of the kind just noted. The first generations of schoolteachers were more inclined to argue for teaching *about* the language and culture, the kind of knowledge that could help Modern Languages hold their own alongside established, prestige subjects like the classical languages. "Mere" fluency could always be "picked up" later. More recently, promoting the acquisition of communicative skills has become accepted as the main goal of school language teaching, and classroom activities have changed accordingly. Methodological shifts have also arisen in response to changing beliefs about how language acquisition works. One example is the effort to promote classroom use of the target language since the late nineteenth century, even if it only gained ground in the mainstream from the 1980s. More recently, focus has shifted to using the target language in a way that recent research suggests is most likely to aid language acquisition (e.g. with an emphasis on actual interaction). But the importance accorded classroom target language use is also bolstered by the conviction that using the target language actively is what today's learners will most want to do in the 'real world'. Here it is worth highlighting the fate of a mainstay of language manuals for many centuries up to around 1800, the bilingual dialogue, which has almost completely disappeared (except in some teach-yourself materials). The concern to present authentic conversational language resurfaced in the twentieth century, but minus the faith in the value of providing a parallel translation, which is more likely to be viewed as an interference with acquisition, rather than as an aid.

It is heartening to see from Chapter 4 that, observed over the long term, change in teaching practice is not only an endless pendulum swing – though there is some evidence of that – but also shows genuine improvements: in describing the language (beginning with the emergence of the first grammars in the sixteenth and seventeenth centuries); in the development of exercises targeted at particular grammar points or functions, exercises which have undergone much evolution and differentiation since the earliest examples emerged in the second half of the eighteenth century; in understanding how a language is acquired and how it can be taught (including grading of material and a growing appreciation of what teaching is likely to be useful when); and in the technological support available. Indeed, it is striking how many of the lasting changes in practice are the result, not only of new insights, but of wider technological developments – the availability first of printed manuals, then of illustrations, of audio, video and CALL – although, as we saw in Chapter 4, predictions of the precise impact of a new technology on teaching have rarely got it right.

7.6 How do we measure language learning success?

Beliefs about the ultimate purpose of language learning are encoded not only in how we teach, but also in how we measure language learners' success – which in turn, in a washback effect, influences classroom practice. Chapter 5 presented a first, albeit far from comprehensive, outline of the history of foreign language assessment in Britain, as a step towards fleshing out the language testing history field mapped out for English as a Foreign Language by Weir and colleagues (Weir 2013; O'Sullivan & Weir 2016). We saw that since the nineteenth century, school language assessment has shifted markedly in the direction of testing communicative performance. Measuring declarative knowledge about a language system or about its culture has lost ground – gone are questions asking for recall of the third person preterite of a given verb; likewise tests of the ability to analyse and explain linguistic and cultural phenomena, except at advanced levels, and to a more limited extent. School languages assessment has thus come closer to assessment of adults' proficiency in professional settings, setting tasks intended to resemble the expected real-life needs of language users. Whereas exam candidates in the nineteenth century were expected to produce no language of their own at all, either in speech or in writing (only to translate a set text), actually producing language is now far more prominent in assessment. Another clear trend has been the increasing concern (not unique to languages assessment) to be precise about what is being measured. Tasks such as translation and dictation – once valued as all-round tests of mastery – have been replaced by a much wider range of tasks intended to measure individual skills. Finally, assessment became much more differentiated in the latter part of the twentieth century. Assessment and accreditation schemes that recognize achievement even at relatively low levels of proficiency – from the CSE and the Foundation tier in GCSE in England, to the Common European Framework of Reference and the Languages Ladder – all reflect the will to promote language learning as an enrichment to anyone's education or cultural experience, and to recognize even levels of achievement that are unlikely, in the cold light of day, to be immediately useful, except as a benchmark from which to measure further progress.

7.7 Outlook

Readers may wish to challenge the tentative conclusions drawn here on the basis of the history presented in the previous chapters. I hope, however, that the themes explored – language learning choices, sociocultural history, and the history of teaching methods, of assessment, and of advocacy and policy – will resonate with readers not only in Britain but also in other parts of Europe, in other Anglophone countries, and beyond. I hope, too, that this history will inspire further research on these themes, and on others (such as the representation and construction of culture in language teaching, only touched on here in Chapter 4), both in Britain and Europe, and in other parts of the world, such as Asia and Africa, of whose language learning and teaching traditions far too little is known.

Notes

1 One strand not considered in detail here, but one that would reward closer scrutiny, is cultural representations in language teaching (as examined for the history

of teaching German in McLelland 2015a; see also McLelland & Smith (2017b, Vol. III), for these tell us much about our views of ourselves, of the Other, and of groups within our own and the other society too (e.g. gender and migrant identities).

2 The utility argument also pits one language against another – one language must be more useful than another – and the evidence of non-English speaking countries is that such instrumental motivation drives choice of a single, dominant foreign language, English.

3 See Lanvers and Coleman (2013) for a recent analysis of the public discourse of a language learning crisis.

4 For comparison, in the Republic of Ireland, Irish is a compulsory subject at the Leaving Certificate, and admission to many courses at the major universities requires another, foreign language.

Bibliography

Adam, J. B. (1970). *Non-school examinations: Examining modern languages*. London: CILT.
Adams, J. B. (1901). *The self-educator in German*. London: Hodder and Stoughton.
Adams, M. and F. B. Knight. (1929). *The basic drills in a minimum vocabulary of French: For first-year students*. Chicago: Rand, McNally & Co.
Adamson, B. (2004). *China's English: A history of English in Chinese education*. Hong Kong: Hong Kong University Press.
Aedler, M. (1680 [1972]). *The high Dutch Minerva*. Facsimile reprint. Menston, England: Scolar Press.
Ahn, F. and J. Pfeiffer. (1868). *New, practical and easy method of learning the German language: New edition, considerably enlarged and improved upon from the original French edition by Johann Pfeiffer*. London: T. J. Allman.
Agard, F. B., Clements, R. J. et al. (1944). *A survey of language classes in the Army Specialized Language Training Program*. New York: Commission on Trends in Education.
Ahn, F. (1834). *Praktischer Lehrgang zur schnellen und leichten Erlernung der französischen Sprache*. Cologne.
Ainslie, S., S. Purcell and Centre for Information on Language Teaching and Research. (2001). *Mixed-ability teaching in language learning*. London: CILT.
Ajax. (1916). *The soldiers' language manual, no. 2: English-German*. London: E. Marlborough and Co.
Alexander, R. (2010). *Children, their world, their education: Final report and recommendations of the Cambridge primary review*. London: Routledge.
Alston, R. C. (1985). *The French language: Grammars, miscellaneous treatises, dictionaries*. [S.l.]: Printed for the author.
Andersson, T. (1955). Teaching modern languages to young children in the United States. In: *The teaching of modern languages. A volume of studies deriving from the International Seminar organized by the Secretariat of UNESCO at Nuwara Eliya, Ceylon, in August 1953*, ed. T. Andersson. Paris: UNESCO, 182–195.
Angiolillo, P. F. (1947). *Armed forces' foreign language teaching: Critical evaluation and implications*. New York: Vanni.
Annan, N. G. (1962). *The teaching of Russian: Report of the Committee appointed by the Minister of Education and the Secretary of State for Scotland in September, 1960*. London: HMSO.
Anon. September 1797. [Review]. Uttiv, J.: A complete practical German grammar. Göttingen: Vandenhoeck & Ruprecht 1796. *Allgemeine Literarische Zeitung* 3 (285): 632. http://zs.thulb.uni-jena.de/receive/jportal_jparticle_00014711.

Arthur, L. (1996). Adults learning languages. In: Hawkins (1996), pp. 53–60.
Ashby, M. and J. Przedlacka. (2017). Technology and pronunciation teaching, 1890–1940. In: McLelland and Smith (2017a), forthcoming.
Association of German Governesses in England. (1876). *Statutes, annual reports, etc.* London.
Atherton, Mark. 2010. 'The globe of language': Thomas Prendergast and applied linguistics in the 1870s. *Language & History* 53.1: 15–26.
Audra, E. (1955a). The Linking of Schools. In: *The teaching of modern languages. A volume of studies deriving from the International Seminar organized by the Secretariat of Unesco at Nuwara Eliya, Ceylon, in August 1953*, ed. T. Andersson. Paris: UNESCO, pp. 209–215.
Audra, E. (1955b). The linking of schools. In: *The teaching of modern languages: A volume of studies deriving from the International Seminar organized by the Secretariat of UNESCO at Nuwara Eliya, Ceylon, in August 1953*, ed. T. Andersson. Paris: UNESCO, pp. 209–215.
Auroux, S., K. Koerner, H.-J. Niederehe and K. Versteegh, eds. (2000–2006). *History of the language sciences: An international handbook on the evolution of the study of language from the beginnings to the present (HSK 18:1–3)*. Berlin: de Gruyter.
Bahlsen, L. (1905, rpt. 2002). *The teaching of modern languages*, translated by M. Blakemore Evans, 2nd ed. Boston: Ginn. Rpt. in Howatt and Smith (2002, V: 333–435).
Bale, J. (2011). The campaign for Spanish language education in the 'Colossus of the North,' 1914–1945. *Language Policy* 10: 137–157.
——— (2017). Spanish as Ersatz: Advocacy for Spanish language education in the United States, 1914–1945. In: *The history of learning and teaching languages: Vol. III across cultures*, ed. N. McLelland and R. Smith. Oxford: Legenda, forthcoming.
Baretti, G. (1775). *Small talk for the use of young ladies that wish to learn the colloquial part of the Italian language.* London: Printed for G. Robinson.
Barlement, Noel van. (1639). *New dialogues or colloquies, and a little dictionary of eight languages. Latine, French, Low-Dutch, High-Dutch, Spanish, Italian, English, Portugal, etc. (Colloquia & dictionariolum octo linguarum, etc.)* London: E. G. [Edward Griffin] for Michael Sparke Junior.
Barlet, S. (1885). French teachers and teachers of French. *Educational Times* Jan. 1, 1885: 11–16.
Barrier, P. (1955). International school correspondence and the teaching of modern languages. In: *The teaching of modern languages: A volume of studies deriving from the International Seminar organized by the Secretariat of UNESCO at Nuwara Eliya, Ceylon, in August 1953*, ed. T. Andersson. Paris: UNESCO, pp. 199–208.
Barton, A. and J. Bragg. *'Discovering Languages' Project – Evaluation (Phase 3) December 2010.* Online at www.escholar.manchester.ac.uk/uk-ac-man-scw:113130
Bayley, S. (1991). Modern languages: An 'Ideal of Humane Learning': The Leathes report of 1918. *Journal of Educational Adminstration and History* 23(2): 11–24.
——— (1989). Life is too short to learn German: Modern languages in English Elementary Education 1872–1904. *History of Education: Journal of the History of Education Society* 18: 57–70.
Beck-Busse, G. (2014 [1999]). *Grammatik für Damen. Zur Geschichte der französischen und italienischen Grammatik in Deutschland, England, Frankreich und Italien (1605–1850).* Habilitationsschrift FU Berlin. Published in 2014 as *Grammaire des*

dames, Grammatica per le dame: Grammatik im Spannungsfeld von Sprache, Kultur und Gesellschaft.
Beckwith, E. G. A. (1917). *The soldier's manual: military expressions in English, French and German [. . .].* Philadelphia: D. McKay.
Beiler, B. (1731). *A new German Grammar. Whereby an Englishman may easily attain to the knowledge of the German Language, especially useful for merchants and travellers: To which are added, several useful and familiar dialogues.* London: J. Downing for the Author.
Bellot, J. (1580). *Le maistre d'escole Anglois [. . .] The Englishe Scholemaister.* London: Thomas Purfoote, for Henry Dizlie.
Berlemont, N. D. (1637). *The English, Latine, French, Dutch, Schole-master. [. . .].* London: A. G. for Michael Sparke.
Beuzemaker, J. J. (1892). Old and new methods of teaching modern languages. *Educational Times* 1892: 505–509.
Bevis, R. and A. Gregory. (2005). *Mind the gap! Improving transition between key stage 2 and 3.* London: Centre for Information on Language Teaching and Research.
Bischoff, D. (1939). Deutsch und Französisch im britischen Bildungswesen unter besonderer Berücksichtigung der Entwicklung in Schottland. *Internationale Zeitschrift für Erziehung* 8: 180–202.
Bithell, J., ed. (1932). *Germany: A companion to German studies.* [S.I.]: Methuen.
Blamires, D. (1990). British knowledge of German before the High Dutch Minerva. *German Life and Letters* 43: 102–112.
Bloomfield, L. (1933). *Language.* London: Allen & Unwin.
——— (1944–1945). *Spoken Dutch.* New York: Henry Holt & Co.
Blusch, M., ed. (1992). *Ein italienisch-deutsches Sprachlehrbuch des 15: Jahrhunderts. Edition der Handschrift Universitätsbibliothek Heidelberg Pal. Ger. 657 und räumlich-zeitliche Einordnung des deutschen Textes.* Frankfurt a/M: Peter Lang.
Board of Education. (1903). *List of holiday courses on the Continent for instruction in modern languages and other subjects.* London: HMSO.
——— (1930a). *Foreign languages in 'modern' schools.* London: HMSO.
——— (1930b). *Memorandum on the teaching of foreign languages in certain types of schools.* Educational Pamphlets, no. 82. London: HMSO.
——— (1930d). *Second Interim Report of the committee on education for salesmanship. Modern Languages.* London: HMSO.
——— (1931). *Final report of the committee on education for salesmanship.* London: HMSO.
Board, K. and T. Tinsley. (2015). *Language trends 2014/15: The state of language learning in primary and secondary schools in England.* London: CfBT. Online at http://cdn.cfbt.com/~/media/cfbtcorporate/files/research/2015/r-language-trends-2015.pdf.
Boer, M. G. de (2012). *Ecrire la grammaire italien aux Pays-Bas.* Amsterdam & Münster: Stichting Neerlandistiek VU Amsterdam & Nodus Publikationen.
Boiling, G. (2005). *Secret students on parade: Cold-war memories of JSSL, Crail.* Powys: Old Station Offices.
Brebner, M. (1898, 3rd ed. 1904; rpt. 1909). *The method of teaching modern languages in Germany being the report presented to the Trustees of Gilchrist Educational Trust on a visit to Germany in 1897, as a Gilchrist travelling scholar*, 3rd ed. London: Clay and Sons.

Brereton, C. (1930). *Modern language teaching in day and evening schools with special reference to London*. London: University of London Press.
Brereton, C., D. L. Savory, W. Rippmann and F. B. Kirkman. (1908). Report on the conditions of modern (foreign) language instruction in secondary schools. *Modern Language Teaching* 4: 33–38, 65–68.
Breul, K. (1894). The training of teachers of modern foreign languages (Paper read at the evening meeting of the College of Preceptors, April 11, 1894). *Educational Times* May 1: 225–231.
——— (1897). Großbritannien. In: *Handbuch der Erziehungs- und Unterrichtslehre für höhere Schulen*, ed. A. Baumeister. Munich: Beck. 1: 737–892. Online at https://archive.org/stream/handbuchdererzi01baumgoog#page/n518/mode/2up
——— (1899). *The teaching of modern foreign languages in secondary schools*. Cambridge: Cambridge University Press.
——— (1902). The Neuphilologentag at Breslau. *Modern Language Quarterly* 5(3): 160–166. Online at www.jstor.org/stable/41057945
Bridge, G. F. (1921). French and German in higher education. *Contemporary Review* 120: 805–810.
Brigstocke, W. O. (1905). Oral examinations. *Modern Language Teaching* 1: 110–112.
Brockey, L. M. (2007). *Journey to the East: The Jesuit mission to China, 1579–1724*. Cambridge, MA: Belknap Press of Harvard University Press.
Brown, H. (2009). Women translators in the Sprachgesellschaften. *Daphnis* 38: 621–647.
Bruézière, M. (1983). *L'Alliance française: histoire d'une institution*. Paris: Hachette.
Brunfaut, T. and C. Clapham. (2012). Assessment and testing. In Byram and Hu (2012), 52–59.
Bruschi, A. (2017). Learning vernaculars, learning in vernaculars: The role of modern languages in Nicolas Le Gras' noble academy and in teaching practices for the nobility (France, 1640-about 1750). In: *Language choice in Enlightenment Europe: education and sociability*, ed. V. Rjeoutski and W. Frijhoff. Amsterdam: AUP, forthcoming.
Buckby, M. and Schools Council Project on Graded Tests in Modern Modern Languages. (1981). *Graded objectives and tests for modern languages: An evaluation*. London: Schools Council, distributed by the Centre for Information on Language Teaching and Research.
Byram, M. (1997). *Teaching and assessing intercultural communicative competence*. Clevedon: Multilingual Matters.
——— (2008a). *From foreign language education to education for intercultural citizenship: Essays and reflection*. Clevedon: Multilingual Matters.
——— (2008b). Researching residence and study abroad. *Auslandsaufenthalte in Schule und Studium: Bestandaufnahmen aus Forschung und Praxis*, ed. S. Ehrenreich, G. Woodman and M. Perrefort. Münster: Waxmann, 19–27.
——— (2014). Languages, choice of languages, and other priorities in the Leathes report to the British government (1918). *Documents pour l'histoire du français langue étrangère ou seconde* 53: 153–174.
Byram, M. and A. Hu. (2012). *Routledge Encyclopaedia of Language Teaching and Learning*, 2nd ed. London: Routledge.
Cabau, B. (2014). The 'language tournament' within the Swedish school system (1849–1946). *Documents pour l'histoire du français langue étrangère ou seconde* 53: 65–90.

Calbris, B. A. M. (1797). *The rational guide to the French tongue. [. . .]*. London: Debrett.
Cambridge Assessment. (1994). *General Certificate of Secondary Education. French - Syllabus code 1525*. Cambridge: Cambridge Assessment.
Cambridge Assessment/UCLES. (2008/1858). *University of Cambridge: Examination of students who are not members of the University. Examination papers, with lists of syndics and examiners, and the regulations &c. for the examination held in December 1858* (facsimile reprint 2008). Cambridge: Cambridge University Press.
Caravolas, J. (1994). *La didactique des langues: Précis d'histoire I. 1450–1700. Anthologie I. A L'ombre de Quintilien*. Tübingen: Narr.
——— (2000). *Histoire de la didactique des languages au siècle des Lumières: Précis et anthologie thématique*. Tübingen: Narr.
Cassella, M. E. (1837). *Memorietta Italiana, per le fanciulle; o Conversazioni familiari in italiano ed in francese, etc. Ital. & Fr*. Londra: J. Souter.
Centre for Information on Language and Research. (1982). *Portuguese*. London: CILT.
Chambaud, L. (1750). *A grammar of the French tongue: With a prefatory discourse, containing an essay on the proper method for teaching and learning that language*. London: Printed for A. Millar [. . .] [Available online through ECCO].
——— (1762). *Exercises to the rules of construction of French-Speech* [. . .], 3rd ed. Dublin: Printed for James Potts and Samuel Watson, Bookseller.
——— (1765). revised ed. published as *The Art of Speaking French: or the French language methodised for the use of the English*. Dublin: Hulton Bradley.
——— (1767). *Exercises to the rules of construction of French speech, consisting of passages extracted out of the best French authors. With a reference to the grammar-rules, to be turned back into French* [. . .]. *The fifth edition, etc*. London: A. Millar
——— (1772). *The Art of Speaking French*. Dublin: Printed by Thomas Walker, at Cicero's Head, in Dame-Street.
Chandla, N., P. Grewal and J. Anderson. (2007). *Curriculum guide for Panjabi*. London: CILT.
Chaney, E. (1998, revised ed. 2000). *The Evolution of the Grand Tour: Anglo-Italian cultural relations since the Renaissance*. London and Portland, OR: Frank Cass; revised ed., London: Routledge, 2000.
Chappell, H. and A. Peyraube. (2014). The history of Chinese grammars in Chinese and Western scholarly traditions. *Language & History* 57(2): 107–136.
Christ, H. (1985). *Fremdsprachenunterricht unter staatlicher Verwaltung: 1700 bis 1945: eine Dokumentation amtlicher Richtlinien und Verordnungen. Bd. 6 Prüfungsbestimmungen für den Fremdsprachenunterricht*. Tübingen: Narr.
——— (2005). Du Maître de langue au 'Neuphilologe': La formation des enseignants de français en Allemagne au cours du 19e siècle. *Documents pour l'histoire du français langue étrangère ou seconde* 33–34: 47–62 (online pagination, which I have used, 1–12).
CILT. (1970). *Examining modern languages: Abridged proceedings of a conference [. . .]*. London: CILT.
——— (2005). *Language Trends 2005: Community language learning in England, Wales and Scotland*. London: CILT.
——— (2007). *Language Trends 2007: Languages in secondary schools*. London: CILT.
——— (2010). *HE language students in the UK 2002–2003 to 2008–2009: Annual analysis of HESA Data*. London: CILT.

Clapton, G. T. and W. Stewart. (1929). *Les Études françaises dans l'enseignement en Grande-Bretagne*. Paris: Les Belles Lettres.
Clark, J. L. D. (1972). *Foreign language testing: Theory and practice*. Philadelphia: The Center for Curriculum Development, Inc.
Clark, J. L. D. and J. Hamilton. (1984). *Syllabus guidelines*. London: CILT.
Cohen, M. (1996). *Fashioning masculinity: National identity and language in the eighteenth century*. London: Routledge.
——— (2001). The grand tour: Language, national identity and masculinity. *Changing English: Studies in Reading and Culture* 8(2): 129–141.
Colbeck, C. (1887). *On the teaching of modern languages in theory and practice*. Cambridge: Cambridge University Press.
Coleman, J. A. (1996). *Studying languages: a survey of British and European students: The proficiency, background, attitudes and motivations of students of foreign languages in the United Kingdom and Europe*. London: CILT.
——— (2001). Lessons for the future: Evaluating FDTL languages. In: *Language learning futures: Issues and strategies for modern languages provision in higher education*, ed. A. Coleman, D. Ferney, D. Head and R. Rix. London: CILT, 7–21.
——— (2012). *Valuing the year abroad: The importance of the year abroad as part of a degree programme for UK students*. London: British Academy. Online at www.britac.ac.uk/policy/Valuing_The_Year_Abroad.cfm.
——— (2013). Study abroad. In: *Routledge Encyclopaedia of Language Teaching and Learning*, 2nd ed., ed. M. Byram and A. Hu. London: Routledge, pp. 679–671.
Coleman, J. A. and CILT. (1996). *Studying languages: A survey of British and European students: The proficiency, background, attitudes and motivations of students of foreign languages in the United Kingdom and Europe*. London: CILT.
Coleman, J. A. and L. Parker. (2001). Preparing for residence abroad: Staff development implications. In: *Teaching languages in higher education: Issues in training and continuing professional development*, ed. J. Klapper. London: CILT, 134–162.
Colsoni, F. (1699). *The English ladies' new French grammar [. . .]*. London: Printed for the author, and John Barnes at the Crown in the Pall Mall.
Cowan, J. M. (1991). American Linguistics in Peace and War. In: *First Person Singular II: Autobiographies by North American Scholars in the Language Sciences*, ed. E. F. K. Koerner. Amsterdam: Benjamins, pp. 69–82.
Cooper, R. L. (1989). *Language planning and social change*. Cambridge: Cambridge University Press.
Council of Europe. (2001). *Common European framework of reference for languages: Learning, teaching, assessment*. Cambridge: Cambridge University Press.
Coverley Smith, F. (1892). *Introduction to commercial German*. London: Macmillan.
Cowman, K. (2014). Getting stuck in the trenches: From makeshift lessons to French phrasebooks, how troops learnt French on the Western Front. *The Linguist* 53(5): 8–9. Online at http://thelinguist.uberflip.com/h/i/27628339-the-linguist-53-5.
Crabb, G. (1800a). *A complete introduction to the knowledge of the German language; or, a translation from Adelung: Arranged and adapted to the English learner. [. . .] To which is affixed, a dictionary*. London: Printed for the author, by C. Whittingham.
Crook, D. (2002). Local authorities and comprehensivization in England and Wales, 1944–1974. *Oxford Review of Education* 28(2–3): 247–260.
Dakin, J. (1973). *The language laboratory and language learning*. London: Longman.

232 Bibliography

Davies, Graham. (2012). CALL – Computer Assisted Language Learning. In: *Routledge Encyclopaedia of Language Teaching and Learning*, ed. M. Byram and A. Hu, 2nd ed. London: Routledge, pp. 98–101.

DCSF (Department for Children, Schools and Families). (2007). *The Languages Ladder: Steps to success.* http://webarchive.nationalarchives.gov.uk/20130401151715/ http://education.gov.uk/publications/eorderingdownload/dcsf-00811-2007.pdf.

Della Gana, D. (1988). *Neue Perspektiven.* London: Longman.

Department for Education. (2013). *National curriculum in England: Languages programmes of study. Key stage 2. Foreign language; Key stage 3. Modern foreign language.* London: Department for Education, DFE-00195-2013.

Department for Education. (2015). *GCSE subject content.* London: DfE. Online at www.gov.uk/government/uploads/system/uploads/attachment_data/file/400854/GCSE_modern_foreign_languages_January_2015.pdf.

Department of Education and Science and Welsh Office. (1991). *Modern foreign languages in the national curriculum.* London: HMSO.

Department for Education and Welsh Office. (1995). *Modern foreign languages in the National Curriculum.* London: HMSO.

Dibbets, G. R. W. (1971–1972). Rond Le Mayre's The Dutch Schoolemaster (Londen 1606). *Taal en tongval* 23–24: 1–14.

——— (2000). Frühe Grammatische Beschreibungen des Niederländischen (ca.1550–ca.1650). In: *History of the language sciences: An international handbook on the evolution of the study of language from the beginnings to the present (HSK 18:1–2): 2 vols, 2000–2001.* ed. S. Auroux, K. Koerner, H.-J. Niederehe and K. Versteegh. Berlin: de Gruyter, 1: 784–792.

———, ed. (1985). *Twe-Spraack vande Nederduitsche letterkunst (1584), edited with an introduction and commentary by Geert R.W. Dibbets.* Assen-Maastricht: Van Gorcum.

Dickson, P. (1986). *Assessing foreign languages: The French, German and Spanish tests.* Windsor: BRK: NEFR-Nelson Publishing Company.

Dobson, A. (2012). European language portfolio. In: Byram and Hu (2012), 232–233.

Doff, S. (2002). *Englischlernen zwischen Tradition und Innovation: Fremdsprachenunterricht für Mädchen im 19. Jahrhundert.* Munich: Langenscheidt-Longman.

Douglas, R. K., rev. H. C. G. Matthew. (2004). Kidd, Samuel (1804–1843). In: *Oxford dictionary of national biography.* Oxford University Press. Online edn, Jan. 2014. www.oxforddnb.com/view/article/15513, accessed 1 Dec. 2014.

Doyé, P., A. Hurrell, and Council of Europe Council for Cultural Co-operation – Education. (1997). *Foreign language learning in primary schools (age 5/6 to 10/11).* Strasbourg: Council of Europe.

Driscoll, P. (1999). Modern foreign languages in the primary school. A fresh start. In: *The teaching of modern foreign languages in the primary school*, ed. P. Driscoll and D. Frost. London: Routledge, 9–26.

Driscoll, P. and D. Frost, eds. (1999). *The teaching of modern foreign languages in the primary school.* London: Routledge.

Driscoll, P., E. Macaro and A. Swarbrick. (2014). *Debates in modern languages education.* London: Routledge.

Duff, C. (1933). *The basis and essentials of French [. . .], being a first approximation to a basic French.* London: Published for the Orthological Institute by T. Nelson.

Edgeworth, M. (1868). *The bracelets; and the good French governess: Two stories for girls.* London: Houlston and Wright.

Ehrenreich, S., G. Woodman and M. Perrefort, eds. (2008). *Auslandsaufenthalte in Schule und Studium: Bestandaufnahmen aus Forschung und Praxis*. Münster: Waxmann.
Eichhoff, J. (1971). German in Wisconsin. In: *The German language in America*, ed. G. G. Gilbert. Austin, TX: University of Texas, 43–57.
Ek, J. A. van (1976). *The threshold level for modern language learning in schools*. London: Longman.
——— (1986 (Vol. I), 1987 (Vol. II)). *Objectives for foreign language learning: Vol. I Scope, Vol. II Levels*. Strasbourg: Council of Europe.
——— and J. L. M. Trim. (1998). *Threshold 1990: Council of Europe*. Cambridge: Cambridge University Press.
Eliot, J. T. (1593). *Ortho-epia Gallica: Eliots Fruits for the French [. . .]*. London: Iohn Wolfe.
Elliott, G. and H. Shukman. (2003). *Secret classrooms: A memoir of the Cold War*. London: St Ermin's.
Els, Theo J. M. van, T. Bongaerts, G. Extra, C. van Os and A.-M. Janssen-van Dieten. (1984). *Applied linguistics and the learning and teaching of foreign languages*. London: Arnold.
Elwes, A. (1876). *A grammar of the Portguese language [. . .]*. London: Crosby Lockwood & Co.
Erondell, P. (1605, later ed. 1621). *The French garden: For English ladyes and gentlewomen to walke in [. . .]*. London: Printed by Edw: All-de for Iohn Grismond [. . .]. Rpt. Menston: Scolar Press, 1969.
Eve, H. W. (1880). *A school German grammar*. London: David Nutt.
Faucher, C. and P. Lane. (2013). French cultural diplomacy in early twentieth-century London. In: *A history of the French in London: Liberty, equality, opportunity*, ed. D. Kelly and M. Cornick. London: Institute of Historical Research, 281–298.
Fenwick de Porquet, L. (1830). *The Fenwickian system, of learning and teaching the French language*. London: Simpkin & Marshall.
Finkenberger, M., ed. (2005). *100 Jahre Fremdsprachenassistentenprogramm*. Bonn: Sekretariat der Kultusministerkonferenz – Deutscher Pädagogischer Austauschdienst (PAD).
Finotti, I. (2010). *Lambert Sauveur à l'ombre de Maximilian Berlitz: Les débuts de la méthode directe aux Etats-Unis*. Bologna: CLUEB.
Fischer, J. (2000). *Das Deutschlandbild der Iren 1890–1939*. Heidelberg: Winter.
Fisher, M. H. (2001). Persian professor in Britain: Mirza Muhammad Ibrahim at the East India College, 1826–1844. *Comparative Studies of South Asia, Africa and the Middle East* 21(1&2): 24–32.
Fleming, J. (1989). The French Garden: An introduction to women's French. *ELH: English Literary History* 56: 19–51.
Flood, J. L. (1999). Ginger beer and sugared cauliflower: Adolphus Bernays and language teaching in nineteenth-century London. In: *German studies at the turn of the century*, ed. R. Gorner and H. Kelly-Holmes. Munich: Iudicium, 101–115.
Florio, J. (1578). *Florio his firste Fruites [. . .] Also a perfect Induction to the Italian, and English tongues, etc. Eng. & Ital*. London: Thomas Dawson, for Thomas Woodcocke.
Fonseca, M. (2017). Londres et les Britanniques dans l'Ancienne Grammaticographie du Portugais Langue Étrangère (XVIIe- XIX e siècles). In: *The History of Language*

Learning and Teaching. Vol. II. 19th–20th Century Europe, ed. McLelland & Smith. Oxford: Legenda/MHRA, forthcoming.
Freeth, F. (1886). *A condensed Russian grammar for the use of staff-officers and others*. London: Trübner.
Fries, C. (1945). *Teaching and learning English as a foreign language*. Ann Arbor: University of Michigan Press.
Gallagher, J. (2014). *Vernacular language-learning in early modern England* (PhD thesis Cambridge).
Gallardo, M. (2001). Thomas Prendergast y su The Mastery of Languages. . . . , un ejemplo de la aplicación de los principios generativos a la enseñanza de lenguas en el siglo XIX. In: *Actas del II Congreso Internacional de la Sociedad Española de Historiografía Lingüística*. Universidad de León. Arco/Libro S.L., 249–256.
Gallichan, W. M. ([1914] and later editions). *The soldier's English-French conversation book*. London: T. Werner Laurie.
Gardt, A. (1999). *Geschichte der Sprachwissenschaft in Deutschland vom Mittelalter bis ins 20. Jahrhundert*. Berlin: de Gruyter.
Gasperin, V. de. (2017). Giuseppe Baretti's multifarious approach for learning Italian in 18th-century Britain. In: McLelland and Smith (2017a), Vol. I, forthcoming.
Geach, J. 1996. Community Languages. In *30 years of language teaching*, ed. Eric Hawkins. London: CILT, pp. 141–152.
Germain, C. (1993). *Evolution de l'enseignement des langues: 5000 ans d'histoire*. Paris: CLE International.
Giesler, T. (2014). School languages between economy and politics: The foreign language curriculum in northern German schools. *Documents pour l'histoire du français langue étrangère ou seconde* 53: 33–48.
Gilchrist, J. (1798). *The oriental linguist: An easy and familiar introduction to the popular language of Hindoostan [. . .]*. Calcutta: Printed by Thomson, Ferris, and Greenway.
Gislot, P. (1824). *The elements of the French language [. . .] particularly arranged for the use of ladies' schools, etc*. Bath: E. Collings.
Giustiniani, V. R., ed. (1987). *Adam von Rottweil, Deutsch-Italienischer Sprachführer*. Tübingen: Narr.
Glass, D. (1996). From Moravia to the Strand: The career of Karl Adolf Buchheim. In: *Exilanten und andere Deutsche in Fontanes London*, ed. P. Alter and R. Muhls. Stuttgart: Heinz, 41–76.
Glehn, Dr. von. (1912). A brief sketch of the theory and practice of what is generally called the direct method which it is attempted to carry out in this school. [i.e. the Perse School, Cambridge]. Appendix to *Board of Education Circular 797*.
Glück, H. (2002). *Deutsch als Fremdsprache in Europa vom Mittelalter bis zur Barockzeit*. Berlin: de Gruyter.
——— (2013). *Die Fremdsprache Deutsch im Zeitalter von Aufklärung, Klassik und Romantik*. Wiesbaden: Harrassowitz.
——— (2014). The history of German as a foreign language in Europe. *Language & History* 57(1): 44–58.
——— and M. Häberlein, eds. (2014). *Militär und Mehrsprachigkeit im neuzeitlichen Europa*. Wiesbaden: Harrassowitz.
——— and B. Morcinek, eds. (2006). *Ein Franke in Venedig: Das Sprachlehrbuch des Georg von Nürnberg (1424) und seine Folgen*. Wiesbaden: Harrassowitz.

Goldberg, D., D. Looney and N. Lusin. (2015). *Enrollments in languages other than English in United States institutions of higher education, Fall 2013.* Online at www.mla.org/pdf/2013_enrollment_survey.pdf.

Gräf, H. T. (2014). 'Gott daimie und wer weiß wie all das andre heist' – Zum Unbehagen der hessischen Offiziere im anglophonen Milieu des britischen Militärs in Nordamerika. In: Glück and Häberlein (2014), 151–166.

Graves, M. and J. M. Cowan. (1942). *Report of the first year's operation of the intensive language program of the American Council of Learned Societies, 1941–1942.* Washington, DC: American Council of Learned Societies.

Grimani, S. (1788). *The ladies new Italian grammar [. . .].* London: Printed by W. Smith [. . .].

Groot, J. de (2013). 'Euery one teacheth after thyr owne fantasie': French language instruction. In: *Performing pedagogy in early modern england*, ed. K. M. Moncrief and K. R. McPherson. London: Ashgate, 33–52.

Guilherme, M. (2012). Intercultural competence. In: *Routledge Encyclopaedia of Language Teaching and Learning*, 2nd ed., ed. M. Byram and A. Hu. London: Routledge, 346–349.

Guthke, K. (2011). Deutsche Literatur aus zweiter Hand: Engl. Lehr-und Lesebücher in der Goethezeit. *Jahrbuch des Freien Deutschen Hochstifts* 163–237.

——— (2015). Deutsche Literatur aus zweiter Hand: Englische Lehr- und Lesebuecher in der Goethezeit. In: *Geistiger Handelsverkehr: Streifzüge im Zeitalter der Weltliteratur*, ed. K. Guthke. Tübingen: Francke, 1–55.

Gwosdek, H. (2013). *Lily's grammar of Latin in English: An Introduction of the Eyght Partes of Speche, and the construction of the same. Edition and introduction.* Oxford: Oxford University Press.

Häberlein, M. and C. Kuhn, eds. (2010). *Fremde Sprachen in frühneuzeitlichen Städten.* Wiesbaden: Harrassowitz.

Halls, W. D. (1970). *Foreign languages and education in Western Europe.* London: Harrap.

Hamilton, J. (1829). *The history, principles, practice, and results of the Hamiltonian system [. . .].* Manchester: Printed by T. Sowler, Courier and Herald Office.

Hammar, E. (1991). *"La française": Mille et une façons d'apprendre le français en Suède avant 1807.* Uppsala: Uppsala Studies in Education, 41.

Hardach-Pinke, I. (2000). German Governesses in England. In: *Prinz Albert und die Entwicklung der Bildung in England und Deutschland im 19. Jahrhundert: Prince Albert and the development of education in England and Germany in the 19th century*, ed. F. Bosbach, C. Filmer-Sankey and H. Hiery. Munich: K.G. Saur, 23–32.

Harding, A., B. Page, and S. Rowell. (1980). *Graded objectives in modern languages.* London: CILT.

Hargreaves, P. H. (1961). Modern language classes. *Adult Education* 34: 23–27, 37.

Harris, E. F. (1915). *French for the front.* London: Marlborough.

Hauch, E. F. (1929). *German idiom list.* New York: Macmillan.

Hawkins, E. (1987). *Modern languages in the curriculum*, Revised edition. Cambridge: Cambridge University Press.

———, ed. (1996). *Thirty years of language teaching.* London: Centre for Information on Language Teaching and Research.

Hay, M. (1962). [letter to the editor, in response to the January issue of *Journal of Adult Education* 34]. *Journal of Adult Education* 34: 31–33.

——— (1966–1967). Language confusion. *Journal of Adult Education* 39: 290–294.
Hayden, D. (2011). Poetic law and the medieval Irish linguist: Contextualising the vices and virtues of verse composition in Auraicept na nÉces. *Language & History* 54(1): 1–34.
H. B. (1887). The 'Neuphilologentag' at Frankfurt. *The Educational Times* 1887, July 1: 273–274.
HEFCE (Higher Education Funding Council for England). (2005). *Strategically important and vulnerable subjects. Final report of the advisory group*. London: HEFCE.
Hellgardt, E. (2001). Einige altenglische, althoch- und altniederdeutsche Interlinearversionen des Psalters im Vergleich. In: *Mittelalterliche volkssprachige Glossen*, ed. R. Bergmann, E. Glaser, and C. Moulin-Fankhänel. Heidelberg: Winter, 261–296.
Henkel, N. (2009). Glossierung und Texterschließung. Zur Funktion lateinischer und volkssprachiger Glossen im Schulunterricht. In: *Die althochdeutsche und altsächsische Glossographie. Ein Handbuch*, ed. R. Bergmann and S. Stricker. Berlin and New York: de Gruyter, 1: 468–496.
Hickel, Raymond A. (1965). *Modern language teaching by television: A survey based on the principal experiments carried out in Western Europe*. Strasbourg: Council for Cultural Co-operation.
Hicks, W. C. R. (1944). Language learning for adults. *Journal of Adult Education* 16: 172–184.
Hoffa, W. (2007). *A history of US study abroad: Beginnings to 1965*. Carlisle, PA: Forum on Education Abroad.
——— and S. C. DePaul, eds. (2010). A history of U.S. study abroad: 1965 to present (A history of U.S. study abroad, Volume II). Carlisle, PA: A publication of *Frontiers: The Interdisciplinary Journal of Study Abroad*.
Holmes, D. (2011). A short history of French studies in the UK. In: *French studies in and for the twenty-first century*, ed. P. Lane and M. Worton. Liverpool: Liverpool University Press, 12–24.
Hoogvliet, J. M. (1908). *Elements of Dutch [. . .]*, 7th ed. The Hague: Martinus Nijhoff.
Hooper, E. (1873). *Our nurseries and school rooms: Remarks on home training and teaching. [. . .] Specially dedicated to ladies engaged in tuition*. London: Hatchards, Piccadilly.
Hope Simpson, J. B. (1967). *Rugby since Arnold: A history of Rugby school since 1842*. London: Macmillan.
Hornberger, N. H. (2006). Frameworks and models in language policy and planning. In: *Introduction to language policy: Theory and method*, ed. T. Ricento. Oxford: Wiley-Blackwell, 24–41.
Howatt, A. P. R. (1984). *A history of English language teaching*. Oxford: Oxford University Press.
——— (1994). H. E. Palmer (1877–1949). In R. E. Asher,. ed. *Encyclopaedia of Language and Linguistics*, vol. 7. Oxford: Pergamon, p. 2915.
——— and R. Smith. (2014). The history of teaching English as a foreign language, from a British and European perspective. *Language & History* 58(1): 75–95.
——— with H. G. Widdowson. (2004). *A history of English language teaching*, 2nd ed. Oxford: Oxford University Press.
Howell, J. (1650). *Instructions and directions for forren travell. [. . .]*. London: Printed by W. W. for Humphrey Moseley.

Hughes, K. (1993). *The Victorian Governess*. London: Hambledon Press.
Hüllen, W. (1995). The path through an undergrowth: A Royal Complete Grammar, English and High German (1715). *Paradigm* 17. http://faculty.ed.uiuc.edu/westbury/paradigm/.
——— (1997). Review of *Colloquia, et dictionariolum octo linguarum Latinae, Gallicae, Belgicae, Teutonicae, Hispanicae, Italicae, Anglicae, Portugallicae*, ed. Riccarda Rizza et al. (Viareggio-Lucca-Italy: Mauro Baroni editore s.d. [1996]). *Henry Sweet Society Bulletin* 29: 53–55.
——— (1999). *English dictionaries 800–1700: The topical tradition*. Oxford: Clarendon.
——— (2005). *Kleine Geschichte des Fremdsprachenlernerns*. Berlin: Erich Schmidt.
——— (2007). The European tradition of early foreign language teaching. In: *Geschichte der Sprachtheorien. 6.2 Sprachtheorien der Neuzeit III/s. Sprachbeschreibung und Sprachunterricht. Teil 2*, ed. P. Schmitter. Tübingen: Narr, 479–499.
Hulshof, H., E. K. Wakernaak and F. Wilhelm. (2016). *Geschiedenis van het taalonderwijs in Nederland. Onderwijs in de moderne talen van 1500 tot heden*. Groningen: Uitgeverij Passage.
Hunt, F. (1987). *Lessons for life: The schooling of girls and women 1850–1950*. Oxford: Blackwell.
Hunt, T. (1991). *Teaching and learning Latin in thirteenth century England*. Cambridge: Brewer.
Incorporated Association of Assistant Masters. (1949). *The teaching of modern languages*. 2nd ed. London: University of London Press.
Incorporated Association of Assistant Masters in Secondary Schools. (1929). *Memorandum on the teaching of modern languages*. London: University of London Press.
Incorporated Association of Assistant Masters in Secondary Schools. (1952). *The teaching of modern languages*, 2nd ed. London: University of London Press.
Ising, E. (1966). *Die Anfänge der volkssprachlichen Grammatik in Deutschland und Böhmen: Dargestellt am Einfluss der Schrift des Aelius Donatus. De octo partibus orationis ars minor. Teil I: Quellen*. Berlin: Deutsche Akademie der Wissenschaften zu Berlin.
Johnson, K. (1994). Teaching declarative and procedural knowledge. In: *Grammar and the language teacher*, ed. M. Bygate, A. Tonkyn, & E. Williams. Hemel Hempstead: Prentice Hall, 121–131.
Johnstone, M. (2014). Languages over the past 40 years: Does history repeat itself? In: *Debates in modern languages education*, ed. P. Driscoll, E. Macaro and A. Swarbrick. London: Routledge, 9–21.
Johnstone, R. and J. Trim. (1996). Research in the UK and Europe. In: Hawkins (1996), 299–318.
Jolles, F. (1968). The hazard of travel in medieval Germany: An attempt at an interpretation of the *altdeutsche Gespräche*. *German Life and Letters* 21: 309–319.
Jones, B. (1996). Contacts with the foreign country. In: *30 years of language teaching*, ed. Eric Hawkins, ed.. London: CILT, 238–244.
Jones, M., C. Kitetu and J. Sunderland. (1997). Discourse roles, gender and language textbook dialogues: Who learns what from John and Sally? *Gender and Education* 9(4): 469–490.
Jones, R. (1993). Survey of German at A-level. In: *German Studies in the United Kingdom. A Survey of German in Schools and Universities*, ed. R. Jones and R. Tenberg. London: European Business Associates, 43–80.

Kapcia, A. and L. A. Newsom. (2014). *Report on the state of UK-based research on Latin America and the Caribbean.* London: Institute of Latin American Studies, School of Advanced Study, University of London.
Kaplan, R. B. and R. B. Baldauf. (1997). *Language planning from practice to theory.* Clevedon: Multilingual Matters.
Kaye, E. (1972). *A History of Queen's College.* London: Chatto & Windus.
Kaye, J. M. (1966). *Placita corone: or La corone pledée devant justices.* London: Quaritch.
Keane, A. H. (1873). *True theory of the German declensions and conjugations.* London: Ahser & Co.
Keefer, L. E. (1988). *Scholars in foxholes: The story of the army specialized training program in World War II.* Reston, VA: Cotu Publishing.
Kelly, L. (1969). *Twenty-five centuries of language teaching.* Rowley, MA: Newbury House.
Kelly, T. (1950). *Outside the walls: Sixty years of university extension at Manchester, 1886–1946.* Manchester: Manchester University Press.
Kibbee, D. (1991). *For to Speke Frenche Trewely: The French language in England, 1000–1600: Its status, description and instruction.* Amsterdam: Benjamins.
Kinloch, A. (1890). *Russian conversational grammar: With exercises, colloquial phrases, and extensive English-Russian vocabulary.* London: W. Thacker.
Kirk, S. (2016). 'Whatever you do, do not let a boy grow up without Latin': A comparative study of 19th-century Latin textbooks in English and Prussian education (unpublished PhD thesis). University of Nottingham. Available online at http://eprints.nottingham.ac.uk/33080/.
Klippel, F. (1994). *Englischlernen im 18. und 19. Jahrhunderts. Die Geschichte der Lehrbücher und Unterrichtsmethoden.* Münster: Nodus.
―― (2015). Classroom-oriented teacher research in modern languages in the reform movement. Paper presented at the Colloquium of the Henry Sweet Society for the History of Linguistic Ideas, Gargnano, Sept. 2015.
Kloss, H. (1971). German as an immigrant, indigenous, foreign, and second language in the United States. In: *The German language in America*, ed. G. G. Gilbert. Austin, TX: University of Texas, 106–127.
Klöter, H. (2010). *The language of the Sangleys: A Chinese vernacular in missionary sources of the seventeenth century.* Leiden and Boston: Brill.
Koch, K. (2002). *Deutsch als Fremdsprache im Rußland des 18. Jahrhunderts.* Berlin: de Gruyter.
Koischwitz, O. (1933). *Deutsche Fibel.* London: Harrap.
Kok Escalle, M.-C. (2015). Between academic discipline and societal relevance: Professionalizing foreign language education in the Netherlands, 1881–1921. In: *The practice of philology in the nineteenth-century Netherlands*, ed. H. Zuidenvaart and T. van Kalmthout. Amsterdam: Amsterdam University Press, 53–78.
―― and M. van Strien-Chardonneau. (2010). Le français aux Pays-Bas (XVIIe–XIXe siècles): de la langue du bilinguisme élitaire à une langue du plurilinguisme d'éducation. *Documents pour l'histoire du français langue étrangère ou seconde* 45: 123–156. Online at http://dhfles.revues.org/1364.
König, J. (1715). *A royal compleat grammar, English and High-German [. . .].* London: gedruckt for Wilhelm Frieman, und bey B. Barker und Charl. King, 1715.
Kricher, R. (2016). Language attitudes among adolescents in Montreal: Potential lessons for language planning in Quebec. *Nottingham French Studies* 55(2): 239–259.

Kuhfuß, W. (2014). *Eine Kulturgeschichte des Französischunterrichts in der Frühen Neuzeit: Französischlernen am Fürstenhof, auf dem Marktplatz, und in der Schule in Deutschland*. Göttingen: V&R unipress.

Kuhn, C. (2010). Fremdsprachenlernen zwischen Berufsbildung und sozialer Distinktion: Das Beispiel der Nürnberger Kaufmannsfamilie Tucher im 16. Jahrhundert. In: Häberlein and Kuhn (2010), 47–74.

Kuiper, W. (1961). *Historisch-didactische aspecten van het onderwijs in het Duits. Beschouwingen over de ontwikkeling van het Hoogduits op de Nederlandse scholen voor voorbereidend hoger en middelbaar onderwijs*. Groningen: J. B. Wolters.

Kultusministerkonferenz. (2004). *Bildungsstandards für die erste Fremdsprache (Englisch/Französisch) für den Mittleren Schulabschluss. Beschluss vom 4.12.2003*. Munich: Luchterhand.

Lado, R. (1957). *Linguistics across cultures: Applied linguistics for language teachers*. Ann Arbor: University of Michigan Press.

Lamartine, E. W. (1914). *The pictorial French course [. . .]*, 14th ed. London: Modern Language Press.

Lambley, K. (1920). *The teaching and cultivation of the French language in England during Tudor and Stuart Times*. Manchester: Manchester University Press; London: Longman.

Landfester, M. (2012). Neo-humanism (CT). In: *Brill's New Pauly*. Brill Online, 2013. http://referenceworks.brillonline.com/entries/brill-s-new-pauly/neo-humanism-ct-e1508000, accessed June 2013.

Lang, H. (2010). Fremdsprachenkompetenz zwischen Handelsverbindungen und Familiennetzwerken: Augsburger Kaufmannssöhne aus dem Welser-Umfeld in der Ausbildung bei Florentiner Bankiers um 1500. In: Häberlein and Kuhn (2010), 75–92.

Language Teaching Library, Centre for Information on Language Teaching Research, and British Council. (1980). *Contrastive studies/error analysis: German-English*. London: Language Teaching Library.

Languages Lead Body. (1993). *National language standards: Breaking the language barrier across the world of work*. London: Languages Lead Body

Lanvers, U. and J. A. Coleman. (2013). The UK language learning crisis in the public media: A critical analysis. *The Language Learning Journal* 45: 1–23.

Law, V. (2003). *The history of linguistics in Europe from Plato to 1600*. Cambridge: Cambridge University Press.

Lawrence, J. (2005). *Who the devil taught thee so much Italian? Italian language learning and literary imitation in early modern England*. Manchester: Manchester University Press.

Le Mayre, M. (1606). *The Dutch schoole master, wherein is shewed the true way to learne the Dutch tongue*. London: G. Elde for S. Waterson.

Leathes, S. (1918, 2nd ed. 1928). *Modern studies: Being the report of the Committee on the position of modern languages in the educational system of Great Britain*, Cmd 9036, 2nd ed. (Leathes Report), 1928. London: HMSO.

Lee, J., D. Buckland and G. Shaw. (1998). *The invisible child: The responses and attitudes to the learning of modern foreign languages shown by Year 9 pupils of average ability*. London: CILT.

Lemercier de Neuville, L. (1901). *Trois comédies pour jeunes filles: pièces à jouer dans les familles et dans les pensionnats*. New York: Holt.

Lepschy, A. L. (1974). *A case for Italian: Report on the teaching of Italian in Great Britain*. Strood, Rochester: Association of Teachers of Italian.

Lepschy, A. L. and A. R. Tamponi. (2005). *Prospettive sull'italiano come lingua straniera*. Perugia: Guerra Edizioni.
Lindemann, M. (1994). *Die französischen Wörterbücher von den Anfängen bis 1600: Entstehung und typologische Beschreibung*. Tübingen: Niemeyer.
Linn, A. R. (2016). *Investigating English in Europe: Contexts and agendas* (English in Europe, vol. 6). Berlin: de Gruyter Mouton.
——— (2017). Modern foreign language teachers get a voice: The role of the journals. In: McLelland and Smith (2017a), Vol. II, forthcoming.
Little, D., F. Gouillier and G. Hughes. (2011). *The European language portfolio: The story so far (1991–2011): A history of the ELP*. Strasbourg: Council of Europe. Online at www.coe.int/t/dg4/education/elp/elp-reg/History_ELP/History_EN.asp.
Loonen, P. L. M. (1991). *For to learne to buye and sell: Learning English in the Low Dutch area between 1500 and 1800: A critical survey*. Amsterdam: APA-Holland University Press.
Lorch, M. (2016). A late 19th-century British perspective on Modern Foreign Language Learning, Teaching and Reform: The legacy of Prendergast's 'Mastery System'. *Historiographia Linguistica* 43(1–2): 175–208.
——— (2017). For the tongue oft proclaims the man: The biographical sources of Thomas Prendergast's Mastery System of language learning. In: McLelland and Smith (2017a), Vol. II, forthcoming.
Louis, A. (1954). *German grammar: An approach to reading*.
Low, L. (1999). Policy issues for primary MFL. In: *The teaching of modern foreign languages in the primary school*, ed. P. Driscoll and D. Frost. London: Routledge, 50–64.
Lowell, A. L. (1900). *Colonial civil service*. London: Macmillan.
Ludolf, H. W. (1696 [1959]). *Grammatica Russica*. Oxford: e Theatro Sheldoniana. Facsimile reprint ed. Boris Unbegaun, Oxford: Oxford University Press.
Macht, K. (1986–1990). *Methodengeschichte des Englischunterrichts*. Vol. 1: 1800–1880. Vol. 2: 1880–1960. Vol. 3: 1960–1985. Augsburg: University of Augsburg.
——— (1992). Englischmethodik an der Schwelle zum 19. Jahrhundert zwischen Spätaufklärung und Neuhumanismus. In: *Fremdsprachenunterricht 1500–1800*, ed. K. Schröder. Wiesbaden: Harrassowitz, 109–123.
——— (1994). Practical skills or mental traning? The historical dilemma of foreign language methodology in nineteenth and twentieth century Germany. *Paradigm* 14. Online at http://faculty.ed.uiuc.edu/westbury/paradigm/macht.html.
Mairs, R. (2017). 'A Dragoman for Travellers': Popular Arabic instruction books and their authors in late nineteenth-century Egypt. In: McLelland and Smith (2017a), Vol. III, forthcoming.
Mandel, H. H. (1989). *Geschichte der Gymnasiallehrerbildung in Preussen-Deutschland, 1787–1987*. Berlin: Colloquium Verlag.
Mandich, A. (2005). Préparation et vérification des compétences des professeurs de langues vivantes en Italie aux XIXe–XXe siècles. *Documents pour l'histoire du français langue étrangère ou seconde* 33–34: 63–78 (online pagination, which I have used, 1–12).
Marcel, C. (1820). *Practical method of teaching the living languages, applied to the French, in which several defects of the old method are pointed out and remedied*. London: Hurst, Robinson.
——— (1853). *Language as a means of mental culture and international communication: Or, manual of the teacher, and the learner of languages*. London: Chapman and Hall.

Maréchal, R. (1972). *Histoire de l'enseignment et de la méthodologie des langues vivantes en Belgique des origines au début du 20e siècle*. Paris: Didier.
Martinez, L. (2014). De hispanófilo a hispanista. La construcción de una comunidad profesional en Gran Bretaña. *Ayer: Revista de Historia Contemporánea* 93(1): 139–161.
——— (2015). *Cultural diplomacy: A hundred years of the British-Spanish society*. Liverpool: Liverpool University Press.
Martyniuk, W. and S. Slivensky (2012). European Centre for Modern Languages (ECML). In: Byram and Hu (2012), 231 (single page).
Matthew, R. J. (1947). *Language and area studies in the armed forces: Their future significance*. Washington, DC: American Council on Education.
McLagan, P. (2006). *My languages portfolio: European language portfolio, junior version*. London: CILT.
McLelland, N. (2000). *Ulrich von Zatzikhoven's Lanzelet: Narrative style and entertainment*. Cambridge: Boydell & Brewer.
——— (2004). Dialogue and German language learning in the Renaissance. In: *Printed voices: The Renaissance Culture of Dialogue*, ed. D. Heitsch and J.-F. Vallee. Toronto: University of Toronto Press, 206–225.
——— (2009). Understanding German grammar takes centuries... In: *Landmarks in the history of the German language*, ed. N. Langer, G. Horan and S. Watts. Oxford: Lang, 57–84.
——— (2011). *J.G. Schottelius's Ausführliche Arbeit von der Teutschen Haubtsprache (1663) and its place in early modern European vernacular*. Oxford: Wiley-Blackwell.
——— (2012). Walter Rippmann and Otto Siepmann as Reform Movement textbook authors: A contribution to the history of teaching and learning German in the United Kingdom. *Language & History* 55: 125–145.
——— (2014). French and German in competition in British schools, 1850–1945. *Documents pour l'histoire du français langue étrangère ou seconde* 53 (Special issue, ed. Marcus Reinfried: *French, English and German: Three Languages in Competition Between 1850 and 1945*): 125–151.
——— (2015a). *German through English eyes: A history of language teaching and learning in Britain, 1500–2000*. Wiesbaden: Harrassowitz.
——— (2015b). Teach yourself Chinese – how? The history of Chinese self-instruction manuals for English speakers, 1900–2010. *Journal of the Chinese Language Teachers Association* 50(2): 109–152.
——— (2015c). German as a foreign language in Britain – The history of German of a 'useful' language since 1600. In: *Angermion Yearbook for Anglo-German Literary Criticism, Intellectual History and Cultural Transfers*, 8(1): 1–34
——— (2016). German global soft power, 1700–1920. In: *Les politiques linguistiques et culturelles extérieures des États européens (XVIIIème–XXème siècles)*, ed. M.-C. Kok Escalle and K. Sanchez. Amsterdam: University of Amsterdam Press, 45–68.
——— (2017a). *Der Schüler ist fleißig*. Learning German in colonized China, ca. 1906. In: McLelland and Smith (2017a), Vol. III, forthcoming.
——— (2017b). Mining foreign language teaching manuals for the history of pragmatics. *Journal of Historical Pragmatics*, forthcoming.
McLelland, N. and R. Smith, eds. (2014). Building the history of modern language learning. *Special Issue of Language & History* 57(1): 116.
——— (2017a). *The history of language learning and teaching. I. 16th–18th century Europe. II. 19th–20th century Europe. III. Across cultures*. Oxford: Legenda.

——— (2017b). The history of learning and teaching languages in Europe. *Language Learning Journal* (special issue, forthcoming December 2017).
Meidinger, J. V. (1783). *Praktische Französische Grammatik*. Frankfurt.
Menzies, G. K. and H. Truman Wood. (1935). *The story of the Royal Society of Arts: Abridged from Sir Henry Truman Wood's official history and brought up to date by G.K. Menzies*. London: Murray.
Michael, I. (1987). *The teaching of English: From the sixteenth century to 1870*. Cambridge: Cambridge University Press.
Milton, J. (2007). French as a foreign language and the Common European Framework of Reference for languages. Paper originally presented at LLAS conference: *Crossing frontiers: Languages and the international dimension*, 6–7 July 2006. Available from www.llas.ac.uk/resources/paper/2715.
Minsheu, J. (1617, rpt. 1978). *The guide into the tongues [. . .] at the charges of Iohn Minsheu published and printed: anno 1617*. Rpt. Delmar: Scholars' Facsimiles and Reprints.
Mitchell, R. (2014). Debates in modern languages education. In: *Debates in modern languages education*, ed. P. Driscoll, E. Macaro and A. Swarbrick. London: Routledge, 203–217.
Modern Language Association of America. (1901). *Report of the Committee of Twelve of the Modern Language Association of America*. Boston: D. C. Heath.
Mombert, M. (2001). *L'enseignement de l'allemand en France 1880–1918: entre 'modèle allemand' et 'langue de l'ennemi'*. Strasbourg: Presses Universitaires de Strasbourg.
More, H. (1799). *Strictures on the modern system of female education: With a view of the principles and conduct prevalent among women of rank and fortune. In two volumes*. Vol. I. London: Printed for T. Cadell Jun and W. Davies in the Strand.
Morgan, B. Q. (1928). *German frequency word book based on Kaeding's Häufigkeitswörterbuch der deutschen Sprache*. New York: Macmillan.
Morton, A. (2014). Sandhurst and the First World War: The royal military college 1902–1918. *Sandhurst Occasional Papers*. Sandhurst: Central Library, Royal Military Academy. Online at www.army.mod.uk/documents/general/rmas_occ_paper_17.pdf.
Moys, A. (1996). In-service training and support for teachers. In: Hawkins (1996), 286–293.
——— et al. (1980). *Modern language examinations at sixteen plus: A critical analysis*, compiled and edited by A. Moys . . . [et al.]. London: CILT.
——— (1984). *Foreign language examinations: The 16+ debate 1981–83*. London: CILT.
Muckle, J. (2008a). *The Russian language in Britain: A historical study of learners and teachers*. Ilkeston, Derbyshire: Bramcote Press.
——— (2008b). Russian in the university curriculum: A case-study of the impact of the First World War on language study in higher education in Britain. *History of Education* 37(3): 359–381.
——— (n.d.). Ivan Nestor-Schnurmann (1852–1917): A pioneer of the teaching of Russian in Great Britain. Online at: www.russianpresence.org.uk/index.php/studyingrussia/3036-nestor-schnurmann.html, accessed 2015.
Müller, J. 1969 (rpt. of 1882). *Quellenschriften und Geschichte des deutschsprachlichen Unterrichts bis zur Mitte des 16. Jahrhunderts*. Mit einer Einführung von Monika Rössing-Hager. Hildesheim: Olms.

Munoz, C. and D. Singleton. (2011). A critical review of age-related research on L2 ultimate attainment. *Language Teaching* 44(1): 1–35.

Murphy, J. J. (2000). Grammar and rhetoric in Roman schools. In Auroux et al. (2000), 1: 484–492.

National Curriculum Council. (1991). *Modern foreign languages in the national curriculum: A report [. . .] on the statutory consultation for attainment targets and programmes of study in modern foreign languages.* New York: National Curriculum Council.

——— (1992). *Modern foreign languages examples of information technology-related tasks* (Poster. Published as part of Modern Foreign Languages Non-Statutory Guidance).

Nestor-Schnurmann, I. (1884). *The Russian manual [. . .]*. London: Sampson Low, Marston & company.

Newmark, P. (1963–1964). Thoughts on machines and language teachers. *Adult Education* 36: 311–319.

Niederehe, H.-J. (1994). *Bibliografía cronológica de la lingüística, la gramática y la lexicografía del español (BICRES) desde los comiienzos hasta el año 1600 (BICRES).* Amsterdam: Benjamins.

——— (1999). *Bibliografía cronológica de la lingüística, la gramática y la lexicografía del español (BICRES II). Desde el año 1601 hasta el año 1700.* Amsterdam: Benjamins.

Noordegraf, Jan. 1992. Hoogvliet versus van Ginneken. Dutch Linguistics around the Turn of the Century. In: *The History of Linguistics in the Low Countries* (Studies in the History of the Language Sciences 64), ed. J. Noordegraaf, K. Versteegh and E. F. K. Koerner. Amsterdam: Benjamins, 273–304

Nott, D. (1996). University degree courses. In: Hawkins (1996), 61–69.

Nuffield Foundation. (1974). *Vorwärts.* York: University of York, Language Teaching Centre. Leeds: E.J. Arnold.

Núñez, L. P. (2010). *El arte de las palabras: diccionarios e imprenta en el Siglo de Oro.* Mérida: Editora Regional de Extremadura.

Offelen, H. (1687). *A double grammar for Germans to learn English and for English-men to learn the German tongue: Zwey-fache gründliche Sprach-Lehr, für Hochteutsche, englisch, und für Engelländer hochteutsch zu lernen. [. . .] London.* London: Old Spring Garden by Charing Cross.

Ölinger, A. (1587). *Duodecim dialogi apprimi elegantes clarissimi [. . .].* Spirae: Typis Bernardi Albini.

Orme, N. (2006). *Medieval schools: From Roman Britain to Renaissance England.* New Haven, CT: Yale University Press.

Ortmanns, K. P. (1993). *Deutsch in Großbritannien: Die Entwicklung von Deutsch als Fremdsprache von den Anfängen bis 1985.* Stuttgart: Franz Steiner.

O'Sullivan, B. and C. J. Weir. (2016). *Assessing English on the global stage: The British council and English language testing, 1941–2016.* London: British Council Monographs on Modern Language Testing.

Otter, H. S. (1970). Research by examining boards. In: *Examining modern languages.* London: CILT, 46–49.

Otto, E. and J. Wright. (1889). *Materials for Translating English into German with Grammatical Notes and a Vocabulary. Revised by Dr J. Wright. First Part.* 6th ed. London: David Nutt.

Padley, G. A. (1985, 1988). *Grammatical theory in Western Europe 1500–1700: Trends in vernacular grammar.* Cambridge: Cambridge University Press.

Page, B. W. and W. M. Shortt. (1970). The influence of GCE examinations on teaching modern languages. In: *Examining modern languages*. London: CILT Reports and Papers 4, 7–24.
Palmer, Harold E. *The principles of language study*. London: G. G. Harrap
Palmer, H. E. and A. S. Hornby. (1937). *Thousand word English*. London: G. G. Harrap & Co.
Parry, J. H. (1965). *Report of the committee on Latin American studies ('Parry Report')*. London: HMSO.
Parsons, D. and Titmus, C. J. (1962–63). Language Laboratory Colloquium. *Adult Education* 33: 36–39.
Patrick, H. and K. Reid. (1980). Universities and the PGCE: An historical perspective. In: *Developments in PGCE courses*, ed. R. Alexander and J. Whittaker. Leeds: Published by the Teacher Education Study Group, Society for Research into Higher Education, 6–16.
Peers, E. A. (1944). *Spanish – Now*. London: Methuen.
Peeters-Fontainas, J. F. (1965). *Bibliographie des impressions espagnoles des Pays-Bas méridionaux*. Nieuwkoop: de Graaf.
Pennycook, A. (2012). History: After 1945. In: Byram and Hu (2012), 312–319.
Phillips, D. and C. Filmer-Sankey. (1993). *Diversification in modern language teaching: Choice and the national curriculum*. London: Routledge.
Pienemann, M. (1984). Psychological constraints on the teachability of languages. *Studies in Second Language Acquisition* 6(2): 186–214.
Plumon, E. (1917). *Vade-mecum for the use of officers and interpreters in the present campaign: French and English technical and military terms*. London: Hachette & Company.
Porny, M. (1784). *The practical French grammar [. . .]* Dublin: Printed by H. Chamberlaine, No. 5, College-Green.
Prendergast, T. (1864). *The mastery of languages, or, the art of speaking foreign tongues idiomatically*. London: Bentley.
Proescholdt, C. W. (1991). The introduction of German language teaching into England. *German Life and Letters* 44(2): 93–102.
Protassova, E. (2017). Teaching second languages at pre-school age: The Russian experience. In: McLelland and Smith (2017), Vol. II, forthcoming.
Puff, Helmut. (1995). *Das Bild im Fremdsprachenunterricht: eine Geschichte der visuellen Medien am Beispiel des Französischunterrichts*. Tübingen: Francke.
Puren, C. (1988). *Histoire des méthodologies de l'enseignement des langues*. Paris: Nathan-CLE International.
——— (1994). *La didactique des langues à la croisée des méthodes: Essai sur l'éclectisme*. Paris: CRÉDIF-Didier.
Purin, C. M. (1929). *The training of teachers of the modern foreign languages*. New York: Macmillan.
QCA (Qualifications and Curriculum Authority). (2008). *Grade standards in GCSE modern foreign languages*. Online at www.all-london.org.uk/Resources/severe_grading/qca-08-3570-Grade_standards_in_GCSE_MFL.pdf.
Quick, R. H. (1874). *A German primer: Giving the essentials of German grammar, with a selection of proverbs, poems etc for learning by heart: also easy exercises in the use of common German words*. Harrow: Samuel Clarke.
——— (1875). The first steps in teaching a language. *Educational Times* 1874–1875: 279–282.

Raban, S., ed. (2008). *Examining the world: A history of the University of Cambridge examinations syndicate*. Cambridge: Cambridge University Press.
Radtke, E. (1994). *Gesprochenes Französisch und Sprachgeschichte: zur Rekonstruktion der Gesprächskonstitution in Dialogen französischer Sprachlehrbücher des 17. Jahrhunderts unter besonderer Berücksichtigung der italienischen Adaptionen*. Tübingen: Niemeyer.
Raffe, D. and K. Spours. (2007). *Policy-making and policy learning in 14–19 education*. London: Institute of Education (Bedford Way Papers), 1–32.
Rambeau, A. (1894). Remarks on the study of modern languages. *Die neueren Sprachen* 9: 261–276.
Reiff, C. P. (1853). *English-Russian grammar*. Karlsruhe: [s.n.].
Reinbothe, R. (2006). *Deutsch als internationale Wissenschaftssprache und der Boykott nach dem Ersten Weltkrieg*. Frankfurt: Lang.
Reinfried, M. (1992). *Das Bild im Fremdsprachenunterricht: eine Geschichte der visuellen Medien am Beispiel des Französischunterrichts*. Tübingen: Narr.
——— (2012). Audio-visual language teaching. In Byrman and Hu, 68–70.
Render, W. (1799). *A concise practical grammar of the German tongue*. London: H.D. Symonds.
Reuchlin, J. (1517 [1993]). *On the art of Kabbalah: De Arte Cabalistica*, translated by Martin Goodman and Sarah Goodman. Introduction by G. Lloyd Jones. Ed. with introduction by Moshe Idel. Lincoln and London: University of Nebraska Press.
Richards, D. (Joint Council of Language Associations). (1976). Teaching children of moderate ability. In: *German in the United Kingdom: Problems and prospects*. London: CILT, 56–59.
Ridley, R. (2010). *Dear Friends, Liebe Freunde*. lulu.com (self-published).
——— (2014). *All quiet on the western front?* Waterlord Publishing (self-published).
Ripman, W., S. Alge and S. Hamburger. (1917). *Dent's new first German book*. New York: Dutton.
Risager, K. (2006). *Language and culture: Global flows and local complexity*. Clevedon: Multilingual Matters.
——— (2007). *Language and culture pedagogy. From a nation to a transnational perspective*. Clevedon: Multilingual Matters.
Rival, S. (2012). *L'échange des assistants de language vivante entre la France et l'Allemagne avant la Seconde Guerre mondiale: les 'directeurs de conversation' et la 'langue de l'ennemi'*. Université de Lorraine. Online at http://docnum.univ-lorraine.fr/public/DDOC_T_2012_0366_RIVAL.pdf.
——— (2013a). Les premières années de l'échange d'assistants de langue entre la France et l'Allemagne (1904–1939). *Revue d'Allemagne et des Pays de langue allemande* 45: 141–164.
——— (2013b). Drei Fremdsprachenassistente in der Zeit des Nationalsozialismus. In Klippel, Friederike. Ellisabeth Kolb, Felicitas Sharp, eds. *Schulsprachenpolitik und fremdsprachliche Unterrichtspraxis*. Munich: Waxmann, 49–62.
Rjéoutski, V. and A. Tchoudinov, eds. (2013). *Le Précepteur francophone en Europe: XVIIe–XIXe siècles*. Paris: L'Harmattan.
Roach, J. (1971). *Public examinations in England 1850–1900*. Cambridge: Cambridge University Press.
Robins, R. H. (1994). William Bullokar's *Bref grammar of English*: Text and context. In: *Anglistentag 1993 Eichstätt: Proceedings*, ed. G. Blaicher and B. Glaser. Tübingen: Niemeyer, 19–31

Robson, E. H. A. (1929). *How shall we train the teacher of modern languages?: A textbook on modern language method for use in training colleges, and for all interested in the study and teaching of modern languages.* Cambridge: W. Heffer & Sons.

Roche, E. [1883]. *French plays for girls by various authors: With explanatory notes of difficult idioms by M. Emile Roche, professor of the French language and literature.* London: Allman & Sons.

Rocher, R. (1968). *Alexander Hamilton (1762–1824): A chapter in the early history of Sanskrit philology.* New Haven, CT: American Oriental Society.

Roeming, R. F. (1967). Foreign languages as weapons for defense. *Foreign Languages and the Schools: A book of readings*, ed. M. R. Donoghue. Dubuque: Wm. C. Brown Company Publishers, 53–59. First published in *The Modern Language Journal* 46: 53–59 (November 1962), 299–303.

Rossebastiano Bart, A. (2000). La tradition des manuels polyglottes dans l'enseignement des languages. In: Auroux et al. (2000), 688–698.

Rothwell, W. (1992). Chaucer and Stratford att Bowe. *Bulletin of the John Rylands University Library of Manchester* 74: 3–28.

Rowbotham, J. (1824). *A practical German grammar.* London: Printed for Baldwin, Cradock and Joy; Harvey and Darton; and Boosey and Sons.

Rowles, D. and V. Rowles. (2005). *Breaking the barriers: 100 years of the language assistants programme.* London: British Council.

Rowlinson, W. (1967, 1980 2nd ed.). *Sprich mal Deutsch 1.* Oxford: Oxford University Press.

Rowlinson, W., L. Lehnigk and G. Schladebach. (1993). *Deutschland hier und jetzt.* Oxford: Oxford University Press.

Rowntree, J. (1961–62 [sic]). Languages by Radio. *Adult Education* 24: 264–266

RSA (Royal Society of Arts). (1857–1870). *Examination papers of the Society of Arts: 1856–1870.* Held in the RSA archive, PR.ED/100/17/1.

——— (1857–1870). *Examination papers of the Society of Arts: 1857–1870.* Held in the RSA archive, PR.ED/100/17/2

——— (1902–1906). *RSA programme of examinations (1902–1906).* Held in the RSA archive, PR.ED/100/17/9.

——— (1933). *RSA examination papers 1933.* Held in the RSA archive PR.ED/100/17/71.

——— (1942–1946). *RSA examinations: Prisoner of War Camps 1942/1946.* Held in the RSA archive PR.ED/100/10/9.

——— (1994). *RSA examination papers: Language courses, 1994.* Held in the RSA archive, PR.ED/100/17/172

Rühle, C. (1881). *French examination papers: Being an entire series of French papers, set from 1876 to the year 1880 to candidates for Woolwich and Sandhurst; first appointments to the Royal Marine artillery and light infantry; the staff college; at the local examinations of the university of Oxford and Cambridge; and the London University; and to candidates for the civil service of India & Ceylon. Especially adapted for the use of Schools and students reading for competitive and other examinations*, 3rd ed., entirely new and enlarged. London: David Nutt.

Rühle, C. (1884). *German examination papers: Being an entire series of German papers set from 1879 to the Year 1881 to candidates for Woolwich & Sandhurst etc.* London: Dulau & Co.

Ruiz, R. (1984). Orientations in language planning. *NABE Journal* 8: 15–34.

Rybak, S. and British Broadcasting Corporation. (1980). *Learning languages from the BBC: Research into courses for adults*. London: BBC.
Salmon, V. (1996). *Language and society in early modern England: Selected essays 1981–1994*. Selected and edited by Konrad Koerner. Amsterdam: Benjamins.
——— (2003). Some notes on the life and work of John Minsheu (1560–1627). *Historiographia Linguistica* 30(3): 259–272.
Salverda, R. (2004). A hundred years of explaining the Dutch language to speakers of English, from Hoogvliet's *Elements* (1908) to the present. In: *Thesaurus polyglottus et flores quadrilingues: Festschrift für Stanislaw Predota zum 60. Geburtstag*, ed. S. Kiedron and A. Kowalska-Szubert. Wroclaw: Oficyna Wydawnicza ATUT, 357–382.
Sánchez Escribano, F. J. (2006). Portuguese in England in the sixteenth and seventeenth centuries. *Sederi* 16: 109–132.
Sánchez Pérez, Aquilino. 1992. *Historia de la enseñanza del español como lengua extranjera*. Madrid: SGEL.
Sanderson, T. H. (1913). *A history of the Royal Society of Arts [. . .] with a preface by Lord Sanderson, etc*. London: Royal Society of Arts.
Sandhurst, T. H. (1859). *Examination papers used at the examinations for admisson to the Royal Military College, Sandhurst, in June 1859*. London: Harrison.
Saunders, M. J. (1919–1920). A plea for the study of German. *Modern Languages* 1: 177–179.
Schäfer, J. (1978). Introduction. In: *John Minsheu, Guide into the tongues*, ed. J. Schäfer. New York: Scholars' facsimiles and reprints.
Schleich, M. (2013). Die Anfänge des internationalen Schülerbriefwechsels. In: *Schulsprachenpolitik und fremdsprachliche Unterrichtspraxis*, ed. F. Klippel, E. Kolb and F. Sharp. Münster: Waxmann, 139–152.
——— (2015). *Geschichte des internationalen Schülerbriefwechsels. Entstehung und Entwicklung im historischen Kontext von den Anfängen bis zum Ersten Weltkrieg*. Münster: Waxmann.
——— (2017). Connecting cultures through letter-writing: The scholars' international correspondence (1896 to 1914). In: McLelland and Smith (2017a), Vol. III, forthcoming.
Schottelius, J. G. (1663). *Ausführliche Arbeit von der teutschen Haubtsprache*. Braunschweig: Zilliger. Facsimile ed. Wolfgang Hecht 1967, Tübingen: Niemeyer.
Schröder, K. (1987, 1989, 1992, 1995, 1996, 1999; new ed. in prep.). *Biographisches und bibliographisches Lexikon der Fremdsprachenlehrer des deutschsprachigen Raumes, Spätmittelalter bis 1800*. 6 vols. (A-C, D-H, I-Q, R-Z, Nachträge und Ergänzungen zu A-K, Nachträge und Ergänzungen zu L-Z). Augsburg: Universität Augsburg.
——— (2000). Die Traditionen des Sprachunterrichts im Europa des 17. und 18. Jahrhunderts. In: Auroux et al. (2000–2006), 734–741.
——— (2006). Didaktische Ansätze im Sprachbuch von Georg von Nürnberg. In Glück and Morcinek (2006), 51–64.
Schwanke, I. (2010). Lernen bei Sprachmeistern und im Kontor: Die Ausbildung Augsburger Patriziersöhne in Lucca und Lyon 1620–1627. In: Häberlein and Kuhn (2010), 93–102.
Sculthorp, M. A. C. (1961–1962). The language laboratory. *Adult Education* 34: 249–253.

Secombe, T. 2004. 'Wanostrocht, Nicholas [Nicholas Felix] (1804–1876)', rev. Gerald M. D. Howat, *Oxford Dictionary of National Biography*. Oxford: Oxford University Press. www.oxforddnb.com/view/article/28667, accessed 24 Feb 2015.

Self, E. (1939). *The complete self educator, etc.* London: Odhams Press.

Sewel, W. (1706). *A compendious guide to the Low-Dutch language [. . .]*. Amsterdam: Printed for the widdow [sic] of Stephen Swart.

Sidwell, D. (1987a). *Teaching languages to adults.* London: CILT.

—— (1987b). *Adult learning strategies and approaches: Modern language learning. Trainers' handbook; Tutors' handbook.* Leicester: NIACE (National Institute for Adult and Continuing Education).

—— and P. Capoore (1983–1985). *Deutsch heute* (Part 1 1983, Part 2 1984, Part 3 1985; new edition 1990–1994). Walton-on-Thames: Nelson.

Skinner, B. F. (1957). *Verbal behavior.* London: Methuen.

Smith, G. H., G. Martin and W. Hedley. (2010). *Professionally speaking: The Chartered Institute of Linguists Centenary 1910–2010.* London: Chartered Institute of Linguists. Available for purchase from the Institute.

Smith, R. C. (1999). *The writings of Harold E. Palmer: An overview.* Tokyo: Hon-no-Tomosha.

—— (2009). Claude Marcel (1793–1876): A neglected applied linguist? *Language and History* 52(2): 171–182.

—— (2016). Building 'Applied Linguistic Historiography': Rationale, scope and methods. *Applied Linguistics* 37(1): 71–87.

Sørensen, L. M. (2010). *Teach yourself? Language learning through self-instruction manuals in nineteenth-century Scandinavia.* PhD thesis, University of Sheffield. Available online at: http://etheses.whiterose.ac.uk/904/2/SORENSEN_FINAL.pdf.

Spaulding, R. K. (1948). *How Spanish grew.* Berkeley: University of California Press.

Stack, E. M. (1960, 3rd ed. 1971). *The language laboratory and modern language teaching.* New York and Oxford: Oxford University Press.

Steadman-Jones, R. (2007). *Colonialism and grammatical representation: John Gilchrist and the analysis of the 'Hindustani' language in the late eighteenth and early nineteenth centuries.* Oxford: Blackwell.

Stegmann, T. D., ed. (1991). *Vocabulari Catalá-Alemany d l'any 1502 [. . .]* . Frankfurt: Domus Editoria Europaea.

Stern, H. H. (1963, 1967). *Foreign languages in primary education: The teaching of foreign or second languages to younger children: Report on an international meeting of experts, Hamburg, 1962.* Hamburg: UNESCO Institute for Education. Revised ed. published by OUP in 1967, with a revised introduction, some new notes, and a new final chapter. I have consulted this 1967 edition.

—— (1983). *Fundamental concepts of language teaching.* Oxford: Oxford University Press.

Stern, H. H. and Modern Language Association. (1965). *Modern languages in the universities: A guide to courses of study in five European languages at universities in the United Kingdom.* London: Macmillan.

Stevenson, W. H. (1929). *Early scholastic colloquies.* Oxford: Clarendon Press. Rpt. New York: AMS Press, 1989.

Storr, F. (1891). *German declensions and conjugations by help of reason and rhyme.* London: William Rice.

Stray, C. (1998). *Classics transformed: Schools, universities, and society in England, 1830–1960.* Oxford and New York: Clarendon Press and Oxford University Press.
Sumillera, R. G. (2014). Language manuals and the book trade in England. In: *Translation and the book trade in early modern Europe*, ed. J. M. Pérez Fernández and E. Wilson-Lee. Cambridge: Cambridge University Press, 61–80.
Sunderland, J. (2013). Gender in language learning. In: Byram and Hu (2012), 265–268.
Suso López, J., ed. (2005). *Documents pour l'histoire du français langue étrangère ou seconde* 33–34 (special issue) *L'enseignement du français en Europe autour du XIXe siècle. Histoire professionnelle et sociale.*
Swan, H. (1893). Gouin's Series Method of teaching languages. *Educational Times* 1893: 282–286.
Sweet, H. (1899). *The practical study of languages: A guide for teachers and learners.* London: Dent.
Tavoni, M. (1998). Renaissance Linguistics. In: *History of linguistics, Vol. III: Renaissance and early modern linguistics*, ed. G. Lepschy. London: Longman, 1–122.
Taylor, L. (2009). Assessment literacy. *Annual Review of Applied Linguistics* 29: 21–36.
Terrell, T. D., E. Tschirner, B. Nikolai and H. Genzmer. (1992). *Kontakte: A communicative approach.* New York: McGraw-Hill.
Teufel, P. C. (1906). *Grammatik für Chinesen zur Erlernung der deutschen Sprache.* Jentschoufu: Druck und Verlag der katholischen Mission.
Tharp, J. B. (1934). *A basic French vocabulary.* Washington, DC: The Modern Language Journal (National Federation of Modern Language Teachers).
Thierfelder, F. (1957). *Die deutsche Sprache im Ausland.* Hamburg: Decker.
Thimann, I. C. (1955). *Teaching languages: A notebook of suggestions and recollections.* London: Harrap.
Thomas, A. (2005). A la conquête d'un statut professionnel: les enseignants de français en Angleterre et leurs associations (1880–1914). *Documents pour l'histoire du français langue étrangère ou seconde* 33–34: 214–226 (online pagination, which I have used, 1–10).
Thomas, D. M. (2003). Introduction. In: Elliott, G. and H. Shukma, *Secret classrooms: A memoir of the Cold War.* London: St Ermin's, 1–5.
Thomas, J. B. (1990). Victorian beginnings. In: *British Universities and teacher education: A century of change*, ed. J. B. Thomas. London: The Falmer Press, 1–18.
Timbs, J. (1858). *School-days of eminent men: I. Sketches of the progress of education in England, from the reign of King Alfred to that of Queen Victoria. II. Early lives of celebrated British authors, philosophers, etc.* London: Kent & Company.
Tinsley, T. (2012). *Asset Languages briefing note.* Online at Association for Language Learning: www.all-languages.org.uk/uploads/files/Committees/World%20Languages%20Group/Briefing%20note%20re%20Asset%20Languages.pdf.
——— (for the British Academy). (2013). *Languages: The state of the nation.* London: British Academy. Online at www.britac.ac.uk/policy/State_of_the_Nation_2013.cfm.
Titone, R. (1968). *Teaching foreign languages: An historical sketch.* Washington, DC: Georgetown University Press.
Torriano, G. (1639). *New and easie directions for attaining the Thuscan Italian tongue* London: Printed by R. O[ulton] for Ralph Mab [. . .].

——— (1640). *The Italian tutor, or a new and most compleat Italian Grammer [. . .]*. London: Printed by T. Paine.
Torriano, G., J. Martyn and J. Allestry. (1657). *Della lingua Toscana-Romana: Or, an introduction to the Italian tongue [. . .]*. London: Printed for J. Martin, and J. Allestrye [. . .].
Townend, M. (2002). *Language and history in Viking age England: Linguistic relations between speakers of Old Norse and Old English*. Turnhout: Brepols.
Townson, B. (1886). *Easy German stories*. London: Rivingtons.
Trim, J. (1978). *Some possible lines of development of an overall structure for a European unit/credit scheme for foreign language learning by adults*. Strasbourg: Council of Europe.
Tyler, E. M. (2011). *Conceptualizing multilingualism in medieval England, c.800–c.1250*. Turnhout: Brepols.
UCLES [University of Cambridge Local Examinations Syndicate (1858–). *Local Examinations and Lectures Syndicate to the Senate of Cambridge University (Reports and Examinations)*. Held in Cambridge University Library, Cam.c.11.51.1-.
——— (1949). *Report on the work in School Certificate French, July 1949*. Held by Cambridge Assessment Archives.
——— (1987). *UCLES SR8 1987 = University of Cambridge local examinations syndicate SR8 (1987). Report on the June 1987 Examinations. Part 8 Modern Languages*. Cambridge: UCLES. Held by Cambridge Assessment archives.
Usher, H. J. K., C. D. Black-Hawkins and G. J. Carrick. (1981). *An Angel without Wings: The history of University College School 1830–1980*. London: University College School.
Valette, R. M. and R. S. Disick. (1972). *Modern language performance objectives and individualization: A handbook*. New York: Harcourt Brace Jovanovich.
Van der Lubbe, F. (2007). *Martin Aedler and the High Dutch Minerva: The first German grammar for the English*. Frankfurt: Lang.
Van Essen, A. (2012). History: From the reform movement to 1945. In: Byram and Hu (2012), 307–312.
Varnava, G., ed. (1975). *Mixed-ability teaching in modern languages*. Glasgow: Blackie.
Velleman, B. L. (2008). The 'scientific linguist' goes to war: The United States A.S.T. program in foreign languages. *Historiographia Linguistica* 35(3): 385–416.
Vidal Rodeiro, C. L. (2007). *Uptake of GCSE subjects 2000–2006: Statistics report series no. 4*. Cambridge: Cambridge Assessment. Online at www.cambridgeassessment.org.uk/images/111061-uptake-of-gcse-subjects-2000-2006.pdf.
Viémon, M. (2016). Histoire de quelques règles de prononciation pour savoir lire le français: de Berlaimont (1527) à Reixac i Carbó (1749). In: McLelland and Smith (2017a), Vol. I, forthcoming.
Viëtor, W. (published under the pseudonym Quousque Tandem). (1882, 1905). *Der Sprachunterricht muss umkehren! Ein Beitrag zur Überbürdungsfrag*e. (Pamphlet) Heilbronn: Verlag von Gebr. Henninger. 1905 ed. Leipzig: O.R. Reisland.
Villoria-Prieto, J. and J. Suso López. (2017). The use of dialogues in the teaching of foreign languages (XVIth and XVIIth century): Circulations, adaptations and transpositions. In: McLelland and Smith (2017a), Vol. I, forthcoming.
Vineis, E. and A. Maierù. (1994). Medieval linguistics. In: *History of linguistics: Vol. II Classical and medieval linguistics*, ed. G. Lepschy. London: Longman (Italian original 1990), 134–346.

Walford, G. (2006). *Private education: Tradition and diversity*. London: Continuum.
Wall, C. H. (1882). *A practical grammar of the Portuguese language, on Dr. Otto's conversational system. (Key)*. London: David Nutt.
Wanostrocht, N. (1780). *A practical grammar of the French language*. London: Printed for J. Johnson and J. Boosey.
Watson, F. (1909). *The beginnings of teaching modern subjects in England*. London: Pitman. Rpt Wakefield: S.R. Publishers, 1971.
—— (1921). German in England, History of the teaching of. In: *The encyclopaedia and dictionary of education: A comprehensive, practical and authoritative guide on all matters connected with education, including education principles and practice, various types of teaching instruction and educational systems throughout the world*, ed. F. Watson. London: Pitman, Vol. 2: 693–694.
Watts, A. (2008). Cambridge Local Examinations 1858–1945. In Raban (2008), 36–70.
Watzke, J. L. (2002). *Lasting change in foreign language education: A historical case for change in national policy*. Westport, CT: Praeger.
Weber, A. (2006). Der Frühsozialist Thomas Hodgskin und die Anfänge der Germanistik in Großbritannien. *Internationales Archiv für Sozialgeschichte der deutschen Literatur* 31(1): 51–75.
—— (2012). Karl Völker (1796–1884). Turner, Germanist und Pädagoge im englischen Exil. *Euphorion* 106: 387–415.
—— (2013). Karl Heinrich Schaible (1824–1899): Eine Fallstudie zur Germanistik und der deutschen Kolonie in London. *Euphorion* 107: 229–258.
Wegner, A. (2017). The other in the history of German language teaching: England and France 1900–2000. In: McLelland and Smith (2017a), Vol. III, forthcoming.
Weir, C. J., with contributions by I. Vidakovic and E. Dimitrova-Galaczi (2013). *Measured constructs: A history of Cambridge English examinations 1913–2012*. Cambridge: Cambridge University Press.
Wells, S. W. and J. Adams (1938). *Teach yourself German: A book of self-instruction in German based on the work ["The Self-Educator in German"] by Sir John Adams [. . .]*. London: English Universities Press.
Welsh Government. (2015). *Global futures: A plan to improve and promote modern foreign languages in Wales 2015–2020*. Online at http://gov.wales/topics/educationandskills/publications/guidance/global-futures-a-plan-to-improve-and-promote-modern-foreign-languages-in-wales/?lang=en.
Wendeborn, G. F. A. (1774). *The elements of German grammar*. London: C. Heydinger.
—— (1797). *Exercises to Dr. Wendeborn's introduction to German grammar [. . .]*. London: Printed for the author [. . .].
Wheeler, G. (2013). *Language Teaching through the Ages*. London: Routledge.
Whitehead, M. (1996). From 'O' level to GCSE – the impact of examinations. In: Hawkins (1996), 198–207.
—— (2004). Siepmann, Otto (1861–1947). In: *Oxford Dictionary of National Biography*. Oxford: Oxford University Press. Online edn, Oct. 2009 www.oxforddnb.com/view/article/36088.
Whitehouse, J. C. (1963–64). Language laboratories and adult students. *Adult Education* 34: 324–328.
Widgery, W. H. (1888). *The teaching of languages in schools*. London: David Nutt.
Wilhelm, F. A. (1993). Training foreign language teachers in the Netherlands (1795–1970): An historical outline. In: *Five hundred years of foreign language teaching in*

the Netherlands, 1450–1950, ed. J. Noordegraaf and F. Vonk. Amsterdam: Stichting Neerlandistiek VU: 67–87.

—— (2017). Foreign language teaching and learning in the Netherlands, 1500–2000: An overview. *Language Learning Journal* (December 2017, forthcoming).

Williamson, H. R. (1947). *Teach yourself Chinese*. London: Hodder & Stoughton for the English Universities Press.

Willis, J. (2003). *Foreign language learning and technology in England from the 17th to 21st centuries: An investigation into the functional and symbolic values attributed to foreign languages in England over four centuries of technological change* (Doctoral thesis). University of Surrey. Available online at http://epubs.surrey.ac.uk/1000/.

Witt, H. de (1873). *Recueil de Poésies pour les jeunes filles. (Class-Book of French Poetry for young girls)*. London: Hachette.

Wörsching, M. (2012). Foreign language assistants in schools: Making sure of the future. In: *Schools for the future Europe – Values and change beyond Lisbon*, ed. J. Sayer and L. Erler. London: Continuum, 117–134.

Wringe, C. (1976). *Developments in modern language teaching*. London: Open Books.

—— (1989). *The effective teaching of modern languages*. London: Longman.

—— (1996). Training to teach modern languages. In: Hawkins (1996), 269–277.

Zettersten, A. (1986). *New technologies in language learning*. Oxford: Pergamon.

Zwartjes, O. (2012). The historiography of missionary linguistics. *Historiographia Linguistica* 39(2–3): 185–242.

Index

academic value and birth of school subject 46–7
The Active-Service French Book for Soldiers and Sailors 42
actors in language advocacy 176–80
Adams, M. 114
adult language learning 48, 61–4, 81
Aedler, M.: *The High Dutch Minerva* 22, 94
Ahn, F. 19, 37n13, 99, 100–1, 102, 103, 115
Ajax: *Soldier's Language Manual, No. 1* 42, 82n4
A-level (Advanced Level) 27, *29*, 30, 32, *33*, 34, 45, 48, 53, 61, 62, 63, 83n19, 122, 127, 130, 132, 133, *134*, *136*, 137, 138, 140, 143, 146, 148, 151, 153–5, 157, *158–9*, 168, 169, 170n10, 173n39, 183, 189, 191
Alfred House Academy 125n10
Allgemeiner Deutscher Neuphilologen-Verbund 83n28
Alliance Française 75, 220
Alston, R. C. 35
America's International Correspondence Committee 77
Angiolillo, P. F. 81
Anglo-Dutch trade 81
Annan, N. G. 36, 119, 191; Report 215n29
AQA 35, 130, 132, 133, 141, *142*, 145, *166*, 169; Teacher Resource Bank 172n26
Arabic 27, 28–30, 32, 34, 35, 36, 38n27, 44, 82n6, 128, 156, 178, 191; combination of two or more foreign languages *31*; GCSE Examination figures *29*; UK higher education institution offering *74*
Arnold, M. 37n4

Arnold, T. 37n4, 47
Ascham, R. 84n30, 87
Ashby, M. 126n18
assessment 127–68; dictation 131, *134*, 135, 141–3, 144, 146, 147, 151, 169; four skills 144–53; grammatical knowledge 60, 119, 139–41, *162–3*; learning success 188, 223–4; levels of attainment 60, 128, 141, 151, 155–65, *161*, 168, 172n31, 173n34, 173n40; listening comprehension *142*, 145, 150, 151–3, 168; non-language knowledge and skills 128, 153–5; reading comprehension *135*, 138, 144, 145–6, 169; speaking 146–8; test constructs/what to measure 133–44, 66; translation from the target language into English 137–9; translation into the target language 135–7; validity, reliability and comparability 130–3; who tests, how and for whom? 128–30; writing 148–51
Association des Institutrices Françaises en Angleterre 67, 83n28
Association of Language Testers 130
Association of Teachers of Russian 26
ASTP *see* U.S. Army Specialized Training Program
attainment 60, 128, 141, 151, 155–65, *161*, 168, 172n31, 173n34, 173n40
Audio Visual Language Association 111, 179, 214n7
Audra, E. 81

Baldauf, B. 176, 213n5
Bale, J. 192, 193
Baretti, G. 125n2; *Small talk for the use of young ladies that wish to learn the colloquial part of the Italian language* 13

254 *Index*

Barlet, S. 66–7, 68, 70
Barrier, P. 81
Bata, A. 35
BBC 81, 112
Beck-Busse, G. 81
Bedford College 70, 105
Bellay, J. du 93
Bengali 27, 28, 32, 34, 44; GCSE Examination figures *29*; typeface 38n22
Berlaimont, N. de 40, 81, 93, 102, 125n5
Berlitz, M. D. 61, 107
Bernays, A. 129, 170n10
beyond classroom learning 39, 64, 75–80
Blonde d'Oxford 10
Bloomfield, L: *Spoken Dutch* 115
Board, K., 36, 38n28, 178
Boer Wars 18, 44
Boccaccio 12
Bolton Technical College 62
Brebner, M. 61, 122; *The Method of Teaching Modern Languages in Germany* 177
Brereton, C. 127, 170n8
Breul, K. 70, 71, 73, 106, 170n10, 177
Brigstocke, W. O. 146–7
British Academy 80, 216n33
British Association for Language Teaching 214n7
British Council 72, 84n34, 178, 191, 220
British Library 16
British Red Cross Society 170n6
Brunfaut, T. 130
Byram, M. 81, 85, 177
Bryce Commission 50
Bücklin, K. 88
Burstall, C. 178, 188; *Primary French in the Balance* 187
Byron, Lord 15

Calbris, B. A. M.: *A French Plaidoyer Between Five Young Ladies* 59
CALL *see* Computer Aided-Language Learning
Cambridge Assessment 127, 130, 133, *136*, 148, 150, 152, 156, 171nn11–12
Cambridge Board *see* University of Cambridge Local Examinations Syndicate: Cambridge Board
Cambridge Certificate of Proficiency in English 143, 153
Cambridge International Examinations 130
Cambridge Local Examinations *see* University of Cambridge Local Examinations Syndicate: Cambridge: Local Examinations
Cambridge Senior School Certificate *see* University of Cambridge Local Examinations Syndicate: Cambridge: Cambridge Senior School Certificate
Cambridge Syndicate Junior School Certificate *see* University of Cambridge Local Examinations Syndicate: Cambridge: Cambridge Syndicate Junior School Certificate
Cambridge Examination of Women *see* University of Cambridge Local Examinations Syndicate: Cambridge Examination for Women
Cambridge Primary Review 215n24
Cambridge Teacher Training Syndicate: *On the Teaching of Modern Languages in Theory and Practice* 71
Cambridge Training College for Women Teachers, 61, 71–2
Cambridge University Library 133
Cantonese 29, 30, 38n28, 125n4
Capoore, *Deutsch Heute* 122
Caravolas, J. 4n1, 87
Carroll, P.: *The Dutch Language Simplified* 18
Cassella, M. E. 59
Catherine of Aragon 14
Caxton, W. 11
CEFR *see* Common European Framework of References for Languages
Central Bureau for Educational Visits and Exchanges 72, 84n34
Centre for Information on Language Teaching (CILT) 19, 29, 32, 36, 53, 72, 130, 156, 175, 178, 189, 197, 201, 214nn9–10, 215n30
Centre for Languages, Linguistics and Area Studies 216n33
Centre for Language Teaching Research 116, 128
CHA *see* Co-operative Holiday Association
Chambaud, L. 59, 105, 124, 125n8, 222; *Grammar of the French Tongue* 95–7, 98
Chartered Institute of Linguists 40–1, 171n12
Chartered Institute of Secretaries 170n6

Chaucer, G. 10
Cheltenham Ladies College 104
Chinese 5, 6, 9, 28, 30–1, 32, 34, 35, 36, 38n28, 42, 63, 90–2, *91*, 114, 120, 125n4, 173n40, 178, 191, 213, 222; combination of two or more foreign languages *31*; GCSE Examination figures *29*; UK higher education institution offering *74*; Proficiency Test, 130; *see also* Mandarin
Chio Chiu grammar 91
Chomsky, N. 104
Christ, J. 72, 81, 96, 170n1, 171n22
chronological bibliography of reports and policy documents in modern languages education, 1890–2015 202–13
CILT *see* Centre for Information on Language Teaching
City Literary Institute 62
Civil Service Commission 25, 128, 129
Clancy, S. 83n22
Clapham, C. 130
Clapton, G. T. 35
Clarendon Commission 47, 60
Clarendon Report 177
Clark, J. L. D. 172n32, 173n35
Clark, S. 173n35
Clarke, H. B. 15
cognitive validity, 130, 132, 133, 138, 140
Cohen, M. 60, 81
Colbeck, C. 66, 68, 217–19; *On the Teaching of Modern Languages in Theory and Practice* 71
Coleman, J. A. 81, 225n3
College of Preceptors 65, 66, 68, 70, 84n30, 128, 170n6, 177
Comenius 84n30, 108, 179
Comfort, T. 184, 189
Commercial Certificate 15, 16, 51, 146, 154, 217
Commercial Correspondence for French and German 129
Commercial Dictionary 25
Committee of Twelve 172n29, 179, 184, 185, 195, 196, 197, 198, 202
Committee on Research and Development in Modern Language (CRDML) 28, 30, 174, 178, 179, 186, 188, 194, 197, 198, 201, 215n29
Common European Framework of References for Languages (CEFR) 137, 141, 148, 151, 155, 156, *158–60*, 168, 180, 215n23
community languages 5, 19, 27–30, *29*, 32, 37n20, 129, 198
Complete Self-Educator 61
Computer Aided-Language Learning (CALL) 113–14, 223
construing 95, 96, 125n8
Contemporary Russian Language Analysis Project 26
context validity, 131, 132, 133, 138, 140, 141, 149, 151, 155, 168
Cooper, W. 22
Co-operative Holiday Association (CHA) 6, 76
correspondence learning 77, 83n17, 83n17, 156, *159*; commercial 132
Council of Europe 2, 130, 137, 179, 184, 214n12; Charter for Regional or Minority Languages 180; Language Policy Unit 179; Modern Language Project 156
Council of Military Education 128
Coverdale, M. 41
Cowan, J. M. 81
Cowman, K. 42
Crabb, G. 67–8
CRDML *see* Committee on Research and Development in Modern Language
Crimean War 25
Cross Commission 70
cultural awareness 123, 172n34, 173n36, 189, 218

Dakin, J. 110
Dante 12
Defence Centre for Language & Culture 128
Della Gana, D.: *Neue Perspektiven* 122
dictation 71, 131, *134*, 135, 141–3, 144, 146, 169
direct method 107, 112
discipline in higher education 72–5
Disick, R. S. 155, 157
Doff, S. 81
Dominicans 91
Donatus, A. 88; *Ars minor* 6–7, 87–8
Driscoll, P. 188, 215n19
Ducie Street School 50
Dutch 5, 6, 16–19, 20, 23, 27, 32, 34, 35, 36, 44, 94, 120, 141, 147, 219; -English manuals 55, 81; Dutch-English/Flemish manuals 94; GCSE

Examination figures *29*; grammars 93; manual 64; *Twespraak* 93; UK higher education institution offering *74*; Bloomfield, L: *Spoken Dutch*; Le Mayre, M.: *Dutch Schoolmaster*
Dutch-Anglo trade 81

East India College 27, 36
East India Company 27; Military Seminary 28
Edgeworth, M. 59
educational infrastructure 64–80
Eliot, J.: *Ortho-Epia Gallica* 66
Elliott, C. 20
Elwes, A. 19
English Baccalaureate 175, 181
English Board of Education 77
English-Dutch/Flemish manuals 94
English Language Teaching (ELT) 5, 20–2, 35, 41, 56, 107, 198, 224
English speakers learning language 220–2
Erasmus scheme 79, 179
Eton College 47
European Centre for Modern Languages 179
European Day of Languages 180
European Language Portfolio 156, 180
European Ministers of Education 179, 197
European Year of Languages 180
Eve, H. W. 68, 126n13, 177
Exeter College 79

Ferienheimgesellschaft 76
Filmer-Sankey, C. 215n25
Fleming, J. 55, 81
Flemish 16, 17; /Dutch-English manuals 94
Flood, J. L. 81
Florio, M. A. 12
Florio, J. 5, 64, 220; *First Fruits* 12
Fonseca, C. 36
four skills 115, 117–19, 128, 132, 133, 144–53, 157, 168; listening comprehension *142*, 145, 150, 151–3, 168; reading comprehension *135*, 138, 144, 145–6, 169; speaking 146–8; writing 148–51
French 1, 4nn1–2, 5, 9–12, 13, 14, 15, 16, 17, 18, 19, 21, 22, 23, 25, 26, 31–2, 34, 35, 37, 37n6, 37n11, 37n18, 42, *43*, 44, 45, 46, 47, 48, 49, 50, 51, 52, *54*, 55, 58, 59, 60–1, 62, 63, 64, 65, 66, 67, 68, 69, 70, 71, 72, 73, 74, 75, 76, 77, 78, 79, 81, 82n6, 82n12, 83n21, 86, 95, 98, 102, 103, 104, 107, 108, 109, 112, 114, 116, 120, 121, 122, 124, 125n10, 128, 129, 131, 132, 133, *134*, 136, 137, 140, 141, 145, 147, 149–51, 155, 170n6, 171nn12–14, 171n21, 172n25, 172nn28–9, 179, 181, 184, 185, 186–7, 188, 189, 190, 191, 192, 195, 198, 218, 219, 220, 221, 222; A-level *33*, 148, 153; Anglo-Norman 35, 37n8; Cambridge Local Examinations *8*, 171n12; combination of two or more foreign languages *31*; -Dutch 40, 93; -English 40; grammar 97; Higher School Certificate 154; JMB 153; Junior 138, 169; language candidates at Cambridge Local Examinations *8*; Latin 125n7; O-level 150, 153, 168, 169, 187; Senior School Certificate 173n36; -Spanish 153, 183; spoken 60, 71, 147, 157; UCLES Higher School Certificate 143–4; ICLES Junior 169; UK higher education institution offering *74*
Fries, C. 116
Fugger, J. 89

Gallagher, J. 13, 15, 35, 55
Gasperin, V. de 125n2
Gaspey, T.: *Englische Konversationsgrammatik* 101
GCE *see* General Certificate Examination
gender in language learning and teaching 47, 53–61, 83n15
General Certificate Examination (GCE) 16, 62, 127, 130, 155, 192
George I 22, 64, 86
Germain, C. 87
German 1, 5, 9, 13, 15, 16, 18, 22–4, 32, 34–5, 36, 37n18, 41–4, 46–7, 48–51, 55, 56, 60–1, 62, 63, 64, 69–71, 72, 73, 75, 76, 77, 78–9, 82n12, 83n16, 83n21, 83n28, 87–8, 89, 93, 100–1, 103, 104, 108–9, 110, 112, 114, 116, 117, 118, 119–20, 121, 122, 123, 125n7, 126n11, 126n25, 128, 129, 131, *136*, 141, 145, 146, 149, 151, 154,

155, 170n6, 171nn12–13, 171n16, 171n22, 172n23, 172n29, 172n32, 173n36, 178, 179, 183, 184, 185, 186, 187, 189, 191, 192, 195, 196, 198, 214n14, 216n32, 218, 219, 220, 221, 224n1; A-level *33*; Cambridge Local Examinations 8; -Catalan 81; combination of two or more foreign languages *31*; -French 54; grammar 64, 65, 94, 95, 96–9, 100, 102, 126n13; Italian 81, 92; Juniors 138; language candidates at Cambridge Local Examinations *8*; manuals 82n6; O-level 140, 152; Seniors 139, 169; spoken 4n1, 25, 82n3, 147; teaching 39–40, 67–8; UCLES Higher School Certificate 144, 149–50; UK higher education institution offering *74*
German House of Hanover 22
Gilmour, G. 15
Gislot, P. 59
Glehn, Dr. L. von 106
Glück, H. 35, 39–40, 82n3, 86
Goethe, J. 23, 154
Goethe Institute 75–6, 220
Goethe-Zertifikat 129
Goldsmith, O. 173n36
Graded Objectives 128, 155, 156, 168
Grammar Schools Act 126n15
Grammatica Anglo-Lusitanica 19
grammatical knowledge 60, 119, 139–41, *163*
Grand Tour 2, 12, 45, 49, 58, 75
Granthan, H. G.: *An Italian Grammar* 12
Great Pronoun Theft 114
Greek 9, 44, 48, 58, 73, 103, 124, 125n1, 129, 182, 191, 218, 219; Ancient 8–9, 35, 37n4; GCSE Examination figures *29*; language candidates at Cambridge Local Examinations *8*
Grimani, S.: *The Ladies' New Italian Grammar* 13
Gujarati 10, 28; combination of two or more foreign languages *31*; GCSE Examination figures *29*

Häberlein, M. 81, 82n3
Hamilton, A. 125n2, 172n32
Harding, C. L. M. 83n20, 155
Hargreaves, A. 68
Hargreaves, P. H. 62, 82n21
Harris, E. F.: *French for the Front* 42–3

Harrow School 47, 68, 71, 104
Hartley, H. R. 83n24
Hartley Institute 68, 83n24
Hartmann, M. 76
Hawkins, E. 1, 126n24, 214n10
Hay, M. 63
Hayter, W. 215n29
Hebrew 36, 41–2, 58, 64; GCSE Examination figures *29*
Henry II 37n8
Henry VIII 8, 14
Hermaneumata 87
Hickel, R. A. 111
Hicks, W. C. R. 62, 63
Higher School Certificate 13, 19, 127, *136*, 143–4, 154, 169
Hindustani 27, 28, 32, 36, 44, 68, 83n24
history of language advocacy and policy 174–213; actors 176–80; chronological bibliography of reports and policy documents in modern languages education, 1890–2015 202–13; how many languages should pupils learn 180, 182–3; languages for all 180–1; policy direction changes 180–93; rationales by policy actors to advocate foreign languages 193–200 (*see also* Leathes Report; National Languages Strategy); Spanish advocacy and growth 191–93; when to start learning a language 184–90; which language to learn 191–3
history of language learning 39–81; academic value and birth of school subject 46–7; adults 48, 61–4, 81; beyond the classroom 39, 64, 75–80; discipline in higher education 72–5; educational infrastructure 64–80; gender 47, 53–61; learners 47–64; native speakers/non-native speakers 66–9; reasons for learning before compulsory schooling 39–47; military 42–5; religion 41–2; social class 30, 39, 48–53, 82n8, 183; social prestige and leisured cultural enrichment 45–6; teachers' professionalization and qualifications 69–72, 178; trade and commerce 40–1
Hoffa, W. 81
holiday courses 21, 75, 81

Hollyband, C. 64, 65; *The Italian Schoolemaister* 12
Holmes, B. 200, 213n2
Holmes, D. 81
Hoogvliet, J. M. 37n13; *Elements of Dutch* 18
Howatt, A. P. R. 20, 22, 35, 85, 86, 104, 105, 107, 117, 125n2; *English Grammar* 21
how languages have been taught and learned 85–124; up to around 1600 87–93; 1600–1750: first foreign language grammars and "full" textbooks 93–4; 1750–1800: "practical grammar" and exercises 25, 95–9, 106, 126n11; nineteenth century: grammar and translation, and patented methods 99–105; 1920–70: scientific period I 107–16; 1965–2000: scientific period II 117–19; cultural knowledge 121–3; four communicative skills 119; Reform Movement and beyond 1, 2, 20, 71, 77, 81, 85, 87, 105–7, 112, 118, 179, 185
how many languages should pupils learn 180, 182–3
Hu, A. 85
Huguenots 21, 64, 105
Hüllen, W. 4n1, 35, 81, 87, 93
Hulshof, H. 4n1
Hundred Years War 10
Hunt, F. 82n9
Hunt, T. 35

IAAM *see* Incorporated Association of Assistant Masters
Incorporated Association of Assistant Masters (IAAM) 132, 133, 135, *135*, 140, 149, 171n13, 185, 191
Institute for Research in English Teaching 107
Institute of Chartered Accountants 41
Institute of Chemistry 52
Institute of Linguists *see* Chartered Institute of Linguists
Institute of Mechanics and Electrical Engineers 52
Instituto Cervantes 76, 220
Introito e porta 40, 81, 125n5
Irish 6, 23, 27, 89, 175, 225n4; GCSE Examination figures *29*; Leaving Certificate 27, 48, 225n4; Northern 130, 137

Italian 4n2, 5, 12–13, 15, 16, 19, 23, 26, 32, 34, 35, 43, 48, 58, 59, 61, 62, 64, 65, 73, 75, 83n21, 86, 89, 103, 112, 116, 120, 125n2, 128, 129, 147, 150, 153, 170n6, 191, 219, 220; A-level *33*, 153; combination of two or more foreign languages *31*; German 40, 81, 92; UK higher education institutions offering 74

James I 14, 46, 58
Japanese 32, 34, 44, 173n40, 183; GCSE Examination figures *29*; UK higher education institution offering 74
Jespersen, O. 83n28
Jesuits 36, 90–1, 92
JMB *see* Joint Matriculation Board
Joint Matriculation Board (JMB) 35, 130, 132, 133, *134–5*, 141, 147, 148, 149, 150, 151, 153, 170n10
Jones, B. 81
Jones, D. 109
Jones, R. 38n29

Kapcia, A. 36
Kaplan, R. B. 176, 213n5
Keane, A. H. 68, 83n24
Keefer, L. E. 81
Kelly, L. 87, 100, 126n13
Kennedy, B. H.: *Latin Primer* 6
Kibbee, D. 9, 10, 35, 37n7, 45–6
King's School Canterbury 47
King's College London 15, 129, 170n10
Klippel, F.4n2, 100, 126n25
Klöter, H. 90, 91, 92
Knight, F. B. 114
Knox, J. 41
Koischwitz, O. 108
Kok Escalle, M.-C. 4n2, 53, 81
König, J. 49, 64
Koschwitz, E. 37n17
Kuhfuß, W. 4n2

Lamartine, E. W.: *Pictorial French Course* 56, *57*
Lamb Guildhouse 63
Lambley, K. 35
language "charts" 31–5
languages English speakers want to learn 5–36; Chinese 30–1; Dutch 16–19; English as a foreign or

second language 20–2; French 9–12; German 22–4; Italian 12–13; language "charts" 31–5; languages of empire to "community languages" 27–30; Portuguese 19–20; Russian 24–7; Spanish 14–16
languages for all 180–1
Languages in Europe report 193
Languages Ladder 156, *158–60*, 224
Languages Lead Body 156
languages of empire to "community languages" 27–30
Language Teaching Assistantships 77
Lanvers, U. 225n3
Latin 5, 6, 7–8, 9, 12, 17, 23, 24, 30, 31, 35, 37n4, 40, 45, 46, 48, 51, 56, 58, 60, 73, 86, 87–9, 91, 93, 96, 103, 123, 124, 128, 182, 183, 218, 219; French 125n7; ; grammar 94, 108; language candidates at Cambridge Local Examinations *8*; "mental gymnastics" 97; Russian 24; textbooks 117
Latin American Studies 36, 78, 192
Lawrence, J. 35
LEA *see* Local Education Authority
learners in language learning 47–64, 222
learning success 188, 223–4
Leathes Committee 185, 195, 198
Leathes Report on Modern Studies 16, 26, 73, 180, 182, 183, 189, 191, 194, 195, 196–7, 198, 200, 213n1
Leeds Central Higher Grade Board School 50
Le Mayre, M.: *Dutch Schoolmaster* 40, *41*, 86
Lemercier de Neuville, L. 59
Lennox, S. 65
Leonard, T. A. 76
Lepschy, A. L. 13, 35
Lessing, G. E. 23, 154
Lindemann, M. 81, 125n5
Lineker, G. 199
Linguaphone 61, 109–10
listening comprehension *142*, 145, 150, 151–3, 168
Livre des Mestiers 11, 40
LLAS (Subject Centre for Languages, Linguistics and Area Studies 214n10, 216n33
Local Education Authorities (LEA) 62, 72, 77, 79, 175, 178, 181, 186, 188
Locke, J. 87, 136

London Chamber of Commerce 129, *134*, 170n6
Loonen, P. L. M. 36, 81, 86, 94, 123
Lorch, M. 38n21
Louis XI 143
Louis XIV 20
Low, L. 188, 190
Ludolf, H. W.: *Grammatica russica* 24, *24*, 125n6
Luquien, F. B. 192

McDonald, T. 199
McLelland, N. 1, 4n1, 35, 36, 40, 44, 68, 81, 82n1, 83n25, 108, 121, 123, 126nn11–12, 126n14, 173n36, 222n1
Maddison, J. 24–5
Mairs, R. 81
Manchester Central Higher Grade Board School 50
Manchester Grammar School 76
Manchester Metropolitan University 28–9
Mandarin 30–1, 32, 34, 38n28, 90, 156, 220; *see also* Chinese
Marcel, C. 106; *Practical Method of Teaching the Living Languages* 104
Maréchal, R. 4n1
Marlborough College 47
Marriette, A. 129
Marshman, J. 30: *Clavis Sinica* 30
Martínez, L. 36, 81
Mary (Queen) 14, 41
Matthew, R. J. 81, 82n7
Mauger, C. *True Advancement of the French Tongue* 94
Meidinger, J. V. 95, 97, 98, 99
Menzerath, P. 109
Michael, I. 35
Miège, G. 108; *Nouvelle Mèthode* 21
Mieille, P. 76
Military Academy at Woolwich 43, 128, 129
military language education 42–5; *see also* Sandhurst
Ministry of Defence 174
Minsheu, J. 14; *Guide into Tongues* 46, 64–5
Modern Language Association 69, 73, 76–7, 83n27, 177
Modern Languages 2, 6, 31, 62, 68, 69, 70, 73, 74, 75, 78, 80, 174, 177, 178, 185, 194, 195, 197, 198, 199, 200, 217, 223

Modern Languages in Comprehensive Schools 52–3
More, H.: *Strictures on the Modern System of Female Education* 59
Morville, Hugh de 37n8
Moys, A. 81, 130, 133, 137, 138–9, 145
Muckle, J. 25, 26, 32, 36, 81, 84n38, 178
Müller, M. 47, 140, 146, 171n21

Napoleon 15
National Association of Language Advisors 72, 178, 187
National Centre for Languages 189, 214n9; see also CILT
National Congress on Languages 178
National Curriculum for England 9, 29, 35, 114, 122, 123, 135, 141, 151, 153, 157, *161–7*, 168, 169, 172n34, 174, 175, 181, 194, 198, 199–201, 215n28
National Defense Education Act 176, 186, 188
National Languages Strategy 29, 38n26, 156, 178, 180, 194, 198, 201, 213n4; "Languages for All"180; *Language Learning* 194
National Language Standards 156, *158–60*
National University of Ireland 175
National Vocational Qualifications (NVQs) 156, 172n33
native speakers/non-native speakers as teachers 66–9
natural method 105, 106, 107
Navy Japanese language School 82n7
Newmark, P. 110–1, 124
Newsom, A. 36
Newsom Report: *Half Our Future* 181
Nextor-Schnurmann, I. 82n5, 83n17
Niederehe, H.-J. 125n5
non-language knowledge and skills 128, 153–5
Norman Conquest 9
Nott, D. 79
Nottingham High School 52, 68
Nuffield Foreign Languages Teaching Materials Project 26, 112, *113*, 178
Nuffield Foundation 178, 186–7, 215n26, 215n29
Nuffield Languages Enquiry 178
number of languages pupils should learn 180, 182–3
Núñez, L. P. 81, 125n5

Nuremberg, Georg von 89, 92
NVQs *see* national vocational qualifications

OCR 19, 20, 129, 130
Offelen, H. 49; *Double Grammar* 64, 121
O-level comprehension 32, 45, 127, 130, 132, 133, 134–5, 137, 138, 145, 148, 155, 170n10, 181; French 150, 153, 168, 169, 187; German 140, 152; JMB 141, 151; Spanish 169
Ölinger, A. 94, 125n7
Ollendorff, H. G. 84n30, 100, 101, 102, 103, 115
Order of St. John of Jerusalem Prisoners of War Department 170n6
Ortmanns, K. P. 36n3
Otto, E. 101, 102, 103, 115
Oxford, Cambridge and RSA Examinations (OCR) 19, 20, 129, 130

Page, B. W. 134, 137, 144
Palmer, H. E. 21, 107, 115; *Principles of Language Study* 114; *Thousand-Word English* 114
Palmgren, K. E. 179
Parry, J. H.: centres; 215n26; Report 36, 192
parsing, 103, 125n8
Passy, P. 83n28, 109
Pearson, W. 15
Pearson Education 20, 130
Peers, E. Allison 15, 36, 192
Peeters-Fontainas, J. F. 81, 125n5
Peninsula War 15
Persian 27, 28, 36; GCSE Examination figures 29
Philip III 14
Phillip of Spain 14
Phillips, D. 215n25
Pictorial French Course 56, *57*
Pleco 114
Ploiche, P. de 64
Plötz, K. 100, 103, 126n13
policy direction changes 180–93
Polish 26, 37n20, 86, 183; GCSE Examination figures 29
Porny, M. *Practical French Grammar* 47
Portuguese 5, 19–20, 32, 34, 35, 36; GCSE Examination figures *29*; UK higher education institution offering *74*

"practical grammar" and exercises 25, 95–9, 106, 126n11
Practical Grammar of the Russian Language 25
Prendergast, T. 21n38, 104, 105
prisoners of war 44, 170n6
Promoting Language Learning and Linguistic Diversity report 183
prose composition 135–7, 144, 148, 149, 153; *see also* translation
Puncher, S. 38n23, 170n2
Punjabi 28; GCSE Examination figures *29*
Puren, C. 4n1

Queen's College 21, 70, 75, 105
Quick, R. H. 68, 104, 177
Quousque Tandem Society 83n28

Radtke, E. 82n1
Raffe, D. 213n4
Rambeau, A. 65, 70, 71, 73, 221
rationales by policy actors to advocate foreign languages 193–200; *see also* Leathes Report; National Languages Strategy
rationalist approach to policy learning 176, 213n4
reading comprehension *135*, 138, 144, 145–6, 169
reasons for learning before compulsory schooling 39–47; academic value and birth of school subject 46–7; military 42–5; religion 41–2; social prestige and leisured cultural enrichment 45–6; trade and commerce 40–1
Rees, J. *Pictorial Courses* 108, 109; *see also* Linguaphone
Reform Movement 1, 2, 20, 71, 77, 81, 85, 87, 105–7, 112, 118, 179, 185
Renaissance 12
Render, W. 22–3
residence abroad 77, 78, 79, 80, 81, 147, 153; *see also* year abroad: teaching assistantships
Reuchlin, J. 42
Revolution of 1917 26
Richardson, J.: *A Vocabulary Persian, Arabic, and English* 38n22
Ripman/Rippman, W. 21–2, 37n17, 69, 70, 75, 105, 106, 170n10, 177, 197, 199; *English Sounds* 21; *A First English Book for Boys and Girls Whose Mother-Tongue Is Not English* 21; *First German Book* 100–1; *Hints on Teaching German* 100; *The Sounds of Spoken English* 21
Rjéoutski, V. 4n2
Roche, E. 59
Rocher, R. 28
Rossman, J. P. : *Lehrbuch der französischen Sprache* 179
Rottweil, Adam von 93
Rowbotham, J. 68, 99
Rowles, D. 81
Rowles, V. 81
Rowlinson, W. *Deutschland hier und jetzt* 56–7; *Sprich Mal Deutsch* 119
Royal Society of Arts (RSA) 16, 19, 129, 130, 132–3, *134*, 146, 168, 170n4, 170n6, 170nn9–10, 171n14, 172n28
RSA *see* Royal Society of Arts
Rugby School 9, 37n4, 47
Rumiantsev (Count) 25
Russian 1, 5, 13, 20, 24–7, 32, 34, 35, 36, 43, 44–5, 62, 73, 78, 81, 82n6, 83n17, 83n21, 84n38, 103, 112, 116, 119, 150, 153, 170n6, 187, 191, 219; A-level *33*; Annan Report 215n29; combination of two or more foreign languages *31*; GCSE Examination figures *29*; grammar 125n6; Polish 183; UK higher education institution offering *74*
Rybak, S. 81

Salverda, R. 17, 36
Sánchez Escribano, F. J. 36
Sánchez Pérez, A. 36
Sandhurst Military College 28, 44, 128, 129, 131, 133, 139–40, 141, 146, 149, 151, 170n3, 171n12, 171n16, 171n19, 173n36
Sanford, J.: *Introduction to the Italian Tongue* 12
Sanskrit 27, 28, 35, 128
Saunders, M. J.: "Plea for the Study of German" 24
Sauveur, L. 106
Schleich, M. 81
Schmidt, F. *Lehrbuch der französischen Sprache* 179
Schoell, C. 171n21
Scholars' International Correspondence 76
Schottelius, J. G. 94, 96
scoring validity 131
Scott, W. 15
Scotland 26, 36n3, 75, 77, 172n32, 175, 178, 183, 184, 188, 190,

221; Scottish CILT 178; Scottish Education Department 78; Scottish Government Languages Working Group 183; Scottish Secretary of State 215n29
Sculthorp, M. 63
Second Interim Report of the committee of education for Salesmanship 177
Seidenstücker, J. H. F. 99, 100
Self-Educator in German 61
Sheffield Central Higher Grade School 17, 50, 130
A Short and Easy Way for the Palatines to Learn English 21
Shorte Introduction of Grammar 8
Shrewsbury School 47
Sidwell, D. 72; *Deutsch Heute* 122
Siepmann, O. 9, 105, 106, 110
Single Honours degrees 74, 78
Smith, C. 68
Smith, R. 4n1, 85, 86, 107, 117, 125n2, 224n1
SNPF *see Société Nationale des Professeurs de Français en Angleterre*
social class 30, 39, 48–53, 82n8, 183
social gender 53, 58
social prestige and leisured cultural enrichment 45–6
Société Nationale des Professeurs de Français en Angleterre (SNPF) 67
Somerville College 69
Southey, R. 15
Spanish 2, 5, 12, 14–16, 18, 19, 20, 23, 26, 32, 34, 35, 36, 37n10, 40, 43, 44, 61, 63, 64, 73, 74, 75, 79, 81, 82n6, 83n21, *91*, 93, 103, 112, 116, 129, 133, 147, 148, 150, 170n6, 183, 186, 187, 189, 190, 191–3, 194, 201, 218, 219, 220; advocacy and growth 191–3; A-level *33*, 62; combination of two or more foreign languages *31*; "Exemplar Material" 172n26; -French *54*; grammar 36n1; IMB 153; O-level 138, 169; UCLES Higher School Certificate 143–4, 169; UCLES Junior 169; UK higher education institution offering *74*
Spanish Armada 14
Spanish Peninsula War 15
Spanish War of Independence 15
speaking assessment 146–8
Spottiswoode, R. 43
Spours, K. 213n4
Stack, E. M. 115
STANAG 128, 132, 155, 157, *158–60*, 168

Stead, W. T. 76
Steadman-Jones, R. 36
Stevens, J. 14
Stewart, W. 35
Strategically Important and Vulnerable subjects 175
Stray, C. 35
Strien-Chardonneau, M. van 4n2
Subject Centre for Languages, Linguistics and Area Studies 214n10
Sumillera, R. G. 35
Sunderland, J. 53
Suso López, J. 81

Tamponi, R. 35
Taunton Commission and Report 60, 177
Tchoudinov, A. 4n2
Teachers' professionalization and qualifications 69–72, 178, 222
Terrell, T. D. 118
test constructs/what to measure 133–44, 66
Thimann, I. C. 52, 77
Thomas, W.: *Principal Rules of the Italian Grammar* 12
Thomas, D. M. 45
Three Character Classic 90
Threlford, W. L. 129
Tinsley, T. 30, 36, 184, 189
Titone, R. 87, 100
Torriano, G.: *Della Lingua Toscana-Romana* 13; *Italian Tutor or a new and most compleat Italian grammer* 13
Towles, C. 17
trade and commerce 40–1; *see also* commercial
"The Training of Teachers of Modern Foreign Languages" 70
translation from the target language into English 137–9
translation into the target language 135–7; *see also* prose composition
Trim, J. 156, 178, 190
Trithen, F. 25
Turkish 28, 44; GCSE Examination figures *29*
Tyler, E. M. 35
Tyndale, W. 41

UCLES *see* University of Cambridge Local Examinations Syndicate
UNESCO 179, 186
University College London 15, 28, 30, 46, 83n24; Latin American Studies 78; Nottingham 17

University of Cambridge 23, 25, 64, 65, 66, 71, 79, 103, 128, 130, 137; Parry Centres 215n26; school of Spanish 15; *see also* Cambridge Assessment; Cambridge Certificate of Proficiency in English; Cambridge International Examinations; Cambridge Primary Review; Cambridge Teacher Training Syndicate; Cambridge Training College for Women Teachers; Cambridge University Library; Oxford, Cambridge and RSA Examinations

University of Cambridge Local Examinations Syndicate (UCLES) Cambridge Board 15, 20, 36n3, 47, 133, 154, 155; Cambridge Examination for Women 13, 32, 61, 70, 149; Cambridge Local Examinations 8, *8*, 15, 20, 26, 35, 47, 51, 103, 138, 145, 171n12; Higher School Certificate 13, 19, 127, *136*, 143–4, 154, 169; Cambridge Senior School Certificate 8; Cambridge Syndicate Junior School Certificate 18

University of Liverpool 15
University of Oldenburg 214n10
University of Ulster 175
Uppingham School 47
Urdu 5, 10, 28, 29, 30, 38n25, 96; combination of two or more foreign languages *31*; GCSE Examination figures *29*; Punjabi 183
U.S. Army Specialized Training Program (ASTP) 44, 45, 81, 115, 176; Foreign Languages programme 44
Uttiv, J.: *Complete practical German grammar* 97–8

Valette, R. M. 155, 157
validity, reliability and comparability 130–3; cognitive validity, 130, 132, 133, 138, 140; context validity, 131, 132, 133, 138, 140, 141, 149, 151, 155, 168; scoring validity, 131
Velleman, B. L. 45, 81, 115
Vidal Rodeiro, C. L. 36, 38n28, 183
Viëtor, W. 20, 37n17, 71, 75, 106, 110

Wakernaak, E. K. 4n1
Wales *see* Welsh

Wall, C. H.: *Practical Grammar on Dr. Otto's Conversational System* 19–20
Wanostrocht, N.: *Livre des enfans* 125n10; *Practical French Grammar* 65, 97, *98*,
Waren, 67, 179, 184
Watzke, J. L. 176, 191, 213n1, 214n13
WEA *see* Workers Education Association
Weber, A. 81
Weir, C. J. 2, 127, 130, 143, 151, 153, 224
Weißenburg, O. 88
Wells, H. G. 26
Wells, S. 120
Welsh 35, 130, 137, 183, 221; Baccalaureate 183
Wendeborn, G. F. A. 126n11; *Elements of German Grammar* 46, 98–9
Westminster School 36
when to start learning a language 184–90
which languages to learn 191–3, 219–20
Whitehouse, J. C. 110
who tests, how and for whom? 128–30
Widgery, W. H. 71, 106, 185
why teach languages 217–19
Wilhelm, F. A. 4n1
Wilkins, C.: *Grammar of the Sanskrita Language* 38n22
Williamson, H. R. *Teach Yourself Chinese* 120–1
Witt, H. de 59
women, education of *see* gender),
Woodhouse, R. 19
Woolwich Military Academy 43, 128, 129
Worde, W. de: *Lytell Treatise for to lerne Englisshe and Frensshe* 11
Workers Education Association (WEA) 62, 63
World War I 21, 23, 28, 34, 42, 44, 68, 186, 220
World War II 23, 26, 44, 79, 92, 110, 115, 116, 122, 196, 220
Wringe, C. 81
writing 148–51

year abroad: teaching assistantships 78, 79–80, 84n39, 222

Zwartjes, O. 82n2